Contents

Acknowledgments . . . . *ix*

Foreword . . . . *xi*

Introduction . . . . *xvii*

Coming to *El Norte* 1

"An Excellent Education" 27

"A Desire to Serve My Country" 49

Barrio Americanism: Constructing a Veterans'
    Movement 74

The Felix Longoria Incident 104

The Beginning of a Protracted Struggle 140

The Fifties: Best of Times, Worst of Times 172

Unity as Politics but No Unity in Politics 208

From the Halls of D.C. to the Barrios of Aztlán 251

Lifelong Pursuit of Justice 288

Bibliographical Note *314*

Bibliography *317*

Index *364*

Acknowledgments

It is not uncommon to dedicate a biography to the spouse of the person discussed. And in this case Wanda Fusillo García more than merits the honor. It is, however, uncommon to dedicate a book to the archivists who helped compile the information. In this case it would be quite unfair not to do so. Besides being great friends, Tom Kreneck and Grace Charles have been intellectual fellow travelers with me in trying to tell the story of Hector P. García and his civil rights work in Texas. Tom was the first person to realize the García papers had much to offer scholars interested in Mexican American studies. Painstakingly, he worked with an often feisty García and his family to have the hundreds of boxes moved to the Special Collections Room of the Texas A&M University library in Corpus Christi. His next most important decision was to assign Grace Charles to be chief archivist of the collection. Grace, who had been a student of mine, then undertook the difficult task of reading every letter, report, telegram, speech, news clip, and document in the collection. She then set about cataloguing every item in the hundreds of boxes. While the work is still unfinished, her efforts have already proven to be of great benefit to numerous scholars.

Needless to say, both were enthusiastic when I chose to write a biography on Hector P. García. What followed over the next several years was a collaboration made in Heaven. I spent hours talking to both Tom and Grace and other members of the staff, and every summer that I spent in the collections I came home more encouraged that this was the right topic and I had fallen into a gold mine by divine providence. One of my great scholarly concerns has been that not enough collections are available—though that is changing—and not enough archivists see Mexican American collections as a priority. There are some very good archivists scattered around the country, but they are a small group and possibly the best of them are a dying breed. Luckily, I found Tom and Grace. Spending time at the Special Collections at Texas A&M University in Corpus Christi has been an intellectual experience that profoundly affects those who have shared in it. Over the last five years, I spent hours conversing with Tom and Grace and other scholars who were researching Hector P. García, the American G.I. Forum, Mexican American reform in general, and many other peripheral issues. Tom would remember something he read in García's boxes and Grace would be the only person to know where it was. At other times, Grace would tell us about a new item she had discovered in the boxes and a long conversation would ensue. How they were able to do any work with me around was amazing.

There were others who provided an encouraging word. Pat Carroll, a colleague at Texas A&M University in Corpus Christi, was one of the first to suggest I do a work on García even though he was doing one himself. Alan Lessoff helped me see the difficulties, while Jesus Rosales and Javier Villarreal believed I was one of the few people capable of doing it. José Angel Gutiérrez, Rudy Acuña, and Armando Navarro provided a historical perspective on the life of García and the American G.I. Forum and offered much other advice on this project. Carl Allsup, the first scholar to do work on the Forum was also very helpful in providing insight and some valuable documents. The few hours I spent with him talking about the project helped me orient myself toward a better biography. In the end, it was Nicolás Kanellos of Arte Público Press who became the person most responsible for the writing of this book. He offered to make it part of his press's civil rights series and offered me the resources to do the research and the writing. Brigham Young University supported this effort with several grants, and my colleagues in the history department proved extremely supportive with generous advice and patience as I talked constantly about this project. I was also blessed with a good research assistant, Dan Combs, who helped tremendously with the bibliography.

My family again proved to be crucial in this endeavor with their support. I have always written for them. Now, with four grandchildren I feel even more the need to chronicle the life of my people. For this new burst of energy I thank Cristian, Citlali, Adrian, and Caleb.

Foreword

At the end of World War II, Mexican American servicemen and women who had supported their nation to defeat totalitarian nations abroad returned to their communities here in the United States to confront continuing social, political, and economic discrimination. Across the southwestern and midwesten United States, Mexican American community conditions and constraints on civic participation, upward mobility, and public respect were akin to those facing former slaves of African American descent in the South. Given their many accomplishments abroad — their demonstrated valor in combat, their effectiveness as soldiers, nurses, and battlefield leaders, and in many cases their real heroism[1]—these circumstances proved unacceptable to the generation of Mexican Americans who served America in war. These individuals had fought overseas against foreign racism and repression. The irony and the harsh reality of returning to institutional racism here at home were too great to overlook.

This was especially the case when, in 1949, a white-owned funeral home in the small South Texas town of Three Rivers refused to provide memorial services for a Mexican American soldier whose body was returned after more than a three year journey home from the Philippines, where he was killed in combat. Against this backdrop of public insult and disdain directed to the Mexican American people, a young physician named Hector P. García and his organization of returning Mexican

---

[1]Mexican Americans were drafted and killed during World War II in proportions far greater than their share of the U.S. population of the time. Most saw frontline combat duty and those who did not fortified American war efforts with exemplary supportive service in every branch of the armed services. Not a single Mexican American soldier was ever reported to have deserted during these years and, per capita, Mexican Americans serving during World War II received more Medals of Honor than any other group of American combatants.

American veterans, the American GI Forum, emerged. García mobilized local Mexican Americans to successfully challenge the funeral home and to have the felled soldier, Private Felix Longoria, buried with honors.

During ensuing years, with support (even if at times begrudging) from American leaders no less significant than Lyndon B. Johnson, the Kennedys, and later, Ronald Reagan, García and the American GI Forum would transform American political and civic culture relative to Spanish-speaking communities in profound and unprecedented ways. García and his Forum allies would develop a new order of Latino community leadership and strategy. They would help to expand Hispanic community access to essential human services, social opportunities, and political rights by dramatically increasing community participation in public and civic affairs. They would introduce massive voter registration campaigns that for the first time positioned Mexican Americans as strategic participants in public elections. They would file and win landmark lawsuits to remedy systemic violations of Mexican American civil rights, desegregating schools, county hospitals, government housing, and other public facilities. García and the Forum would help to position Mexican Americans (and other Latino groups) as meaningful participants in national policy formation and debate.

These accomplishments are sadly overlooked today, largely because Hector P. García, although substantially chronicled in sections of important books and articles on his times, has never been the subject of a dedicated biography. Now, Ignacio M. García (no relation to Hector) has changed that. His work, presented in the pages that follow this foreword, provides a first time public glimpse into the life of the man who Hector García actually was. It ably chronicles his early life experiences, his informative motivations, his style of leadership, and his heretofore easily misunderstood political philosophy. In well-written and objective, yet sensitive and giving analysis, Ignacio M. García uncovers Hector's complexity and at times his contradictions.

Hector García was a man of unique determination, energy, and commitment to his cause. He was also—like many accomplished individuals—extremely intentional about his quest for a place in history. Indeed, he was prepared to pay dearly to advance that quest, often failing to care for his own family and physical well-being. Strong-minded and in essence religious in his personal convictions, García often made it difficult, even impossible, for friends and enemies alike to disagree with him.

Hector compensated for these shortcomings by putting his money where his mouth was. He worked harder and with greater personal sacrifice and impact than any of his GI Forum followers, or for that matter any of his Latino community leadership contemporaries (with the arguable exception of farm labor leader César Chávez). He was furthermore remarkably giving in his public service to the poor and needy, providing for more than fifty years (at great personal expense) low- or no-cost medical services to indigent Mexican American (and other) individuals and families in and around his hometown of Corpus Christi, Texas. Finally, García had many endearing personal qualities that were often missed in the course of his public journey. He loved simple things, much preferring to conduct important business lunches at the nearby fast-food What-a-Burger in his neighborhood, rather than any high-end restaurant. He also took child-like pride in his many personal relationships, contacts, and mementos involving significant white public officials. No visit to his office was complete without a substantial review of these marks of his political influence.

It was a harsh blow to him in his later years to become less and less relevant to important U.S. political figures. When we participated at a 1983 meeting with then president Ronald Reagan and a small group of Latino community organizational leaders, Hector—by that time ailing and in his seventies—was effectively left out of the conversation, except for Reagan's mention that he would soon be bestowing an important recognition on the doctor for his many past good works. (The award turned out to be the prestigious Presidential Medal of Freedom, which Reagan presented to García the following year.) After the meeting, García sat next to me on the escort bus that transported us from the presidential meeting site, his eyes sad and tearful, a look of frustration on his face as he gazed out the window, too proud and discreet to reveal or acknowledge his emotions.[2] Years later, I learned

---

[2]Gratefully for Hector and all of us who attended that meeting, its outcome was somewhat significant. The following day before the national convention of the American GI Forum, Reagan publicly reversed his previously harsh objection to federally supported bilingual education programs.

from Carlos Martínez, director of the GI Forum's National Veteran's Outreach Program how deeply hurt Hector was towards the end of his life when Texas governor Ann Richards stopped returning his phone calls.

Such unfortunate slights concerning recognition of García's life force in more recent years have not been limited to politicians. Latino historians have also effectively overlooked the dynamic life and legacy of Hector García. Many of these scholars, products of the radical student and community movements of the 1960s that protested much of the patriotism and goals that García valued, have considered him too *bourgeois* and conservative a subject to warrant serious study or meaningful acknowledgment.

Hector P. García: In Relentless Pursuit of Justice opens a too-long-closed door of understanding about an individual who has probably had more to do than any other individual with contemporary Latino advancement in American society and institutions. It is a long overdue work that should help both Latino and non-Latino readers to better appreciate Hector García and his many contributions to American civic culture. Ignacio M. García's book reminds us that Hector was an unusually able—if at times controversial—leader on behalf of his people. But the book equally makes clear in ways that may surprise readers that Hector García was more than just a Mexican American advocate. He was finally a champion of American democracy and values, of all poor and disenfranchised people, and of fundamental notions of justice. As the author observes:

> Hector saw the essence of being American not in speaking perfect English, being middle-class, or assimilating into a homogeneous culture. Becoming American meant believing in the fundamentals of citizenship, democracy, pluralism and equality for all. It meant giving one's self to a life of service for the nation and for one's community, as well as being willing to make the ultimate sacrifice for that life. Anyone, of any color, national origin or race could do this. This was, in his mind, the beauty of American society. It was for everyone, native-born, immigrant, rich or poor, male or female, white or colored.

These notions of what is unique and special about America—

whatever it's many continuing contradictions and our imperfect efforts to make good on basic constitutional promises—are as timely and relevant today as when Hector García began his public journey more than fifty years ago. At a time of growing ambivalence and resistance relative to our nation's expanding multiculturalism and global role, it is too easy to forget what is important and positive about the American experiment. It is too easy to overlook that what is in progress here, however elusive and unsatisfactory, represents something worth appreciating, something worth celebrating, something worth fighting for.

Hector P. García: In Relentless Pursuit of Justice is an important new entry in a larger effort by Arte Público Press to develop an Hispanic Civil Rights Series. With support from major funders including the Charles Stewart Mott Foundation, the Ewing Marion Kauffman Foundation, and the Rockefeller Foundation, the Series is intended to educate and inform readers—both Latino and non-Latino, young and old alike—about the many important contributions of U.S. Hispanic leaders and groups to contemporary American life. As Latinos emerge to comprise the nation's most significant minority population, the Series is especially timely and important. The work that follows offers particularly important lessons and information about major Latino contributions to American democracy and social justice during the second half of the twentieth century. It is essential reading for all who wish more fully to understand the true meaning of being an American as we enter the twenty-first century.

Henry A. J. Ramos
Executive Editor
Hispanic Civil Rights Series, Arte Público Press

Introduction

Tireless in the pursuit of decency and justice, generous in support of just causes and in aiding his less fortunate brethren, Hector García will need no monument of stone or metal to be remembered by posterity. His deeds speak for themselves, and those deeds will not soon fade from the memory of his people.

—George I. Sánchez

If George I. Sánchez had been a prophet, this biography would simply enhance the known story of Hector P. García. Sánchez, however, proved only to be a good educator and reformer, but not much of a seer. The sad fact is that Hector García not only merits a biography, but he also needs one to be remembered. When he died in 1996, old veterans, aging reformers, and smart politicians attended the funeral. Many others in his own community wondered what all the commotion was about. The man who had given most of his life to reforming American society to be inclusive of Mexican Americans would not even be the most known citizen in his own community of Corpus Christi, Texas. That distinction would go to the slain Tejano singer Selena. Friends often laughed when I called Hector García the most famous unknown reformer in our community. It would be difficult to study reform in the Mexican American community without finding some mention of his name or his organization, the American G.I. Forum. García surely does not belong in the file of the forgotten. It would be difficult to identify someone else that most represented his era. If there is a Jeffersonian Age, then there needs to be the acknowledgment of a García Age in Latino history of the United States. He was that important, if only because he worked so hard and reflected so well the ambitions and aspirations of many Mexican Americans of his generation desirous of being considered Americans.

Just as certain about his life is how little people know of him beyond his founding of the American G.I. Forum and his triumph over segregation in the rural community of Three Rivers, Texas. Young people do not remember him, Chicano scholars have largely ignored him, and American historians fail to mention him. Beyond two introductory works on the American G.I. Forum, nothing else has been written on his life. His life in social reform has "aged" so quickly, despite his having died less than ten short years ago. This lost memory is as much a reflection of the politics of today's Hispanics as it is of America's traditional "amnesia" about its Mexican-origin citizenry. At a time of ethnicity and power politics by special interest groups, García's brand of social reform and partisan politics seems too accommodating and, at times, archaic. The fact that he never became the darling of the liberal media, as César Chávez once was, meant to many Mexican American leaders that he had not made it. Those, of course, are the perceptions of the generation that succeeded him. More will be said about them later. But it must be said that their analysis is a false reconstruction that has developed because many problems continue to plague the Chicano community. We have often fallen, as Mexican Americans, into the trap of seeing our own in the context of how American society at large responds to them. With that litmus test, only a few become worthy of biographical study.

García is worthy of a biography. After studying his life, it is tempting to describe him as a quintessential American, although an American with an ethnic background. After all, what he most wanted was to have his community be seen as American and for it to behave as American. But his life was much more complicated than any term could describe. This complexity came from the reality that all Americans of Mexican descent must navigate a social, cultural, and political minefield that is the Mexican American experience. This minefield, then and now, is not only about cultural differences and economic disparities, which are in themselves a serious challenge, but also about historical legacy. Mexican Americans have a history that is tied to two nations, and often convergence is common, but so is divergence. Most Mexican Americans see the United States as a hostile heaven, a place of opportunity and possibility, but one that constantly reminds them that their inclusion is always conditional.

Mexican Americans have learned to accommodate this duality, but rarely do they see the same reciprocal efforts from the larger society. Thus Mexican Americans develop a complex, nuanced way of constructing their American identity. They are positive and optimistic but guarded and vigilant. They trust American ideals but are not too sure about American policy-makers. They enthusiastically participate in the larger society when included but rarely assume that the invitation is a standing one. Hector's life and his efforts at social reform exemplified that complexity of living in a hostile heaven. He loved the United States but he remained vigilant up until his death.

When his parents crossed the border north from Mexico, they never looked back. Instead, they built a transitional Mexico that provided their children a secure environment, even as they grew into Americans. By their own accounts, the García children did not confront an identity crisis, did not face gross discrimination, nor did they find integration into their new society difficult. By every measure, they should have struggled and at least one or two of the eight children should have succumbed to the reality that was the South Texas of their time. But none did. Almost all went to college, became professionals, and were financially stable by Mexican American standards. Some became civic leaders, with Hector becoming the most prominent, if only because his tenacity, work ethic, and commitment to his community were the greatest. The other thing Hector had over his other siblings was his willingness to give up economic security and professional recognition, as well as to sacrifice his family and health for his political beliefs. One may argue with García's politics or question the value of his "ideals," but it is impossible to deny his wholehearted commitment to social reform and his willingness to pay any price and travel anywhere for his *raza*.

Yet, Hector P. García is not an ideological hero today. Few remember his words, and even those who followed him and worked at his side would have trouble remembering catchy phrases or profound philosophical statements pronounced by him. His writings are not likely to be compared to Jefferson's, Du Bois's, or Anthony's, and his rhetorical skills will never be compared with those of Lincoln, King, or even Chávez. The fact is that a dissected Hector P. García is not likely to be of great interest to a general or even a scholarly audience. García, or

Hector as I will refer to him throughout this biography, is valuable as a sum of *all* his parts. Once known, I believe, Hector will take his place in the American century. And it is in the American century that he belongs: an immigrant child, a Depression youth, a wartime soldier, and a postwar reformer. All these experiences came together, but the war would be one of the dominant themes in Hector's life. War gave him and many others like him an opportunity to "prove" themselves brave soldiers and loyal Americans. Even those who came from elite families were proud to wear the uniform, and they sought to be as good and possibly better, than their Anglo American counterparts.

Probably no generation before or after has felt as compelled to compete as this G.I. generation did. Those before had never felt capable of such direct competition, and succeeding generations have felt no need to prove anything. But this generation of Mexican Americans was given a place and time in which to show its capabilities and to directly measure itself against a population group that had so discriminated against it. And in war Mexican American soldiers dispelled so many of the disdainful stereotypes: cowardice, slothfulness, inefficiency, lack of intelligence, and selfish individualism. In the process of proving their valor, a transformation occurred that would have a profound impact on their communities after the war. For individuals like Hector, who already had developed important leadership characteristics in his youth, the war enhanced their vision of America and the place of Mexican Americans within it.

It was an auspicious time for Hector to turn to reform in Texas immediately after the war. In the Lone Star state the Cold War had meshed with blatant discrimination and Anglo American feelings of superiority to create an extremely hostile climate. Adding to the challenge was a pervasive sense of inferiority among many Mexican Americans who had tasted Anglo Texan malevolence for decades. While reform had been part of Mexican American history since Texas's separation from Mexico in 1836, by the end of World War II many old reformers and their organizations had succumbed to patriotism's pitch or to its heavy hand. Tired of waging war, many had simply decided to join the wave of optimism that permeated the country, or they chose to take what they could get. Hector would be part of a new generation of reformers who shunned ideology, whether nationalist or of the left, and concentrated on reform to solve immediate problems and open the doors to future prosperity.

For them, being Mexican had become part of the past, possibly a nostalgic past but surely one that was inconsequential to their future. This does not mean that they abandoned their identity or attempted to assimilate into Anglo American society. They also did not simply become ideological reformers, as many American liberals did. They did not forget culture and language, and most of them remained in the barrio. Rather, they set out to reconstruct the world of the American of Mexican descent. The constructors of a new barrio Americanism were few, but they had an enormous impact on hundreds of thousands of other veterans and their families. The leaders were predominantly middle-class and their followers working-class. They had a great impact because they had the field to themselves. Unlike African Americans, Mexican Americans had few Anglo Americans advocating for them and even fewer federal agencies concerned about their plight. Neither white nor black, but still concerned about their niche in American society, Mexican Americans were ready for someone to lead them toward equality.

Even before the war, there had been a core of leaders developing in the barrios of the nation. Most of these were professionals, educators, and lawyers. In the barrio there had always been competing classes: the poor, the well-off, and the professional. The latter two were at times synonymous, but more often they were not. The well-off were descendants of rich exiles from the Mexican Revolution or from the landed families that had survived the Americanization of the Southwest. There were also those immigrants who had made money by providing services to their community. The professionals were their children or the few who had pulled themselves up by their bootstraps. These latter were usually from poor parents who had some level of education. The circumstances in Mexican America simply did not offer too many working-class children from poor parents an opportunity to better themselves. Consequently, the Mexican American middle class had little challenge to its leadership.

The professional class had become the core of the leadership, and most of its members were concerned with economic issues and the attainment of legitimacy. That is, they sought the fruits of American society and consciously sought respect and validation from the larger society. Often devoid of ideology, they found structure for their activism in the tenets of their professions. That is, Mexican Americans were discriminated against so blatantly and their lives at times were so disrupted that any effort at bringing order to them proved a major accomplishment. These reformers simply sought to bring their fellow brothers and sisters up to par. The gap between them and the status quo was so wide that reform seemed distant and unattainable. And it was. But that type of catch-up reform did not provide the foundations for an ideology or a way of life. So they grabbed at Americanism and made a social/cultural philosophy into a basis for activism. Their yearning was to be mainstream, and they added reformist tendencies and cultural pride to it. Their own desires and those of their people to enjoy the benefits of an abundant society meshed with their deep Mexican *orgullo,* or pride, in making Americanism a new way of life. This *orgullo* was not so much pride *of* being Mexican as it was pride that came *from* being Mexican. Veteran status provided them something that few Mexican Americans had had before. The benefits that came from that status—the G.I. Bill, housing and education loans, and preference in federal hiring—gave them a lift that no other Mexican American generation had ever received. When government dragged its feet in providing them those fruits of service and victory, Hector backed into the crusade that thrust him onto the national scene.

Ironically, Hector needed little of this lift to enjoy the benefits of American society. Other than a housing loan, Hector had little need for direct government benefits. While he benefited from treating veterans medically, he did not build his reform crusades, as some had done in the past and would do in the future, on the professional needs of his constituency. Hector's reform activities came out of genuine concern for the plight of his fellow veterans. First, he empathized with them because of the government's failure to respond to their medical needs and later to their educational and housing needs. Then he became concerned over the needs of their families, both nuclear and extended. Then he came to realize that their lives reflected the challenges of most Mexican Americans in South Texas and the rest of the nation. His concerns would eventually reach out to the lowest rung of Mexican America, the migrant workers. Eventually, in his mind, all Mexican Americans *were* veterans or potential ones. Mexican and Mexican American G.I.s had made sacrifices on behalf of all of those in the barrios and *rancherías* of the United States. War had become the great vicarious experience for many, and they became veterans by proxy, worthy of all that America had to offer. Hector combined the heroism of the veterans with the daily struggles and needs of migrant workers to create a reform agenda that was inclusive of all Mexican Americans.

Never before had anyone looked at reform in such a way. Much more inclusive than organizations like the League of United Latin American Citizens (LULAC) and more pro-status quo than those like the Congress of Spanish-Speaking People, his American G.I. Forum would lay the foundation for the kind of inclusive and accommodating organizations that exist in the present. But while ethnic in its make-up, the American G.I. Forum would refrain from becoming an organization focused on ethnic politics. Hector's concern for his people went beyond them being discriminated against. He wanted them to cease to be "invisible." In this he would take up the call of earlier reformers who believed that Mexican Americans were a forgotten people, absent from the history books, government policy-making, and the American conscience. Out-of-sight often meant out-of-mind. And being out-of-mind meant that their inclusion and equality would be difficult to achieve. It also meant that it had to be achieved without the help of outsiders. Mexican Americans would see little outside advocacy and very few resources from outside the barrio.

Hector, like numerous other reformers of the time, was a true believer in pluralism. Like the members of LULAC who had preceded his activism, Hector wanted the benefits of American society for his people, but unlike them he did not practice the "unofficial" politics of class by moving away from the monolingual Spanish-speaking or the resident aliens. His organization would, at least initially, concentrate on bread-and-butter issues that affected a large part of the Mexican American working class. And while he became a middle-class hero, he remained even more popular among the working people of South Texas as well as among the average veteran who saw him as an incredibly brave reformer. His own ability to mingle with the poor, the lower working class, the elderly, and the youth rendered him a respect that few others in his time would achieve. In his worldview, most Mexican Americans could see themselves as part of the larger American Dream.

Hector's dream might well have been the last hurrah of the melting pot. It had to be, for in no other era had the prosperity, confidence, and attractiveness of the United States been so obvious. If there was a time of inclusion, it was then. The baseball color barrier had been broken, African American entertainers were dominating the charts, segregation among Mexican Americans was crumbling legally, and liberalism had begun to achieve dominance in the political arena by the end of the 1950s and through much of the 1960s. People were optimistic and, notwithstanding the Cold War, were again believing that their nation could solve all problems and was a place where all who worked hard and kept clean of ideological entanglements could accomplish anything they set their minds to doing. In this climate, Hector believed that Americans could be generous and compassionate, especially to those who had offered their lives to make the nation great.

But this generosity and compassion turned out to be both shallow and discriminating. White Americans, including many of their liberal leaders, showed little inclination to voluntarily share the abundance of America, nor did they seem that open to an ample discussion of the conditions of ethnic Americans, especially for those not black. While African Americans faced rigid segregation and all-too-common lynching, Mexican Americans confronted disdain, neglect, law enforcement violence, and invisibility. Mexican American reformers busily worked to challenge segregation, win court cases, and articulate their concerns, but white Americans rarely listened or noticed. After each court and political battle they won, the school districts, public facilities, and policy-makers found ways to simply do the same thing while avoiding the legal consequences. The legal victories of the 1940s and 1950s helped, but not enough to make Mexican Americans feel like first-class citizens.

The continual denial of first-class citizenship had a negative impact on Mexican Americans. While there is no doubt that there was resistance to their marginalization, it was often fragmented and individualistic. It was also discriminating, as individuals and organizations picked and chose those battles they felt they could win. They defended what was near and dear but often avoided entanglements or conflict outside their areas of influence. A form of defensive nationalism permeated the barrios that made segregation bearable and sustained its internal community structure. The positive aspect of this nationalism was that it kept the community vibrant as Mexican Americans found an environment in which they felt some sense of control.

The negative aspect was that it enhanced the rigidity of segregation as Mexican Americans reenforced their side of the walls of separation. Those who chose to break out often found resistance not only on the outside but also from those on the inside. This caused some reformers to be slightly ambivalent about their people's ability to rise above their condition. For this reason many reformers and reform organizations worked on changing their people's attitudes even as they sought to change American society in general. These reformers stressed English-language acquisition, citizenship obligations, education, voting, and even beautification of the barrio. Their stress on Americanism resulted in part because they saw their own people as lacking some of the characteristics necessary to be good Americans.

Hector came into the barrio with a different attitude. While he understood the deficiencies in the barrio, he did not stress them as a part of his reform activities. Unlike past reformers who sought to "correct" their constituencies so they could become good Americans, Hector believed that Mexican Americans could only become good Americans if they were treated as such. If given their rights, respected for their contributions, and rewarded for their sacrifices, Mexican Americans would respond as good Americans. He had been a witness to Mexican American service to the country on a scale unseen before. He knew the commitment that Mexican Americans were willing to make, and he had seen their abilities in combat and heard of their efforts on the home front. His own actions during the war were a testament of what the Mexican American soldier could do. The men and the community had performed above and beyond the call of duty. That they had received no more training or resources than the white citizenry testified to their equality. The fact that he and other overachievers like him had become officers and leaders in the armed forces attested to what Mexican Americans could do if given the opportunity.

Since Hector had a self-centered view of the world, what he saw and experienced was, in his mind, what actually occurred. This self-centeredness allowed him to focus on the tasks at hand, but it also permitted him to block out those experiences that disrupted his worldview. Consequently, his view of the war experience was devoid of segregation, discrimination, and race-based combat duty. The fact that as a medical officer he had escaped the trenches and the extreme front meant that his perception of the war remained glorified. That no one in his family served or became a victim allowed him to see the war in political and ideological terms. While most combat soldiers would wait a decade before romanticizing the war, by 1948 Hector had already canonized the experience as pivotal in the Mexican American twentieth-century experience. And for the rest of his political life he would retain an almost spiritual connection to the great conflict.

The war would legitimize Mexican American valor, hard work, commitment, intelligence, and loyalty. No matter what happened before, World War II had proved the worth of the American of Mexican descent. Hector soon discovered that many veterans felt the same way. And if they did not, they would come to do so through his promptings. Calling them to social reform from all walks of life, he emphasized their service to their nation and made patriotism a pseudo-ideology whose tenets could change along with the national mood and style. What did not change was that Mexican Americans had paid the ultimate price and thus earned the right to be called and treated as American. This patriotism, which I call barrio Americanism because it could best be understood in the context of the barrio, allowed Mexican Americans to live a vicarious life. Becoming Americans to themselves and their barrio peers allowed them to live the American Dream that was a reality to many other Americans because of postwar prosperity.

This prosperity actually circumvented most Mexican Americans, but enough felt an upward economic adjustment to proclaim that good times had arrived. This "feeling" of prosperity meshed with a slight but nonetheless significant softening of segregation and blatant racism in many quarters to provide some elbowroom for reform. Feeling good about themselves, they felt good about their nation, even if they were not too keen on their local political and social structures. Local politics and social dynamics did not change much for Mexican Americans immediately after the war, but the nation's optimism despite the Cold War fears—a contradiction hard to explain—invited Mexican Americans to be national citizens. This national citizenship held the promise of being inclusive. After all, those who spoke the "national" language of citizenship spoke a rhetoric that transcended local and regional politics, race relations, and legal statutes. The fact that outside the traditional Southwest and some Mexican American pockets in the Midwest, most Anglo Americans had no profoundly developed racial views of Mexican Americans meant to some that America was definitely better than any of its parts.

Hector, and others like him who found ways to circumvent the realities of their localities, quickly grasped the "goodness" of national America and rallied Mexican American veterans around it. With the founding of the American G.I. Forum, social reform became a call to "reenlist" in a new crusade against an enemy much closer to home. Calling them to battle as veterans and as patriots meant building on the valor developed in battle. These men were no longer afraid nor intimidated in demanding their fundamental rights as Americans. They felt certain that their patriotism and war service shielded them from accusations of being un-American, and so they responded with passionate but controlled fervor.

For Hector, social reform became not only a way to change America but a way to change the Mexican American's place in America. While major accomplishments in reform came in the late 1940s and throughout most of the 1950s, the greater impact of Hector's efforts came in the 1960s. Joining a number of other bright, articulate, and ambitious Mexican American lawyers, politicians, and bureaucrats, Hector cracked open the doors to the federal government and, for a fleeting half-decade, captured the ears of the president of the United States. He negotiated with cabinet members, congressmen, high-level bureaucrats, and was sought out by powerful politicians and candidates.

During this time Mexican American concerns became a topic of discussion at the highest levels of government. Through his efforts and that of others—most of whom followed his lead—younger reformers came to see the federal government, and the national political arena as the place in which to struggle for civil rights. Hector's battle was a battle for inclusion. He wanted the nation to include Mexican Americans in its policies, its government, and its rewards. But he also wanted Mexican Americans to include this nation in their hearts and souls, to become loyal citizens.

Because Hector saw the American Dream as real and tangible, he chose not to associate closely with those who challenged the basic goodness of American society. While he and others occasionally spoke of alliances with African Americans and other alienated groups, Hector never did work closely with such groups. Their rhetoric and their actions often troubled him. He could often be fiery and would push hard against the "system," but he always knew the limits. He did not always feel the same way about others. Rather than a radical approach, he took a militantly moderate course. He worked passionately for mainstream approaches to uplift his people. He devoted time and money, and tenaciously recruited Mexican Americans to register and vote. But initially—until he became a dyed-in-the-wool Democrat—the greater goal was participation and civic duty, not necessarily electing a "particular" kind of candidate. He fiercely challenged school segregation with marches, litigation, and moral persuasion, but rarely if ever did he challenge the fundamental biases of the curriculum or seek to fire the racists within school faculties. He sought instead to change them, to make them live up to their creed as educators. He believed, at least until a ripe old age, that people could change their views.

He lobbied presidents, senators, governors, and other policy-makers for inclusion, but only to get Mexican American input and not to challenge the direction of policy-making. Unlike other reformers who challenged the United States' wars, or its alliances with dictators, or its harmful economic policies, Hector instead remained steadfast in his loyalties. He did not propose new ideas to the nation; he simply looked at the existing ones he thought best, and promoted them with all the passion and tenacity he had.

Hector did not suffer from naiveté. He simply saw no other vision greater than the American Dream. This was the only place a young immigrant boy with little money and no English-language skills could become a doctor, dine with presidents, and become a savior to his people without bloodshed or revolution. No other place had the ideals and the liberty or provided the elbowroom for people to rise above their humble beginnings. He loved all that was successful in America. History for him was to be found in important American individuals, events, and institutions. And history indicated to him that no greater accomplishment existed beyond the founding and development of this nation. Mexican Americans did not have to work for fundamental changes but rather for inclusion. Becoming American would remain for Hector the ultimate prize.

Becoming American, however, was a collective achievement for Hector, not an individual's personal odyssey. He harshly criticized those reformers of the past and those contemporaries who worked to open the doors to upward mobility for the individual. He had no patience for those who stopped advocating when their personal situation or that of their families became comfortable. He hated the elitism of earlier organizations that would have loved for the barrios to disappear and everyone become like their Anglo American counterparts.

Hector saw the essence of being American not in speaking perfect English, being middle class, or assimilating into a homogeneous culture. Becoming American meant believing in the fundamentals of citizenship, democracy, pluralism, and equality for all. It meant giving one's self to a life of service for the nation and for one's community, as well as being willing to make the ultimate sacrifice for that life. Anyone, of any color, national origin, or race could do this. This was, in his mind, the beauty of American society. It was for everyone, native-born, immigrant, rich or poor, male or female, white or colored.

The obstacles to becoming American came not from any flaws inherent in the American way but from those who did not understand or simply did not believe in the American Dream. In time he would come to see Republicans and conservatives as nonbelievers, although he found numerous exceptions among them. He also felt the same way about those on the left. While ambivalent at first about the Chicano nationalists, he eventually rejected their anti-Americanism too. Adjustments, fine-tuning, and committed patriotism were needed to make Americanism work, not radical change or "foreign" ideologies.

For Americanism to work, much had to be done to change the way Anglo Americans practiced it. Militancy became necessary because Mexican Americans had been kept from the mainstream so long that most Anglo Americans considered them outsiders, and too many Mexican Americans felt they did not belong. Consequently, Hector pushed hard and his actions often seemed militant, and to some even radical. He had to uplift Mexican Americans from so far down that often his work was radical. Mexican Americans not only had to raise their educational level, their economic position, and their social standing, but they had to raise their expectations and their hopes. They had to make the transformation from being Mexican, Hispano, Latin American, Spanish American, etc. to being American. This transition required not only a change in political values and social outlook, but also a commitment to do it against a hostile resistance by many Anglo Americans, and in spite of a disdainful criticism from within the barrio by those who had stopped trying or believed it could not be done. Hector knew there were many from within who were hostile to this transformation. This group consisted of nationalistic old-timers who continually looked south, of barrio politicians who needed a dependent community, of assimilated Mexican Americans who were ashamed of their people, and finally of self-haters who believed Mexican Americans were incapable of being first-class citizens.

In barrios across the land, where misery, discrimination, violence, self-destructive behavior, poor health, segregation, and social isolation had brewed for years, change was difficult. For Hector there was no alternative to Americanism. Unlike Mexican exiles of the past who wanted to return to Mexico, or Chicano militants of the future who sought redemption from within, Hector saw American ideals, civic virtue, and participation in the electoral process as the road to victory. And he saw no group in the nation as imbued with those ideals as were the Mexican American veterans. The preparation for war and the war itself had instilled in them a strong belief and hope in the United States. The combat experience and the ultimate victory against fascism, Nazism, and Japanese imperialism had consolidated their hope. Like a refiner's fire, the war experience had purified them and transformed them into Americans. Taking them as a core group who had been willing to pay the ultimate price, he simply recruited other Mexican Americans who through some political or philosophical osmosis would come to share the same ideals. That is one reason why Hector never questioned the country's wars or military conflicts. Each one provided new members of the core group, and each reemphasized a total commitment to the American way of life. Even more important, each one contributed to a familial and friendship network that could be brought into the movement to reform the barrios and challenge discrimination in the United States.

Hector had no morbid attraction to war nor was he necessarily militaristic. He simply saw service to the nation as the premier example of one's civic duty. Like a Turnerian process of Americanization, militarization pruned Mexican Americans of those characteristics useless in becoming good citizens. But it also refined those qualities that were good, such as loyalty, teamwork, valor, comradery, and self-sacrifice for a good cause. Hector truly believed that his people had as much to give as they needed to receive. Americanization was not a hugely asymmetric equation to the advantage of Anglo America.

Unlike the salad-bowl theorists of today's multiculturalism, Hector believed in a melting pot, but one that kept changing flavors and colors and becoming richer and not more bland. Notwithstanding his concerns about Mexico's undocumented hordes, he had confidence that his people were a benefit and not a deficit to his country. There was a strong sense of hope in Hector's generation that things would get better and that Mexican Americans would take their place as builders of this nation. This hope and enthusiasm for the future was the result of the nation's prosperity, hard-won civil rights victories, and the reformers' own rhetoric. A prominent sector of the Mexican American community came to believe that things were getting better.

Ironically, Hector's success would decline in proportion to his victories. Unlike other new activists who appeared in the 1960s and 1970s, Hector did not adapt to the new political realities. The Vietnam War, working-class antagonism, and student radicalism would challenge and compete with Hector's views of American society. Even those who rejected Chicanismo's nationalism and leftist politics were drawn away from Hector's Americanism because they saw his politics as those of another age. The politics were either too militant or not militant enough.

While Mexican Americans continued to join the armed forces in large numbers, there were fewer veterans to organize and recruit. This was because, unlike those who went to war and came back, new recruits were making the service a career and thus becoming unavailable for the American G.I. Forum for several decades. Also, liberal Mexican Americans, once a source of support for Hector, had become critical of American foreign policy and less likely to use patriotism as an ideology. Ethnic politics, to which Hector had inadvertently contributed, moved away from consensus politics and created schisms between middle-class reformers and working-class activists. Finally government, once a political and economic ally to reformers like Hector, began to move away from providing safety nets and promoting social equality. By the late 1970s and early 1980s, a new generation of Anglo American politicians came to power who had little connection to Mexican American reformers. Some sought to avoid minority politics and others had already cemented a solid and often exclusive relationship with America's "real" minorities: African Americans and white women.

A greater handicap facing Hector would be the changing nature of political recruitment in American society. Mass movements for social reform gave way to special interest lobbying and political-action money influence. The American G.I. Forum had been a mass movement with democratic principles that positively affected Mexican Americans and the nation. While eventually accepting corporate and government funding for its training and employment services, the organization never had much of a budget and it never quite developed a lobbying mechanism that could compete against those of other groups.

Worst of all, as Hector's health declined, not one of his disciples was able to step up and carry the torch as forcefully as he had. No one else had the same charisma, tenacity, audacity, and willingness to make personal sacrifices. The new generation of social reformers was composed of professional "advocates," unwilling to drive across the nation, live off the kindness of their people, speak in dilapidated churches and halls, and mingle with the powerless. Hector loved to mingle with the high and mighty, but he never lost his ability or willingness to associate with the downtrodden. In this he shared more with the Chicano militants he rejected than with the new social advocates he engendered.

The story of Hector P. García is part of the story of America's search for a just society. It is also a story of a time that called for extraordinary measures by extraordinary people. With few resources but a full commitment to justice and equality, Hector created what historian Rodolfo Acuña calls a "constituency," a group of people loyal to his view of American society. This constituency was created more than simply brought together. While numerous other social reformers used the concept of patriotic service as a denominator for recruiting people, none used it as eloquently and effectively as Hector. With this constituency, he engaged in activities that had been the domain of individual or of small groups of reformers. He used litigation, protest, lobbying, denunciation, and threats to accomplish his goals, but they all meshed in the process of collective reform. Mexican American veterans and their families and friends rallied into a movement to challenge the segregated culture of their communities. Through this process they became concerned about justice, equality, democracy, and social mobility.

Reformers of the past and even some of Hector's contemporaries could not handle all the issues at once. They emphasized general equality and opportunity. They also sought to promote Americanism, but few succeeded in making Americanism the sum part of all the other "isms" for which Americans were fighting. Hector did. Yet, that Americanism rarely challenged people's sense of being Mexican or Mexican American. Americanism was not the absence of Mexicanism but its evolution into something even better or grander. In other words, Americanism was both a process and the culmination of the process. And it was open to anyone who believed in it and was willing to pay the price. Americanism was not coercive but inviting.

Because Hector took that attitude, he would see the demise of his efforts by the mid-1970s. More about this will be said in the body of this book, but it is important to mention it now. Vietnam, the civil rights movement, Johnson's retirement and Richard Nixon's impeachment proceedings destroyed the moral foundation on which Hector based his social reform movement. Legitimacy was important. It was only important to be American if America represented all the core values it promoted. Hector believed it did, and so the underlying message of all his reform activities was that America was great. When many Americans and a growing number of Mexican Americans stopped believing in that, or simply did not make it a predominant part of their civic belief system, Hector's appeal waned. He became part of the past and not a model for the future.

Simultaneously arising with the cynicism toward American ideals was the notion that government or foundations had to pay for activism. Reform became a professional rather than a moral endeavor. When many young Mexican Americans entered government service or established social service agencies, they provided parameters to activism that had not been there before. Reformers and activists of the past had been engaged in such activity without the idea of remuneration and mostly on their own time. By the twilight of Hector's reform career, most barrio advocates were either politicians, social workers, bureaucrats, party officials, or poverty lawyers. While articulate and often with more resources than Hector could ever muster, they had restraints that he never had. Hector eventually did accommodate to politicians and government policy-makers but he did so not because he had to, but because he wanted to. The medical practice gave him the freedom that his father had promised him. He owed his job to no one and he escaped much of the economic and social pressure that other Mexican Americans received when they engaged in reform activities. By the 1970s, the only others who could claim that kind of political freedom were Chicano activists who rejected any kind of government connection or compensation.

With government providing the funding or the positions for social reform, the protests became more sophisticated and a lot more complex. By the 1970s, the politics of identity had become the politics of ethnicity and those had become entangled with feminism, abortion, environmental issues, bilingual education, immigration reform, and foreign policy debates to make social reform much more complicated. It became harder to develop the kind of constituent loyalty that the American G.I. Forum had depended on.

Leadership styles also changed. These new leaders were enlarging their agendas from simple inclusion of those on the outside to fundamental changes in the way government operated. Opportunities gave way to entitlements. Loyalty to the nation was replaced by an adversarial approach to politics and reform. Old social reformers were replaced in the mainstream with advocacy lawyers, government employees, politicians, and social workers. The constituency also changed. It became demographically polarized between young people and faithful old-timers. The youth of the 1960s and early 1970s simply did not stay or did not join. With college campuses often becoming the new battlegrounds, the college students stayed active until they left. Most simply never returned to activism on the outside. Others who did not become active in college or who did not go to college were often not recruited to social activism.

The new leadership was also more pluralistic and often narrowly focused on single issues, and it became difficult for old leaders to retain their status or for new leaders like Hector to arise. They often reflected a constituency less interested in being "good" Americans and more committed to having their rights as citizens respected; they were more interested in enjoying the benefits of an abundant society. If Anglo Americans who had gone through Vietnam, Watergate, Central American wars, the Iran hostage situation, race riots, and a severe recession were less motivated toward patriotism, Mexican Americans, who could add the Chicano Movement and heightened racial tensions to the equation, were no different.

The battle for civil rights also gave way to the fight for economic upward mobility. This meant that the new leadership of organizations, such as the American G.I. Forum and the League of United Latin American Citizens, shifted their agendas somewhat. While many of the problems they had faced were still around, finding jobs and training people to escape poverty became more important; In order to be responsive, they had to occupy themselves in getting funding for job training programs. This, in turn, allowed them to hire their best and brightest that were not professionals, and also gave them staff and some operating funds. The entrance into the job-training arena also provided them ties to corporate America. Within a short time, most of these organizations' conferences and conventions were being sponsored by major corporations, particularly those that sold beer to the community.

Hector's work had been mostly with politicians and government officials. With a slight antibusiness bias, he felt more at ease working with politicians and government officials who could be lobbied, coerced, or persuaded to a particular point of view. He was not a stranger to boycotting businesses that did not serve Mexicans, and he had been involved in the Coors beer national boycott. But by the time his Forum and others began negotiating with corporate America, he was in his sixties. He also found himself becoming an icon to which young reformers and Anglo American politicians came for advice. The last twenty years of his life would involve speaking out on issues and trying to keep the G.I. Forum from collapsing. It also involved keeping his story alive. Hector understood that times had changed and that he and others like him were in danger of being forgotten. More important, the lesson of the great Mexican American struggle for civil rights seemed overshadowed by the new politics of the conservative right and the postmodern politics of the liberal left. In the process of remembrance, he made himself the icon of the past. He personalized history and by retelling his story to aging audiences of veterans and to public school youth, he became a living memoir of the struggle of his people.

The biography of Hector P. García is then the collective biography of one. The story of the immigrant, the scholarship boy, the committed patriot, the health crusader, the social reformer, the friend of presidents and politicians, and the historical icon all come together in the life of Hector. His life chronicles the life of upwardly mobile Mexican Americans in the twentieth century as few can. Because such is the value of the man in understanding Mexican American history, this biography is neither traditional nor topical, although at times it incurs both of those tendencies. It is a collective biography through the life of one man.

The first three chapters are rather straight narratives. After these, the rest of the story follows a somewhat chronological style but focuses more on themes and issues to tell us about Hector. His letters and the responses to them, his speeches, his conversations, and his actions are interpreted and reconstructed to provide us a picture of his community. The story of his people becomes as important as his. This approach does justice to his story because his story is the story of his people. No matter his idiosyncrasies, Hector acted and reacted to the things that happened to his people. At the precise moment that he decided to engage in a lifelong struggle for his people, he left personal history behind. That is why at the end of his years he could speak of his life as if he were speaking of the lives of all Mexican Americans. Rather than being egocentric, Hector was simply expressing history the best way he knew how.

This approach to his biography challenges the "oral history" story that Hector himself told. But it serves to better present the man who might have been the most successful organizer that the Mexican American community ever produced, with the exception of César Chávez. Peones to presidents listened to his advice, and among an elite group of strong-willed reformers, he was first among equals. But more important to his history, and to him personally, the average person believed in him and often acted on his word. True, he did not reach all Mexican Americans. In fact, he reached mostly those who shifted their sights toward American society. But he reached many and he came to symbolize their yearnings and their demands. He not only wanted the things they wanted, he taught them to demand them with dignity and honor. For him, the average Mexican American was a greater ally than most of his contemporaries in social reform. Often the reformers' yearnings for the American way seemed tempered by the politics of the day and by the alliances to which they belonged. In contrast, most Mexican Americans simply wanted the opportunities of American citizenship. They believed with him, or he with them, that citizenship was the most important catalyst for getting ahead. In this respect, Hector was a man of the people. Far from ideological, he was practical, as most Mexican Americans have learned to be. Thus, his story is a big part of their story.

I tell this story in the context of his political and social reform activities. While much will be learned about Hector, the person, this book is about him as a reformer and about his influence on those politics that impacted his people's struggle for civil rights. This book is not about the American G.I. Forum that he founded. The Forum's story cannot be written without placing Hector at its center, but his activist life expanded beyond his beloved organization of veterans. Hector was an extremely complex man. People who knew him never could describe him without admitting that his actions as well as his idiosyncrasies often made a mockery of their analysis. They also grudgingly admitted that, no, they did not always understand him, although they might well have known all his goings and comings. Tom Kreneck, head of the archives that house most of Hector's papers and an accomplished biographer himself, shared his many personal dealings with Hector. But he admitted several times that while he knew much about Hector, he did not fully "know" Hector.

Speaking to some of those who disliked his politics and took issue with his view of his people, it is obvious that they admired his tenacity and his commitment to his people. José Angel Gutiérrez wanted to make sure that I fairly "place him in the context of his times." He was a worthy adversary. The historian Rudy Acuña emphasized that Hector had a "constituency." He said this to me when we were both at a badly-attended activist meeting. When I asked him how Hector would have impacted such a meeting, he answered, "There would be many more people here." Others, after criticizing his ways, his Democratic Party politics, and his "middle-class" views, always came back to how tough it must have been in his time to do the things he did.

This work does not purport to understand Hector any more than his closest associates or harshest critics did. What it does seek to do is to shed light on his activities and provide glimpses of his personality. It also begins the process of putting Hector back into the history of his people, where he so deserves to be. He has been ignored for too long, and his people have been the worse for it.

Coming to *El Norte*

It seems quite appropriate that Hector P. García came into this world in the midst of an evolving revolution. Born in Llera, Tamaulipas, on January 17, 1914, his life would be a whirlwind of activity, social reform, and political battles, some of which would take place in areas where everyone took sides and no one was spared. Mexico, torn by violence and ideological contortions, seemed no place to raise a family, and so José and Faustina García chose to leave the capital city of Ciudad Victoria and follow extended family across the border to the United States. Hector, only four years old at the time of the move, did not remember much except the fighting. "A kid is impressed very much when they shoot all around you," he would say later.

As teachers in Mexico's lower middle class, José and Faustina were in constant danger. Besides the possibility of being killed by a stray bullet, they had to worry about which group took power and who would be the next target. Hector remembers his father as having been politically neutral, but his sister Cleotilde, the family genealogist and the García most in tune with family history, would describe her father as initially sympathetic to the Mexican Revolution. As a budding intellectual, he was most distressed by the power of the Catholic clergy and its suffocating hold on much of Mexican society nearly sixty years after the War of Reform had legally curtailed its power.

Unfortunately, as a teacher he would find the government's action in the field of education to be disappointing. After the military government—which had replaced the first revolutionary government— raised national spending on education, a succeeding group of revolutionaries reduced the budget, mainly to punish those who chose to stay in the classroom rather than join the numerous revolting groups.

The Constitution of 1917 secularized education and subsequent governments would introduce socialist tendencies into the curriculum. While José did not stay long enough to experience the shift, he would have likely opposed such actions. His subsequent actions as an exiled immigrant indicate he was very much a positivist, and positivists, not being socialistic, no longer fit in Mexico. Aside from the danger of angry revolutionaries, a devastating drought had killed off much of the livestock on a small ranch that José owned. With few economic resources and a dangerous and chaotic society around him, José chose to leave in 1917, along with hundreds of thousands of his countrymen, to relocate to the United States.

José chose to join his second oldest brother, Antonio, an irrigation worker who lived in Mercedes, Texas. His mother and father had moved there years before, and so had most of his siblings. The border area was initially attractive because the García family had a land grant near the border town of Camargo, which was in the vicinity of Mercedes. This land grant came as a result of José's ancestors' participation in the Escandón mission to New Spain. As Spanish Jews, they sought to escape the Catholic Church's Inquisition, and so they preceded many other Jews who made Mexico their home. Some of the family members settled in Monterrey—even becoming leading citizens there—while others went north to the border region. Dispersed, they worked to conceal their identity as Jews and to build a better life for themselves. But like many other Jews in Mexico, they found a precarious stability that depended on their skills and ethics but which could easily be threatened by their identity. So well did they hide their identity that the younger Garcías would have to wait for genealogical research to learn their ancestry was Jewish. By then they were all Catholics.

Hector remembers the family loading "something like a wagon" and heading toward *el norte*. The memory of the wagon was a child's romantic remembrance as the family actually boarded a train and arrived at the small border outpost of Río Rico that faced the Río Grande River on the northern edge of the state of Coahuila. The irrigation company for which Antonio worked stood across the river and it provided the ferry for the crossing. Once across, José never looked back and never took his family back to visit Mexico. Unlike many other Mexican refugees, he did not live his life in transition, waiting for the chance to return to the mother land. He feared the revolutionaries and he feared not being able to come back to the United States if he did not like what was happening in Mexico. Hector remembered that their status as Mexicans on American soil made his father cautious about calling attention to himself or his family.

José, Faustina, and the children arrived first in Thayer, Texas, where the elder García found work with the American Rio Grande Land & Irrigation Company. But after a short stay there, they moved to Mercedes. They arrived at that small community at a time when army troops were still stationed there. Years later, Hector still believed that the soldiers were there because of World War I. The truth is that they were there because of border conflicts, leftover tensions from the Black Jack Pershing Expedition, and because of the fear that the Mexican Revolution would spill over. Pancho Villa, the famous Mexican revolutionary leader, had actually come to Mercedes, but refrained from looting and burning as he would in his famous raids in New Mexico. The soldiers were also there to put down the *revoltosos*, Mexican and Mexican American guerrilla fighters who had taken up arms against local authorities to protest their harsh treatment. Although he misunderstood their presence, Hector nonetheless admired their uniforms and came to view them as different from "the other people." Thus would begin a love affair with the military and the ritualism of the soldier that would stay with him until his death. It would be in Mercedes that he met his first military doctor.

When his parents left Mexico, they were flirting with middle-class status, something they would struggle to attain in the Rio Grande Valley. Faustina came from a moderately well-to-do home governed by a widow who believed in educating her daughters. She moved the family from Llera, a small town, to the provincial capital of Ciudad Victoria so her daughter could pursue a teaching career. But once married, Faustina became a full-time mother and wife. By the time they came to the United States, Faustina had given birth to José Antonio, Hector, Emilia, and Cleotilde. With the exception of Emilia who would return to Mexico as an adult, those children would be the most accomplished of the García family. Five more children were born to her in the United States.

José had initially wanted to be a lawyer, but the revolution disrupted his studies and so he became a teacher. A stern disciplinarian with profound intellectual tendencies, he never got used to the fact that as a Mexican immigrant, he could not use his professional skills, except with his own children. For a short time upon their arrival, the family lived on a leased ranch named *Campesario,* where José tried farming. But José found no joy in this kind of work and even found it humiliating. He not only did not like farming but he did not look the part. His children would remember him as tall, with green eyes and very white complexion. He was "Spanish-looking," and one of his daughters remembers his extended family as having been disdainful of those with Indian features. Yet neither his children nor his neighbors remember José having had such prejudices.

In Mercedes José got together with his four other brothers who had established the Antonio G. García and Brothers department store. Antonio had established the store in 1913. His brother Odón joined it around 1916, and Moisés and Hector became part of it in 1920. The dry-goods store sold plows, work clothing, tools, and most other things needed in this rural community. Customers came from as far away as Brownsville, Raymondville, and Rio Grande City, well-established communities close to the border. It was said that anything you were looking for "you could find it at García's." Within a few years, Moisés opened a dance hall right behind it, making the store an important town center for the Mexican American and Mexican community. The store provided the kind of stability that few other Mexican immigrants acquired. It provided a job, merchandise for the family, a company car—which allowed the García children to drive—and an opportunity to integrate into the community. For a time, one of the few stores in the Mexican side of town, it attracted both Mexican and Anglo American customers.

Eventually, José opened his own clothing store even as he remained an employee in his brothers' store. The fact that he had the largest number of dependents in the extended family meant that he used the store's resources the most. This caused resentment among the other brothers, and so he decided to augment his finances and depend less on the store's merchandise. José also moved his family into a small house less than two blocks from the store. The area was "nothing like upper class," but neither was it the more traditional barrio. Their house stood within the business district and was the closest thing to a middle-class neighborhood that Mexicans could occupy. Well-known writer, educator, and Mercedes neighbor, Rolando Hinojosa-Smith remembered the neighborhood as a five- or six-block area of town where a particular brand of *mexicanos* lived. There were recent immigrants, longtime residents, and native born. What separated them from the rest of the townspeople was their closeness, their desire to succeed, and their lower-middle-class status. This status was often cultural and intellectual rather than economic. Most Mexicans were poor in Mercedes, but some simply navigated life there better than others.

While the family had few belongings, José had a stable job, and hunger or deprivation did not play a daily part in their lives as it did for many other Mexicans in the region. As immigrants, they fell in between the dichotomy of the elite exiles and the peons. They would be limited by the difficulty of acquiring luxury items, but they could count on having enough to live on. In 1920s rural Texas, that meant living modestly. This modesty often came by choice. José worked at the store but he did not put his heart and soul into it. He also had no illusions of having one of his sons or daughters take over the store. He envisioned them as professionals, not merchants. He never allowed them to become too preoccupied with helping with family finances, although some of them did make it a priority. Their role was to get educated, even if it meant that the family as a whole would just barely get by.

The world into which José and Faustina brought their family resembled nothing of the past world, except in its convulsions and tensions. No open warfare existed, but the conflict between Anglo Americans and Mexicans and their native counterparts raged just as profoundly. Only two years earlier, Mexican *sediciosos*, or revolutionaries, had risen up in arms, proclaiming a campaign to end "gringo dominance" and form a nation in the Rio Grande Valley region. There were all kinds of armed groups, and it took the U.S. cavalry and a ruthless Texas Ranger campaign to put the insurrection down. In the years preceding the García arrival, Texas Rangers and Anglo American vigilante groups had lynched hundreds of Mexicans. Calm had returned to the region by the time of the family's arrival, but it was a class- and race-based accommodation.

Many of the Mexicans who remained after the U.S.-Mexico war, or had come early on and survived the loss of land and the violence, had integrated into the larger society and played a significant role in communities such as Mercedes. However, there were many more who had been pushed into a mass of working-class laborers. And except for a few counties on the border, the Mexican and Mexican American community had lost much of its political and social power. Political bosses, most of whom were Anglo Americans, ruled South Texas and the Rio Grande Valley. The few existing Mexican American leaders were not particularly interested in their people's welfare, despite some of them railing against "gringo" prejudices and discrimination. Like the *caciques* in Mexico, they rarely questioned the social disparities among their people. In most of Texas, racial discrimination was rampant and Mexican American elites had to hold on to what they had by creating alliances or simply staying out of politics and avoiding any conflict with Anglo Americans.

José understood well the complexities of the social reality that was the Rio Grande Valley. That and his positivist views made him a strict disciplinarian. He taught his children that the main purpose of life revolved around an education. School fulfilled that purpose and nothing else. Seeing the poverty and the illiteracy among most of the Mexican and Mexican Americans in Mercedes, and seeing how that lack of education made them targets of discrimination, José made up his mind to press his children incessantly. He understood that they had little margin for error, if their lives were to be different from that of their other countrymen. For him, athletics, extracurricular activities and girlfriends and boyfriends were a distraction and forbidden. In the United States educational system, athletics and extracurricular activities were a sign of the Progressives' entrance into the educational arena. These reformers saw athletics and other educationally sponsored activities as a way to Americanize many of the foreign immigrants and a way to teach moral values and loyalty to the American way of life. It was also a way to homogenize the different economic classes by providing an environment where all children, regardless of nationality or background, could find an even playing field. This of course did not apply to most of the colored immigrants.

The American public school system provided a worldview that was attractive to the middle class and to those who wanted to be middle class. José must have understood that this kind of system benefited those who began life on an equal plane. Most Mexican immigrant children did not fit. They had to focus on catching up. Besides, the Mexican school system did not provide these extracurricular activities, and they were new to José who, trained under the old system, believed in rigid schoolwork and discipline. Starting out unequal was an apparent trap from which few Mexicans could escape. His children were going to be different.

It may be valuable to point out that in the 1920s, American youth became a more dominant sector in the culture of American society. Parental control loosened, families became more nurturing, and youth became more focused on their liberties and their future. Schools, clubs, and recreational activities became the domain of unsupervised youth. José was likely alarmed by this and probably saw that this youthful lifestyle was more conducive to middle-class white youth than to immigrant youth. Mexican American youth had so little leeway in how to live their lives.

José expected his children to pay strict attention to their teachers, behave and then run home as soon as school ended. Once home, they were to tend to the store, do chores, and study. If they did not respond to the verbal command, he responded physically. Using a time-tested Mexican form of punishment, he would belt his sons. Hector defended his father's actions, as most children and spouses do, by taking blame for the elder García's temper tantrums. Hector seems to have been the one son who most tested his father's social parameters. As the most independent of all the children, he played sports and dated, something that worried his father. He also snuck away when his father's vigilance slacked off. Hector sometimes failed to show up at the store, and his father knew where to find him. In a sight that might have become routine for the kids of Mercedes, José would chase his wayward son from the football or baseball field to home, where Faustina came to the rescue. Despite his strictness, the elder García threatened a spanking more than he delivered.

The escapades revealed the energetic and independent-minded side of Hector. He credited his father for that energy, although it is likely that his father would rather have seen him expend it in studying and working at the family store. Hector used this joy for life to live as much of the youthful life as he could. Years later his energy exhausted even his closest friends and fellow reformers. His friends would most remember the tenacity with which he lived life and the fact that he rarely got tired of doing what he set his mind to doing. Hinojosa-Smith, several years his junior, remembered him as the handsome guy with girlfriends up and down the Valley. His good looks, good manners, and "likeliness to succeed" made him a great catch, especially for the Mexican American girls of the area's elite families. But Hector, showing an early egalitarianism, did not make class distinctions in his amorous relationships.

Yet, by his own admission, he had more interest as a young boy in sports than "anything else." He liked football, the great emerging American game and played halfback and guard for at least one season. He was tall and husky for a Mexican, but he nevertheless eventually moved to less physical sports. Track became his real love and turned out to be the only sport he engaged in long enough to get a varsity letter. He ran the 440- and 880-yard races, and the mile. Track would fit his nature better. While remembered as a founder and leader of an organization and a promoter of collective action, Hector remained the individual, the loner within the collective. Running alone made him solely responsible for himself, and the results were an indication of his abilities and his efforts.

Whether the thrill of competition or the satisfaction of personal achievement, he loved the challenge. Hector also placed second in an interscholastic district meet in typing, at a time when women did not dominate this skill. As a blooming overachiever, Hector learned to compensate for his flaws. His penmanship was awful, and so he learned to type.

Whether a technical skill impressed his father is unknown, but it is apparent that his father's influence did have a lasting impression on Hector. Years later, he defended his father's rigid discipline, characterizing him as a "very good man who was interested" in his children succeeding. Having forgotten his great need to define himself as an individual while young, Hector would ask an interviewer: "Why [was I] playing football or basketball [anyway]?" As an educator, José demanded his children commit themselves to learning and acquiring skills for a career. As a positivist he believed in education as a panacea for peoples' troubles. This is one lesson Hector never lost. José taught his children history, language (Spanish), and mathematics. He even taught them calculus because the high school did not offer it. This extra education, along with the discipline, meant advantages for the García children that other Mexican children lacked. José understood that his children confronted segregated education at the lower levels and a competitive environment in the high school. Learning would be difficult because the other Mexican children would be of little help and the Anglo American children would be hostile.

Life with José not only meant discipline but also exposure to a world larger than their home or work. Respected because of their knowledge and their service to community, José and Faustina attracted many to their home and place of business. Outside of the family store was a bench where older men sat and discussed the issues of the day, tidbits of history, the Mexican Revolution, the Texas Rangers, and other topics of interest. They would argue, agree, laugh, and tell anecdotes, but more important, they created a much-needed space where Mexicans could come to display a public presence. Young boys would come to hear about Mexico and to be exposed to adult ideas. In an ambiance like that, the young boys of the area could gain a sense of identity. It was a place that helped those who hung around to construct their own identity as Mexicans.

José resembled many other Mexican exiles that escaped the revolution and sought to make a better life for themselves in the United States. But life presented a particular challenge. No matter their education or their economic position in Mexico, in this new land they were foreigners, *meskins* and second-class citizens. Only those with significant wealth could easily establish themselves in their new home, and then only because they had the means to put barriers between themselves and the outside world. For others with less money but the same class consciousness, hard work, education, and personal pride had to be of utmost importance. Their characteristics were reenforced by a strong nationalism. Not the nationalism of the revolution but the one of the Porfirio Díaz dictatorship and the early, optimistic years of the revolution, when Mexico had been ready to assume its place in the higher echelons of world society.

Fighting a constant battle for the soul of the Mexican nation were the old conservatives with their creole pride, their Catholicism, and their European focus, against the new mestizos with their revolutionary rhetoric, their adulation of the indigenous, and their liberal corporatism. While the conflict was first political, it later became ideological. The *exiliados*, both conservative and liberal, would spurn a generation of liberal reformers as well as revolutionaries, unionists, and leftists on the northern side of the border. Both sectors of the *exiliado* community were important for the cultural maintenance and creation of a Mexican community in the United States, but in the long run they held diametrically opposed visions of Mexican American destiny.

While José served as the educator, the disciplinarian, and the promoter of Mexican culture, Faustina provided the nurturing and instilled the faith. Her children remembered her as a loving mother who took time to be with each one of them. A tall, beautiful woman, she had been a beauty queen in her state of Tamaulipas, Mexico. In Mercedes, she became the trusted one among the women who came to her for advice and to gossip. They admired her intellect and her sophistication in a place where most of the women were working class and had little to offer their children in terms of culture and education. They could admire a woman who kept her house clean, helped run a dry-goods store, and still had the time to sit her children around her in the afternoons and read them excerpts from *La Prensa*, a state-wide Spanish-language newspaper. The newspaper represented the *exiliado* class in San Antonio who sought to maintain a Mexican ambience among the exile and immigrant community. The newspaper published essays, poems, proverbs, and numerous articles on culture and language. Its call for order, tradition, and cultural maintenance did much to rejuvenate Mexican culture in the northern communities that fought both assimilation and segregation at the same time.

Children from the neighborhood ran in and out of her house, confident that this loving woman would always have some treat or some kind word for them. A loving and devoutly religious person, she insisted her children go to church and learn the Catechism. She taught them to be charitable. Although the family, had little extras, she found ways to give to her neighbors, extended family, and the poor of Mercedes. Working closely with the sisters of the local convent, she helped provide a community safety net. This was important in communities like Mercedes, where most of the people were migrant farmworkers who earned barely enough to subsist, and for whom disease and poor housing were a constant problem.

Hector vividly remembered his mother's charitable acts and found them to be an inspiration for his own charity work. He found in her a sweetness of soul and a positive outlook that was often missing in his father, who seemed always burdened by his bad luck. Hector often brought her flowers and told her that he loved her. Her patience and unwillingness to complain were characteristics Hector learned and used effectively, even as he gained a reputation for being strong-tempered and impatient. Her religiosity also remained with him, although it would be affected by his father's aloofness from the church. Hector would be a dedicated Catholic, but unlike other religious social reformers, he never based his activities on religious premises and rarely used the church as a base of operations. José's lack of religious fervor coincided with his apolitical attitudes once in the United States. Not much is known about his political activities; his children later described him as anticlerical and antiradical. As an immigrant, he avoided political involvements as many other Mexican immigrants did to avoid calling attention to himself. But unlike many other immigrants, José never revealed a desire to return to México. He seemed content in making a life for himself and his children in the United States.

Still, both José and Faustina were proud to be Mexican. They were Mexican to the day they died, refusing to become American citizens. Both of them sought to inculcate in their children a respect for their mother country. Three of their sons born in the United States were named after Aztec emperors: Cuauhtemoc (he died young), Xicoteutactl, and Cuitlahuac. This inducement for their children to be proud of who they were was manifested in daily activities. It was the political discussions outside the store, the reading of *La Prensa*, the numerous classes on Mexican history, and the acquisition of the Spanish language that emphasized their Mexicanness.

José and Faustina could count on the *exiliados* and the Mexican elites of the Rio Grande Valley to help them out. This community promoted newspapers, traveling theater groups, patriotic festivals, debates, political discussions, and role models. Confronting a hostile Anglo American world, and being disdainful of it, community leaders promoted Mexican culture tenaciously. The fact that most Mexican immigrants were segregated from the larger society meant that those who chose to could create a Mexican world around them. Ironically, the more secure the immigrants were in this Mexican world, the more probable it became that they could move out successfully into the American world.

For the García children this promotion of culture and nationality had the desired effect. They would grow up bilingual, remain tied to their community, and appreciate their ethnicity. But they never allowed it to become a detriment to their Americanism. José and Faustina would never have wished it any other way. As positivists, they did not look back. They were in a new country and, while they could not see fit to give up their nationality or their allegiances, they were not about to make their children Mexicans when the United States held all the promise. The promotion of middle-class values and educational skills, along with a stress on public service, was crucial in their Americanization. In the end, this type of rearing allowed the García children to forge an identity that served to integrate them into American society without the conflicts, tensions, and contradictions common to many other Mexican children.

This assurance of a bilingual identity helped Hector and his siblings adjust well to the public school system in Mercedes. Segregation was a way of life in the whole of the Rio Grande Valley. Segregation was complete in the elementary grades, partial in middle school, and less so physically in high school. There, students were often separated by slow or advanced classes, restrictions in school club memberships, and in treatment by their teachers. In Mercedes, Mexican children greatly outnumbered their Anglo American cohorts, so the mixing in high school was unavoidable. But even there the culture of segregation permeated. Social historian David Montejano has argued that segregation as practiced in Texas was a two-way street. Anglo Americans believed segregation necessary and appropriate, and constructed the political, economic, and social barriers to maintain their world free of Mexicans. Many Mexicans came to accept segregation as unavoidable and a way to minimize conflict. Thus, they too created barriers, some molded by resentment and others by fear or inferiority complexes. While many Mexicans and Mexican Americans resented segregation and fought against it, even with violence, they failed to change the situation. So many simply found ways to survive it.

Into this world entered Hector. The segregated, educational world was anything but static. Thousands of students poured into the school systems throughout Texas. Attracted by agricultural expansion, new railroad lines, and industrialization, hundreds of complete families moved into South Texas and the Rio Grande Valley. The school systems vacillated between providing services and educational instruction to the Mexican children and keeping them out. Teachers felt overwhelmed by the numbers of Mexican students, but also by the difficulty in integrating them into the American educational system. Numerous efforts were promoted to educate the children. These educational techniques usually depended on a strong Americanization effort. Early in the century, state educational officials were promoting more state involvement in education. They correctly perceived that local school districts could not handle the influx nor develop curricula fast enough. The state had to provide resources, and university educators had to participate in the creation of new methodologies. Accompanying the growth of resources and methodologies was a greater effort at Americanization.

In the 1920s, the state superintendent called for an English-only law mandating English not only in the state schools but also in the parochial ones. Numerous religious and private schools had been established in Mexican communities as an alternative to segregation.

These schools, financed by the local Mexican communities or the local Catholic churches, provided instruction in Spanish, courses in Mexican history, Spanish literature, and grammar. Texas educators believed that the existence of such schools only compounded the Mexican community's resistance to Americanization. State educators also debated the application of vagrancy laws. They found that in some schools Mexican and Mexican American children were only required to attend at the beginning of the school year, when per-pupil funding was allocated by the state. Afterwards, few school districts exhibited any concern for Mexican children's absences.

Many educators in Texas believed that most Anglo American parents simply did not want their children going to school with Mexican children, many of whom confronted problems of illness, illiteracy, lack of appropriate clothing, and language deficiencies. Parents protested loud and often against educators who brought the children together. Segregation seemed the only solution, even for those educators who felt sympathy for the plight of Mexican children. They felt that segregation in the schools only reflected the reality of the public arena. Mexicans and Mexican Americans lived in separate neighborhoods, participated in separate celebrations, and stayed in their own separate spheres, even at job sites that were integrated. Anglo Americans did the same thing and were even more conscious of their separate spheres. Bringing the children together seemed only to invite trouble. Both Anglo and Mexican children felt uneasy with each other.

The fact that most Mexican and Mexican American children worked with their parents only compounded the problem and made it easier to segregate them. Many Mexican students missed hours of school because of work and eventually dropped out as they grew older and their familial responsibilities grew larger. Also, the farmers and the agricultural capitalists were opposed to having their workers learn "schooling," as this might lead them to desire a better wage. It was an accepted fact that educating Mexicans would make them want to stop working. Keeping them literate enough to perform their jobs, but not so much that they would aspire to other jobs, was crucial. While possibly discomforting to many educators that these children would drop out, it was however a lessening of the load and the challenges. The

Texas public school system reflected the reality of the larger society, and few educators and even fewer parents wanted to experiment with anything that disrupted the social order.

There were, however, Mexican American children who went to school, survived difficult situations, and performed adequately or even well. The Garcías were part of these overachievers. They entered school without a knowledge of the language, and more than once the García children went to schools without money or appropriate clothing, but they never doubted they would succeed. They were part of that group of Mexican children of the 1920s and 1930s who had the tenacity and the courage to overcome the constant obstacles placed in their path. Once these elite Mexican students proved they had the background, parental assistance, or simply the tenacity and intelligence, they did well in school. The public school curriculum in the rural schools did not serve as much of a challenge to bright students. And these students, unlike most other Mexican children, came with tremendous advantages: educated parents, economic stability, language and grammar skills (even though it might be Spanish), and a confidence that they were as good as their Anglo American counterparts. Most also had parents who did not let them succumb to discrimination or the other difficulties inherent in a segregated environment.

Hector's advantage over other Mexican children hinged on his quick learning of the English language. None of the García siblings had problems with the language. The García experience confirmed what educational scholars would say years later: students with an educated background and with study skills have little trouble acquiring language skills. By the time Hector and his brothers and sisters entered school, they knew how to speak, read, and write Spanish correctly. They were also efficient in mathematics. Their father stressed learning algebra, calculus, and some trigonometry, as well as history and literature. After school and chores, they studied both school-related subjects and material José believed crucial to their education. "He wouldn't let anyone go to bed without studying," remembers Cleotilde.

Having such skills must have endeared Hector and his siblings to the Anglo American teachers in the public schools. They confirmed this in their recollections. Guadalupe San Miguel, in his study of public school education in Texas, points out that there were many well-intentioned teachers who were simply overwhelmed by the educational deficiencies of many of the Mexican children they taught. Over time, frustration led to the notion that these students were inferior, either intellectually or culturally. These students lacked the basic skills of reading, writing, and speech in the English language. That they lacked confidence, seemed clannish, and were usually bored with schoolwork only confirmed the teacher's suspicions. Thus, efforts to establish basic and limited learning environments simply lowered the educational and intellectual ceiling for these children. Learning basic English so they could function in the local and regional labor markets would couple with domestic and "usable" skills to define a functional Mexican schooling.

The Garcías and other children of the Mexican elites were different because they came with writing skills, they could read, multiply, and, more importantly, they had usable functions for these skills. They came with the view that education connected with economics, mobility, accomplishment, and even leadership. That positivist view of education was more rigorous, scientific, and elitist than the kind of American educational view in rural America, and this meant that the García children were not only the cream of the crop in the Mexican community but also some of the brightest in the educational world of the Rio Grande Valley. While this may well have engendered disdain or even jealousy among the Anglo American teachers and students, Hector and his siblings recalled few instances in which racial discrimination affected them. The opposite occurred, as they would later recall.

This absence of malice from an insensitive American educational system occurred because the Garcías constructed a singular educational space with which to navigate through the gaps and crevices of segregated schools, racist or at least insensitive teachers, and hostile Anglo American students. Hector saw little wrong with his school environment, except maybe that it lacked flexibility. This environment provided him with status, organized activities, learning—which he loved, and opportunities to excel in sports, typing, and academics. The space that Hector and his siblings constructed around themselves also provided them a buffer from those other Mexican children who were not like them. The fact that the family was not wealthy meant that they were physically part of the masses; however, they were intellectually capable to lead and to traverse the Anglo American world.

With skill, confidence, and discipline they quickly gravitated away from the Mexican kids and many of the rural Anglo American children who dreamed of taking over the farm or assuming a professional position within the region. The whole of South Texas retained a low-attainment ceiling which the Garcías and a number of other Mercedes elite quickly surpassed. Given this advantage, the García children enjoyed school. "I was happy in school," Hector said decades later, after spending many years fighting school systems he characterized as bad. In fact, he remembered all of the family as being satisfied with the educational experience. "There were not racial (sic) feelings at the time or anti-racial feelings toward us," he repeated near the end of his life.

It seems incredible now to believe that Hector remembered a good educational experience in one of the worst anti-Mexican periods of the Texas educational system. He would have been fifteen years old when the League of United Latin American Citizens (LULAC) was formed to fight that which Hector had not experienced. The organization was founded only a couple of hours from where he lived, and it was in areas like Hidalgo County and communities like Mercedes where LULAC focused its efforts. His father, having been an educated man and a merchant, would surely have been contacted by LULAC reformers for assistance in their struggle. The late twenties and the early thirties saw the heyday of segregation in Texas, and the rise of Mexican American middle-class reform that proved to be unrelenting until the arrival of the nationalistic Chicano Movement in the 1960s. Texas was a whirlwind of racial antagonisms, but Hector and his siblings passed through it unscathed.

Yet, the Garcías were not as detached from the reality of a racist society in South Texas as Hector would have many believe. Cleotilde, his closest sibling, remembers the Texas Rangers unexpectedly barging into their home one night. She would never know why they did so—possibly to look for moonshine—but she did know that this was not uncommon in the Rio Grande Valley. Searching without warrants, arresting Mexicans without cause, and engaging in violence without provocation were things for which Texas Rangers were known. This experience and other similar ones stayed with José, for when Hector came home one day with his uniform from the civilian military training corp, he quickly told him to take it off. It looked too much like a Ranger uniform.

Only in bits and pieces of recollection did Hector speak about his life in the segregated and discriminating Rio Grande Valley. But he saw them as experiences rather than blatant acts. Sometimes they were even funny to him as when one of the substitute teachers was scandalized by his cousin's name. "Jesús," said the young man when asked his name. "Jesús," he answered when asked to repeat it. "My god," screamed the teacher, "he is named after Jesus Christ." But though funny years later, Hector admitted that for a time he believed his cousin had done something wrong.

Interestingly and maybe not surprisingly, the Garcías constructed a space that did not include too many other Mexican children in school—at least not to the extent that Hector took note of how the other children were faring. When asked many years later whether the Mexican children in Mercedes were having difficulty in school, he answered, "We had no contact with them other than when they bought at our store . . . so how did I know they had problems?" He would later contradict himself by remembering all the Mexican "kids" as his friends. The discrepancies of having all of them as "friends" but knowing little of them may have reflected a spatial dichotomy in the public and private lives of Hector. For Mexican elite children there have always been two worlds, the school and the home. Social class always played a part.

American society dealt then and now with class by dichotomizing the home from the public sphere. The public schools also provided an imaginary classless world that gave way to the real world at the end of the day. Hector further dichotomized this reality by living in his world even as he shared their world. This would be the case for Hector most of his life. In living his own activism he shared the "others'" world, but philosophically he mostly stayed in his own. Thus, he remained positive about American society, even as he spent most of his time fighting its unfairness.

It is hard to tell much from the records of his relations with non-Mexican students, though he did associate with them through his participation in track and football. His academic achievements made it likely that he interacted mostly with Anglo American youth. In spite of the number of elite Mexican children from Mercedes who went on to achieve success, most of the Mexican youths were dropouts and low achievers. Thus, if he competed or if he made academic friendships, they were likely to be with Anglo Americans. "Even the richest Anglos in town were nice to me," Hector would recall. This recollection came late in his life when even the richest Anglo Americans in Corpus Christi were nice to him. Yet it is quite possible that for an overachiever like himself, who also happened to be tall, white-complexioned, and spoke English well, interaction with Anglo Americans was not only possible but quite frequent.

In fact, Hector remembered that his white skin provided him an advantage over his fellow students. His teachers and some of the Anglo citizens in town often referred to him and some of his siblings as "Spanish." The term served as a way to de-Mexicanize those who might be found acceptable to the larger society. Quite early after the U.S.-Mexican War, the term "Mexican" had become derogatory and demeaning. Even among Mexican Americans, the term had come to denote second-class citizenship and a host of character deficiencies. Many elites had begun to call themselves Spanish American or Latin American to avoid using the term Mexican. In places like New Mexico, a whole mythology had arisen that envisioned Mexican Americans as descendants of the early Spanish explorers and not the Mexican settlers. But the Garcías would have none of that.

José resented the suggestion that he was a Spaniard—although his family had come from Spain—and his children, though cautious and courteous, tried to tell people that they were not Spaniards but Mexicans. Throughout his life Hector never exhibited any embarrassment or shame for being a Mexican. Years later, he would privately criticize those Mexican American reformers who tried to avoid using the term "Mexican." Hector's Americanism did not grow out of his shame of being a Mexican, but rather grew out of his pride of being who he was.

The confidence he felt as a Mexican allowed him to ease into his Americanism. It also allowed him to navigate between the two without ambivalence.

Without doubt, the confidence that came with his "learning" advantage helped in that navigation. While many Anglo Texans may have found an educated and confident Mexican a threat to their class and race structure, Hector, like a number of other elites, never flaunted his advantages nor sought to disrupt the order of the day. Rather, he sought to carefully thread the precarious fabric of American society by never offending anyone. Yet, he never felt or acted inferior to anyone. His teachers and some of his classmates came to appreciate this "special" young man. No doubt part of this strategy was defensively learned in places where Mexican Americans and Anglo Texans interacted. But it was also a natural part of a young man who had learned propriety, courtesy, and respect at home. Hector might have been careful, but more likely he was being proper.

That he had friends on both sides of the racial divide indicates that there were junctures of interaction between the two groups. It also reflected Hector's ability to serve as a bridge between the two worlds, something he would later do quite often in his political and social crusades. This bridge-building helped him create a fluid space in which he navigated his reality of being an overachieving Mexican American in a Anglo American world. This fluidity allowed him to be at ease with high-level Anglo American politicians as well as poor migrant farmworkers. This fluidity meant that his school years were years of preparation for his social reform.

As noted before, despite his father's objections, Hector participated as much as he could in school activities and made many acquaintances. It is hard to say how many close friends he had. In his adult life, Hector attracted loyal followers and created strong partnerships, but with a few exceptions, he rarely gave the impression of being anybody's "buddy" or close friend. He befriended many but he rarely became intimate with anyone. He was congenial and he had a good sense of humor, but his priorities usually revolved around getting people to do things that needed to be done. Thus, most people that associated with him were always doing something for him and taking orders from him. He also had a propensity for being attracted to people with power. This seems quite evident even in his youth when teachers were the most important people in his life. He believed that they had done a good job in teaching him. This is not likely to have been the feeling of most other Mexican and Mexican American children, but it was consistent with the experience of other elite Mexican children.

Hector could recall no ugly encounters in his school years, but he did remember one teacher telling his brother Antonio that "as far as she was concerned, no Mexican student would get an A in English." Hector, however, did not see that necessarily as discrimination but rather meanness, and even that was questionable. Seeing most teachers burdened by Mexican students' illiteracy, Hector sympathized with them. At the height of his social reform years, Hector would be greatly bothered that "qualified" Mexican Americans were discriminated against, while slightly understanding how Anglo Americans might misjudge poor Mexican farmworkers.

Interestingly, Hector did remember one case of discrimination. It involved a young girl who came from mixed parentage. The school officials, unsure of her ethnicity, placed her in a Mexican school. The problem was that she knew the English language well and had an Anglo surname. More important, her father did not want her in a learning environment full of Mexican students with educational deficiencies. He demanded she be transferred to a non-Mexican school, but the school officials vacillated until the father threatened the principal with bodily harm. Hector saw the young girl as a victim of discrimination because she was forced to attend a Mexican school.

Beyond the case of his brother and that of the white girl, Hector could not recall much about racial or cultural issues in his school years when he was interviewed years later. He believed that his parents had never made distinctions among races, so he remained oblivious to ethnicity or religious differences. Everyone that was non-Mexican or black was Anglo American. And the few African Americans in town were called "negritos," a term often used by Mexicans to sound more sympathetic, although it might well be a term that continually traps African Americans into a childlike character, for "negrito" would translate into "little black person."

Detached from the Mexican kids, with few African Americans in town, and oblivious to class and other ethnic distinctions, Hector came out of high school with little understanding of the racial, ethnic, and class conflicts that were prevalent in rural Texas in the twenties and thirties. "We were lucky," he would say later, "because . . . we were good students." One of his brothers was valedictorian of the high school and Hector would finish with the third highest GPA in his senior class. His academic achievements shielded him from the conflicts inherent in his community. "Not only did I not notice it (discrimination), I didn't face it, neither did I feel it. I didn't," he would insist years later.

In contrast, his brothers and sisters did remember numerous cases of discrimination. They also remembered that Hector was sensitive to what he saw around him. They noted that he was acutely aware of the poverty in the neighborhood and the unhealthy conditions in which so many of the other children lived. It is quite possible that Hector did not remember his own feelings of sympathy; after all, his life was flooded with so many instances of others' poverty, illness, hunger, and suffering. They may have all fused into one, and it became hard for him to remember them all. It may have also been that in his innocence he simply took each instance at a time and made no connection to a larger question of suffering. Consumed with doing what his father told him to do, and engaged in the activities of an overachieving and gregarious young man, Hector would store this knowledge to call upon it during his activist times. For Hector, youthful innocence remained important.

For Hector, this naiveté toward the reality of discrimination was natural for a young boy. It would, however, be more correct to say that it was natural for a capable Mexican boy with educated parents, good skills, modest financial stability, and tremendous tenacity. He had entered school with little knowledge of English, but he quickly learned. He read a lot and spent countless hours in the Mercedes school library. What Hector did, he did with passion. No doubt, his parents instilled in him a desire to be more than a laborer or a victim. It was also quite apparent to see what awaited a Mexican without an education. If Hector did not realize it quickly enough, his parents probably did.

Although his parents avoided most social functions, they did retain a loyalty to their neighborhood. With homes so closely aligned, it was impossible not to participate in birthday parties and other extended family activities. Church activities also served to keep the García children actively involved with their neighbors. Much like other Rio Grande Valley Mexican towns, Mercedes saw the creation of internal communities. Mexicans and Mexican Americans, often unable to cross racial and cultural boundaries to become part of mainstream society, founded their own institutions and their own celebrations. His uncle Antonio encouraged Hector and Cleotilde to give speeches during the Mexican Independence Day celebrations. A family theater allowed them interaction with many other Mexicans and Mexican Americans who loved watching the silent American movies. While the political arena may not have been a large part of the internal community, there were other aspects of society to which Hector became exposed.

In the Mexican part of town, Hector saw the small Mexican merchant class, from peddlers to small businessmen like his father. He probably understood that there were elites, politicians, intellectuals, and movers of festivities, such as the Salinas and the Hinojosa families who established businesses and sought at times successfully to be part of the larger society. There were also those like his uncle Antonio who served as a bridge to the Anglo American world by associating with them through business dealings or by simply going fishing with them as Antonio often did. Antonio provided Hector and his brothers a social context outside the home and the barrio. While José served as the disciplinarian, the teacher of academic values, and the instiller of a work ethic, Antonio showed Hector a glimpse of the life in the larger society. He took Hector hunting and fishing, allowing him a freedom of expression and action that he lacked at home. Hector would later remember him as having a great influence on him. Antonio also introduced him to the Anglo world by having him meet some of his fishing buddies. This was an opportunity few Mexican children were afforded. Meeting Anglos outside an institutional framework, Hector learned to feel at ease with them, something few Mexican American youths in Texas could claim.

The store also helped in this acculturation to American society as the García children became the facilitators between English-speaking customers and Faustina and José, who never mastered the English language. The store would stay open until 1:00 a.m. to accommodate out-of-town ranchers and farmers who could only come after all the chores were done. In their capacity as translators and store clerks, they assumed a role few other Mexican children, or adults for that matter, ever played. Being the clerks and future owners of one of only two dry-goods stores in town allowed them to negotiate from strength, especially in the wee hours of the day when few options existed for the customers.

Hector graduated from high school in 1932, when the Great Depression began to devastate the rural economy in Texas. The Depression changed drastically the economic base of the García family. The store barely survived for a time, but people could not stop buying completely. The fact that the Hidalgo County Bank & Trust Company survived the economic depression of the 1930s contributed to the survival of several of the businesses in town. But over time, as the people became more cautious in their purchasing, the store did succumb to the bad economic climate. Hector remembered that rice, beans, and tortillas were always available. And like many other Mexican families in the region, the Garcías also complemented their diets with fruits and vegetables that the packing sheds could not market. Since the Valley had ample fruits and vegetables—thirteen different distributors of fruits and vegetables existed in the community—there was always some to distribute to those who worked the fields and sheds.

The Garcías had friends and relatives who brought them fruits and vegetables. Other times, Hector went to the sheds himself to see what was available. Cleotilde remembers going to the loading docks where she would petition the workers for fruits and vegetables. There was always soup at home to accompany the vegetables. "I don't remember being hungry," said Cleotilde. But, "There were no in-between meals . . . just three meals. We would run from school to home . . . to eat and then run back." The Depression was complicated by several hurricanes, widespread flooding, and malaria epidemics that struck the area. These events made life hard, but it did not change the course for the García siblings.

For Hector, his childhood was precious. It set a strong foundation for his views of what the educational and growing-up experience should have been for all Mexican American students. What most bothered him later as an adult was that other children's experiences could not be as enjoyable or productive as his. He had attentive teachers who liked him. He found education intriguing and fun. He participated in sports and other extracurricular activities, and he found room to experiment. Outside of school he had supportive parents who could teach him skills. He learned responsibilities by working at the family store, and he interacted with Anglo Americans on an equal plane.

While the family fought through the obstacles of being an immigrant family without much financial foundation, it never lost its confidence in its ability to prosper or to achieve. José, who never found fulfillment in Texas—at least not the economic or professional kind—dedicated his life to seeing his children succeed. He disciplined them by regimenting their lives, keeping them busy, and teaching them responsibility at a young age. Cleotilde played the piano and ran the movie camera in the theater, while Hector sold newspapers and worked in the store all through high school. The other children would do similar things. José instilled in them an urgency to succeed that would later serve them well at the university and in their professions. Whether consciously or not, José prepared his children to confront the paradox of South Texas: underachieving Mexican Americans and Anglo Americans who saw themselves as superior. He made sure his children began school ahead of other children and kept them ahead through a regimen of after-school academic work, daily chores in the home, and more work in the store. He also seemed to have avoided letting the South Texas paradox invade his home. His children would never feel inferior to anyone.

Hector and his siblings, once experiencing success in school, took it upon themselves to continue their overachieving. In education, they found the elite status that their few elite Mexican American friends had found in their prosperity. Their overachieving attitude eventually helped them enter the middle class without much difficulty. Equally important for Hector, nothing in his youth taught him about limits to his potential or to his achievements. Personal responsibility, hard work, and an ability to block out setbacks or distasteful moments kept him focused on overcoming the limitations the family had arrived with. Education, but an education that came from home, school, work, personal activities, and reflection, was for Hector the key to overcoming obstacles. Years later he promoted this process by urging Mexican Americans to participate in the civic life of their communities and to keep their children in school. Civic participation provided them experiences and maturity while school provided them skills. Hector never learned to articulate that principle well in the written word, but his speeches to small groups and in Forum meetings, and his personal example were great teachers to those who paid attention.

"An Excellent Education"

For many Mexican Americans, high school graduation even today is a rite of passage that introduces them to the world of work. From that moment they cease being "students" or "young" and they engage in a lifelong endeavor that offers limited mobility and often chips away at their identity as individuals. They become part of the labor pool of Mexican workers that occupies the lower echelons of American jobs. This was particularly true in the midst of the Depression, when few Americans had the resources or the inclination to attend college. Working-class Americans and especially those of color were rare on college campuses. For Mexican Americans who had no colleges of their own and who also faced the barrier of language, going to college was a luxury that only a few could enjoy. This makes it particularly impressive that Hector and his brothers and sisters never doubted they would attend college. The main concern was where and how to pay for tuition and living expenses.

Antonio, the brightest and oldest of all the García children, had gone directly to the University of Texas, where the elite Mexican American youth of South Texas attended school. But the University of Texas was expensive for two Garcías, at least relative to the family finances, and so José decided that Hector would attend Edinburg Junior College, located about thirty miles north of Mercedes. While Hector had the intelligence and work ethic to attend a major university, it turned out better for him to go to a smaller place. Hector had enjoyed high school and often remembered many of his teachers fondly, but there is no record to indicate that he learned much from them. It is accurate to say that he learned many of his hard subjects at home and most of his social skills working at the store. Junior college served as a bridge from high school to the university. Hector still had many of the fun-loving characteristics of the high schooler. He enjoyed participating in activities, despite time limitations, and he enjoyed excelling above others.

For an experienced hitchhiker like Hector, the thirty-mile journey proved a small, although unwelcome problem. Hector remembers hitchhiking to and fro from the beginning. But other family members remember him taking the bus the first year. When Cleotilde entered Edinburg the following year, she got the bus fare and he hitchhiked. While unusual by today's standards, hitchhiking was a common way of getting back and forth in the Rio Grande Valley. Most people asked for rides and most drivers obliged. That is not to say that doing it did not create a burden, especially after a long day in school. Hector usually did it without complaining, but once in a while he had to be reminded of why he did it. Once, after a hard day, he grumbled to his father about his misfortune in having to travel so far by thumb. His father, conscious of not only the sacrifice but of its necessity, snapped back, "That's the price of an education." Hector likely never complained again to his father, and by the end of his schooling, he had acquired his father's attitude.

Hector planned to become a teacher like his father when he first entered college. He remembered it was his childhood dream to emulate his father. But by his second year, he also contemplated a military career. As a member of the Citizens Military Training Corp (CMTC), he regularly trained and eventually earned an officer's commission. More will be said about the CMTC in the next chapter, but suffice it to say that, by the time he was a sophomore in college, Hector had an offer from the military to go to Alaska for $400 a month, a nice sum during the height of the Depression. By this time, his father had lost the store, and most of Hector's friends who had not gone to college were already working. In fact, most Mexican Americans he knew had chosen to work their way through the Depression, working at any job they could get their hands on. In the end, practicality won out. No doubt his father and other family members convinced him that a higher education provided better opportunities. It is also likely that Hector felt the same way. He had dreams of being an important person, and college and medical school seemed to offer the best opportunities.

Eventually, all of the García children entered the medical profession. José had encouraged it because it represented an independent profession that no one could take away. It also meant economic stability, something none of the García children had known. With Antonio already on his way to medical school—he graduated early from the University of Texas—Hector figured it would be relatively easy for him to get into the medical profession. Hector, thus, chose a medical career early because it seemed like the "right and logical" choice and not because of any early discernible love for the profession. Yet, he would become a good doctor because that was expected of him, and he came to love it because he always committed himself to everything he did. This practicality allowed Hector to circumvent all the doubts and insecurities inherent in making important decisions. It would be a trait that spared Hector the depression and frustrations that other social reformers experienced constantly. Hector seems to have had an acute ability to quickly choose the right path for himself and to move forcefully forward, rarely regretting his actions and even more rarely admitting he had made a wrong choice.

Hector's initial desire to be a teacher arose in part from his performance in school and his ability to learn quickly. History, languages, science, and most other subjects came easy to him in high school. It was no different in Edinburg, thus prompting a number of his teachers to encourage him toward that goal. It is likely that they believed he could do much for his own people, and possibly they saw few other career options for a Mexican American overachiever. But his pragmatism and his father's advice pointed him in another direction. Although he later talked of wishing he could have taught, he never admitted regret on the choice of professions.

It would come as no surprise that Hector enjoyed his time at Edinburg. He made some friends, but enjoyed the interaction with his teachers more than with friends. He remembered years later that his teachers took "an exceptional liking" to him. He believed that several of them really liked the Mexican people. They were not anything like one of his high school teachers who had once told him that Mexicans were dark because they drank too much black coffee.

For Hector, the experience of being "away from home," at least for several hours, proved exciting. The distance from his father allowed him to feel more like a man and less like a regulated teenager. While he went home every evening and helped out, he also spent less time around his father's restrictive space. He now had teachers that he could respect for their knowledge, and choosing his own courses allowed him the kind of independence that he found neither at home nor at the store. Hector benefited greatly from his father's discipline and teachings, but it was not until he left home that he began to blossom. José taught his children well but he also suffocated them. Antonio was the first to leave home as soon as he could, and when it came time, Hector proved just as anxious.

At Edinburg, Hector found a number of other Mexican American students. His priorities and his obligations kept him from really being close to too many people, but the few Mexican American students at Edinburg Junior College felt a bond out of being there together, despite the obstacles they encountered in a racist and hostile setting. They were truly exceptional cases and they appreciated that fact.

His Pollyannaish view of education allowed him to surmise that he received an "excellent" education. "The teachers were very nice to me . . . they [were ready] right away to help me and direct me . . . guide me, compliment me," Hector remembered years later. It is hard to imagine that a small, rural, mostly technical school could provide an "excellent" education to anyone, much less a Mexican American student. But again, it is important to remember Hector's worldview. He went to school with a deep respect for his teachers, believing they had important knowledge to impart. He arrived with excellent learning skills and an enthusiasm to learn. And he believed himself to be lucky to have the opportunity to attend school. Throughout his youth, Hector never exhibited a belief that anyone or any institution had an obligation to provide him an education or any other benefit. He was supposed to earn everything he got. His immigrant mindset never allowed him complacency. Consequently, when his teachers were nice and took an interest in him, he saw it as an honor. This awe of education and educators allowed him to appreciate what he could get, and made him work harder. This in turn brought him recognition—something he enjoyed very much—and made him try harder, and the process kept repeating itself.

To keep himself in school Hector had to earn funds anyway he could. Usually that meant traveling thirty-one miles to McAllen to work at a department store for two dollars per eight-hour shift. This made him part of the cheap labor pool that roamed the Rio Grande Valley, but he never allowed himself to be trapped into a depressing work cycle. Hector had already sold newspapers, distributed circulars, manned a store, shined shoes, and helped run a theater. He had also worked sporadically in the fields. There were few things Hector had not done and would not do to keep himself afloat and to help his family. In this respect, he was like most Mexican youth of the region who sought to make ends meet. The difference hinged on the fact that Hector worked in order to continue his schooling, as well as to help the other siblings do the same. His brother Xico (Xicoteutactl) remembers that many other youths, when they found steady agricultural jobs, tended to stay with them until they ran out, whereas Hector used them as a temporary stopgap to meet his economic needs.

By seeing those jobs as temporary and peripherally important to his future, he never became dependent on them. In fact, the whole family approached Depression-era employment as an investment in the future. This kept them from becoming dependent on menial work and from making the economic accommodations a permanent job required. While all the García children contributed to the household finances, it was not their highest priority. In a community where the household and the family were the most important entities, the Garcías were practicing the American style of promoting and endowing the children of the family rather than the family itself. This allowed the García children to get on the American fast track while many of their neighbors were settling into a difficult life of poverty and under-employment.

Being a strict traditionalist yet a strong believer in education must have created a conflict for José. Mexican familial traditions required that sons make "helping out" a priority. A son was recognized as a man when he contributed to the family's finances. But José recognized that a steady job in the fields or packing plants was a temptation away from the university. And that steady job would turn into a life of poverty and low achievement. The conflict of lifestyles also crossed into the economic and cultural domains of García's life. Without land or a thriving business, José had nothing to keep his children near once they became professionals. At this time, most Mexican sons and daughters remained close to home. Once removed physically, they would become susceptible to assimilation and estrangement from the culture. Most working-class Mexican parents might not have understood this until it was too late. José could see it coming but decided that his children's future was much too important. He could only hope that things would turn out right.

At the end of two years, Hector was ready for the university. Little thought went into where he would go. His brother had already blazed the trail, and the school to attend for success was the University of Texas in Austin. Anglo American elites from throughout the state attended there, and so did the most exceptional of the Mexican elite children. Along with Hector—although not at the same time—those who attended form an illustrious list of who's who among Mexican Americans. It was the largest state institution, had the most modern facilities, and the most famous faculty. That it was at the center of Texas government made it all the more important as an institution of higher learning.

Before enrolling at the university, Hector had been there once to visit his older brother Antonio. The trip had been rather unpleasant for the whole family. José hired a chauffeur to drive them to Austin because he had never ventured out that far from Mercedes. Aware of the tales of discrimination common among Mexican Americans who traveled to the larger cities, he refused to stop at any restaurants on the way or to stay at a hotel overnight. So the family ate and slept in the car. The García children did not receive a lengthy explanation but simply were told that this was the best way to avoid conflict. José tried hard to avoid making discrimination and prejudices a central concern of his children. As an educated man with pride in his heritage and in his family, these experiences must have been painful and frustrating. He chose, however, to downplay them to show his children that life could still be lived normally.

His children had to learn to do the things that people in normal circumstances did: learn good habits, get an education, find a profession, and get along with people. José shared this philosophy with many Mexican exiles who, while conscious of discrimination—and they fought hard against it—still tried to live normal lives. In carving out their lives as best they could, they felt they had greater control of them than if they simply reacted to Anglo American hostility. There was practicality in this approach. Being in a foreign society, they took what they could get, resisted when they could, and accepted what they could not change. This was not a passive approach to them but a practical one that allowed them the opportunity to truly protest when it was appropriate. For as long as he could, José served as a shield for his children against the outside world. But rather than providing a nurturing world, he provided a training ground where they refined their social skills, their academic learning, and their discipline. Home was a training camp. Every experience they encountered was an opportunity to develop a skill, eliminate a fault, or strengthen a weakness.

Following his father's practical approach, Hector made his tenure at the university very rewarding. He liked the facilities, the companions, the teachers, and the variety of courses offered. This was so much better than at the Edinburg college. Like a child in a candy store, Hector marveled at the opportunity to immerse himself in great culture and learning. At the university he found companions who also enjoyed learning and who challenged him to be better. The library facilities towered over anything he had experienced, and the faculty inspired a respect that surpassed anything he had felt for his prior teachers. The large structures, the wide-open campus, the stadium and baseball field, the stately classrooms, and the orderly gardens all gave a sense of importance and grandeur to the place. The University of Texas was the premier institution in the state and it surpassed anything that Hector had ever visited. "Privileged" was the way Hector described his situation. The university may well have also been one of the few places where a poor Mexican American could rub shoulders with the Anglo American elites of Texas. For an overachiever with high aspirations and a humble background, the university was as good as it got . . . for the time being.

Being at the university also provided an extra bonus that he would appreciate even more when he became immersed in social reform activities. In that intellectual environment, he met some brilliant Mexican American students and faculty. Rather early upon his arrival, he met Gustavo García of Laredo, Texas, who became part of the first Mexican American team of lawyers to argue and win a case before the U.S. Supreme Court. Hector would remember him as an impressive, articulate, and good-looking student who spoke almost perfect English to go along with his impeccable Spanish. An aggressive individual, he formed part of the Laredo contingency of bright young men from elite families who came to the University of Texas to prepare to launch their careers. Gus, as he came to be known, lived with his mother and brother, who had moved to Austin to be with him while he attended the university.

Along with Gus, he met Carlos Cadena, another aspiring Mexican American lawyer who would eventually became known for researching the *Pete Hernández v. State of Texas* (1954) case, which won Mexican Americans protection under the Fourteenth Amendment. He also wrote the brief that took the case to court.

Hector also met George I. Sánchez, one of the preeminent Mexican American scholars in the nation at the time; he was also a committed social reformer. By this time, Sánchez had waged educational battles over segregation, bias testing, and anti-Mexican prejudices in the curriculum for almost a decade. A committed New Dealer, Sánchez worked with LULAC and other organizations advocating on behalf of the Spanish-speaking. No intellectual would influence Hector's generation more than Sánchez. The professor of education taught Hector and other bright Mexican American students about the plight of their people. Hector remembered him as the "brains" behind an effort to prepare students to be leaders in their communities. He taught them not to be satisfied with "making it." Sánchez not only remained a mentor but also a friend to many of his students who became involved in social reform in Texas. He became a lifelong friend of Hector, although their relationship would be strained almost to the point of breaking over political alliances. Sánchez, the intellectual and political ideologue, would clash with Hector, the practical organizer and loyal Democrat.

Carlos Castañeda, a librarian and prolific historian, shared the same intellectual ground with Sánchez at the University of Texas. His interpretation of Texas history would become the dominant view of Mexican American history for several decades. Castañeda, in the words of historian Mario T. García, created a complementary history that sought to resolve the conflicts between the Anglo American and the Mexican American experience in the Southwest. He did this by providing a Christian and pluralistic framework in the retelling of the past. This kind of history would be valuable for Hector's generation because it promoted integration and downplayed the most severe racial and class conflicts between the two groups. In Castañeda's view, most ethnic conflicts could be eliminated if Anglo Americans and Mexican Americans made a greater effort to know each other's history better.

Castañeda met with students and sponsored numerous activities, but to Hector's recollection, he never became close to the students. This is probably because at the time of Hector's stay in Austin Castañeda was plunging into a period of tremendous scholarly production while facing some difficult financial struggles. Unlike his colleague Sánchez, he never became a community reformer. He did, however, serve as president of the League of United Latin American Citizens and associated with many other reformers of his time. Castañeda was deeply concerned about discrimination, segregation, and law enforcement violence in the barrio, but saw his greatest contribution coming from his scholarship.

The two scholars provided much of the intellectual impetus for reform activities in the postwar years in Texas and some parts of the Southwest. Ironically, Hector chose not to take any courses from them, and he did not exhibit much interest in learning Mexican American history or culture, this despite the fact that one of his minor fields was history. As a reformer, his historical anecdotes were rarely from a period before World War II or his own childhood. Whatever historical perspective he had came from learning American history and from the talks he heard other reformers give. As a young man, he had witnessed old-time reformers such as Alonso Perales, Manuel González, J. T. Canales, and others rally the Mercedes Mexicans to be concerned about their rights and their treatment. These were either World War I veterans or reformers from the turn of the century. They impressed Hector because they were articulate in both languages, they were professionals, they spoke with confidence, and they stood out in a community with little else to distinguish it. He would get to know and befriend some of these reformers in his own time. But his own American G.I. Forum would be a reaction, in part, to the politics of that past generation.

These reformers were middle-class elites who promoted Mexican American rights but often couched them within a critique of their own communities' shortcomings. They spoke to the issues of discrimination—rarely using the term "racism," since they considered themselves Caucasians—but rarely dealt with class. They saw themselves as equals to Anglo Americans but worried that most of their fellow Mexican Americans were not. They saw history as a chronicle of Anglo American achievement and Mexican American underachievement, as a story of Anglo American disdain for Mexican Americans and their inability to respond to that disdain. Through their efforts they sought to create a "new" Mexican American because the old one was susceptible and at times responsible for Anglo American discrimination. The "old" *mexicano* fought for his or her rights and dignity but did not understand the "privileges and duties of his American citizenship." The "new" *mexicano* or Mexican American knew he or she had to incorporate themselves into American society. The answer lay not in defending what they were but in becoming something new, something more sophisticated, more competitive, more American.

In order to accomplish this incorporation, the Mexican American had to find historical periods of convergence with the Anglo American experience. The nineteenth century simply did not offer any examples except those few Mexican Americans who sided with the Anglo American onslaught of the Southwest and California. But these elites were not historians and it would take Castañeda in the 1940s to find other examples. Thus, disillusioned with the nineteenth century, abhorring the early part of the twentieth, they chose World War I as a watershed event in the Americanization of the Mexican American. Yet, relatively few Mexican Americans participated in that conflict.

Only future elites did, and so history was personified in their personal experiences. This history then became a history of events and personal experiences that "implied" what Mexican Americans were capable of if they simply chose to and were allowed to become Americans. No collective sense of positive history came from their political speeches, despite their striving to motivate and inspire their *raza* through anecdotes and tidbits of history.

Hector never fully grasped the value of Mexican American history, culture, or literature. If he had, he might have been a more active participant in the discussions and activities occurring at the University of Texas among his fellow students and acquaintances. Years later he downplayed any political consciousness-raising at the University of Texas. He would later say, "I was a premed student, that's all I was." Hector concentrated on his studies and on preparing to enter medical school. No doubt the exposure to so many capable individuals would eventually prove useful, but his education came first. Thus he avoided most political discussions and agitations, and years later accepted the fact that he was ignorant of his rights. Besides, he would defensively argue, there were so few Mexican Americans at the university that they attracted little discrimination. This would contradict the experience of many other Mexican Americans who were also a tiny minority in other American colleges.

One person who was there just before Hector was Mike De La Fuente, a young Mexican baseball pitcher. De La Fuente was also an overachiever, but on the baseball diamond and not in the classroom. Because of baseball, he had many more Anglo American friends than Hector and he was a more valuable commodity to the school—especially since he did not lose a game in his first three years. Yet, he constantly had to verbally and physically defend himself. He found himself excluded from activities, and only when he became a star did his team fully accept him. While he also loved his experience at the university, he never forgot the abuse he had to put up with. The fact that he proudly and publicly defended his national origins may have been one reason he confronted such difficulties, but in his experience it was the only way to retain his dignity.

It is not known what kind of problems Hector faced because he told no interviewer or chronicler about them. Did he fight back, walk away, or try to reason? We will probably never know. What is clear is that there were others like him who would go on to social reform who also downplayed or simply denied that they had been discriminated against. Ernesto Galarza, Ed Idar, Jr., Edward Roybal, Jr., and others would depict a wonderful college life devoid of ugly encounters or embarrassing situations.

Having the ability to navigate hostile domains and actually enjoy their educational experiences allowed these reformers to be committed to American higher education. It also allowed them to create for themselves a stable nostalgia of fond memories, thus avoiding resentment against Anglo Americans, for the most part. This did not mean that they were blind to discrimination or that they never felt bitter or angry against American society. They often did, but they could call upon memories of better times to balance out their anger. Thus, they were less distrustful of Anglo American intentions than reformers of the nineteenth century or the activists of the Chicano Movement. These two groups never learned to trust Anglo American good intentions, and thus made resentment and distrust a foundation of their struggle.

In Austin, for his two years at the university, Hector stayed at the Saldívar House, a boarding home run by two sisters from Mexico. He shared the home with eight other Mexican American students. It cost him $30 a month for room and board. The meal plan extended for six days, and on Sundays Hector had to eat when and where he could. Luckily, Hector had some friends from Port Lavaca, a seaside town on the Gulf of Mexico, who often received fish, oysters, and shrimp from home and were rather generous in sharing them. Throughout his academic years, Hector created relationships that provided him a helping hand or a meal when he needed one. Interestingly, most of these relationships were not intimate but based rather on the fact that he was likeable, and people felt genuine admiration for his work ethic, his manners, and his positive attitude.

For Hector those associations were even more important because he had no social life. It must have been difficult for Hector, who was known throughout his part of the Valley as very sociable, despite his father's rigidity. But there were no funds to spend on dances, dinner dates, or trips outside of Austin. Some of the other Mexican Americans were well-off financially and this no doubt caused Hector some frustration. But he worked it off by concentrating on his studies. The fact that he was bright did not mean that he had been well-prepared in the small rural schools he had attended. He had to study hard.

Not much else is known of Hector's university life, as he kept no journal and rarely mentioned it in his letters or conversations. But by 1936, he graduated with a bachelor's degree in zoology and minors in English literature and ancient history. Lack of money and the fact that he owned no suit kept him from the graduation ceremonies. In moments like those, it became apparent how much of a struggle it had been for the García children to attend college. There were simply no frills, no activities that were not directed toward the goal of getting an education and succeeding in life. Hector had no time or resources to bask in the success attained so far. Had his family had money, each met goal would have been seen as an accomplishment on the way to a better life or a distinguished career. But being poor and insignificant meant that the only judgment or celebration would be the final one.

In selecting medical schools, Hector chose to follow the García beaten path: he accepted entrance to the University of Texas Medical School at Galveston because his brother Antonio had already been there. Hector believed that Antonio's performance there would facilitate his reception, and having a positive reception mitigated any problems associated with being one of a handful of Mexican American students accepted. His status as a minority student at the University of Texas would be nothing compared to the even smaller group he would encounter in Galveston. Hector had no desire to be a ground-breaker. Following a brother who had excelled in every academic endeavor he had undertaken meant following a well-prepared path.

Although Hector later gained a reputation for combativeness and for opening doors, throughout his educational odyssey Hector avoided conflict and found ways to circumvent rather than eliminate obstacles. He did not challenge the closed doors nor did he seem conscious that others behind him would not be able to slip past the obstacles as he did. But avoiding conflict allowed him to focus on his studies and eventually his profession. In the long run, this approach mitigated any serious challenge in his early life and provided him the skills he would need years later. Hector had no other alternative vision. He might have followed Sánchez's disciples in becoming involved in community issues, but even they did not challenge the university's hostile environment. They too saw it as a necessity to get a degree and move out. Back then, the university was not the place where one demonstrated for civil rights.

Once at the medical school, Hector found the course work difficult, especially chemistry and physics. But as in Austin, he enjoyed the challenge and even found that his Spanish came in handy in making the Latin terms easier to remember. He tried to build on his strengths and survive his weaknesses. He saw himself as an average student at the medical school, and felt fortunate to survive as he saw students who had been with him in Austin not survive their first year. Of course, the course work was not the only problem that confronted a new medical student. Socializing in a very formal environment, making new friends, and finding places to relax from the tension of medical school were also very important. For Hector, Galveston became a much lonelier place than Austin. Still, Hector made acquaintances and a few friends. There were, to his knowledge, at least four other Mexican American students in the medical school, but he did not take classes with any of them, and there is no record of whether he befriended any of them.

The time in Galveston allowed Hector to be more active in his community. While in Austin, he had often wondered why so few local Mexican Americans attended the University of Texas. He saw in Austin a rather beaten down community, but chose not to get involved or do more than wonder. But in Galveston Hector felt prompted to do something, to get to know the community and to serve it. This action was probably spurred by the fact that he worked in two hospitals with many African American, Mexican American, and poor white patients. He studied at John Sealy Teaching Hospital (Galveston) and practiced in Jefferson Davis Hospital in Houston. He found that he enjoyed working with these patients because they had faith in him and listened intently to his instructions. Hector treated each patient seriously, taking time to explain the procedures and medications and often going the extra mile in providing them health care. For the Spanish-speaking, it was the first time that anyone had spoken to them in their language in that setting. But even the other patients found in Hector someone extremely sensitive to their pains and concerns. This trust meant that the patients were more open to Hector's inquiries and allowed him more freedom to learn than most middle-class patients would have permitted.

Hector found he could communicate well with the poor and often illiterate patients that came to be treated. It is probable that they came apprehensive about their treatment, since they had little money and limited experience with doctors. It is also probable that many could recall bad experiences with young medical students who saw them as "samples" on which to experiment and learn. Being sick, poor, and of color in 1930s America was not a pleasant experience. Meeting someone who spoke their language, felt at ease with their poverty, and cared about their illnesses was rather astounding to them. While working with these patients Hector may well have developed his crusader's zeal as he tenaciously sought to find remedies for their medical problems. But hospital treatment was not sufficient for all that ailed them. He quickly grasped the idea of prevention as he realized that poor diets, unsanitary homes, and unsafe work environments meant a constant attack on their health.

During his stay in Galveston, then, Hector organized a group of mostly Houston residents and some medical students to launch a disease-prevention program for the Latino community. He and other medical students taught the Houston residents about hygiene, disease prevention, immunization, diabetes, tuberculosis, and cancer. The volunteers sought to head off most diseases before they began because treatment was long, expensive, and sometimes unavailable to the community. Unused to such attention, most of the patients were so appreciative that they befriended Hector and the other volunteers and often invited them to their homes for lunch and dinner. Hector, who always depended on the kindness of others to keep his stomach full, graciously accepted as many invitations as he could. In no time his personality, charm, and his dedication to their good health won most of the people over. In Hector they found a young man they could be proud of.

Aside from lecturing on hygiene and disease prevention, the group also translated educational material from English to Spanish. In this effort they were assisted financially by a well-to-do Italian family in Houston who often provided the resources to produce the printed material. The group visited schools and churches to pass out literature, lecture, and answer questions that residents rarely ever had an opportunity to ask. Given the opportunity to participate in maintaining their own health, many Mexican Americans and Mexican immigrants responded eagerly to the meetings. This was still at the height of the Depression, but few of the poor found similar concern from many of the New Deal agencies. Acts of service and charity were deeply appreciated. This thus endeared Hector to that part of the Houston Mexican American community affected by the work of his organization, so much so that they made him part of their Cinco de Mayo and Diez y Seis de Septiembre celebrations. This, of course, made him an even more integral part of the active community and gave him his first taste of civic life in a major urban center such as Houston.

It also allowed Hector to attend the large Mexican dances in Houston without having to pay or wear a tuxedo. These dances were the biggest attraction during weekends, offering an opportunity to meet new friends and particularly companions of the opposite sex. The home-cooked meals, the free dances, and the socializing outside the medical school were a tremendous benefit for someone with limited funds who depended on his doctor's frock for clothing. The experience also allowed Hector to learn to navigate class lines within the Mexican American community. As a doctor-in-training, he was allowed into the higher levels of the community, and his charitable service created a place for him among the poorer members of the community. This smooth navigation among different constituencies would teach Hector about organizing among the different classes of the Mexican community.

One of Hector's friends, Vicente Eduardo Jiménez from Floresville, was dating the Mexican consul's daughter at the time, and that opened the doors to the immigrant community. Once having the opening, Hector, in what would become customary fashion, rushed in to do service. The organization that he founded in this first organizing effort—the Federación Regional de Organizaciones Mexicanas Confederación Estatal de Galveston—gave him a certificate of appreciation for his work. He was so proud of it that he kept it safely stored for the rest of his life.

The years in Galveston proved to be a productive time in his young life. For the first time, he became involved in an effort that went beyond meeting his own needs or accomplishing his own goals. While participating in these activities enhanced his skills and gave him an advantage in his residency years, he did it out of his concern for the Mexican American community. The hard workload, the limited funds—his father had to sell his life insurance policy to pay for Hector's school, and the demands of being a minority could well have kept him busy and self-consumed. Instead, he committed himself wholeheartedly and displayed the tenacity and inexhaustible energy that characterized his later organizing activities.

Hector discovered that he had a mission to fulfill that would take him back into the barrio. This was not simply a disposition to do charitable work or to give back to his community. This was a desire to do something for the community that it could not do for itself. By maintaining a strict commitment to his studies, as his father had taught him, he was now in a position to do what his mother had taught him to do: charitable work. The fact that he brought with him a dedication to learning and self-improvement meant he distinguished himself from others who lacked one or the other characteristic or simply had had no opportunities. But coupled with these character strengths, he brought with him a closeness to the poor and the working class that few medical students could match.

Being concerned ideologically with the poor would be one reason a number of his generation's reformers got involved. For Hector, becoming involved in his people's plight did not result from ideology or politics but rather from a concern for their well-being. Hector developed a sense of mission, admitting to his brother shortly after the war that he had a special role to play in his community. While Hector would later come across at times as arrogant and overbearing, even his enemies acknowledged his love of community. This love no doubt was learned in part at home. But it revealed itself and refined itself in his work among the poor in Houston. Seeing their pain and befriending them allowed him to bond with them in a way that other social reformers could not. Staying connected with them gave him an empathy toward them that transcended ideology.

Hector graduated in 1940 and this time he did attend the commencement ceremonies to receive his medical degree. He had no more money than he did after his first graduation, but this time Cleotilde's husband had a suit to lend him. Hector then took the customary hitchhike and arrived in Galveston in time for the ceremonies. Years later, he fondly remembered the festivities as a "thing of beauty." At the time, he realized that he was one of the lucky few to accomplish such a goal. Hector would forever appreciate and love the pomp and circumstances of events such as these, and he had no qualms in enjoying recognition for his achievements. His financial difficulties and the fact that he came from an undistinguished family, moreover, may have motivated his constant search for attention and honors that became obvious in his later years. While he did not engage in charitable acts or social reform for the sake of publicity or honors, he enjoyed basking in the attention they brought.

Hector spent little time in Mercedes after graduation, moving to Omaha, Nebraska, to begin his internship and residency. He would have rather stayed in Texas, but his own misgivings about how he would be treated in his home state led him elsewhere. Several of his professors and probably a dozen of his colleagues had advised him to avoid an internship in Texas. The rest of the Southwest did not provide much more hope. Luckily, Grace Collins, director of nursing at John Sealy Hospital, had encouraged him to apply to St. Joseph's Hospital, a branch of Creighton University's medical school. That it was a Catholic hospital made him feel more at ease in moving so far away. So following his custom, he hitchhiked to Omaha with little money and few clothes, hoping that the physician's uniform would compliment his wardrobe. With $50 a month, room and board, and a uniform, he survived two years of residency there. Only once did he visit his home, and that was when his mother died.

Faustina's death proved a major blow to Hector. He loved his mother dearly. All throughout his youth, when rigidity and work seemed to be the norm, she had provided an oasis of love and peace. She comforted him in his moments of sadness and when he seemed ready to be overcome by the despair that was the Rio Grande Valley. She spent time talking to him about things other than school or business. For an overachiever who had so many dreams, she served as the patient audience who always encouraged him. Hector would never write about his mother or say anything in public about her, but he carried her memory with him throughout his life. He would never find another nurturer in his life like Faustina. Without her, he would also find it difficult to give of himself to family, as he had before.

The teaching physicians soon took a liking to this odd fellow from Texas. They were impressed by what he knew and his ability to learn quickly. It amazed them that he could deliver babies, and perform spinal punctures on his own. Even some of these doctors had not done those procedures. Having volunteered so much and been given access to poor patients in Houston meant that he knew more than most interns, especially those trained in private hospitals or who had never done any charity work. Most paying patients would have been horrified to have students providing medical attention. Poorer patients had little choice but to allow their bodies to be laboratories. This meant that Hector got a chance to do more at the hospital and this allowed him to expand his knowledge, even as others were learning what he already knew. This would be another important trait of Hector's, his wide range of experiences that kept him ahead of others, even those much brighter than he. Never one to abuse time or downplay experiences, he walked around with a surplus of knowledge that prepared him to confront most situations. His hard work and his medical knowledge simply put him in position to endear himself to his instructors.

In Omaha, Hector met his first sizeable group of Germans, Poles, Czechs, and other ethnic Europeans. It offered him a new experience since those groups, while well represented in Texas, lived far from South Texas and the Rio Grande Valley. This experience taught Hector that not all Anglo Americans looked or acted the same. Diversity, a cornerstone of his philosophy, began to take shape outside of the segregated valley. Omaha showed him that different groups could

work together, although admittedly they were all white. During this
period, Mexican American reformers were still advocating Caucasian
status for the barrio residents.

In the Midwest, Hector met the first Mexican Americans who
were not from Texas. Most of them worked in the packing plants and
slaughterhouses of the region. Interestingly, he saw them as "well-
off," probably in comparison to the mostly migrant farmworker families of the Rio Grande Valley. They had stable jobs, humble homes,
and for the most part their children were in the public school system.
Most had arrived there several years earlier as children of Mexican
laborers who had helped build the railroads and pick the crops.

Hector's perceptions were skewed by his limited contact with
those Mexican Americans. Unlike in Galveston and Houston, his stay
in Omaha did not produce the same type of relationships with the community. There were simply fewer Mexican Americans, and they were
less organized. Most Midwest Mexican Americans would have told
him that poverty, unemployment, segregation, and discrimination were
every bit as bad as they were in South Texas, possibly even worse.
There was less of an internal community structure, there were no Mexican American politicians or reformers to defend them, and the winters
were horrible to live through in their dilapidated homes. But Hector
may have been right in one perception: they were not yet as structural-
ly subjugated as they were back home in Texas. And since they were
relatively small in number, they were not seen as much of a threat.

The war ended Hector's educational career earlier than expected.
He did not finish his residency before he donned an army uniform.
Yet, despite its abrupt end, his educational odyssey served him well.
Few Mexican Americans would travel the road he did and learn so
much about the things he needed to do. Hector's educational odyssey
had served to transform him from a Mexican boy into an American
man. In his mind, Hector had disproved any notion of his inferiority,
if there ever was one. He had also proven to be as good as any of his
classmates.

The fact that Hector endured this journey in such horrible financial
straits served to help him prioritize his goals in life. Throughout his
educational career he had barely survived, and for the rest of his life

money played a secondary role. Repeatedly, he engaged in reform activities with limited resources and managed to perform the task after suffering some financial hardships. His efforts never centered on making money or creating the kind of financial stability that many post-war reformers sought out. The medical practice gave him stability and security, but it never afforded him much else. His other brothers and sisters would find a greater economic return for their education, and his nuclear family would resent some of the sacrifices he imposed on them, but Hector had learned only too well to engage in life without the benefit of much money. He did not live in poverty, by any means. By his mature years he had a nice house and enjoyed driving a Cadillac, but little was left over to provide anything other than a middle-class life.

The awe with which Hector perceived educational institutions served to build in him a respect for American ideals. He learned to conform to the parameters of American political philosophy and he never engaged in any action directly harmful to any American institution. Like reformers of an earlier generation, he simply sought to have other Mexican Americans participate in the American experience. His own positive experience in the American educational system convinced him that the problems of Mexican Americans were problems of access. Even during his moment of greatest criticism of the public school system, he never lost that perspective. Since school had been good for him, it could be good for anyone. No fundamental flaws existed, and most problems could be eliminated with a more open policy. This attitude allowed him to engage in an all-out assault on the closed doors of the educational system without worrying about divisive ideological debates on the merit of the education provided. This educational experience would help him define his future strategy of fighting for accessibility and not radical change. It would be appropriate to say at this time that his experiences meshed well with the idea of American pluralism and democratic principles.

In his mind there was nothing a young, poor Mexican boy could not do if he worked hard, maintained discipline, took advantage of opportunities, and acted with modesty and respect. What he had accomplished had been done by playing by the rules. American institutions had been opened to him and Anglo American teachers had responded to his commitment by being kind, encouraging, and sup-portive. None had served as an obstacle. The schools had provided him an education and facilitated his journey to the next step. While discrimination and prejudices abounded, he had never been a victim. By maintaining a positive attitude and never becoming bitter, he had managed to come out of school, college, and medical school without any permanent scars. That he did so is a testament to his will. He was not going to be discriminated against and he was not going to become a victim. He was going to succeed, no matter what. This was the only way for a Mexican American to survive. To fight back at every instance guaranteed closed doors, enemies, and failure. Hector did not see any value in living an adversarial role. His father had taught him there were ways to get ahead, and his experiences in higher education had confirmed to him that view.

"A Desire to Serve My Country"

The attack on Pearl Harbor took Hector by surprise as it had most Americans who hoped that their country would stay out of war. Once the initial shock subsided, he realized a dark cloud of concern had settled over many of the interns, doctors, and nurses. Many were married, and a number had children and worried about having to leave home and go to war. Most could not see themselves as soldiers or even medical officers. They could not fathom mass casualties and the hardships of living in a war zone. A good number came from elite families who expected them to graduate to lucrative practices. Hector remembered one young pharmacist who refused to be a medical officer in the Army, believing the government would simply reassign him to a civilian support hospital. Instead, the Army drafted him into the infantry as a private first class.

Hector did not vacillate in what he wanted to do. He wanted to go. He had prepared himself in the Army Reserves, even as he worked his way to a medical degree. By 1941, he had been in military training for almost twelve years. There was no doubt in his mind that he wanted to serve his country in a time of crisis. In this, he joined thousands of other Mexican Americans who responded to the call from throughout the nation. Despite the treatment they received or the fact that they lived in segregated worlds, or that many of them had experienced exclusion all their lives, they found within themselves a love for their country.

For many of them, the United States still had a promise to keep to them, and they were going to be loyal until the promise was kept. Despite the hostility of much of Anglo America, discussions within the confines of the segregated barrios emphasized the opportunities and possibilities within the nation they had chosen as a home. Mexican Americans clung to the possibilities of America even as they often lost faith in many of its citizens and leaders. The war also represented a greater cause. Along with most Americans, they had followed the news of the war in the newspapers, both in English and in Spanish. The attack on Pearl Harbor had appalled them as much as it did other Americans. For many, World War II was a crusade for democracy and a battle against tyranny.

Mexican American volunteers also saw the war as an opportunity to prove to themselves their valor and to others that they were loyal citizens. Mexican American social reformers encouraged the men in the barrios to enter the service as a way to earn their rights of citizenship. A number of these social reformers had themselves earned this right with their participation in World War I. In fact, several of the founders of the League of United Latin American Citizens (LULAC), at that time the most significant reform organization in the barrio, had been World War I veterans. For this war, the men responded not only from the traditional Southwest but also from every nook and cranny in the vast United States. Raúl Morín, in his book *Among the Valiant*, would write:

> One could always tell where they came from by their manner of speech. . . . It was quite easy to distinguish the fast-English-speaking Angelinos from the slow-Spanish-speaking Texans or New Mexicans. The *caló* talk (slang) of the border inhabitants from El Paso and Ciudad Juárez was in contrast to the homespun Spanish of the Coloradoans or Arizonans. Those that originated from the far away localities where very few of our people live stood out because their knowledge of Spanish was limited and they preferred the English language.

In coming together they reenforced their own sense of identity and created a cross-pollination of subcultures and dialects. It would also become one of the largest regatherings of Mexicans in the nation's history. Hector became part of that mass migration when he enlisted in the Army without even going back to Texas. He had no money for a ticket home, his mother had passed away, and he probably felt that his family had gotten used to him being away. "Looking back," he would say years later, "I really had . . . a desire to serve my country and I wanted to go. I felt a duty to go. I would say, obligated. No! I was not obligated, I felt a duty to go, so I left."

Hector's sense of obligation to his country had begun more than a decade before when he followed a cousin into the Civilian Military Training Corp (CMTC). His cousin Jesús had joined up and had convinced Hector, who took little prodding, to join up as well. Hector had to lie about his age as he was still in high school and not yet sixteen. Not one prone to lying, Hector later justified the fib by rationalizing that he had harmed no one. His age had not been detected, most likely because he stood several inches above most Mexican young men; he was about 5'7" at the time and would grow to almost 5'10" at full maturity. Hector also had a stout build that allowed him to pass for being older. The fact that he was also athletic and took a tenacious approach to all he did helped him keep up with the older enlistees during the hard physical training.

Though Hector remembered it as a New Deal program, the CMTC actually predated the Franklin D. Roosevelt administration by a few years. It was a program begun in the 1920s that took mostly working-class young men and sent them to military bases to receive a month's military training during four summers. At the end of the training the young men could take several examinations to become commissioned infantry officers in the Army Reserves. Hector began his training while in high school and continued it through his time at the University of Texas Medical School. By the time he arrived in Galveston, he was a first lieutenant in the 357th Infantry of the 90th Division of the United States Army Reserve. He kept taking military courses even while studying to become a doctor.

One of the prime reasons that Hector joined the CMTC had to do with finances. The corps provided $50 a month, and he soon discovered that he could be thrifty and save money even as he helped out the family. The other reason he joined had to do with his fascination as a young immigrant with the soldiers on the U.S. border. They distinguished themselves from the Anglo farmers and Mexican laborers in their discipline, youth, and uniforms. Hector's first experience with a doctor had been with a military physician. A number of his teachers had military spouses. More importantly, the respect with which people treated military people had impressed the young Hector.

Military training turned out to be rather rigorous. The schedule began at 4:00 a.m. and stretched through sunset. But Hector loved the physical effort, the leadership role, and the privileges that came with a steady progression of rank. Coming from Mercedes, where the majority of Mexican Americans were an invisible people when it came to the political and economic arenas, leadership proved attractive. He loved the way that his uniform helped him transcend some of the realities of the Rio Grande Valley. When he hitchhiked back to Mercedes after the training, he proudly wore his uniform, which usually got him rides and stares of respect from both Anglo Americans and Mexican Americans.

Not all Anglo Americans, however, felt the same way about a Mexican wearing the uniform of the U.S. Armed Forces. Once, while coming back from training, and looking "darker than the dickens," he found himself accused of impersonating an officer. Some Anglo Americans who had seen him notified the authorities that a Mexican was "masquerading" as an American military officer. When approached by a law enforcement official, Hector proudly exhibited his military identification. Hector later referred to the incident as "interesting," but denied having been offended by the accusation. As far as he was concerned, he had nothing to hide and nothing had come of it. By this early age, Hector had learned to be impervious to circumstances he could not control or that did not have long-lasting effects.

Incidents like this amounted to very little and worrying about them seemed silly to him and a waste of time. "Adaptability has been the source of my being able to succeed," he told a friend years later. As a young officer he saw himself as an American soldier, not a Mexican in an American uniform. He thus did not feel insecure about being seen in uniform and would not admit to being uncomfortable when asked to prove his commission. "I had an ability to adapt myself to what I was doing at the time," he would say. Hector simply became the role he played.

At the end of each month of training at Camp Bullis, near San Antonio, each cadet took a test to qualify for a commission. The courses were designated by color so that cadets could see the progress of their comrades, and the veterans were distinguished from the new recruits. In the final year, the examination involved map reading, battle strategy, and evaluating the other men in the battalion. The cadets seeking a commission led their men through maneuvers and taught them to follow a map. The exams were rigorous and so were the regular training days. Discipline was of the utmost importance and so was physical strength. The post-World War I Army was a place where the grunt soldiers had few rights, and sergeants and officers took it upon themselves to see how far their men could be pushed without breaking.

Hector could be pushed very far. The discipline instilled by his father kept him out of trouble and allowed him to be good at following orders. His tenacity and his enthusiasm for learning and for pleasing his superiors made him a valuable soldier. His cheerful and pleasant disposition endeared him to his fellow cadets and the officers. And his strength and physical abilities allowed him to withstand the rigors of training in difficult terrains and scorching heat. While sometimes pushed to the limit, he always had enough gumption to pull through. His superiors learned to admire this in him.

Once, he was assigned a mule-mounted machine gun company and commanded to maneuver them over San Antonio's hilly country. The climbing over high rocky hills proved extremely difficult for both the men and the mules, especially in keeping them in some kind of formation. The training exercise's difficulty was compounded by cadet officers from various military schools who had come to train the part-timers and show them how the "real" Army functioned. Hector would make a serious mistake while training with these tough and sometimes arrogant cadets who thought little of these summer warriors. After one long march and difficult maneuvers, Hector and the other CMTC officers sat down to eat and rest before they fed and watered the mules. This did not go unnoticed by the military school cadets, and Hector and his CMTC colleagues were severely reprimanded. They had forgotten a critical lesson in leadership. The leader never rests until his men are taken care of first. Hector never forgot the lesson nor did he make the same mistake again. He would remember that summer as one that taught him much about discipline and setting priorities.

After attending for more than the four summers expected, Hector gained his commission and transferred to the Army Reserves. He had moved steadily up the ranks, first as a corporal in 1932 and eventually a second lieutenant in June 1935. In the reserves, he kept attending summer camps and continued to take courses to move from second lieutenant to first, which he accomplished on June 31, 1938. To see his rigid military schedule and realize that at the same time he was facing rigorous premed and then medical studies is to get a glimpse of Hector's abilities and tenacity. That he could do both and excel at them revealed a stable emotional character and a work ethic that few of his fellow students had. The schedule did provide a relief from the reality that he was poor and could not enjoy the kind of social life that others had in college. The fact that he needed the money to pay for school and help out the family whenever he could also motivated him to keep working and advancing in rank. Economics became a great motivator, but these were the economics of survival rather than of profit.

When the war came, Hector sought to use his training and reserve rank to attain an active-duty commission. He wanted to join a unit in Texas, but because he was out of the area, the military seemed reluctant at first to grant him his commission. Hector wanted to enter the service as a medical officer, believing he could get more money, something he desperately needed, and be of greater assistance to the war effort by practicing his profession. He applied for enrollment in the school of aviation medicine on January 25, 1942, but was rejected because he was a reservist. The Army recommended that he join the medical reserve corp and prove himself, but Hector did not want to wait for the summer to enlist. He explained that he was not essential personnel at the hospital because he had finished his internship, and his residency was simply not to his liking. He had already been certified to practice medicine since July 29, 1940. The Army finally accepted him on June 29, 1942.

Hector expected a two- or three-month training period in a military hospital, but instead the Army sent him to Camp Edward in Cape

Cod, Massachusetts, to the 591st Engineer Boat Regiment of the First Engineer Amphibian Brigade. It also denied his request for an advancement in rank. The Army had changed its promotion procedures at the beginning of the new year to make it impossible for reservists to advance in rank without entering active service. Since Hector had not attended a summer camp while doing his residency at St. Joseph's, the Army refused him any promotion, despite the fact most doctors were going in at the rank of captain. In fact, the Army first refused him a medical officer position, and he entered as an infantry officer, which is what he had been in the reserves.

While waiting for his transfer from Omaha to Camp Edwards, Hector wrote his father and siblings some rather tender letters. In them he revealed his love for them and his sense of obligation to help them in their financial struggles. He worried that his military pay was slow in coming, and thus he could not help out a father who was now basically unemployed but who had several children at home and two others in college. In one shipment home, he sent six white doctor's pants for the family to wear. He also sent a box of medical supplies to his brother Antonio, or Tono as he referred to him, who had opened a medical practice in Corpus Christi. In his letters, he took time to ask about each of his brothers and sisters and about relatives and friends. The extended family was important to him and so were his friends.

The bond he felt toward friends and family had grown tighter the longer and farther away he was from them. From 1934, when he had entered the University of Texas, to the time he was called to duty in 1942, he had seen his family for only short periods of time. Most of his life had been consumed with school and military training. He had shown little inclination to return home. The death of his mother had made his father difficult to live with, and there were already some rifts between Tono and his father José. Mercedes also had little attraction for a young man who had been to the university, to Austin, Galveston, Houston, and Omaha. After leaving Mercedes, Hector would never really feel at home there again.

Like many other Americans of the time period that left rural homes, Hector would find his hometown archaic, petty, and at times suffocating. In a later letter to his father, Hector would write, "I would rather you not even open a store at all. In that way you will not have to be mixed up in the daily affairs of a ·. . . town like Mercedes." For a mobile young man who had witnessed the outside world, Mercedes seemed a throwback to another time period. For a Mexican American young man, the little town served to reemphasize the second-class position of his people. Hector may have been angered by such circumstances, but his generation reacted personally and sought to escape and prove themselves better rather than fight back. Not going home, then, became the best defensive mechanism for many like Hector who chose to leave behind the old world.

But Hector was still devoted to the dream of a close-knit family. He loved his brothers and sisters and had a great respect for his father. The further he went from them, the more he longed for the kind of family bonds that build on superficial nostalgia. While all of the García children fondly remembered their loving mother and pledged their respect to a good father, few of them as they grew older revealed a longing for the past, as children of close-knit families do. In the way that parents often later regret, José taught his children to look forward and to go after their dreams, discarding anything that kept them attached to the past or the present.

Richard Rodriguez, in his controversial book *Hunger of Memory*, best articulates the ambivalence and contradictory feelings of many upwardly mobile Mexican Americans. There is a longing for the communal, the affection and the togetherness of the Mexican American family. But the rewards, or potential rewards, and the sophistication and excitement of the outside world, despite its coldness and isolation, are too attractive to give up for the familial. Thus, while the nostalgia is there and the emptiness of the new life is lifelong, the pain is never sufficient to bring most of them back to their geographic or familial roots.

Hector, thus, yearned to have a close bond with his family, but the pursuit of his dreams and incessant necessity to succeed took him away from the family. He had been taught to move ahead, to work hard, to take advantage of every situation, and to be a man of the world, not to be a family man or a simple man of his community. Hector would never really know what it meant to live a life without ambition, without involvement, or with time to enjoy family or some personal hobby. Hector's jovial character and sometimes innocent search for knowledge would always acquiesce to his need to accomplish a task. Thus, he could be a tender letter writer and a devoted provider of funds, while still retaining a distance from all those he loved. Cleotilde, the one sibling most like him, would be the one close relative he had. The war would keep Hector from having to worry about going home and thus spare him the awkwardness of which Rodriguez wrote so vividly.

On his way to Camp Edward, Hector got to see Chicago, Pittsburgh, Philadelphia, and Boston, places he had read about in his history and civic textbooks. No place in which he had lived could compare in size, nor in historical or cultural importance. Houston, Austin, and Galveston were at the time only big towns, still unimportant as metropolitan centers, with little of the cultural and historic importance they would later gain. Without doubt Hector must have played out in his mind what he knew about these cities and added to that information the sights and sounds he experienced. With little knowledge of the severe problems these cities faced during the Depression, he simply basked in the past glory of these great American cities. In between them he saw the American heartland with its family farms, small picturesque communities, smokestack industries, beautiful rivers, grassy plains, and rolling hills. Impressed by its beauty and orderliness, he fell in love with his country, as many immigrants had done before him. The trip served as another phase in his journey from immigrant boy to American soldier.

At Camp Edwards, Hector trained with the unit for three months and then shipped out to Great Britain, from where General Dwight D. Eisenhower administered the Allied effort. He went to Europe as part of the second massive ship convoy to cross the Atlantic. Hector remembered the convoy being attacked several times, but its massive size made it possible for him not to experience combat at sea. Upon arrival, he wrote an undated letter to his family reporting how he had enjoyed his first trip across the ocean. "I hope that the next time . . . will be when we go back to the States, and then we will not be bothered [by] the submarines." Hector arrived in Europe as an infantry officer, although he did assist the battalion as a physician. Still, Hector did not push for his medical status during that early period. By his own admission, he got "caught up" in the excitement of the war effort. Immediately upon arrival he became an instructor, training the soldiers under his command on how to get from the ships to the shore and back.

On August 29, 1942, he wrote his brother Tono. By this time his letters were now all in English, even those to his father, who never really mastered the language. Hector said little of his actual Army experience, except to say that things were going well. It would be an approach he kept throughout the war, never letting on about any danger and reassuring his family that he was fine. In the letter, he told Tono that he had not married as he had planned because of his transfer to Europe. "I guess my girlfriend is disappointed a bit, but she is very nice and will take it alright."

Tono, as well as the rest of the family, must have been surprised at the news. Nothing in his previous letters had indicated that he had developed that kind of close relationship with anyone. Only in subsequent letters did he reveal her name, Constance McArthur. What little he told them described her as a nursing student at St. Joseph's. But for the time that the relationship lasted, she wrote daily. Hector had her write to his family and they to her. He even got his father to send her some Valley fruit. Hector planned on marrying Constance after the war and taking a "long honeymoon into Mexico." He then expected to start a profitable medical practice. "We will win," he wrote Tono, "and then all will go back to enjoy our comforts and American way of living."

Hector revealed such confidence at a time when the United States was just pulling out of the Depression and the war effort was still going the way of the Axis Powers. But he seemed only to see the future. After all, his last twelve years had been spent preparing for a bright future as a professional. His stay in Ireland may have made him feel lucky to be an American. He compared the communities in Northern Ireland with those of the Rio Grande Valley. "The people are very nice," he wrote, "but they do not have the same standards of living as we do." For the duration of the war, he saw mostly poverty, destitute children, destruction, and hunger. Even rural South Texas looked good compared to the war-torn world.

In Northern Ireland the Army finally realized that it could best utilize him as a medical officer, but not until it was certain he was a
physician from a reputable medical school. Hector did not read much
into the interrogation but it provides insight into the Army's uncertainty about a Mexican American being a doctor.

> They asked me, "Are you a doctor?" I said, "Yes." They
> asked, "What medical school did you graduate from? Did you
> go to Spain?" And without letting me answer, they said,
> "Well, did you graduate in Spain?" "No." "In Mexico?" "No."
> I finally told them I was a graduate from the University of
> Texas Medical School in Galveston.

Surprised, they asked him why he was not in the Medical Corps,
and he told them of his initial requests. They immediately removed his
engineer insignia and replaced it with the serpent and pole to signify
his transfer to the Medical Corps. Hector quickly followed the transfer
with a request for a promotion to captain. They refused him the promotion but allowed him to stay with his unit, which suited him fine.

The surprise at his medical training and their refusal to promote
him to a rank more appropriate for his training bothered Hector, but
not because he felt discriminated against. He wanted the promotion so
he could get more pay to send home. The Medical Corps status
allowed him to practice his profession and to keep him from direct
combat. Unlike some veterans who needed to embellish their war
service with combat or at least combat stories, Hector did not feel a
need to be shot at. He saw his service as important to the war effort
and did not try to make of it something it was not. The promotion
finally came in September. By then he was the battalion surgeon for
the engineering group.

The advance in rank and pay did not come soon enough for Hector. Throughout his war years his major concern was his family's economic well-being. He listed his father as a dependent, and the Army
sent the elder García a monthly stipend of $50. Hector added another
$30 a month and he frequently supplemented that amount with
numerous money orders that ranged from $40 to $1200. He divided

his money into a stipend for his father, a payment for life insurance, and deposits to a personal savings account. He also found himself sending money to his brothers and sisters, including for a short time some money to Tono, who already had a small but thriving medical practice. He constantly inquired about their financial circumstances. Few of their letters to him are available, but it is obvious that money was always a topic of discussion. Sometimes, frustration seeped through his letters as he wondered why they could not make it with what he sent them. Over time, he came to believe that his father was saving most of the money and not using it for the intended purposes. His father did not want to be a burden to his son. In a letter near the end of the war, José wrote, "I know that as long as you live, my old age is assured and I will live tranquil and happy," but added that he did not want to be a burden. After all, he was only 58 and in good health. Still, he admitted that maintaining several children in school was draining. He wanted to work and open up another store.

Hector cringed at the thought of his father going back into the workforce. He chastised his father for looking like a poor man. "If you work, then you will . . . have to wear dirty clothing." He told José that he wanted him to be a "gentleman and live like one." He reminded him again that with the money he was receiving, he had more than enough to live decently. After all, Tono was occasionally sending some money and Cleotilde was working in Mercedes. One important reason Hector was sending all that he could was that José had begun to build a new house. But he was trying to do it himself to save money. This frustrated Hector who wanted him to pay someone to finish it faster. For two years he continually chastised his father for not finishing the house, despite the money he was receiving: "I want you to spend it on the house, buying clothing . . . fixing your teeth, buying furniture for the house, buying books, etc. . . . If you put all the money in the bank and still look like a poor man, I'll get downright angry." Hector, by the second year, was demanding his father become middle class and respectable.

A July 24, 1943, letter to his father might well have revealed the often hidden scars of growing up with few resources at home. Up until then he had managed to suppress most feelings of frustration. But in this letter, as he counseled his father to be respectable, he opened his heart and let some of the pain ease out.

> Remember cleanliness, house, books, clothes. I am not asking you to be extravagant. No, I am merely asking you to be practical and modern. I remember when I was a kid I loved my house and I loved you and mother, but I wished so badly to have a nice house like the American kids, a nice stove, a nice living room, a nice library.

Hector pleaded with his father to buy books, and he even sent him several boxes full of books from Europe. He also sent him artwork for the house.

Hector's letter revealed a profound yearning for respectability and middle-class status. While all sons and daughters want the best for their parents, Hector's letter revealed a personal crisis that could only be relieved by a change in his father's identity. Hector never discussed ethnicity as a handicap nor did he reveal a disdain for those below him. But he nonetheless yearned to be like those who were not poor or Mexican. In his youth he had met some other Mexican kids who were better off, but even they judged their circumstances by the status of the Anglo American kids. And what these kids had were good homes, nice furniture, and a library. Thus, they not only separated themselves from the Mexican kids through their material possessions but also through their knowledge and intellect. Books meant education, and for Hector education meant freedom.

For the rest of the war Hector continued to admonish his father, but it seemed to have had little effect. Pride, the loss of his wife, and poor economic circumstances had taken their toll on José. In his old age he would cease to be a hero to his children. The fact that he no longer provided and that he depended on his children was hard to bear. But American society had little to offer someone who spoke limited English and whose skills fit more his native country than his adopted home.

Two other concerns occupied Hector's mind in his letters to the family. One was his older brother's relationship to his father and the other the possibility that two of his brothers might have to serve in the military. Whatever the reason for the conflict between José and Tono, it had reached Hector's attention. Few of the letters to Tono are available, but aside from pleading with him to write more often, they revealed that he admired his older brother very much. His letter to his father showed a partial bias toward his brother. The sibling solidarity might well have been based on the fact that Tono was the first achiever, the trailblazer of the family. He was the García children's link to the outside world. It is also possible that Tono's brothers and sisters, Hector included, empathized with him because his father's rigid discipline had first been tested on him. There is no doubt that the Garcías remembered a mellowing José, but the first children knew little of that. Tono had taken the brunt of José's frustration over his personal situation and the fear that his children might suffer some of the same consequences if they did not measure up.

Tono also represented the reality of assimilation to American society by an immigrant young man. While José pushed them toward success, he did not want to lose them from the family or from the community. Tono would actually be the first social reformer in the family, but he took the LULAC route rather than the one blazed by his younger brother. Like that generation of reformers who populated LULAC, he retained a certain class distinction from the working people that Hector associated with. He also never lost sight of the fact that making money was important in American society. Many social reformers, contemporary with Hector, did not prioritize wealth accumulation as the top concern, as some in the past had done.

Still, for the García siblings and particularly for Hector, Tono represented respectability and accomplishment. They idolized him. It is hard to judge Tono's own feelings toward his family. He rarely wrote to Hector during the war and he almost never went to Mercedes to visit his father. From José's letters and Hector's responses, the father-son conflict was serious. Hector constantly admonished his father to patch up the differences. He even advised him to visit Tono, if the elder son was not willing to come to Mercedes. It is not completely clear, but José may have also fretted over the fact that Tono as a practicing physician was not willing to help support the family. Hector would try to alleviate that situation by sending more money and advising his father to forget about Tono's obligation.

In his letter to his older brother, Hector admonished him to stay home and take care of the family rather than enlist in the armed forces. "I am happy 'cause I am an old Army guy," wrote Hector. "But you would find it different than civilian [life]." In another letter he told Tono that one García in the service was enough to beat the Germans. He also reminded Tono that as a physician on the home front he was already helping the cause. No doubt that while Hector was committed to the war effort, he did not relish the thought of sacrificing a family member. Because he always remained optimistic of an Allied victory, he did not see Tono's participation as crucial. The situation with Bone (Cuitlahuac), his younger brother, was different. Bone was in school and subject to the draft. Hector admonished him to stay in school and not enlist but wait to be drafted. He also suggested that he do some reading on medical procedures so he could be in the Medical Corps if drafted. He had the same advice for his schooling: go into medicine. Hector believed that once in medical school, the armed forces would not draft him until he finished, and the war would probably end by then. Unlike many Americans, Hector never believed the Germans would win.

If he had to go, Hector advised him to try to get into the officer corps. "The best way to get into it (officer's school) is to do all [the] work that is asked of you, study the Army regulations, and pamphlets and booklets, and learn all you can. Be just like a student in the Army." He also cautioned Bone against griping—a common activity among G.I.s—and against bragging or being disrespectful to his superiors. "If the officers see that you are earnest and interested in the work, they themselves will recommend you." Bone would eventually get drafted but saw no action. Hector's advice revealed his view of a fair and color-blind society.

Hector experienced life as an "only." "Onlies" are individuals who find themselves the lone person in their group in a particular time and place. While this may often be disadvantageous and frightening, it can also be a situation in which there is less resistance and hostility. The fact that they find themselves in that situation is usually because they

are exceptional, they are less "different," and they tend to adopt quickly. Given those circumstances, they become the "good exception" with
which the majority group might feel comfortable. Having Bone not
gripe, work hard, and be respectable meant distinguishing himself
from the mass of soldiers. Because of ethnicity and physical traits, he
would stand out even more. Once given the limelight, Bone had a
chance to distinguish himself even more and seize the opportunity.
This is what gave Hector the advantages he had. For Hector, all other
desires were fulfilled only after the advantages were seized. In this, he
was different from many post-fifties activists and others from his own
generation who came out swinging from an early age.

From Northern Ireland his unit shipped out to North Africa, where
it followed the advancing Allies from Morocco to Algeria and then
Tunisia. In North Africa Hector saw the first signs of war. There were
sunken ships in the harbor and much destruction in the port city, but
no fighting, as the area had been pacified earlier. Hector saw many
similarities in North Africa to the Rio Grande Valley. The weather, he
told his family, is "like that of Mercedes. A little rain occasionally, but
hot in the day and cool at night. We have oranges, palms, dates, vegetables, tomatoes, carrots, etc., like the Valley."

He could have added that North Africa also had many poor and
destitute people, like those in the Valley. The war, of course, made
things worse, and Hector proved hypersensitive to their plight. While
there, Hector, along with a few others, provided health care for the
poor North Africans. An undated news clipping, probably from the
Army's *Stars & Stripes,* described the procession of poor mothers
with their babies, who lined up to receive medical service. The
reporter described the sick call as a spontaneous thing. "Nobody
ordered them to do this job. Nobody gets anything extra for it, and the
endless line of poverty-stricken people who have no other way of getting medical attention speak their thanks fervently if silently." The
article also singled out Hector. "Capt. García, who speaks French and
Spanish fluently, has also mastered Arabic, and discusses his patients'
ailments most gravely with them." Hector, in the biblical sense, "was
a respecter of no man." He treated everyone the same, and he took as
much time to discuss the diagnosis with his African patients, and put

as much effort into curing them as he did for his soldiers.

From North Africa his unit followed the Allied forces to Naples, Italy, where it served to protect the port and to assist in the loading and unloading of ships bringing supplies for the push toward Germany. Eventually Hector would arrive in Germany with the last leg of the Allied push to end the war in Europe. In the process he impressed his commander. A certificate of merit for outstanding service read:

> Captain García's constant attention to the health of the men of his unit, his personal crusade against venereal disease and threatened epidemics, as well as his insistence on malaria control measures, were invaluable in maintaining morale and health at a high level. García's devotion to duty was outstanding and his desire to do more than his share was demonstrated when he volunteered to take over the duties, in addition to his own, of another medical officer so that officer might return home on account of an emergency.

The citation highlighted Hector's characteristic approach to his responsibilities. He dove right into his work, performing his assignments to the letter, and then searched out additional things to do. Volunteering to help others as they dealt with their personal problems would be a constant with Hector. He loved work and he loved doing things for others. The fact that he did them as part of his routine garnered admiration and respect from those around him. This type of activity allowed time to pass by quickly, but it also provided Hector with new experiences and new ways to measure his character as well as learn new skills.

In a war in which most American soldiers simply went to fight, survive, and go home, Hector learned things about himself and about others. His awe at the way things were done meant he was always learning and, when possible, emulating. Most American soldiers showed little inclination to appreciate the culture, architecture, or history of the places in which they fought. By contrast, Hector enjoyed his time in Europe, taking in all the sights and going out of his way to meet people. He learned French, Italian, Irish, and a bit of German and Arabic. He even came to like the German people, whom he described as hardworking, clean, and methodical. Years later he bemoaned the fact that most Americans simply did not make an effort to connect with people or to learn much about the places where they went.

No doubt, the fact that Hector escaped direct combat gave him the time and inclination to appreciate his surroundings. But it is likely that had Hector been involved in heavy combat, he would still have found something to appreciate in combat strategy, leadership traits, or good use of weaponry. As a young officer, he felt lucky to be exposed to so much beauty and culture. His training in ancient history and literature came in handy because as he visited museums and churches, he understood their significance to Western culture and to his beloved Catholicism. His Eurocentrism was not elitist, but it was prevalent in his thoughts. He had no reason to question its values or its promise.

The Eurocentrism may well have led to the most important action he took while in the armed forces: he married a beautiful, aristocratic Italian woman. When he forgot about Constance is unclear from his letters. But Hector's single-mindedness in performing his work allowed him to forget her quite soon, as he rarely mentioned her in his letters. From the few references of her, it seems she was another part of his development and learning. But given the fact that Hector mostly concentrated on himself and his work, it is doubtful that he spent much time lamenting her loss. That is not to imply that Hector did not care, it is just that he rarely spent time worrying about things he could not control or lamenting roads not taken. Close relationships would be something that Hector did not prove good at nurturing.

Hector met Wanda Fusillo—at least in his recollection—while doing a favor for an old junior college buddy. Lloyd Roberts, an Army officer, lived with an Italian family that had a number of daughters. They, along with their friends, would pester him with questions about the United States and about Italy. Most of the questions dealt with literature and culture, and Roberts had little background or interest on the subject, so he usually found himself embarrassed by the coquettish young women. Hector, having training in literature, a degree in ancient history, and a fascination with Italian history and culture, quickly jumped at the chance to enter the friendly debate. With his tendency to overkill, Hector proved more than a match for the inquisitive young women. He informed them that Garibaldi, the great Italian liberator, had married an Argentine woman, and that the newly-deposed Fascist dictator, Benito Mussolini, had actually been named after Mexican President Benito Juárez. And he asked them numerous questions about European and world history and literature they could not answer, in spite of the fact that some of them had degrees in literature. Among those most impressed was Wanda, the daughter of the superintendent of Naples' schools, who herself would attain a teacher's certification in Italian literature.

Wanda came from a close-knit family that included two brothers. While aristocratic, the family had suffered wartime hardships, as had most other Italian families. To help out the family, Wanda had gotten a job at the port authority. There, a workmate told her about a confident, cultured, and extremely articulate American officer whom she knew and wanted to introduce to her. She met him one day after work and after that, as she would later report, "He never left me alone." He soon started arriving unannounced at her place of work and eventually her home. He took her and her friends on picnics in the Army ambulance. Eventually, he had her, her friends, and brothers roaming throughout Naples having fun. For Hector, courtship was like work: he put everything into it and left no possibilities to chance.

Wanda soon took a liking to Hector's commanding ways. She loved to hear him talk and expound his vast knowledge of literature, history, and culture. He also impressed her with his stories of medical practice among the casualties of war. At first, she was intimidated by this doctor with a self-assurance that bordered on arrogance. But soon, his charm captivated her. Her family also took a liking to him and even suggested that he stay in Italy after the war to practice medicine. There would be many opportunities, they assured him, for an American doctor after the war. But Hector quickly dismissed that idea, confiding in them that he had a "mission" to perform back home with his people. They were waiting for him, he told them. Wanda admitted to not having believed him. She assumed that like most other Americans, he wanted to return home to a place not ravaged by war.

Sometime during his relationship with Wanda, he decided she was the right person for Hector the man and Hector the crusader. She was bright, sophisticated, well-educated, beautiful, and reverential toward him. Like most other decisions he made, Hector made this one based on the things he wanted to accomplish as much as on personal feelings. The years confirmed Hector's love for Wanda, and the pride and joy he felt for his dedicated wife. But they also confirmed that Wanda was the patient wife who took care of business at home while he was away—a constant occurrence—and her properness and education guaranteed no embarrassments and provided him with a distinguished partner. She also sheltered his children from public scrutiny and maintained a sanctuary to which he occasionally retreated. He married up as would be expected of an overachiever, and she married an American with a future, something as important for an aristocratic woman in war-torn Italy as marrying into money and status.

The marriage proposal was vintage Hector. When he decided on Wanda, he made plans for the wedding without letting her know. By then, his unit had been transferred to Germany as the Allies advanced toward Berlin. Hector obtained a military marriage permit that he needed to marry a girl from outside the United States, and showed up at her home with the declaration that they "had to get married" because he had only a few days furlough to accomplish the task and then return to duty. Surprised and a bit overwhelmed, Wanda hesitated. Aristocratic women were not supposed to get married this way. Also, years of planning her wedding to accommodate familial expectations demanded time. But eventually, Wanda gave in to Hector's pleadings and rationalizations. He would not take no for an answer, and she finally said yes. Without thinking about the social concerns or time restraints, Hector forged ahead to get church permission and to make all the complicated legal arrangements for an American soldier to marry a local woman. The wedding, according to Wanda's recollection, attracted many relatives, friends, and a host of curious people who wondered how a quickly planned wedding to an American would turn out.

Soon after the wedding, Hector flew back to Germany without his bride. His dreams of going on a long honeymoon to Mexico, which he often discussed with his older brother, gave way to the reality of war. He would not see Wanda again for any stretch of time for at least eighteen months, not until they both met up in the States. He would be shipped home alone, and she would follow months later with a sixteen-day boat trip to America. Numerous times during the wait to reunite with her American soldier, Wanda must have wondered what she had done. She was leaving home and would return only a few times. She was going to a foreign land and she was going to live with a man whose life she knew would be a whirlwind. However she could not imagine what awaited her as the wife of Hector, the social reformer.

Years later, Wanda told an interviewer that she did not know Hector was Mexican American at the time of their courtship. She thought he was a Spaniard. Whether she knew much about Mexicans before coming to the United States is unclear, but no doubt Hector's white complexion, height, and demeanor made him look European. She recalled that he never spoke to her about his ethnicity, at least not until she came to Corpus Christi. Even after she learned his ethnicity, she still believed almost until his death that his father had been born in Spain. It seems he told her little about his family and hardly prepared her to live in South Texas. It is also apparent that he told his family very little about Wanda. His marriage came as a surprise, particularly to José, who wanted Hector to practice medicine before deciding to get married. In what became typical fashion for them, few of the Garcías showed Wanda much more than acceptance. The family, while not tight-knit, did seem to develop a boundary around themselves, and spouses were accepted but never quite welcomed in the fashion of more loving families.

Hector's approach to his war service and his time in Europe would follow the pattern he had set in his early years. He bore ahead with his work, he provided charitable service wherever he went, he took in as much of the history and culture as he could, and he planned for the future. He also took care to provide for his family. By now he had become convinced that he had something important to do among his people. He had also acquired a propensity for exhaustive work. He simply outworked everyone around him. In fact, that would become his most distinguishing characteristic. Hector never became the smartest, wisest, or most talented of the reformers of his generation, but he did outwork all of them. And hard work, tenacity, and confidence bordering on arrogance would be a valuable trait in the new

America to which he returned.

The new, postwar society would be a society of hard work, tenacity and overachievement. Americans were not interested in philosophizing about life. The Cold War presented a great struggle over ideology, but most Americans were oblivious to the more profound aspects of the conflict. The fear of atomic warfare and the revulsion to socialism were based on the perceived threat to their physical well-being and their material acquisition. Consumerism and getting ahead became the predominant concerns for Americans who had tasted the bitter fruits of the Depression. Those who were to make their mark in postwar America were the overachievers, the company men, and the mainstreamers. They came back not to "fix" America—and there was much to be done—but to leave the horrible memories of war behind and claim their piece of the American pie. They had few quarrels with American society as it was. This, of course, applied mostly to the white soldiers. But it also applied to men like Hector.

Hector had no bone to pick with the United States as a whole. Initially, he felt good about the country that had won the war against fascism and Nazism. Hector, in his own mind, had experienced a prejudice-free war. There was none of the bitterness that other soldiers of color would feel. Hector credited that good experience to the comradery in the military units, the fact that there was a common enemy, and that all Americans were fighting for a good cause. The reality was that Hector had a commission, and that meant privileges and demanded respect. The fact that he commanded the battalion aid station in his area meant he was extremely important and crucial to the fighting men around him. Thus, he became invulnerable to the kind of discrimination or prejudice that some Mexican American enlisted or drafted grunts experienced.

Hector had the luxury of seeing the war experience in its most glorified aspects. He used his singular view of the war experience to continue to learn and achieve. He could be a friend to other doctors and officers, most of whom had graduated from better programs and schools, and he could even afford to defend the rights of "other" minorities. He came to the rescue of Jewish soldiers who felt out of place and who needed a place and time to celebrate their own reli-

gious holidays. He provided medical assistance to the indigent population of North Africa and sympathized with their hardships. Freed
from confronting personal discrimination, he could continue to see
life as good and the future as unlimited.

Hector developed a perspective that life would be difficult, but its
challenges were meant to refine the person and not break him or her.
In a letter to his father, Hector explained what the war experience had
taught him.

> This (sic) three long, weary years of suffering . . . pain . . .
> hardship and heartaches have taught me how to be tolerant
> and how to be patient. I have seen poverty and have seen cru-
> elty and I want to place myself above both of them. I do not
> seek to fight unless it is completely right. I must not magnify
> my own problems and misery because in all the countries I
> have been there are millions of families worse [off].

Though he escaped much of the physical harm that came to many
others, as a surgeon he could not escape seeing its tragic results. This
would add to his training at home and to his mother's charitable
demeanor to develop in him a real empathy for those who suffered.

His sensitivity to the pain and suffering of others is revealed in a
letter, dated September 27, 1945, that he sent a grieving mother of one
of the soldiers in his unit who had died while Hector was away. The
young man, Abraham Roth, had been with him since Camp Edwards,
although at the time of his death he was not under Hector's command.
"This is not an official communication," he wrote. "This is an effort
of mine to . . . mitigate the suffering that you must have undergone. It
is a letter written by a doctor to a mother of one of his men."

He wrote of a dedicated, funny young man who cheered up everyone and who attracted children wherever he went. He wrote of the
hard German winters and the way the constant moving wore out the
soldiers' bodies and attacked their morale.

> But not Roth. He seemed to find comfort and satisfaction
> knowing . . . he was helping some soldier. He always seemed

to find something funny in that desolate and forsaken place. He . . . laughed and his laughter became infective . . . and that would be the end of that cold day.

Hector explained to the mother the obligations of the U.S. Army's Medical Corps. "I trained him and instilled in his noble heart the tradition and the duties of the Medical [Corps]." He reaffirmed to the grieving mother that her son was one of the selfless men who gave as much as was expected, and at times, even more. He was a man who was proud of his country and had a special bond with those around him. "I never saw him falter, I never saw him hesitate, I never saw him fail. His heart was kindness and his aim to help the suffering around him."

Hector could well have written this about himself. Roth had been one of his "boys," someone he had molded into a proud soldier. What Roth and others had learned from Hector was the essence of what he believed about duty, sacrifice, and honor. Hector was a team player, one who believed the best teams were those composed of individuals whose personal commitment to success was voluntary. Unity and solidarity never infringed on individuality in Hector's worldview. Years later, this trait stood out as he organized Forum chapters throughout the country and allowed each of them to define their issues, choose their leaders, and construct their own political and social space. He demanded great loyalty and never hesitated to chastise his followers for not doing it his way, but he always respected their individuality. Hector ended his letter the way he might have wanted someone to end his obituary: "I know that you are proud to have had such a son; I'm proud to have worked together with him, and the Army feels proud to have had such noble men when they were so sorely needed."

Only five days before he wrote the letter to the grieving Jewish mother, Hector had himself received a letter of appreciation from his commander, Lieutenant Colonel Edward R. McCarthy. The commander praised Hector for needing such little supervision and for looking far beyond the immediate surgical needs of the unit. He noted the effective program of sanitation and disease control that Hector had implemented for the engineering corps. In a war fought on such harsh terrains and in the worst of conditions, Hector had managed to create a sanitary environment and convinced the soldiers to be more careful in their personal hygiene.

> Your constant dissemination of basic sanitation principles, venereal disease control methods, emergency measures when epidemics threaten, valuable and practical advice on medical policy, have been invaluable in maintaining the health of the units at a very high level.

Three months earlier, on May 31, 1945, he had been recommended for a Bronze Medal for his work as a headquarters surgeon. "His role," read the recommendation, "was not merely passive but many times he was engaged actively, going beyond the bounds prescribed."

The end of the war found Hector a highly respected Army surgeon, a married man, a cultured student of life, and a leader of men. At thirty-one years of age, he was ready to go home and begin his professional life and respond to the "call" he knew was pending from his community. War had been a refiner's fire, and Hector never forgot the experience. The war had not only given him and others an opportunity to display their courage and show patriotism, it had also defined them as brave men willing to make the ultimate sacrifice. This sacrifice made them the new guardians of American ideals. This responsibility would one day translate into making the United States a better place for everyone. Hector, as a romantic, believed the world had given his country an opportunity for greatness, and individuals like him had to step up to the challenge. The challenge proved invigorating to him and other Mexican Americans, and so they set out for the rest of their lives to prove worthy of the challenge. For Hector, being cast into greatness would define his own life. While others sought to forget the conflict, Hector never did.

Barrio Americanism:
Constructing a Veterans' Movement

While Hector had spoken to Wanda and her family about his "call" to help his people, it would have been just as easy to follow his older brother's and eventually his younger siblings' quest for professional respectability and economic stability. No one in the family and few other Mexican American professionals of his time combined the education, training, disposition, and leadership characteristics with the will to succeed that Hector did. Throughout his public schooling, his medical school years, and the Army, he caught the eye of his mentors and superiors. He turned his modest beginnings and his ethnicity into a plus by becoming an American success story in the making. Those who chose to notice saw a poor Mexican boy become a highly-educated, articulate, and charming military doctor. Those who chose to ignore his ethnicity saw an efficient, loyal, hardworking Army doctor whose postwar career had unlimited potential.

In his letters to Tono and his father, Hector reiterated his anticipation of a successful medical practice that would allow him to live the "American way." Nowhere in them did he mention a life of social reform or of sacrificed financial stability. By 1946, he now had a wife, a daughter, several siblings in college, and a father who could not fend for himself. His status in the Army provided a class position he had never experienced before, and it surely added to his desire to make something of himself. The last twelve years had revealed his ability to compete and triumph over others. Never a creative or innovative thinker, it is hard to imagine him not being motivated by the same concerns and ambitions as other American veterans. The triumphalist euphoria of the American public, the festive coming-home parades, and the outpouring of gratitude from the nation, had the same effect—at least initially—on most veterans coming home.

In the process of coming home, there were many possibilities and much wishful thinking. A private practice, a car, and a house for a lovely bride occupied Hector's mind upon returning. But in more sober moments, Hector contemplated what awaited at home. The positives were a healthy family, a postwar economic boom, and a brother with a medical practice who could be called upon to help. But some stark realities could not be denied. No home of his own awaited, only that of his father and siblings in Mercedes. There were few savings, as family obligations had prevented him from accumulating much. There were two siblings in college who depended on him. He had no car, and he needed money to begin his medical practice. Compounding the personal problems were the racial tensions in Corpus Christi, where his brother lived and which he chose as a place to start his own postwar life. While Hector rarely complained about discrimination, he did not fail to see its ugly head. Despite degree and military commendations, his lack of money and connections reminded him of the precarious situation of most Mexican Americans. He did not fear the challenge nor was he pessimistic, but like most veterans he could not help but be apprehensive about what awaited him.

A severe kidney infection almost derailed all his short-term and long-term plans. It hospitalized him and had him bedridden for several months. The effects were so severe that for many years he would remember when he "almost died." The illness kept him in bed and unable to meet his wife and daughter after their two-and-a-half-week boat ride to America. It also kept him from fully engaging in setting up a practice. Luckily for Hector, his brother Antonio offered him his home to recuperate and as a place for his wife and child. Wanda remembers having stayed a "long time." Hector remained grateful to his brother, even more so after he died, but Cleotilde remembered that the wives did not get along, and that caused strains in the relationship.

Hector eventually opened up an office at the Texas Building in downtown Corpus Christi. Although not his first choice, the place proved to be lucky, helped launch him professionally, and eventually led him to be the crusader that he became. At his new location, he met

Joe F. Geiger, a veteran services official who befriended him and gave his practice an early boost. Like many other veterans' services officials, Geiger dedicated himself to a population that confronted many serious medical problems. His agency was hard hit shortly after the war with a rise in clients at the moment of a decline in federal funding. Having Hector move into the same building proved a bonus for him and those he served. He soon began referring veterans for consultation and treatment, paying two dollars per visit. Hector could not have been luckier. This meant a steady client base with tremendous possibilities for expansion, as most veterans had or would soon have families. Hector must have celebrated his good fortune. Setting up a medical practice meant buying equipment and hiring staff, and that required a quick infusion of money up front. Because of his downtown location and his last name, he expected to attract few Anglo American patients. But the steady supply of veterans allowed him to quickly spread his name and establish a reputation.

This arrangement worked well for the first several years, but when the Veterans Administration stopped paying for their treatment, many stopped coming due to lack of funds, and others continued to come but pled for "barrio credit," a traditional form of payment that meant installments when possible, or payment with commodities: eggs from home-bred chickens and vegetables from home gardens. Any other doctor could have diagnosed where that would lead and would quickly have changed office policy. But Hector was too much in love with medicine and helping people to turn them away. It became a daily ritual over the years to have his secretary try to turn people away, only to have him step out of his office and call out, "Let him in, he's sick." Eventually, he created a partnership with a pharmacy to accommodate his patients, but undermined his profitability by often declaring, "Put it on my bill." He also gobbled up samples from pharmaceutical companies and gave them out to his patients.

Hector followed the same approach with his new Mexican American patients that he had in North Africa, the Mediterranean, and Europe. He took time to listen, converse, and then explain the procedures. He counseled his patients on proper sanitation and good health habits. Since money was not a major consideration, he could build the kind of relationship with his patients usually reserved for those who had money or some kind of insurance. While sometimes overbearing and intrusive—he wanted to know what their sanitary habits were— many of his patients found him charming and caring. His secretaries and nurses found him demanding and at times quite inefficient, but they stuck with him because they ended up believing in what he did. Loyalty would be one emotion Hector seemed able to inspire in most of those with whom he worked.

Beyond their usual inability to pay, the veterans created another dilemma for Hector. They reintroduced him to the world of Mexican American poverty, but with a new perspective. For Hector, poverty had been something to avoid, to grow out of. It had also been a temporary state of being while growing up, going to school, and opening his practice. The reason for going to medical school was twofold: gain social independence and acquire economic stability. He understood that poverty affected his people, as well as African Americans and poor whites, in very complex ways. But in running from it, or in living through it in his early years, he had avoided dissecting poverty and providing it with a face. It was easier that way. One could continue to be optimistic if one could just depersonalize it and see it as a transitory stage, or at least a stagnant reality.

But the veterans he "doctored" shattered that compartmentalization. They brought him into their world, a world of second-class citizenship, low economic attainment, severe health problems, and bad sanitary conditions. While by nature an optimistic bunch, they were nevertheless burdened with a concern over their precarious situation. They were hardworking family men, not slackers. They believed in the American Dream but found it difficult to live it fully. Through them, Hector became exposed not only to wartime health problems but to many other diseases that had nothing to do with fighting the enemies of freedom. For Texas Mexican American veterans, especially those from South Texas, tuberculosis was one of their main killers. The death rate of Mexican Americans from tuberculosis was 209 for every 100,000, a percentage higher than the combined total for Anglo Americans and African Americans. These numbers made Texas the worse state in the Union in that category. Corpus Christi was in the most affected county in the state and had the most infected sector in the county: Molina, a large Mexican American section of town. Molina and other such barrios in town were a breeding ground for diseases. One-third of all houses in Corpus Christi ranked as "substandard," meaning they were too cold in winter, too hot in summer, and potential fire traps. In most parts of the Mexican side of town, there were few sewage pipes, sidewalks, flushing toilets, or running water. Garbage pickup was haphazard, and health services were nonexistent. People usually went to seek medical help at the latter stages of their illnesses because they knew no better or they simply could not afford it.

The diseases combined with the filth and the poverty to create an eerie sense of disillusionment and depression for those hardest hit. Few men had good jobs, few children attended school, and few households seemed prepared to face such dire circumstances. These conditions appalled Hector and brought home to him the reality of the postwar experience for many Mexican American veterans. Seeing disease, poverty, and hopelessness in war-torn Africa and Europe had affected him profoundly. But seeing that kind of environment back home stirred even greater turmoil within him. Rural poverty he had known most of his life, but urban poverty shocked him. The difficult times in Mercedes were often tempered by the existence of elite Mexican families, the overachievers, and by the sense that getting an education and working hard would resolve most of the monetary problems. The rural areas also had a way of hiding some of their misery through space: distance between communities and the isolation among the scattered ranches. Rural poverty could not be totally hidden, but it was often defused to keep it from overwhelming the eye. Urban Corpus Christi, however, could not hide or disperse its poor Mexican masses. It simply segregated them and lumped them into areas that soon reflected the misery and destitution of its residents.

Hector thought long and deep about the problems of his people. It bothered him, even angered him that they were treated so badly. He quickly saw that most of the problems, often blamed on the Mexican Americans themselves, were mostly caused by outside forces. City officials routinely ignored the Mexican side of town when it came to fixing streets, constructing sidewalks, digging drainage ditches, or building hospitals. And employers who discriminated kept Mexican Americans from pulling themselves out of their misery. The health problems were a consequence of the terrible conditions under which these people lived. But always one to be positive, Hector chose a practical way to express his concerns. His approach would emulate that of reformers of the past and those contemporary to him. Self-help became the approach in tackling problems not resolved politically or economically.

As a physician and one who had been involved in disease prevention since his medical school days, for him it was a priority to educate Mexican Americans about the dangers of unsanitary living. He began to speak to whomever would listen that the barrios had to be cleaned up, that their residents had to be taught good hygiene, and that the city had to provide adequate services to the community. He began by meeting with people and groups to spread his gospel of cleanliness and prevention. He found one effective way was to drive around the barrios with a loudspeaker to warn the residents of the ill effects of unsanitary practices. In the process of this campaign, he revealed his leadership traits and discovered a faithful friend and lieutenant in Gilbert Cásares.

Cásares was the local Army recruiter who often went on the radio to encourage young Mexican American men to join the military. He also traversed the barrios in his vehicle outfitted with a loudspeaker system, seeking out the right young men to meet his quota. Sometime during one of his trips, Hector must have seen him or heard him. Not one to spend too much time with introductions or niceties, Hector came to the recruiting office and asked Cásares for his equipment and his assistance in his health crusades. As would be the case with many other veterans, Cásares was intimidated by this reserve officer—Hector was a major by then—with aggressive manners and an air of self-confidence. Without realizing it, the Army recruiter became a recruit himself: into Hector's army. Together they would begin a crusade to educate the poor residents of Corpus Christi about their health, about sanitation, and about disease prevention. Before long, Hector had the local chapter of the League of United Latin American Citizens (LULAC)—which he joined and eventually led as chapter president—providing him information on what areas to target and feedback on how the communities were responding.

The loudspeaker crusades were combined with radio talk shows and his own radio time slot. At the time, radio was the one medium, aside from Spanish-language newspapers, that provided Mexican Americans information important to them. Radio was also the medium through which he could take the time to walk the mothers and wives through an educational process on health issues. He believed most mothers cared about their children but often felt powerless to rear them in such difficult circumstances. He tried to assure them that things could be done at home that might prevent many of the illnesses that afflicted the Mexican barrios.

As Hector participated in these campaigns and as he treated veterans and their families in his medical practice, he realized the problems were greater than first imagined. Having grown up in the Rio Grande Valley had exposed him to poverty and ignorance. But coming from a stable family had spared him the more insidious aspects of those twin tragedies. Now as a physician and a health crusader, he began to fully recognize the impact of years of neglect, poverty, and disease in the Mexican barrios. He soon learned that the problems were even worse outside of Corpus Christi. In no time, his investigating covered the whole county and even further south. In moving down south he confronted the stark reality of the migrant farmworkers' world, and that pushed him into the public arena and into social reform.

He used his meticulous approach to document, report, and publicize what he saw and what he heard from the migrant farmworkers. They told him of long hours of stoop labor in the fields, lack of toilet facilities, regimented breaks for rest and water, and the harsh climate. He saw migrant habitats that were no more than wooden structures with tin roofs that became hotter than saunas in the height of day. These shacks often lacked doors, windows, running water, and electricity. People cooked outside and showered when water became available. The grower provided no furniture, and rarely were there wooden or cement floors in the shacks, only dirt. Sometimes these shacks, or "chicken coops," as they were often called, had to accommodate more than one family. In fact, some of these accommodations had previously served as chicken coops.

The migrant camps were a reminder that as thousands of Mexican Americans had gone off to war, thousands of others had supported the war effort in the fields and packing plants. They had been joined by hundreds of thousands of others from Mexico recruited to replace the men who had gone off to war. The Bracero Program, a contractual agreement between Mexico and the United States, brought thousands of Mexican workers to work in the agricultural fields of the Southwest. While many took the place of those gone to war, others replaced Mexican American farmworkers who wanted better wages and were forced to go further north to get them. The Bracero Program guaranteed "liveable" wages and safe conditions, but over time most growers came to violate not only the letter of the law but also the spirit of the agreement. Hector would make repeal of the Bracero Program— which outlived the war by almost two decades—one of the top priorities of his social reform.

Finding a place for veterans with tuberculosis became another priority for Hector. Cases of tuberculosis were rampant, and yet no Veterans Administration hospital existed in the area, and there were no other treatment facilities for tuberculosis patients. Hector sought to get the local Navy hospital to open its doors, but the base commander was reluctant and eventually only agreed to a small number of beds. This reluctance troubled Hector, who first saw it as a disservice to veterans who had ably served their country. He eventually recognized it as an insult to Mexican American veterans. After all, the nearest Veterans Hospital was more than one hundred miles from South Texas. Having unoccupied beds nearby but not having them available seemed to him very unjust. Traveling was not the only problem for veterans and their families. The cost of staying away from home for several days meant that most families could not be there when their loved ones needed them. It also meant that many were reluctant to be treated for fear of the cost and the isolation.

The conflict over sanitation, disease control, poverty, and the Navy's reluctance opened up for Hector a larger view of discrimination. He quickly understood that the illnesses he saw among the veterans he treated were related to their life experiences in the barrios. In making the connection from the doctor's office to the dilapidated housing and the bad sanitation, he pieced together part of the puzzle. To that he added discrimination in delivery of veterans' benefits and the lack of facilities for them. Seeing the veterans' wives and children suffering from similar ailments and from ignorance led him to look at the public school system and city government. What he found appalled him.

Still beaming with pride over honorable service during World War II, he could not understand nor could he accept the conditions that permeated Corpus Christi and the rest of South Texas. Newspaper and magazine articles confirmed that the situation was the same through-out the state and the rest of the Southwest. Particularly appalling to Hector was the educational system that poorly served Mexican American children. Having viewed public education from the perspective of the overachiever, he only partially understood the problems inherent in segregated education. But seeing it from the perspective of his patients and the neighbors around his office changed his view of its effects. Instead of uplifting the *mexicano*, public education actually reaffirmed his or her place at the bottom rung of society. Segregation reenforced the apparent inferiority of Mexican Americans and the superiority of Anglo Americans. The dropout rate reaffirmed that bar-rio children were having trouble integrating into American institu-tions, even if they were Americanized. The terrible housing problems and the unsanitary conditions also confirmed that *mexicanos* had no place at the political bargaining table.

Hector viewed education the way W.E.B. Du Bois did decades earlier. It was not just to teach a vocation but to magnify the person. It was a means to make the person a contributing member of society and a participant in the democratic process. Men and women of edu-cation could think, reason, and resolve. They appreciated the political process and could be called upon to perform a myriad of tasks. Hec-tor's view of education was positivistic but it also carried a strain of populism. Education was for mass consumption. For Mexican Amer-icans, education remained critical because they suffered more than others when they did not have it. They could not get good jobs, artic-ulate their concerns, or take advantage of the democratic process. Without it they remained victims of ignorance.

Hector felt so strongly about it that he wrote a stinging letter to the editor when the local newspaper announced the arrival of the remains of a dead Mexican American soldier. In it he accused the segregated public school environment for the deaths of many young Mexican American soldiers.

> [I] wonder if some of the lives might not have been lost if those [Mexican] American soldiers had had a better education. Perhaps those soldiers would have learned more and . . . would have been better equipped and trained to defend themselves. . . . They firmly believed in the ideals of democracy. . . . Today they return [dead] to the same land where they were discriminated against and where their brothers, sisters, and their children are still segregated.

In his letter Hector dealt with a number of themes that became a trademark of his reform activities. He affirmed education as a life-and-death issue for Mexican Americans. It was not enough to argue that lack of an education meant low-paying jobs, poverty, and second-class citizenship. Education represented life itself. An educated Mexican American had options: officer school, noncombat assignments, and home front duty. It also meant that an educated mind would be more mindful of military instruction, would ask questions, and could assess better if the preparation for combat had been sufficient.

These soldiers, despite a lack of real preparation, were nonetheless willing to fight for democracy. Instead of bitterness and refusal to die for an unjust society, they chose to fight for the high ideals of American democracy. Their commitment had been to the promise of America rather than to the reality. But their death earned them, and their families, a right to a better America. The price had been paid, the atonement given, so that their community could live in a freer and fairer society. In the critique, he was not denouncing the United States but rather elevating the role of the Mexican American. Death for democracy was the great atoner for the sins of the community: illiteracy, superstition, poverty, and lack of refinement. Once the price had been paid, the doors of opportunity had to open.

Belief in the ideals of democracy became another cornerstone of Hector's social reform. It is likely that in describing Mexican American veterans as "firmly" believing in the "ideals of democracy," he overstated the feelings of his community. The only studies done on Mexican American veterans indicate that many only had some vague notion of fighting for democracy. Hector took this "vague" notion of American ideals and made it a recurring theme in his speeches and conversations. He filled in the spaces of the vagueness. He interpreted the veterans' intentions and worked hard to make them believe in his ideals. Without an organization, this process occurred on an individual basis, on the radio, at his medical practice office, and in his letters to politicians and friends. That many veterans accepted this analysis indicates that veterans were open to integrating into the American mainstream. But even more than simply assimilating into the mainstream, the veterans were buying into a new process of identity-building. This new identity still depended in part on their national origins, but now also on their actions during the war. Their veteran status also provided them legitimacy in American society, something that their national origins could not.

For these veterans, and particularly for Hector, their service during the war gave them a place at the table. From this place they could tackle another important issue: segregation. As long as Mexican Americans were treated differently and categorized as different, they could not truly enjoy the benefits of American society. School segregation proved debilitating, but so did the separate and unequal treatment they received in the public sphere. While rigid segregation had begun to weaken because of capitalism's need for manpower and a more mobile workforce, there were still places where Anglo Americans simply did not tolerate Mexicans. Signs proclaiming "No Mexicans Served" were still abundant in small restaurants, barbershops, and grocery stores in many parts of the state. Swimming pools remained segregated, and so did most parks and other public facilities. In many places Mexican Americans did not serve on juries, and no translation was available for those seeking legal transactions but whose English-language skills were limited or nonexistent. Even the religious realm remained dichotomized, making Sunday one of the most segregated days of the week.

Since they were proud Americans, the status they received as ex-soldiers gave them a sense of belonging. The umbrella of official recognition served as a countermeasure to the discrimination they encountered in their daily lives. For many Mexican Americans who were politically powerless, economically marginalized, and socially disdained, any form of recognition was welcomed. Thus they invested in Americanism with the enthusiasm usually reserved for ethnic nationalism. Veteran status became a badge of courage but also of citizenship and legitimacy. It set them apart from those in their community who were either attached to Mexico emotionally or who were completely alienated from American society. Their status also provided them benefits—when they could get them—from a grateful nation and indicated a commitment from a society that had usually been indifferent to their plight.

While well aware that their veteran status did not free them from the conflicts of a race-conscious society, they could, among themselves and a few appreciative Anglo Americans, find importance in their lives. Their own community bestowed upon them an important status, and the G.I. Bill gave them valuable advantages. With this status and the few advantages in hiring, schooling, and housing, they created an image of themselves that bordered on a new identity. They came to develop a "barrio Americanism" that made being American a priority. This Americanism was barrio-centered because the world outside the Mexican sections of town was often unfriendly territory. But within the barrio, they were war heroes, they were skilled, and they were the natural leaders. They were also more often the most Americanized. This assimilative character, however, was relative. To the outside world they were still just "Mexicans" with limited abilities and questionable loyalties to the American way of life. Thus, in spite of their own constructed American world, they confronted tremendous challenges. Having lived in the military's version of the world, they were even more conscious than those isolated in the barrio that there was a great disparity in opportunity between the two sides of the track. This sensitivity made them more vulnerable to Hector's social advocacy. In their minds, they deserved better, and here was the good doctor telling them so.

Hector's organizing efforts became more intense by the spring of 1948. By then he had decided to organize veterans into a group so that their individual voices could become a loud collective demand for their rights. It is hard to know how developed Hector's organizational plans were at this stage, as he left no writings to that effect. But certainly the LULAC approach seemed not to be the answer for Hector, even though it personally offered him certain advantages. Leadership opportunities surely awaited someone as capable and respectable as a medical doctor with a distinguished military career. His tenacity resembled that of the earlier LULAC founders, and his ability to rally people around a cause surpassed that of the current leadership, which was comprised of sophisticated professionals more likely to lobby and file lawsuits than to organize rallies or marches.

While LULAC offered him an opportunity to mingle with other talented professionals and to be part of an established and reputable organization, it did not satisfy his major concerns. Hector wanted to help veterans who confronted problems in receiving medical assistance, getting their educational and pension checks, and being hired in federal jobs. This predominantly working-class population deserved better, in Hector's view. School desegregation battles—LULAC's main efforts at the time, and the Forum's future concern—were very important, but not the totality of the struggle. Hector may well have decided that veterans shared a unique collective experience that he could tap into in order to organize them.

Hector began calling for meetings of veterans to discuss the problems they faced. These gatherings culminated in a 600-plus veterans' meeting on March 26, 1948, at the Lamar Elementary School in Corpus Christi. Five other veterans joined Hector in preparing for the meeting. Together they sent out thousands of circulars to the surrounding communities and promoted the meeting in the newspapers and on the radio. Hector believed that emphasizing military issues was the way to begin the discussion. The first item on the agenda referred to the lack of representation of "Latin Americans" on local draft boards. He argued that if Mexican Americans were going to serve in the armed forces, they were entitled to representation among those who made the drafting decisions. Hector was among a number of reformers appalled at the thousands of young Mexican Americans rejected for duty during World War II. There might have been other issues that worried Hector, but his letters and public discussions seemed to focus on representation as a payback for war service. One possible concern was the need to influence where Mexican American recruits and draftees were sent and what kind of training they received.

The importance of the issue to Hector did not resonate with the majority of other veterans in attendance. While they appreciated the importance of those positions, they were more concerned about educational benefits and medical treatment for their service-related illnesses and injuries. They also worried about a Veterans Administration notice that pension benefits were to be reduced, unless veterans could prove, with documentation, that the current levels had to be maintained.

Hector, always sensitive to the direction of discussions, opened up the meeting for the veterans' testimonials on the insensitivity of the government agency in charge of their checks and their medical treatment. He then cited a number of cases of veterans whose pensions had been drastically reduced and then read off a list of veterans whose educational stipends remained in limbo or who could not get medical service. Immediately, dozens of veterans rose to testify of their own difficulties. The complaints ranged from the simple hassles of filing documents and waiting for training certification to the more severe concerns with life-and-death medical problems. Hearing their fellow veterans discussing the difficulty in dealing with the VA led others to openly testify about their own negative experiences. It was not long into the meeting before veterans were publicly expressing what they had privately believed for years. Their national origins and their ethnicity remained an obstacle to receiving the services they merited as veterans. Hector navigated the difficult waters of trying to organize veterans who believed in the American way, while letting these same men vent their frustrations over their treatment as members of an ethnic group.

Hector succeeded by blending together the veteran—loyal, disciplined, committed—with the Mexican American citizen—angry, passionate, law-abiding, macho, and family-focused. He did not bend to the left or to the right but sought to find a common ground. Not given to deep philosophical introspection, he saw the practicality of organizing these men under the rubric of veteranism. The men were American citizens who had put their lives on the line in defense of freedom and now demanded their rightful place in society. Extreme ideologies or positions were not necessary, although militancy might be. He galvanized their testimonials with his own statistics, anecdotes from his patients, and patriotic demands on American society. Rather than turning into a session to air complaints, the meeting became a forum for organizing veterans into a potent force. That night the veterans made Hector their president. More importantly, they "anointed" him their spokesperson. If there existed any doubt about Hector's "calling," the veterans erased it that night. He now knew for certain what laid ahead for him.

The meeting produced the American G.I. Forum. It would take a few years for the Forum to fully develop its institutional philosophy and its internal structure, but several of its basic aims and objectives came out of the meeting. Those could best be divided into three areas: assist veterans in receiving all the benefits to which they were entitled, encourage civic participation among Mexican Americans, and defend American democracy from its enemies abroad and within. The last was motivated by increasing tensions between the United States and the Soviet Union. Although the Forum periodically spoke the language of anticommunism and did report suspicions to the FBI, it never developed a reputation as a red-baiter. The other two aims were a result of the conditions of the veterans and their families.

Interestingly, Hector and some of the early Forum leaders did not consider their organization a civil rights entity. They admitted to defending the rights of those who were discriminated against, "but we are not and have never been a civil rights organization," they declared in a Forum statement. They pointed out that upon learning of a civil rights violation, they referred it immediately to the civil rights section of the office of the Attorney General. If that government agency chose not to prosecute, then the case was dropped. Publicity was not to be undertaken until the final results were obtained. "In this way," declared a Forum statement, "the G.I. Forum shows its faith in American institutions and the courts of justice." The Forum leaders expressed their confidence that justice could be obtained through an orderly process. They also expressed their independence by emphasizing that the Forum would solve its own problems "without outside" help.

It seems ironic that an organization hailed as a model civil rights entity refused, at least initially, to take on that identity. More surprising was its emphasis on a "civility" that seemed to disavow militancy, something that became part of its trademark. It might have been an orderly militancy, but it was still passionate and demonstrative. Marches, rallies, letter-writing campaigns, and verbal confrontations became common tactics for most Forum members. A likely explanation might be that Hector's views on social reform were evolutionary. As in his childhood, college career, and military experience, Hector believed in the ideals of discipline and propriety. He was probably also conscious of Anglo American society's assessment that Mexican Americans were not good citizens, lacked self-discipline, and were too emotional. That there were a few Anglo Americans in the early Forum chapters probably led him to be initially cautious in writing down goals.

Probably just as responsible for the civil approach in the Forum guidelines was the part Gus García played in developing the Forum's ideals. Gus had been a college friend at the University of Texas. He came from an elite family in Laredo, Texas, and promoted civility in LULAC. Gus, always a man of many ideas and sophisticated language, sought as the Forum's legal advisor to construct a guiding document that placed Mexican Americans in the highest light, even among their most vehement critics.

Yet, given Hector's aggressive approach in all he did, the civil approach remained a framework that the Forum periodically returned to but never used to restrict its social reform crusades. In no time, Hector was publicizing cases before the "final results" and committing Mexican American lawyers to cases the government prosecutors refused to take. Civil rights became Hector's and the Forum's most enduring cause. Moreover, aggressive social advocacy by Hector and the Forum, while orderly and peaceful, resulted in charges of being "agitators," "radicals," and "Communists."

As noted earlier, non-Mexican American veterans were allowed and even invited to join the Forum. In fact, two of the four officers had Anglo surnames. But over a short period of time and especially when the focus moved away from veterans' issues, the Forum became almost exclusively Mexican American. The loss of Anglo American members allowed the organization to move more aggressively on issues of civil rights and discrimination. This would initially cause many Anglo Americans to be suspicious of the Forum and Hector, in particular. It would take time for many to understand that he had no "nationalistic" hidden agenda that was meant to hurt Anglo Americans. There were many, however, who never learned to tolerate Hector's militancy.

Within days after the large gathering, Hector received a letter from an important acquaintance in the veterans' affairs realm. On March 29, Joe F. Geiger, manager-in-charge of the Veterans Administration (VA) office in Corpus Christi and the man who gave Hector his start in treating veterans, wrote him a long letter. In it he first congratulated Hector on his being named the president of the Forum and on the way he conducted the meeting. He expressed his friendship and praised the character of the new veterans' president. "I feel sincerely," he wrote, "that the group could not have found a man more sincere in his desire to help them than you, nor one with a more comprehensive knowledge of their problems."

The VA official then went on to discuss some of the difficulties that the agency confronted in trying to service so many veterans. But he also sought to politely stress the misinformation contained in some of the veterans' complaints and in some of the speeches given at the Forum's founding. Part of the delays in responding to veterans' request, he wrote, was not indifference or discrimination but largely due to staff limitations. He reminded Hector that the VA suffered numerous postwar cuts on personnel and resources. Yet, in spite of the smaller staff, there were actually few complaints in comparison to the number of veterans requesting and receiving aid. Geiger considered this proof of the agency's commitment to do all it could for the ex-soldiers.

Geiger then pointed out that most veterans who complained actually compounded their own problems or created them in the first place. They did not follow the procedures outlined and often did not read the instructions nor open the letters sent to them by the agency. He cited the case of one veteran who kept in a cloth sack important documents that needed to go back to the VA. Because he failed to open them and send the appropriate ones back, he did not receive his educational assistance. Geiger emphasized that decisions on medical treatment were handled by thoroughly trained personnel. The decisions made by them were also reviewed by a rating board, if the veteran was not satisfied with the decision. This was a highly trained board, said the VA manager, and could not be rotated, as Hector had suggested at the meeting. Hector's suggestion had been an intent to find more sensitive decision-makers, but Geiger termed the rotation impractical, considering the training that it took in VA procedures.

Geiger also took issue with Hector's allegation that the Navy had been unwilling to care for more Mexican American veterans in its hospital in Corpus Christi. He reminded him that the Navy had opened 120 to 125 beds to veterans per year and had exceeded that quota several times, taking in all patients except those with tuberculosis.

> Considering the fact that the Navy agreed to accept only emergent cases, and did not agree to treat post-diagnostic cases, it is most apparent that the local Navy officials, by their lenient and friendly attitude, contributed significantly to the success of the veterans' medical program in South Texas.

Geiger went on to explain that the Navy had to cut its bed quota and would not be able to exceed its initial offer of beds. He admitted this would worsen the case for tuberculosis patients but emphasized that the construction of a tuberculosis hospital would help out.

The letter underscored two important barriers to Mexican American veterans' rights. One was the reduction of resources and the other the veterans' own failure to follow procedures. These two reasons given by Geiger were supplemented by the "fact" that the complaints where few in comparison to the numbers being served. These reasons, the VA manager believed, were enough to exonerate his agency even though he did feel disappointed that the veterans were not being served to their satisfaction. The reasons, if accepted on face value, freed the agency from charges of discrimination or indifference.

If Hector accepted Geiger's explanation, there was not much to do, except lobby Congress and take time to train veterans to respond efficiently to the VA's requests. There is no letter from Hector responding to Geiger. But one might well read the rebuttal to these points in the way Hector conducted his activities on behalf of the veterans. He rejected the letter's contentions by placing the responsibility not on the veterans and Congress but on the agency itself, as well as on other veterans' advocacy groups. First, they had done little to represent the veterans' interest to a cost-cutting Congress. The VA and its supporters had the largest constituency of any other organization in the country. There were nearly sixteen million veterans, and many of them had war-related conditions that needed to be treated. They had been prepared to give the ultimate sacrifice for their nation, and decisions on their future could not be made on the basis of budget-balancing. Second, the VA and its supporters had to make sure that veterans were served, despite their own failings. After all, the nation had not asked them whether they could fill out paperwork but only if they were ready to defend their nation. The VA's sole purpose should have been to help veterans get the treatment and other rights they merited. Those benefits were not based on the veterans' abilities to follow small-print instructions.

More important for Hector was the need for the agency and government, in general, to change operating procedures. Government had to be more sensitive to the people's limitations. It was not ethical nor moral for the nation's bureaucrats to simply wash their hands of the problems when people did not follow the guidelines. In this, Hector went further than other social reformers of the past who simply wanted to be included within the parameters of the law. Hector sought changes in the rules and the procedures so that his people were fully included. If the rules violated basic principles of justice, they had to be changed.

It was not enough for the government to say there was no money, or for the Navy to say that they were making available a limited number of beds. It was also not enough for the VA officials to say that the veterans failed to follow procedures. Government had a moral obligation to provide for the veterans who fought to defend it. And the Navy, if it had the beds, could not simply turn its back on veterans because they were not its first priority. More importantly, the providing agencies had to take responsibility for the plight of Mexican American veterans and their families. Hector believed, and so did many other Mexican Americans, that agency and government officials did not feel any urgency in responding to their complaints because of the ethnicity of those complaining.

Hector's approach for an accountable government went beyond that of many civil rights advocates of his time. While most sought to make available the rights of citizenship to their constituencies, Hector wanted to make government responsible for not only providing those rights but also ensuring that all people received them. In Hector's view, there were many who neither understood nor demanded their rights because they had never been taught them. He was prone to saying that his own family had never demanded their rights because "No one ever told us we had any." With this approach, Hector predated the social welfare activism of the 1960s and stood as one of the early civil rights pioneers who demanded a more activist government on racial and ethnic minority issues. Government activism was not something new as evidenced by the Progressive Movement and the New Deal, but rarely had that activism extended to racial minorities. It had in fact been discouraged as a detriment to the acquisition of true citizenship. Ethnic Americans had to "earn" their rights, like white Americans had done in the past. Hector refused to accept such notions, since Mexican Americans already deserved such merit through their service. And still others "earned" it through their back-breaking labor.

Feeling empowered and obligated by the leadership of the only veterans' organization specifically representing South Texas residents, Hector set out to challenge the American Legion and the Veterans of Foreign Wars to do more for them. In a letter dated April 6, he reminded the American Legion that Congress had given it power of attorney to assist veterans. Hector accused the Legion and other veterans' groups of ignoring the five hundred or so veterans he represented. Their inaction had been responsible in part for the absence of a VA hospital in the region or even a VA doctor, and for veterans not receiving their educational benefits for up to five months.

Hector called for a meeting of all veterans' organizations to share information and plan strategy. In doing so he sought an equal footing for the American G.I. Forum. No doubt he saw himself as equal to all others who lobbied on behalf of veterans, but more importantly, he believed that Mexican American veterans also had to believe themselves to be equal. Rubbing shoulders with other veterans' advocates would provide them that experience. The fact that the Forum made a special effort to recruit Mexican Americans meant their potential for growth far exceeded that of any other veterans' group in the region. The Forum thus gave Hector a big pulpit from which to expound his views.

There is no record of a response by Legion officials, the VFW only responded with a lukewarm endorsement of a working relationship. It is likely that Legion officials were disturbed, if not down right angered, by the letter. In it, Hector had accused them of being calloused toward veterans at worse, or being inefficient at best. Probably astounded by the letter's audacity, they must have been even more concerned with the rivalry that it represented to the Legion's membership pool. They quickly grasped that this young upstart had a high regard for himself and his ability to do more for veterans than an organization with a national staff, national lobbyists, and thousands of members nationwide. Their first perceptions turned out to be quite accurate.

The leadership of the Forum not only empowered Hector to challenge other veterans' organizations but it also provided him the pulpit from which to speak out to the larger Mexican American community. While he had done so for almost two years now, the Forum leadership allowed him to put his words into action. Hector did not badger his people, as some in the past had, but he did try to reorient them toward more important issues. He began calling for rallies and large meetings, and he called on people to leave their baseball games, billiards, and other diversions so they could tackle the problems confronting them. Mexican Americans had, over time, learned to accommodate to the problems they could not solve, and to respond forcefully to those they could not avoid. But Hector wanted them to challenge all the problems that plagued them. Avoidance or selective responses were not options for those who took their citizenship seriously.

Hector's initial efforts depended on rallying to action the numerous civic, social, and cultural clubs in the barrio. This helped to bring numbers into the social crusades while the Forum was just beginning its recruiting efforts. It also allowed greater visibility for the organization. A great motivator, Hector usually succeeded in getting numerous clubs involved, despite the fact that most of them addressed single-issue activities or provided a social space for Mexican Americans in a segregated environment. Their agendas were usually full of fundraising events, dances, and well-publicized charitable functions. Hardly ever did these groups become involved in the large social or political issues that would pit them against established authority. Their club membership provided them a status that could be maintained only if they remained outside political conflict and limited their membership to a defined population.

While membership did not solely consist of middle-class individuals because of their small number in the community, a middle-class mentality nevertheless permeated these clubs. Civic duty was the cry of middle-class idealism at mid-century, and these Mexican American organizations were involved in all kinds of activities to uplift their members, beautify their communities, and define status within the barrios. Still, the kinds of commitments that Hector demanded of them strained even the most enthusiastic clubs. At times, a number of them failed to participate in all the rallies and meetings. As the issues became more complicated and conflictive, more clubs failed to participate.

In a letter to several clubs dated July 5, 1949, Hector chastised many of them for failing to show up at a rally in support of the construction of a tuberculosis hospital in Corpus Christi. He reminded them that of the 9,000 tuberculosis patients in Corpus Christi, almost 8,500 were of Mexican descent. Tuberculosis afflicted one in every five Mexican Americans in that seaside community. He also reminded them that there always seemed to be time for dances, parties, picnics, and other social events, but not enough time to attend meetings of more important significance. Failure of the project, he added, was directly related to their weak commitment to their people.

The lack of spirit and cooperation shown by these clubs indicates that the majority of them are not interested in bettering the conditions of our citizens who so sorely need their help. Let us show the true spirit, Americanism and civic pride.

This call for civic pride and "Americanism" substituted for any organizational philosophy or ideology. It was also something that most of these club members could understand, even if only vaguely. After all, club members tended to engage in being good citizens, serving others, and finding pride in their work as part of their civic duties.

In order to achieve what he denoted as "Americanism," Hector believed that he had to convince Mexican American veterans of their "whiteness." This whiteness was not a rejection of who they were but a confirmation of their equality to their Anglo American counterparts. In a letter to Forum leaders dated September 8, 1948, Hector urged them to call meetings to discuss registration at the local draft boards. In those meetings, they were to instruct their members, and through them the rest of the community, not to register as "Latin Americans" or "Mexicans." He also told Forum leaders to "explain to all veterans that the Anglos are not to be referred to as 'los blancos' (Spanish for "the whites"). Such phrases are not correct and should not be used, as we are all 'white.'" Hector admitted that nationalistic feelings often prompted Mexican Americans to classify themselves by their national origins, but asserted, "That must be stopped."

Some social reformers had been trying to get Mexican Americans to see themselves as whites or Caucasians for decades. But most had little success, since such identification rarely meant any change in the treatment their supporters received. Hector hoped to have more success by tying whiteness to patriotism and military service. Treating whiteness as a category rather than as a racial or ethnic label, he sought to take some of the edge off what seemed to some an abandonment of their heritage. That he connected quite consciously the ethnic label "Mexican American" to the official term "veteran" made it possible for him to make the request. Hector knew a fine line existed between making the veterans see themselves as Americans first and having them turn their backs on their national origin. Yet, he saw no way for Mexican Americans to gain their rights except by occupying the same spaces civically and racially as Anglo Americans. In a class-conscious society, being different meant being treated differently, and that usually also meant being treated poorly. Classified as white, they could demand equal protection under the law, because the law favored whites. Because reformers like Hector did not see themselves as racially different, they could claim ethnic diversity within the white category.

Still, Hector consciously balanced his strong promotion of Americanism by constantly citing statistics and reports that focused on the Mexican American experience in the United States. He wanted as much information as possible on Mexican Americans to be published, and so he tended to befriend journalists and scholars who could provide such research. In his view, all information reaffirmed the importance of his cause. Unlike some of his contemporaries and future Chicano activists, he did not always recognize that some of this "data" added to the stereotypes and, in the wrong hands, strengthened rather than weakened segregation and discrimination. His naiveté allowed him to befriend liberal scholars whose work came under severe criticism and condemnation by Chicano scholars in the 1960s and 1970s. Liberal condescension never became a problem for Hector, except in the political arena. Veterans and other Mexican Americans who fought "invisibility" for years were often less critical about studies on them than future generations. They simply wanted to be recognized. And recognition, Hector understood, could rally veterans around a cause.

Rallying all kinds of groups together proved an important strategy, as long as the Forum recruited and strengthened its own infrastructure. The most important work for Hector continued to be developing the organization. This he began doing in the way that he did everything else, by getting people to listen to him. He went out to surrounding communities, such as Gregory, Mathis, Kingsville, Beeville, and others, and made contacts with club leaders, politicians, or other social reformers. Sometimes he just contacted a veteran that he identified, then urged him to round up other veterans and set up a meeting for Hector and the Forum. Sometimes using his brother Xico as a driver or his recruiter friend, Gilbert Cásares, as helping hands, he conducted recruiting meetings. Hector drove down with a flag, a constitution, and other civic literature and opened a meeting with a long speech about the problems of veterans.

Rather than preparing messages in advance, he spoke extemporaneously about the decades-long problems that afflicted Mexican American communities. He reminded his audiences that these problems had not gone away by themselves and were not likely to in the future. He showed them graphs and emphasized statistics about health problems in the region due to little medical attention, bad hygiene, no running water, no toilets, and no pavement or drainage systems. He reminded them of police brutality and blamed it on low civic participation and inconsistent voting behavior. He got the veterans "all worked up" and clamoring for action, then invited them to join the American G.I. Forum. As unorganized individuals, the future recruits were likely to do very little, but as a collective force they could count on results. Hector then called for an election of officers, assigned a legal adviser, and instructed the officers to call that person if they had a problem. The adviser was usually a lawyer he had recruited. Sometimes, it was just someone who had a bit of knowledge of the election code or about desegregation cases.

Once the officers were selected and the Forum chapter established, he instructed them to pay their poll taxes and vote. He also admonished the veterans to keep their children in school. Then before leaving, he would ask if anyone in the audience knew another veteran in Mathis, Three Rivers, Victoria, or any other surrounding community. Friends, relatives, or simply acquaintances would do. Hector instructed one of his assistants to take down names, addresses, and phone numbers. He called these contacts or had the referring individuals themselves call them and set up meetings in which he repeated the process again and again.

To pay for its activities, the Forum sponsored numerous cakewalks, where participants baked cakes and then they and others paid a small fee to win them in a musical-chairs-style activity. The fundraising served to keep the local chapters going as well as to print flyers and to conduct local radio programs to continue educating the people. There were also dances and picnics and eventually a small membership fee. The fund-raising activities, along with the meetings, helped Hector get closer to those he led. With his wife at his side, or his brother Xico or his sister Cleotilde, Hector projected the image of a family man. But that was only part of the image. He left no doubt that he was in charge and that he had a plan to get the community out of obscurity and into the mainstream. He knew how to speak to the professionals, the older veterans, their wives, and their children. He took everyone seriously and let their concerns become his own. His charisma, his Spanish-language skills, his lack of an accent, his height and good looks, and his beautiful wife all came to play a part in the image of the social reformer that he wanted to portray.

He projected a very confident image because those who knew him, and even those who met him for the first time, came away impressed that such a distinguished individual had committed himself so whole-heartedly to their cause. Many other social reformers also presented a very distinguished look and they spoke immaculate English and even very good Spanish. But many of them projected a slightly paternalistic image. While committed to their people's plight, rarely did they seem as comfortable at the grassroots level as did Hector. Over the years he became the godfather of many children in the barrios of South Texas, and a *compadre* of the elderly. Almost immediately Hector became many things to many people. Those who were more assimilated admired his education and his profession. Those more culturally Mexican respected his Spanish and his deep respect for his culture. The religious were impressed by his religious dedication, and the more political and liberal related to his political savvy and the fact that Anglo Americans did not intimidate him. He made them all feel proud.

Rather than taking his role as that of a burden or simply a responsibility, Hector took it as both an opportunity and a sacred duty. He loved the attention of those around him and he felt empowered by the confidence they placed in him. Their concerns became his own, and so did their pain and their joy. He seemed to transform himself into the answer to their every question and the solution to their every problem. In doing so, he was driven by an obligation to his people and by a personal joy that he felt in working for them. Every other measure of success in life paled in comparison to being his people's hope. The fact that many Mexican Americans searched for a hero meant that they embraced him readily.

Great men seem to come at particular moments in their society's life, and they usually have few competitors with similar traits. Hector's entrance into social reform came at a crucial juncture in the experience of the Mexican American community of Texas. And he entered much better prepared than others to make the commitment. Unlike many other reformers who would eventually join him, he came out of the military with an education and a profession. His profession provided him the economic stability and political independence that would take many others time to acquire. Those who had been there before him took time to adjust to the new constituency of veterans and to the changing economy that freed more Mexican Americans from the rural areas, yet created new challenges in the urban centers. The old social reformers were now litigators and social critics, having created a niche for themselves in American society. What most of them were not was grassroots organizers. Admired by many, they were too distant to passionately follow. They created their own circles of Mexican American middle-class individuals who shared little with their constituency, except that they too were victims of discrimination, although not to the same degree. They cared, but they did not always relate.

Hector also had another advantage. He developed a more expansive social philosophy. He did not want just inclusion but demanded that mainstream society accommodate the Mexican American community. Demanding to be treated like Americans was one thing; demanding to be treated as defenders of democracy and as patriots was another. Citizenship had its merits, but membership in a veterans' organization which had been called to arms again—this time on behalf of their community—was more inviting to the ex-soldiers. Whether Hector understood this immediately or realized it as he worked with the men is unclear, but once realizing it, he played it for all its value. The fact that the military had been a great experience for him made it easy for him to build upon the ex-soldiers' emotional connection to the war experience. No other social reformer of his time ever stressed the war experience as successfully as he did.

Early on, Hector envisioned the American G.I. Forum as a national entity. He knew that Mexican Americans confronted similar problems wherever they lived. His experience in Houston, Galveston, and

Omaha confirmed this. The newspapers and his correspondence with other Mexican Americans told him that others were just as anxious to do something about the plight of Mexican Americans. Once the word got out on the Forum, he began receiving calls and letters from others around Texas and the country who wanted help. They sought information on how to establish a Forum chapter or invited him to speak to their constituencies. More will be said on his national organizing later, but suffice to say here that it became a mission that he fulfilled with the same tenacity that he did in organizing chapters in South Texas.

Within three years of his return from the war, Hector's life had changed dramatically. Making money, having the beautiful house, and taking long vacations in Mexico had given way to working with veterans and on behalf of the barrios of Corpus Christi and South Texas.

Whereas release from the service promised opportunities and time to relax and contemplate, his crusades eroded those promises to himself. Hector would always be a good doctor—he was too conscientious to do otherwise—but he did not progress within his profession. His career transformed into helping patients with those diseases that were a result of the problems of the barrio. It was common for Hector to see as many as forty patients a day. On Saturdays, he conducted sick bay for those who could not afford to pay. Seeing this great opportunity for medical care, many started coming in on other days of the week. The burden became so great that Hector had to send some away or reschedule them for Saturdays. Hector knew that people with no money were also the people with the biggest problems; eventually many of them would turn out to be the most demanding, for they were the most desperate.

He did not have to look far to see the misery in the barrios. Behind his first office on Morgan Street were outhouses used by dozens of children who caught all kinds of stomach illnesses. Most who came to his office were already in the last stages of dehydration. Intervention had to be quick, and it was always too expensive for these patients. So he set up payment plans of a dollar a month or fifty cents a week. This would be the financial ruin of Hector, but deep into his crusades, he cared little. He seemed to find joy in the process of healing. But physical healing was not enough for Hector. Having them as patients meant he had people in position to hear him expound on hygiene, nutrition, civic participation, and paying one's poll tax. Civic health was as important as physical health.

Hector often made his rounds at the hospital around 12:00 midnight or 1:00 a.m. after putting in his hours at the office and committing another full day in reform activities. His patients came to expect being woken up in the early hours of the day, and nurses stayed on their toes because they knew he would pop up in the middle of the night to see if his patients were being attended with all the care they deserved. This kind of hectic schedule had its consequences. Time for the family was limited, and while the bond between Hector and Wanda grew stronger, it became more asymmetric with time. He became the warrior fighting for his people, and she remained the nurturer, always ready when he needed her, but always in the background.

Wanda later remembered he was silent about what he did and even about the discrimination he fought. He spent little time philosophizing; he just did what he had to do. During the first years, she accompanied him to the labor camps and saw the human tragedy he was so intent on changing. But even then they rarely discussed what they saw. She went to his early organizing meetings but did not understand everything, since many things were said in Spanish. What he did confide in her were his frustrations on how slowly things moved and how he could not get people to do things. During these times, she experienced his temper—though not necessarily aimed at her—which flared up quickly. The pressures and frustrations moved him toward his father's temperament. Wanda remembers that he had his mother's modesty, both in private as well as in public, but he only knew one mode of operation. He was hectic to live with, always on the run, always planning a meeting or calling someone to do something.

While most young couples might have used their first years together to establish a lifelong bond, Hector and Wanda built their relationship on the demands of his work and his activism. He rose early, was gone most of the day, came home to read, went out to another meeting or to his rounds, and went to bed late, only to begin the routine again the next day. While a friend to many, he was rarely intimate with anyone. He did, however, eventually find a number of

Trinity Berley

0369 782

close associates with whom to play dominoes to the wee hours of the morning. This, again, took time from the family. Wanda would remember: "We didn't have any time to really enjoy life. It was always work." Never one to offend her husband's reputation, she called everything work. For Hector, it probably was.

After his death, Wanda admitted that she had known two Hectors: the young man who courted her and told her about his many dreams, and the social reformer who seemed never to have time to dream about anything other than the next meeting, rally, or campaign. The humorous young man became introspective and moody. But she learned to admire his tenacity and to vicariously live his exciting life. He, in turn, protected her from the public spotlight and provided her a modest living. Although progressive in many aspects, Hector simply reenacted his parents' own asymmetric relationship. In his generation, that was simply the path to follow.

But Hector had changed in more than personal respect. Xico remembered his brother being profoundly impacted by the war, its destruction, the poverty it engendered, and the resulting sickness. Coming back to see similar poverty and just as much hopelessness among his people made him relive the horrors of war. He could not accept the idea that veterans had to live that way. Nor could he accept paying a poll tax in order to vote. People, especially veterans, should not have had to pay to vote. The misery of his people and the indifference of the majority of white citizens peeled off the passive civility that Hector had constructed in his early years to avoid conflict in a segregated society. All through public school, college, professional school, and military service Hector had simply worked hard, kept his silence, and benefited from the rewards that came to a "good" Mexican. He did not assimilate, did not reject his heritage, but rather tried to help his people when he could, preferably with a minimum of conflict. Three years in Corpus Christi taking care of veterans, however, were enough to transform him into an aggressive advocate willing to take on established authority.

The Felix Longoria Incident

On February 16, 1949, nineteen American soldiers were laid to rest at Arlington National Cemetery amid dignitaries from Mexico, a presidential aid to President Truman, state department officials, and several newspaper reporters. Of the nineteen, twenty-five-year-old Felix Longoria of Three Rivers, Texas, garnered most of the attention. As a greenhorn recruit, Felix would have been impressed that his congressman and senator stood next to his coffin during the ceremony. And that President Harry Truman had sent General Harry H. Vaughn to give his last respects to "that Longoria boy from Texas." Just as shocking to know would be that the first floral tribute came from Mexican Foreign Minister Justo Sierra, accompanied by young army and navy officers of his country. To have his wife, daughter, mother, sister-in-law, and three brothers witness the honors made the occasion almost perfect. But if Felix had witnessed all of this from Heaven, he still would have found it hard to believe the impact his burial had on the state of Texas, on Mexican Americans in general, and Hector P. García, in particular. No other event defined Hector's legacy like getting this young man to the nation's cemetery.

The story of the Longoria "incident," as it came to be known, began a few years before as World War II wound down. At the time he was called to fight for his country, Felix had a four-year-old daughter, a wife, a job in the Texas oil fields, and part-time work as a fence builder. Born and raised in Three Rivers, a rural community in South Texas, he was anything but a typical Mexican. His father, Guadalupe, was one of the original settlers of the town, and though Mexican, was "well-respected" by the Anglo American leaders of the community. He gained that distinction by his hard work and by the fact that most Mexicans and Mexican Americans saw him as their spokesman. He had come to Three Rivers in 1913 and befriended the founder of the town. Like other Mexicans during this period, he believed he could get along with his Anglo American neighbors by working hard, avoiding trouble, and staying on his side of town. For the most part, he succeeded.

But by the time his son Felix was born in 1920, things had changed in Texas. The agricultural revolution had attracted thousands of Mexican migrant workers, and their presence and their willingness to stay instead of going back to Mexico after the harvest frightened Anglo American citizens in communities like Three Rivers. Thus, segregation became more rigid and Anglo Americans were less friendly and more concerned about controlling the new masses. The large armies of foreign workers, moving from farm to farm with little permanency and no possibility of improving their situation, only fed stereotypes and reaffirmed Mexican American second-class citizenship. This massive influx of workers served to re-Mexicanize South Texas and the Rio Grande Valley, and to stir up old conflicts. Mexican Americans who had fought to define and promote their Americanism were again rhetorically and conceptually re-dumped into this cultural-ideological reconstruction of the foreign community. Still, Guadalupe and his family navigated the new social reality well enough to maintain their position as a "good" Mexican family. Anglo Americans were apt to say that, to distinguish them from others.

Felix might have extended that legacy had he not been drafted in November, 1944. By then, even "pre-Pearl Harbor fathers" were being inducted for the final push toward Germany and Japan. The war in the Pacific, where Felix eventually ended up, had turned into an island-hopping, torturous campaign in which every inch of ground was a battlefield. After seventeen weeks of training, Felix had shipped out to Luzon in the Philippines as part of a replacement unit with the 27th Infantry Regiment. He landed on the island as the monsoon season was in full swing. The U.S. Army had taken the upper hand in the fighting, but the Japanese command sought to hold on to its position at all cost. With the rains washing down bridges and making roads useless, and unleashing millions of insects, the war seemed a battle for "feet and yards rather than miles." The struggle had become a war of attrition, with snipers, disease, insects, and depression taking more lives than any sizeable battle, of which there were few, if any. Said one unpublished manuscript: "The reality of the situation translated into the pushing on, day after day and on through the night so that the day before yesterday turned into today, today into tomorrow, and tomorrow blended into a frustrating, uncomfortable, fearful, singular stream of consciousness."

On June 16, 1945, in this violent ambiance, Felix and another companion left their compound to do mop-up work against a retreating enemy. The Army had changed its tactics. Instead of sending entire units against fortified positions, the Army sent out teams of soldiers to disrupt supply lines, attack transit camps, and destroy any Japanese plan of defense. The Philippines had been converted into islands of guerrilla fighters, striking then disappearing, only to reappear later to do the same. Knowing full well that Japanese soldiers were everywhere waiting to strike, Felix and his companion moved cautiously through hilly and dense hardwood forest. They had not been out too long, when they encountered sniper fire. Before they knew what hit them, Felix fell dead. When General Douglas McArthur pulled out the 27th Infantry Regiment only two weeks later, Felix stayed behind with many others, buried in one of those communal graves so common throughout the Pacific. His dead body carried no more significance than those of many others also buried far away from home.

Beatrice Longoria received word of her husband's death in Corpus Christi, where she, Felix, and Adelita had moved before he entered the Army. The horror of death touched her like it did hundreds of thousands of mothers, wives, sisters, and girlfriends. Her Felix was dead, and his body remained across the ocean until after the war, possibly forever. The two years that passed without any word allowed her to go on with life. She dedicated herself to raising her child and finding a new life in her work. She dated and seemed able to put her past behind her when in the fall of 1948, the Department of the Army notified her that Felix was coming back home for permanent burial. Beatrice must have thought long and hard about the new twist in her life. She lived in Corpus Christi and burial there would make it easy for her daughter to be near her father. But Corpus Christi also symbolized a life that had gone forward. Things were different now. She also thought of Three Rivers and realized how much a part he was of that community. His brothers, sisters, and parents still lived there and they still mourned him.

Thinking it best to bury him in Three Rivers, she traveled there and sought assistance from the only mortuary in town, the Rice Funeral Home. She inquired about the cost, and Tom W. Kennedy, the manager, assured her that he could provide all the services for a reasonable price. Unsure of when, during the next six months, his body would arrive, she made only preliminary arrangements. She then boarded a bus to the county seat, where she asked the county service officer to notify the Army about the funeral home in Three Rivers. It was a bitter winter that year, and riding the bus through that familiar but very barren and gray area, she must have thought of the suffering she and her daughter had endured. Still, the end seemed near.

It is hard to know how much she took the Longoria family into account as she made the arrangements. She probably decided to do much of the work herself and notify the family when things were arranged. Like many other widows whose deceased husbands were just returning from the war, she believed a chapter in her life would close without much public notice, as only close friends and relatives would mourn. Thousands of families were going through this ritual as the armed services excavated communal graves and sent home bodies from throughout the theaters of war. Old wounds were reopened, but for many there was finally closure. Beatrice did not see how her ordeal would be any different.

In early January, 1949, the Department of the Army informed Beatrice that Felix's body would arrive in San Francisco on January 13. Shortly after that, a second telegram asked her to confirm the arrangements made for the body. Beatrice traveled again to Three Rivers to make the final arrangements. She took the bus and upon arrival she called Kennedy, who agreed to meet her at the bus depot. Since their first meeting, Kennedy had bought the funeral home. Beatrice later recounted that in the meeting they had gone over the details of the arrival, preparation of the body, and the burial. In this they were both satisfied with the arrangements. A disagreement emerged, however, when Beatrice requested the use of the chapel for the viewing.

"Well, Mrs. Longoria," Kennedy was later quoted as saying, "I have lots of Latin friends, but I can't let this boy rest in the chapel because the whites won't like it." Kennedy explained that the wake would create an uncomfortable situation likely to aggravate racial tensions. Mexican and Mexican Americans had never used the chapel in the past, and it was not a good idea to start doing it now. Beatrice did not know then, but Kennedy had investigated the family, or at least talked to someone about them, and concluded that there were tensions between the widow and her in-laws. As the new owner of the funeral home, he probably wanted to make a good impression among Anglo Americans in his community, who up until that morning had been his only customers. It is also likely that as a recent arrival to Three Rivers and a new member of its Chamber of Commerce, he sought to stay within the mainstream of Anglo businesses. Those businesses, like others in rural Texas, discriminated against Mexicans and Mexican Americans when it was not detrimental to their livelihood. There was fluidity between the races, but it was a regulated one that always favored Anglo Americans.

Beatrice later recalled her surprise at the rejection of her request. She never accused Kennedy publicly of being hostile or even discourteous, but she admitted to having been disarmed by his comments. Without any other funeral home in town and no legal recourse at her disposal, she accepted the reality that the chapel was unavailable. Kennedy, for his part, might well have felt uncomfortable with the situation. Mexicans and Mexican Americans were expected to understand the social parameters in communities like Three Rivers. When they did not, it made things uncomfortable and forced Anglo Americans to enforce those boundaries. Kennedy, while condoning those social boundaries, was not yet adept at enforcing them, so he tried to "suggest alternatives."

Kennedy asked Beatrice if there was another place where Felix's body could be viewed. She told him of the house where she and Felix had lived before they moved to Corpus Christi. It was now empty but still belonged to her. Kennedy then asked her if "it would not be better to take the remains there." Beatrice, however reluctantly, agreed, whereupon they telegraphed the Army about the arrangements. They then drove to the house to plan the logistics of placing the casket and the mourners' chairs. Kennedy offered to provide the chairs and the floral arrangements and prepare the place for the viewing. Then Kennedy drove Beatrice to a relative's home. Before leaving, he assured Beatrice that things would be fine. Felix would have a traditional Mexican viewing at home, where relatives would feel comfortable and where they could avoid tensions with their Anglo American neighbors. He then asked the widow if she felt "satisfied" with the total cost and with the preparations. Beatrice answered that she was.

In Kennedy's mind this had been a good business transaction. He would receive payment for preparing the body for burial while avoiding the disruption of the community's racial boundaries. He might have even felt good about making sure that Beatrice got the best situation that a "separate-but-not-equal" reality could provide. For him the contract had been signed and, except for its execution, the matter was closed. For Beatrice the matter was just beginning. She spoke to her relatives, unsure of how to react to Kennedy's suggestions. Having the wake at home was a traditional way of viewing the deceased for the Mexican-origin population of Texas. But it was also a tradition rooted in the poverty of the community. Bodies were kept at home because funeral homes were expensive for the meager Mexican budgets. Funeral homes were also usually Anglo establishments, where brown bodies were rarely welcomed. Thus, viewing the deceased at home was a reaction to economics and social stratification.

Beatrice, however, could afford the chapel services, and besides the abandoned home, she had no other place to put Felix's remains. For whatever reason, Felix's parents' house was not an option. Another point to consider is that Beatrice was now a working mother who, like other Mexican American working mothers of the postwar era, were more American in their outlook. It is quite possible that using a funeral chapel—something more common in Corpus Christi—was for her the more appropriate way. Whatever the reasons, and no one asked her publicly, she felt dissatisfied with the arrangements, or became so after speaking to her family. Her sister Sara Moreno suggested she consult Hector, having herself been involved in some of the work he and the Forum were doing in the surrounding area. A distraught and shy Beatrice agreed to let her sister initiate the contact.

Hector received the call from Moreno at about 7:00 p.m. on January 7. She expressed both anger and doubt, anger over what she felt to be a denial of chapel services and uncertainty over what could be done. She stressed Kennedy's comments that the "whites would object." Upon more questioning, Hector felt he had the details, and so he called Kennedy. But concerned that a confrontation might lead to charges and countercharges, he asked his secretary to listen on the other phone. Time and time again, Hector revealed a propensity for witnesses and written reports. Since he had nothing to hide, he always tried to make his actions public. The fact that his secretary was an Anglo American meant he had a witness that could stand public scrutiny.

He called the funeral home and Kennedy answered. Hector asked for the owner, and Kennedy replied that he was the owner, having just bought the funeral home only a few days earlier. Assuming power of attorney, Hector declared that the widow had had a change of heart and now wanted the chapel for memorial services instead of an abandoned house. "Oh no, that can't be done, that just can't be done," said Kennedy. When Hector asked why, Kennedy replied that Three Rivers was a small town, and things like that were just not done. "I have to do what the white people want. The white people just [won't] like it."

Hector then asked if Felix's veteran status made any difference. Kennedy answered that it did not and then revealed one of the apprehensions that Anglo Americans had about Mexicans. "You know how Latin people get drunk and lay around all the time," said Kennedy. "The last time we let them use the chapel, they all got drunk, and we just can't control them. So the white people object to it, and we just can't let them use it." Hector, according to a later affidavit, simply responded with, "I understand, Mr. Kennedy, thank you." Interestingly, Hector would later recall the conversation as rather civil, and never mentioned that Kennedy had raised his voice or expressed any hostility. Kennedy, on the contrary, in defending his choice of words said that he had lost his temper during the conversation and said things he regretted. Hector, by his own account, did not react angrily. This is surprising, given that by now he had exhibited a quick temper. Gilbert Cásares recalled that shortly after organizing the American G.I. Forum, Hector began dressing down the veterans, making some even cry. While congenial and sensitive by nature, Hector rarely controlled his frustration among his own followers and in confronting those he believed to be unrelenting adversaries.

It is possible that Hector developed an immediate strategy as he spoke with Kennedy and chose not to reveal any action by his tone. He could also have been taken aback by Kennedy's hostile resistance and characterization of Latinos as drunks. Alcoholism was a problem in the barrios and most social reformers were often quick to acknowledge this problem that afflicted the working class. Their reform restricted itself to the "good, hardworking, law-abiding citizens of the community." For the most part, Hector rarely engaged in a character defense of his people, like Chicano activists would years later. He simply assumed that most people understood that not all Mexican Americans were drunks, lawbreakers, or violent.

Another, and more plausible explanation, was that he did not want to create problems for Beatrice before he could figure out how to help her. After all, the Rice Funeral Home was the only option in Three Rivers, and antagonizing Kennedy without another recourse meant having no place to receive and prepare the body for an honorable burial. While Mexican Americans often expressed anger and resentment over their treatment, they had learned to set aside their personal feelings in order to obtain whatever services they could. Hector understood this and rarely placed his people in worse circumstances than he found them. He knew well that he could always walk away from the problem, but those affected could not. They still had to deal with a society that was prejudiced and that held all the advantages.

Hector, certain that this incident represented all that he stood against, quickly moved to provide a public record. He called George Groh, a reporter for the *Corpus Christi Caller-Times*, at his home. He told him about his conversations with Beatrice and Kennedy. He made sure to let him know he had a witness. Then he told the reporter that the American G.I. Forum would hold a protest rally the following day at the Lamar Elementary School. It is unclear whether Hector had consulted with any Forum leaders before making the comment to Groh. But whether he did or not, Hector had no doubt in his mind that both the Forum members and the public needed to be aware of the issue. That he had less than twenty-four hours to organize the event seemed not to concern him. He knew people would come.

Groh later testified to a legislative committee that after Hector's call, he phoned Kennedy to verify the facts. He described his conversation with Hector to Kennedy and asked him if he indeed had refused to allow Beatrice to use the chapel for Felix's funeral service. According to Groh, Kennedy replied, "We never make a practice of letting Mexicans use the chapel, and we don't want to start now." He added that most "Latins" did not usually request chapel services. Kennedy was right about this, but he did not understand or chose not to mention that this was due to economics and discrimination rather than some propensity for having the wake at home. Kennedy told Groh that the funeral home had never had a Latin service. He would hold to this line throughout the ordeal, despite it contradicting his earlier assertion to Hector about having had trouble with an earlier Latin service. Groh, wanting to make sure that Kennedy did not see this as a conversation between two Anglo Americans speaking about Mexicans, warned him that he was speaking "on the record." He also told Kennedy he had "hold of a hot potato." The funeral director expressed the opinion that the whole thing amounted to very little.

Kennedy later expressed shock at where the "incident" led him and his small South Texas community, but at the time he reacted as most Anglo Americans in Texas had for generations. Conflicts with Mexicans rarely seemed a big deal, and they always were resolved in favor of the Anglos. Mexicans simply had no recourse, especially against prominent members of the community, and Kennedy, the only mortician in town, must have seen himself as such a person. Hector's civil interrogation did not seem much of a threat. Speaking to the reporter might have been trouble, if the Texas public had ever reacted in outrage on behalf of Mexicans before. But Kennedy, a transplanted Pennsylvanian, had never experienced any Anglo American sympathy toward Mexicans and he believed that good white folks would applaud his actions and understand his motives. That was all that counted.

The next morning Groh decided to call him again to confirm the details. It is hard to understand why the reporter called again. It may have been to give Kennedy more details on the protest rally and possibly to emphasize Hector's ability to bring out the crowds and to get the politicians' attention. Whatever the reason—and it might have been that the conversation had indeed turned into "two Anglo Americans talking about a Mexican"—the call did garner a slightly different response from Kennedy. This time he told the reporter that he "discouraged" the use of the chapel, but would not refuse it if the family "insisted." Kennedy had had the night to think about it and he began to wonder if he had done the appropriate thing. After all, he was still new to the community and, while he could see the separation of the races, he was not privy to all the aspects of the social order. It dawned on him that he had momentarily taken on the role of spokesman for the community, and the city leaders might not appreciate it.

For Hector, the night before had been a marathon. Aside from calling Groh, he gathered a number of Forum leaders to discuss the options and plan the rally. They had little time to contact anyone, but they were adamant that a big crowd was necessary. Hector knew he also needed the attention of the state's and the nation's leaders to augment the impact of the protest. That night and early next morning, he sent telegrams to the governor, state attorney general, state board of embalming, the head of the Good Neighbor Commission, a state senator, two congressmen, the secretary of defense, and President Harry S. Truman.

In a more extensive note to U.S. Senator Lyndon Baines Johnson, he summarized the situation and stressed Kennedy's opinion that "other white people" objected to the use of the chapel by Mexicans. He described that opinion as a direct contradiction "of those principles for which this American soldier made the supreme sacrifice." The sacrifice, continued Hector, had been freely given, even for those like Kennedy who now denied the Mexican American veteran the chapel. Hector underscored that this treatment exemplified the kind of discrimination that his people faced repeatedly in Texas. It is obvious from the tone and the urgency of the letter that Hector had found an issue that encapsulated all the grievances that Mexicans and Mexican

Americans had against the state of Texas and its Anglo power structure. It also provided an extreme example of the depth of Anglo American insensitivity.

People had been denied burial services before. Segregated cemeteries throughout Texas attested to this repeated occurrence. But rarely had it happened to a more "worthy" individual. That it happened so soon after the war and to someone who should have been returning to heroes' welcomes, provided the "incident" with a potentially decisive conclusion. All those who spoke about the cordial relations among Mexicans and Anglo Americans in Texas, or those who outright denied the existence of discrimination, had met their Waterloo. This transplanted Pennsylvanian may not have literally spoken for other insensitive Texans, but he had revealed their private thoughts.

Segregation of Mexicans had always had a "reason," or a multitude of them. But refusal to bury a veteran seemed too big an injustice. If segregationists had wanted to reaffirm the status quo, this was not the right case. Most Americans accepted segregation as a way of life. Few lost sleep over segregated housing, schools, cemeteries, or military units. People were supposed to know their place. Keeping different groups apart might serve to keep the peace and avoid retarding one group for the sake of helping another catch up. But segregation was not to infringe—at least not publicly—on American ideals, because to do so weakened the ability to defend it. There always needed to be a plausible reason for its existence. Segregation existed because many Anglo Americans could rationalize their superiority and many Mexican Americans accepted, if only grudgingly, that Anglo Americans were superior. But that opinion was not without its problems, and public events like the incident in Three Rivers threatened to unravel the system because blatant racism infuriated Mexican Americans.

Hector understood the weak points of segregation. He also understood, or would over time, that the movement for equal rights in Texas required cataclysmic events. Slow-moving processes had worn down many past reformers and might also have the same effect on him and the Forum. Hector had tenacity, but he lacked patience. As a military officer, he knew long campaigns were necessary for ultimate victory, but major victories were key to sustaining long campaigns, especially in keeping up morale and commitment among the rank and file. Very quickly it became obvious to Hector that this was the fight that the American G.I. Forum needed. The case represented blatant discrimination, but more importantly, it was one that only the most racist Texans could condone. Yet, as extreme as the case was, it resulted from segregation taken to its logical conclusion.

The flyers distributed early the next day by Forum members and their families called on residents of Corpus Christi to come "hear the evidence in the case of this cruel humiliation." Without using his name, the flyer described Felix Longoria as a "hero-soldier" of the war, and made it clear that all veterans, their families, and the general public had no excuse not to be present. It pointed out that when a funeral home refused to honor the remains of any soldier because of his Mexican origin, it was time for the whole community to protest. The flyer combined patriotic outrage with the personal affront that Mexicans and Mexican Americans lived with. To provide a powerful stimulus for going to the meeting, it "respectfully" called on the mothers of deceased soldiers to attend. It also announced that the widow Beatrice Longoria would be in attendance.

Before the protest gathering, Hector saw the fruits of the previous evening's marathon. First, the *Corpus Christi Caller-Times* printed the announcement of the rally accompanied by Kennedy's remarks. Then by mid-afternoon, Hector began receiving telegrams of indignation and support from most of those to whom he wrote. Governor Beauford H. Jester wrote, "I deeply regret this action," and added that he had consulted with the Good Neighbor Commission and felt sure the funeral could be held at Three Rivers, as the family desired. The attorney general also expressed regrets but pointed out that there was no law broken. Still, he wrote, "The policy [or rather practice] was against such action." The state board of embalming also admitted no jurisdiction but said it had sent Kennedy a telegram requesting his cooperation. Congressman John Lyle, in whose district the incident had occurred, informed Hector that he and U.S. Senator Lyndon Baines Johnson "were conferring as to any possible assistance."

State Representative Rogers Kelley expressed the most outrage, calling the action "un-American" and the conduct reprehensible.

"This type of conduct cannot be condoned," he wrote, "and I thoroughly agree with your indignation and your attitude." Congressman Lloyd M. Bentsen assured Hector that he would work with state officials to do "everything possible" to resolve the issue and have Longoria receive a proper burial. The secretary of defense expressed sympathy and said he would check with the secretary of the army to see if that military branch had any jurisdiction in the matter. Hector even received a letter from William Coney, who headed the Corpus Christi Day at Arlington Cemetery Committee. This committee annually commemorated those from the area who were buried in the national cemetery. The letter was actually a copy of what he sent to Kennedy in Three Rivers. He first pointed out that the persons buried in the Tomb of the Unknown Soldier were not only unknown in terms of personal identity but also in terms of race, national origin, and religious views. "All we do know," wrote Coney, "is that he laid down his life for his fellow man. It is a terribly small country, Mr. Kennedy, when those who live in it forget too quick." He then reminded him that the freedoms fought and died for made it possible for the Rice Funeral Home to function as a free and unfettered business establishment. Coney then ended with the phrase, "Let us be worth the price they paid." One letter that came a few days later called for Kennedy to be run out of town on a rail, and added, "I suppose that the bullet that killed the Mexican G.I. paused a moment to ask if he came from above or below the border."

Given the often frustrating experience of protesting to government officials, it must have overwhelmed Hector to receive such prompt and supportive responses from such a varied and authoritative group. While he knew some and had contacted others over veterans' issues, he did not have a personal relationship with any as yet. Only Congressman Lyle could be said to have known Hector a long time. But that was because Hector had once driven a young soldier to the shipping-out area in North Africa. That young soldier later became a South Texas Congressman and eventually a friend. But in January 1949, all of these men were just barely aware of the existence of this new social reformer. The responses filled Hector with tremendous confidence and made that night's rally a formidable opportunity for him and the American G.I. Forum.

Nearly a thousand veterans, their families, and interested spectators attended the meeting at the Lamar Elementary School cafeteria. Some came because Hector had called, others came indignant that Felix had no chapel for his body, and still others came because they sensed something important was happening in South Texas. The people, mostly working-class veterans, did not hear anything new in the introductions. They had lived through a segregated society, a depression, and an all-encompassing war and had survived as best they could. But they communed with Hector because he articulated so well their deeply-rooted anger and frustration. They also noticed that unlike some of the reformers of the past, Hector did not seem to be asking for justice, he was demanding it.

They also sensed a new approach to organizing in the barrio. There was about him a sense that he wanted to include them in their own liberation. Earlier, *Border Trends*, a magazine that dealt with border issues, expressed a genuine admiration for the way Hector ran the meetings of the Forum. "Everyone," said the periodical author, "could express an opinion and everyone was heard." Hector's willingness to include every last one of the attendees exemplified a grassroots democracy uncommon in many of the hierarchical groups in the barrio. As they spoke and voted, they seemed certain that the final solution was a synthesis of "all" their thoughts.

The meeting at Lamar School exemplified another of Hector's efforts to empower them to resolve their problems. He wanted the veterans and others to understand the plight of Beatrice and to collectively provide a response. Already, the mayor of Three Rivers, J. K. Montgomery, had telegraphed Hector to offer his own home for the funeral services. He stated that upon interviewing Kennedy, he concluded that the chapel had not been refused nor would it be, if requested. The American Legion, added the mayor, had arranged for full military honors and offered its hall, if the family chose not to use the funeral home. Beatrice had also considered the possibility of burial in Corpus Christi and enlisted the Forum founder in finding a suitable place. But neither of the two options could compare with the one Senator Johnson proposed in a telegram that arrived during the meeting.

It had actually arrived earlier in the afternoon, but Hector had not read it before the meeting.

An excited Hector read the telegram to the gathering and did so in a manner calculated to incite the crowd. Johnson's telegram told the gathering that he deeply regretted the prejudice that extended "even beyond this life." He acknowledged having no authority over the Three Rivers establishment, and neither did the federal government. But then, through Hector's emotional voice, he added:

> However, I have today made arrangements to have Felix Lon-goria buried with full military honors in Arlington National Cemetery [in] Washington where the honored dead of our nations' wars rest.

The audience erupted in applause and cheers. Veterans and others looked at each other with amazement, others hugged, and some did not know whether to cry or laugh. But all the feelings stemmed from the same emotion. Pride. At that moment they felt pride in being Americans and having served their nation honorably. Finally, their nation had acknowledged their valor and service. The cheers probably interrupted the second part of the telegram, which offered another alternative. But once everyone quieted down, they found that the senator had also found a closer burial site for the family's convenience. Fort Sam Houston National Cemetery, close by in San Antonio, would also provide a resting place free of charge. It also provided a place where many Mexican American veterans could attend and be a part of the military honors. Johnson ended his telegram again deploring the injustice and expressing happiness in having a part "in seeing this Texas hero . . . laid to rest with the honor and dignity his service deserves."

Beatrice now had a choice of four cemeteries in which to bury her late husband. All had come in less than twenty-four hours, and each one of them brought a particular challenge. Three of the options meant having his body away from the immediate family, and one represented a reminder of the tensions she had known most of her life as a Mexican American woman. The choice would have made for a long discussion among family members, but the "incident" was no longer just a family affair. It was a state and national affair, drawing in concerned citizens and politicians. More importantly, Felix Longoria's fate had now become a concern to the Mexican American community of Corpus Christi, and through it, the larger Mexican American community of the nation. The decision became not only the family's, but the community's.

Hector saw it no other way. Felix not only represented the Longoria family. He represented every Mexican-origin family that sent a son, father, or brother to war. He also represented the hopes of every Mexican and Mexican American who sought and expected gratitude for a job well done. And more importantly, he represented the yearnings for dignity amid an often disdainful society. What happened to his body could no longer be just a familial concern. Hector indicated this much when he opened the question of where to bury Felix to the large audience. It might have surprised Beatrice and her sister who accompanied her, but they understood that Felix had gone from husband or brother-in-law to a symbol of dignity for all Mexican Americans. Whatever the concerns some had about the distance from home gave way to the significance of having one of their own buried in the nation's cemetery with full military honors. He would lay among the nation's heroes, himself a hero, but of a war much closer to home and much longer in length. Burying him in Arlington meant that Felix was coming home, not only to his family and community, but also to his nation. In opening its doors to him, the nation had welcomed them all in.

After deciding the burial site, a call went out for monetary assistance to get the family to Washington, D.C. and back. The funeral and ceremonies were free, but the flight, hotel, and food represented an investment the family could not afford to make. Hector called on those at the meeting to contribute and to seek other contributions from friends and family. The people in attendance responded with about $900, a significant amount in those times for a community beset by poverty and economic struggles. It came to almost a dollar a person, meaning several families shouldered a large commitment. But at the moment, it seemed a small price to pay for the right of Felix to be buried at Arlington National Cemetery. Veterans and others left the gathering committed to raising the rest of the funds.

Hector developed a deep affection for Felix and his family. While never having met them before, they were the type of people to whom he had recently dedicated his life. They were honest, hardworking people who troubled no one and demanded only respect. But Hector understood that the struggle for civil rights transcended family. Felix might have gotten his plot without a rally or the telegrams sent, but that resolution would have been like most others that Mexican Americans had been forced to accept: resolutions without apologies and without correction of the problem, meaning it could all happen again. Mexican Americans always had to beg, plead, and wait until the larger society awakened its pity, or simply found it politically expedient to be charitable. The rally had allowed frustrations to be aired collectively, giving Mexican Americans a sense of unity and strength. Reading the telegram from Johnson and summarizing the others gave them a sense that people in high places were listening. These messages confirmed that their indignation was legitimate. Deciding en masse gave them control of a public matter, and few had ever experienced that feeling before. Contributing and enlisting in raising the rest of the funds extended the empowering process that many felt that night. Every contribution asked would be prefaced by an indignant retelling of the denial and a triumphant declaration of victory. Every penny given became part of that gathering by proxy.

Hoping to build on the momentum and further empower the Forum, Hector took to the airwaves over the next few days and proclaimed a victory for the Longoria family and the Mexican American community. He also declared that "the American G.I. Forum is worthy of praise for its protest efforts." This message of success was reenforced by the letters and comments that poured in following the rally. The day after, President Truman's military aide, Harry H. Vaughn, telegraphed a message confirming that public opinion represented the best, and at this time only, weapon against discrimination and intolerance. Other letters came expressing indignation, praising Hector's actions, and contributing money for the expenses.

The financial secretary of the Campamento Granado No. 3169 of the Woodman of the World sent $10 and a congratulatory note. He also reminded Hector, "Don't forget that we are with you on issues like this." The G.I.s of Lanier High School in San Antonio sent $67 and best wishes in the "meritorious work." Members of the Sociedad Mutualista Mexicana de Jornaleros of Waco praised Hector and expressed their "gratitude for this demonstration of concern and interest for our [Mexican] people." Raoul Cortez, president of LULAC, sent $100 and thanked Hector for his "efforts to alleviate incidents such as this case." Hector also received letters from individuals personally offended by the Three Rivers case. Juan and Manuela Maya, after hearing of the incident on the radio, gathered what they could to send. Acknowledging that their large family of eleven children left them little money, they nonetheless decided to donate 50 cents for each member of the family. "And this way all of us *mexicanos* can unite and it will not be a heavy burden (author's translation)." J. O. García sent $3 to "become a participant" in the efforts to provide a burial worthy of someone who gave his life for his country. Many others from throughout the country, white, black, and brown, wrote and sent money.

Hector even received support from a rival organization, the American Legion. The James Edmond Post 121 of Waco passed a resolution condemning the conduct of the funeral home and demanding an immediate investigation and reprimand of those responsible for the "un-American act." The resolution declared that Americans of all races, creeds, and religions had fought bravely for their nation and were entitled to all rights provided by the Constitution. They called on the government to force the Three Rivers funeral home to receive the body.

There were others who showed support but did so by interpreting the incident as an aberration rather than a common reality. They deplored the action because it stained the good name of Texas and it invited a militant action from reformers. State Representative O. E. Cannon represented those more "moderate" conservatives who were appalled by Kennedy's action but frightened even more by the reaction to it.

> It is . . . hoped that in working out . . . problems [such as the Longoria incident], we can keep our friends in Mexico and people everywhere from [thinking] that such actions are usual

in Texas and that it is official policy . . . you and I know that such an attitude is *not* held by most of us in Texas.

The problem, as Hector understood it, was that indeed too many white Texans did have that attitude.

There were those who wrote to thank Senator Johnson for prompt action. Within days of his action, he wrote to Beatrice to tell her that many people from around the country had written to express their dismay at the action in Three Rivers and to praise his quick action. The Longoria family would join that chorus of gratitude. Four days after receiving the offer of a burial at Arlington and accepting it, they sent a letter signed by both families thanking him for his "kind offer and generosity" and declaring the burial at Arlington National Cemetery as the greatest honor that Felix could receive. "We regret," they wrote, "that we have caused you to be criticized, but you are still one of the greatest leaders of our country." No doubt Johnson, the consummate politician, appreciated the Longoria letter. For him, the Three Rivers incident allowed him to fulfill a promise he had made long before and at the same time to gain political capital. That was the way it was for the Central Texas politician who had learned to perfect the tactic of being both conservative and liberal, pro-segregation and pro-civil rights, friend of Texas rednecks and Mexican American reformers. Johnson cared deeply for the disadvantaged but he also cared for his brand of politics. When he combined both, he was the happiest. Usually, he simply balanced one action with another and kept both his friends and rivals unable to figure him out.

As a young schoolteacher in Cotulla, Texas, Johnson had experienced Mexican American poverty firsthand. The children that attended his classes often came without shoes or school materials and had not had a healthy breakfast. They tried but they could not keep up. Their parents cared about education but often had pressing economic problems that forced them to take their children out of school and put them in the agricultural fields. Johnson had also experienced the prejudices and bigotry of some of his fellow teachers. Never one to challenge unfairness unless he had overwhelming odds on his side, he simply made note of the injustices lest he forget them. Years later, he revealed a promise he had made as a young educator. If ever he had the chance, he would do something for Mexican Americans. He would repeat that story several times during his presidency.

But there was another side to the man most remembered as LBJ. Political success ranked first among his priorities. While often sympathetic to the poor and the discriminated, he rarely took up their cause if it meant political fallout. Thus, when provided an opportunity, he delivered wholeheartedly, as in the case of Felix Longoria. He must have surmised quickly that public opinion favored a positive resolution. Also, the Arlington National Cemetery burial meant sidestepping a potential conflict in his home state. There would be those siding with the funeral home director, but in the long run even they would appreciate a quick resolution.

Another political factor, however, weighed on the senator. Just about the time of the Three Rivers incident, the United States and Mexico were preparing to engage in serious negotiations over contract labor. Since the latter part of World War II, American farmers and industrialists had depended on labor from Mexico, first to replace soldiers in war and then to meet the labor demands of an expanding economy. The arrangement benefited both countries, but Mexican officials were nonetheless ill at ease with the treatment their countrymen received once on American soil. A year earlier, Mexican negotiators had rewritten the agreement to exclude the state of Texas as a recipient of Mexican laborers. The constant complaints of mistreatment and the Texan attitude of superiority had been too much even for Mexican officials who coveted the safety valve that American labor demands provided.

When the Longoria incident was reported in the *New York Times*, Mexican officials expressed an interest in the case. Paul J. Reveley of the state department immediately called John Connally of Johnson's staff and advised him to call the Mexican ambassador to alleviate concerns. Connally did so and assured the Mexican representative that the case was an isolated one that did not reflect the "feelings of the vast number of Anglo American Texans to the Texans of Latin American extraction." Upon hearing this and of the potential burial in the nation's capital, the Mexican ambassador expressed satisfaction, although journalists and other politicians in his country were not as easily appeased.

Reveley had hoped to include Texas in the new agreement and worried that the incident could derail the talks. He advised Connally to tell Johnson to press for the burial at Arlington and not Fort Sam Houston. And he asked for an individual burial rather than one combined with eighteen other soldiers. Reveley believed the burial did not alleviate all the concerns of the Mexican public, but a failure to resolve the issue promptly and sensitively would surely destroy any negotiations. He understood that Mexican government officials faced pressure at home to end contractual labor agreements with the United States. He also knew that the Mexican press was always vigilant to sensationalize any abuse of its citizens. Repatriation, when thousands of Mexican-origin workers had been coerced into leaving the United States during the Depression, was not yet fully removed from the minds of many Mexican officials and politicians.

The quick action by Johnson seemed rushed to some, but in fact it had been a series of calculated moves preceded by important decision-making. One decision involved confirming Hector's telegram, which Johnson did by calling Robert Jackson, publisher of the Corpus Christi newspaper. Both Jackson and Bob McCracken, the political writer for the paper, confirmed the details of the telegram. They also told the senator that they had published an article on the upcoming protest and on Kennedy's remarks. Johnson's staff also called Tom Sutherland of the Good Neighbor Commission, who immediately set out to investigate the story of the denial of the chapel. Sutherland reported back that Kennedy did not refuse to hold the services, but had strongly discouraged it. According to Sutherland, Kennedy had told him the funeral home was too small to accommodate a Mexican funeral, along with that of a white person. Having the two together might lead to a conflict he wanted to avoid. By this time, Kennedy had started to waiver on his earlier assertions. By the time Sutherland called him, he had been questioned by a reporter, the mayor, the county judge, and now the director of the commission. He told Sutherland that if the family insisted, the service could be held in the chapel.

The commission director, seeking to provide some perspective on the case, told Connally that "it was not germane to the case whether or not Kennedy had 'refused' or 'just discouraged' holding the chapel service." In the social context of Texas, he told Connally, Mexican Americans did not need a direct no or refusal to interpret the funeral director's words as a rejection. Sutherland was more willing to acknowledge the asymmetric relationship between the races than most other state politicians. Anglo Texans believed their "advice" was to be taken seriously, and Mexican Texans believed that all "advice" directed to them had an implied coercion. Both groups knew well that all communication between them had to be evaluated within the context of the social ambiance of the state. This implied, but far from implicit, relationship allowed Anglo Texans to deny any direct discrimination, even as they retained the asymmetric relationship. For Mexican Americans, the language allowed them to explore some flexibility in the social stratification, but it also delineated dangerous ground.

At whatever stage in the process he made the decision to offer burial at Arlington National Cemetery, Johnson did so after believing that it would meet his twofold criteria. It would alleviate some of the pain and anger many Mexican Americans felt and it would gain him political mileage as a peacemaker and a denouncer of the crudest form of discrimination. He believed that even staunch conservatives, leery of national attention, would appreciate the act because it would not of itself undermine the social structure. Felix might get a ceremonious funeral in Washington, D.C., but Three Rivers Anglo Americans would retain their segregated chapels. The quick decision, however, did not dispel all of the Anglo American's concerns. The Bexar County Central Council of the American Legion accused "careless and immature people in high and honorable places" of humiliating and embarrassing the people of Three Rivers. It declared that its own investigation conducted by "competent and unbiased" investigators had simply not found any trace of discrimination or "un-American activities." The resolution praised the people of Three Rivers for enjoying "most pleasant relations among all races." To the Legionnaires, the Longoria incident revealed another instance of Mexican American overreaction and an effort by a national politician to gain political mileage. In their view, a misunderstanding had been the only thing that occurred between Kennedy and Beatrice.

The Three Rivers' Anglo community reacted much the same way

as the legionnaires. In a full page response in the *Three Rivers News* on January 20, community leaders countered the nationwide criticism. Through a series of articles they sought to characterize the incident as a misunderstanding aggravated by reckless politicians and activists. The newspaper led off with an article claiming that city officials, the postmaster, newspaper editor, and Chamber of Commerce leaders had been subjected to derogatory, abusive, and obscene letters from throughout the state and nation. Most of the writers, said the newspaper editors, misunderstood the circumstances. For one, the body had not yet arrived in Three Rivers and would take almost another month before doing so. Upon its arrival, "the people of Three Rivers hope to arrange to have his burial."

The article emphasized that the Longoria family stood in the highest esteem among the town's citizenry and that the Chamber of Commerce, which represented the town's elites, regretted the situation that had developed. "No town," continued the article, "in South Texas enjoys better relations with Americans of Mexican descent than does Three Rivers." People who knew better had already written in defense. The article quoted the president of the chamber, S. F. Ramsey, who charged that Senator Johnson had aggravated the situation by acting "hastily" without contacting anyone in the community before taking action. The newspaper printed a letter from Felix's brothers, Guadalupe and Alberto, indicating that they had contacted the commander of American Legion Post 413 for military honors at the proposed local funeral. The commander, Harold C. Smith, promised a firing squad, color bearers, color guard, and bugles.

Continuing its efforts to prove a misunderstanding, the newspaper carried a statement by Kennedy, who repeated that he had encouraged Beatrice to use her house. But he reiterated that he asked the widow several times if she was satisfied. She, according to Kennedy, had never said otherwise. He then admitted a heated exchange with Hector. "In the heat of the argument [I] undoubtedly made . . . statements that could be possibly misunderstood," said Kennedy. He then expressed concern over a rumored conflict between Beatrice and Felix's family. He did not want that familial animosity to spill over into the funeral services, since he could not deny entrance to the chapel to anyone. "I did use the words that the 'whites would not like it,'" said Kennedy. "I was referring to the fact that the whites would not like the disgrace of a public disturbance at a funeral in the chapel." Kennedy ended with the assurance that if Beatrice had had any dissatisfaction, he would have been glad to "have found a way to satisfy her."

The accusation of familial conflict was to appear several times over the next month. It centered on Beatrice dating another man. It is possible that she stayed in Corpus Christi to avoid conflict with her in-laws over how long she should have waited before dating again. No doubt the conflict had become one between families. There was an added twist in that Kennedy revealed later that the two Longoria brothers had requested information from him, fearing that the widow might not share it with them. Beatrice never directly dispelled the rumors, but her sister Sara Moreno did. She admitted Beatrice had had a conflict with the family, but all had been resolved. This was obvious, said Moreno, by the fact that Beatrice wanted the body buried in Three Rivers, where his immediate family could come to visit the deceased. Another rumor had Guadalupe Sr. angry over Hector's involvement. Felix's family denied any estrangement from Beatrice and expressed gratitude for the doctor's assistance. Without doubt, not all things were right with the two families, but they were willing to work together to have Felix receive a proper burial.

The attempt by Kennedy and others in Three Rivers to paint family conflict as a determining factor in the denial was an old Anglo Texan trick. It sought to cast doubt on the morality of the family and its ability to act civilly in such an important event. By casting Mexican Americans in this light, Anglo Americans could discriminate on the grounds of protecting community standards and even the conflicting families themselves. It also sought to make Mexican Americans uncomfortable about pursuing a just cause. Not only the facts were contested but also the family's morals and reputations. Of course, this was done in the public arena, where Mexican Americans were at a disadvantage. Unused to public discourse, with no access to public forums to present their side and lacking articulation in the English language, they knew the disadvantages and usually chose to avoid a public fight. Anglo American racists and others with little sympathy for Mexicans understood the advantage they had. Thus, public humiliation was another trick to keep the Mexican Americans silent.

The defense of Three Rivers continued with an open letter to Johnson from Della Goebel, editor of the newspaper. In it, she criticized Johnson for making a controversial decision without consulting city leaders. She chided Kennedy's "youthful inexperience" in making rash judgments, but accused the senator of doing the same. In an accompanying byline article, Goebel added that the decision to bury Felix in Washington, D.C. was made mainly to satisfy "selfish interests of persons who either wished to pay political debts or who wished to stabilize their position in public opinion."

The editor then reiterated the positives of the community by citing an example of collective goodwill toward an injured Mexican boy. A high school athlete named Juan Díaz had been partially paralyzed in a football game. The community, said Goebel, had come together to assure the boy received medical attention. His medical bills were paid with local public school funds, and the Rotary Club had donated more than a thousand dollars to buy orthopedic equipment. Now back in school, "both Anglo Americans and Latin Americans help him by moving his chair about the building and the grounds." The article ended with the declaration that Three Rivers had been a "pioneer" in providing equal education facilities for all children. Education, said the article, was desegregated in all aspects. Only children who did not speak English were separated but quickly reintegrated as soon as they learned the language.

The newspaper articles did not use disparaging terms, nor did they try to defend the denial of the use of the chapel. In the minds of the editors, they had simply presented both the "facts" of the incident and the "reality" of Three Rivers. They felt confident that Texans across the state would empathize with them upon hearing their side. After all, what they described reflected in their minds the reality of the state. Mexican Americans often misunderstood good intentions, and liberals (or at least moderate conservatives in the case of Johnson) created ethnic tensions to advance their political careers. Race relations were never an issue because Anglo Americans were happy with the social structure, and Mexican Americans rarely complained, except for the troublemakers.

Hector may have fumed over the newspaper's rationalization but he was not surprised. Anglo Texans were not willing to accept that they had done anything wrong. In his own lifetime he had seen segregation develop and become more rigid. He had seen blatant discrimination become more subtle but remain just as insidious. He had also seen Mexican American reformers marginalized as troublemakers and malcontents. Throughout this time, only a few, lonely Anglo American voices had spoken out. The few liberals in Texas rarely engaged in a sustained campaign to better the lives of Mexican Americans. They concentrated on the "Negro problem" and in supporting labor unions, but even then they played only a small role in the social and political affairs of the state. Even those entrusted with the welfare of Mexican Americans in the state often revealed ambivalent feelings about this population. Welfare agencies were often hostile or indifferent to Mexican Americans, and even more so to the immigrant. So were law enforcement agencies, which instead of protecting, tended to brutalize those in the barrios. Even in the Good Neighbor Commission there were those who put most of the burden to resolve racial conflicts on the back of the Mexican American victim. For the sake of civility and the state's reputation, Mexican American victims of discrimination had to avoid responding with antagonism. Said one member of the Commission on the Longoria incident:

> We all agree that the happening at Three Rivers is to be regretted [but] we must bear in mind that the reputation of Texas will be at stake in history's recording of our handling of this very delicate matter . . . all Texans and the children of Texas now living will feel the effect of the criticism, and we all know that none of them has anything to do with [the incident] . . . she (Beatrice) has an opportunity to contribute to one of the *finest acts* towards this better understanding—and she is the only one who can do it.

The "finest acts" simply meant that Beatrice had to accept burial at Three Rivers for her husband and avoid making any more negative news. Hector had seen this before and he counseled against succumbing to that kind of pressure. He had seen this approach to blame the victim so often in the past that he came to accept it as "typical" for Anglo Texans. Mexican Americans suffered from prejudicial acts, but were then expected to turn around and be good sports, lest the reputation of the offender be injured. Mexican Americans could best express their civility and citizenship by turning the other cheek. But for Hector, this type of beatitude might be fine for individual conflicts, but not among two groups. Texans had been given enough time to change their attitudes after witnessing Mexican American passivity for years. But instead of softening their hearts, most had seen the passivity as an affirmation of the asymmetric relationship. Hector now "hungered and thirsted" for justice.

The most those appeals to civility got were a note from Beatrice. She expressed regret over the bad publicity and thanked the community for the offer to bury Felix but added that it was too late. She had accepted Johnson's offer to have him interred at Arlington National Cemetery. The letter said nothing about discrimination nor did it seek to rationalize the decision. It was simply a polite notification that things would not be resolved in the traditional manner. This woman, supported by the American G.I. Forum, Mexican Americans throughout the state, and enraged Americans nationally, made a decision not to do it the Texan way.

This bold act encouraged others in the Longoria family to speak out. Guadalupe, Sr. had been under pressure to denounce the offer from Senator Johnson and to disassociate himself from Hector. He had actually met twice with several community leaders who pressured him to sign a letter admitting conflicts with Beatrice and expressing that "everyone was his friend in Three Rivers." Guadalupe refused to sign, but the men insisted until he became ill and his children took him to Laredo to avoid any more contact with the city mayor, the Chamber of Commerce president, and Kennedy. Guadalupe later signed an affidavit denying any conflict with Beatrice and expressing his gratitude to Hector. He had, he swore, even volunteered to help with the fund-raising. He expressed regret for the problems caused to the community but added that he was not responsible for the conflicts

in Three Rivers. He stated, "I think we would only be fooling our-
selves to try to leave the impression that people of Mexican descent
are treated the same as anyone else throughout the state."

That was exactly the message Hector had hoped to disseminate
across the state and the nation. Blatant discrimination was easy to
identify and attack. But the daily, simple acts of prejudice and the
"suggestions" of the Kennedy-types paralyzed the daily lives of Mexican-origin people. These actions often occurred in private or simply
out of the larger public's view, and thus they were rarely discussed or
resolved. While these acts often reenforced the second-class citizenship of Mexican Americans, they did so in a way that allowed many
Anglo Americans and some Mexican Americans to assume relations
between the two groups were "good." Those with no enthusiasm for
blatant discrimination could soothe their guilt with the thought that
Mexican Americans were happy with their lot in life.

Just as he had exposed the Veterans Administration's disinterest in
Mexican American health problems, Hector unmasked Texan benevolence in its day-to-day treatment of Mexicans. Both had been based on
making the Tejano responsible for his or her own problems. The VA
did it by blaming them for not following procedures or asking for help
when they needed it. Texas community and political leaders did it by
promoting the view that Mexican Americans were happy with their lot
and simply did not try hard enough to rise above their situation. Neither one of the two views cast any guilt outside of the barrios. By
denouncing both the Veterans Administration and the Three Rivers
officials, Hector undermined the premise of Mexican American collusion in their victimization. Hector did not stop at simply denouncing
the attitude at Three Rivers, but set out to prove the town leaders'
claims as false or at least misleading. He knew South Texas too well
to accept at face value the claim that this community did not fit the
mold of rural towns in Texas.

In vintage Hector fashion, he set out to investigate the conditions
in the town and to interview its Mexican and Mexican American citizens. What he found was anything but atypical. Like most rural communities, a railroad track dissected the town, dividing one group from
the other. Only five Mexican families lived in the Anglo American

side of town, while a few Anglo families described as "transients" lived in the river bottoms, the Mexican side of town. The conditions on that side reflected the same reality of other "Mexican sides": poor or no drainage, unpaved streets, and no sidewalks.

The claim of voluntarily integrated schools proved nothing more than an illusion. Up until 1948, when a state court ordered a partial school desegregation, separation had existed up to the fifth grade. Now, grades three, four, and five were integrated, but students continued to be segregated within the same school and grades. The Mexican school, where Mexican-origin children attended the first two grades, was located outside the city limits. The Mexican parents had raised the money to provide a hard surface on the road leading up to the school because city leaders had ended the road eighty feet from the school. Once inside the school, students found small, crowded rooms, poorly lit, with no fly proofing nor adequate heating in the winter. The children would also not find any recreational equipment on the hard barren ground in the school yard.

Other Mexican children from surrounding communities came to the school in buses. These buses picked up both Mexican and Anglo American children. They first dropped off all the children attending the latter three grades in the regular school and then proceeded to the Mexican school out of town. Even children of those Mexican families living on the Anglo side of town attended the segregated two grades without the benefit of testing to determine their language proficiency. The segregation in the school simply reflected the situation in the rest of the town. The barbershops were segregated and so were the pool halls. Other public areas also suffered the same fate. In most cases there was no need to put up signs denying entrance to "Mexicans," although some establishments did so anyway. Mexican Americans had come to understand their geography and rarely wandered into hostile areas. This separation had been "suggested" by city leaders and an occasional vigilante.

Had Felix been buried in Three Rivers, his body would have occupied a lot in the Mexican cemetery and not in the principal resting place of the town. In 1924, a delegation of Anglo American citizens had approached Felix's father about a concern they had. In their view, the cemetery was "getting too crowded." Translated, that meant that too many Mexicans and Mexican Americans were dying and occupying valuable lots in the privately owned cemetery. They "encouraged" him as the spokesman of the Mexican community to mobilize his people to build another cemetery. The Mexican American community did so by buying up the land adjacent to the cemetery and burying their dead there. Soon after, they were encouraged to build a fence dividing the two resting places.

This process of separation in Three Rivers duplicated those instituted throughout the Southwest in the 1920s and 1930s. Laws, practices, and customs developed to keep the growing Mexican population from mingling with or overwhelming the established Anglo American communities. But the growing separation was tempered by certain realities of the Southwest. Mexican Americans and Anglo Americans often had to work together and participate in public functions together because the small communities could not duplicate all the services or provide equal space. So they often did business with each other, pleaded their cases in the same judicial halls, and shopped in the same stores. But wherever they could, Anglo Americans made sure the races remained segregated, and through this separation they reminded Mexicans of their dislocation from the social and political space of the community.

Anglo Americans could claim that things were okay and point to some interactions as proof of friendly relationships. Their children attended some of the same schools, the men worked at some of the same jobs, and the women shopped in the same few large stores in the town. Mexicans and Mexican Americans, however, had a different view. They saw their children in segregated schools and classrooms, and disdained on the playgrounds. They saw their men in low-paying jobs and always taking orders from Anglo American bosses. Women knew that the specialty shops were often off limits to them, even when they could afford the prices. Finally, families understood that theaters, restaurants, and some parks were off limits. So were the public swimming pools.

Mexican American reformers and others continually protested against such practices, but often their voices were muted by newspaper editors who branded them as troublemakers and by politicians and

administrators who found ways to circumvent Mexican American victories in the courtrooms. More important, Anglo American elites kept
the majority of the population unaware and unconcerned about the
demand for change. Given the amount of reform activity in the 1930s
and the 1940s, and the growing number of court victories achieved by
Mexican Americans during these years, it is amazing how little attitudes had changed among most Anglo American citizens and how
recalcitrant their leaders were.

Felix's body had not been in Arlington National Cemetery more
than a few days when several state legislators began clamoring for the
abolition of the Good Neighbor Commission for its alleged part in the
Longoria incident. State Representative J. F. Gray introduced a bill to
do so, and while the bill had little chance of succeeding because of
labor negotiations with Mexico, it stirred up debate and added what
one observer described as "a dash of gasoline upon the smoldering
fires of racial controversy in Texas." Unfortunately, even those who
protested the denial of the chapel services described the incident as an
aberration and not a sentiment of most of the citizenry. Thus, they
could attack the bill and wash their hands of any responsibility for the
attitudes that permeated the state. Content with believing that they
were different from the Kennedy-types, they took exception to
reformers like Hector, who reminded them of flaws in Texas society.
Said one journalist, "The agitators and the misinformed [will] use this
bill as an excuse to brand all Texans as racists."

While not all Texans may have been racists, there were enough of
them in the Texas legislature disturbed by the "bad publicity" to
approve a request by the same state legislator for an investigation into
the Longoria affair. The legislature chose a committee and appropriated $1000 for the investigation. Again, those in opposition saw the
action as opening the door for more controversy. "Segregation [is] a
reality among racial minorities," said one journalist. "To rediscover
that in hearings [will] serve no purpose." There were those who saw
hearings as a way for Hector to keep promoting his agenda. Said Bob
McCracken of the *Corpus Christi Caller-Times*, "That (investigation)
will be water on [Hector's] wheel."

McCracken's complaint found company. While most major politicians did not criticize Hector, lest they be seen as supporting the chapel denial to a veteran, there were numerous local politicians and organizations who did not hesitate to blame Hector for the "misunderstanding." In this they received a boost from the legislative report that came out in early April. The 372-page report that included the testimony of nineteen witnesses gave a blow-by-blow accounting of the incident. In it, committee members highlighted the familial conflicts, the community leaders' offer to bury Felix, and the funeral director's apology for the misunderstanding. The committee downplayed Beatrice's intimidation by Kennedy, the statements of "white objection," and the asymmetric relationship between the races. It chose to portray a misunderstanding made worse by Hector's interference and Johnson's overreaction. The majority of the committee declared, "This committee therefore concludes that there was no discrimination on the part of the undertaker at Three Rivers, Texas relative to the proposed burial of the body of Felix Longoria."

Ironically, on March 11, the day the committee held hearings in Three Rivers, another blatant act of discrimination was taking place right next to the proceedings. Juventino Ponce, 29, filed the following affidavit:

> I went to a barbershop located next to the Rotary Club . . . and a man wearing a white jacket . . . asked me, "What can I do for you?" I answered, "I need a haircut." He said, "I'm sorry but we don't serve Latin Americans." I said nothing but merely walked out.

The hearings themselves were quite tense as many came to see whether Anglo Texans' dominance of Mexican Americans would remain or whether it would be successfully challenged. Good Neighbor Commission director, Tom Sutherland, would later tell a reporter that the atmosphere resembled "high noon in a western movie." Some Texans brought knives into the courtroom while hostile law enforcement officers angrily stared at Hector, Sutherland, and the Longoria family. "A bunch of low-down greasers," was the way one court visitor described the grieving family.

Despite threatening letters and vicious telephone calls, Hector did not let the report go unchallenged. In a letter dated April 21 to friends and members of the Forum, he used the term "racism" for the first time in referring to the legislative report. He had testified, provided evidence, and done everything possible to have the committee understand the situation, as most Mexican Americans saw it, but his testimony found few sympathizers on the committee. In an earlier letter, he had written to a Miss Kibbe accusing the legislative committee of setting out to "whitewash the whole deal." They had also, he wrote, sought to brand him a troublemaker, but were unsuccessful. Hector charged the committee with knowing that there was discrimination, but being unwilling, owing to the political and social climate in Texas, to admit that it had found discrimination in the case. Gus García, who served as the family's counsel, went further and charged the committee with having "made up its mind in advance" that denial of the chapel to a Mexican was simply not an act of discrimination.

In spite of the outcome, there were those deeply impressed by Hector's testimony before the investigative committee. Said Lyle Saunders, a University of Texas professor, "I hope the hearings went well and . . . you were as impressive on your second appearance as you were on your first." He added that based on the evidence, the committee could not find "anything but discrimination." A reader of the *Pathfinder* wrote: "Permit me to extend hearty congratulations for the fine job you did toward securing . . . the full military honors that were finally awarded the hero." Another letter writer compared Hector to Lincoln, Washington, and Jefferson for his actions in the Longoria case. He regretted the innuendos and accusations that had been made during the investigation: "You are indeed honored by their elevation given you to the ranks of many made honorable by their sacrifices, and you will long be remembered for this."

These praises were undoubtedly welcomed. Hector loved the praise but he must have been particularly pleased with the letter from Alonso Perales, one of the original founders of LULAC and one of the most distinguished reformers of the twentieth century. Perales had already logged more than a quarter of a century of reform activity. Hector had in fact been quite impressed by him as a young man when he heard him speak in the Valley. To have Perales praise him must have indicated to Hector that he was on his way to becoming a major player in Texas reform activity. The old reformer congratulated Hector for "the firm stand you took at the hearing in Three Rivers recently. You made an excellent showing and won your case."

The letters of praise all came before the committee's final report. Their optimism about an eventual victory seemed to indicate that Hector had presented his case well. The majority of legislators did not agree with the assessment, but Hector's words and those of others did have an impact on a minority of the committee members. Representative Frank Oltorf of Marlin, Texas, dissented from the majority opinion stating, "I could not concur in [the] majority report without violating both my sense of justice and my intellectual honesty." Oltorf based his dissent on Kennedy's statement of "white objection." In his view, as well as those of many Mexican Americans, Kennedy simply reflected a communal attitude that discriminated against nonwhites. Shortly after the report went public, Representative Byron Tinsley, another committee member, requested the report to be withdrawn, and if not, to have his name removed from the document. That was followed by a denunciation of the report by Rogers Kelley, another legislator, who called it a "slap in the face of more than one million Latin American citizens of the state of Texas."

The public debate did not prevent the legislature from endorsing the report, but it did prove crucial to civil rights activity in Texas. The wide publicity given the Longoria incident exposed the hypocrisy of most Texas politicians, forcing many of them to choose between defending the old ways or publicly denouncing them. The governor, attorney general, and numerous other officials had to acknowledge, if only indirectly, that discrimination was present in Texas. Even in calling it an "aberration" they undermined discrimination because they defined it as wrong. With the state becoming a target of criticism from the nation's citizenry, the state's congressional delegation was forced to take a firm stand against discrimination. While some like Johnson, Lloyd Bentsen, and John Lyle had been uncomfortable with Texas attitudes, they found it difficult to publicly attack them. The Longoria incident provided them a forum to denounce discrimination once and for all. Had the controversy lingered, it might have been detrimental to their political careers, but the quick resolution provided them a moral victory without really troubling most Texans or challenging their attitudes toward Mexicans.

The unity of the Mexican American community must have surprised the politicians. But they saw potential political gain in the letter writing campaign from what they had considered a "silent" community. Mexican Americans now seemed a potential new group of voters who could be marshaled to change the nature of Texas politics. It would be a long time before they truly became crucial in Texas politics, but these politicians started paying attention. The emergence of Hector was another positive for them. The doctor from Corpus Christi had rallied people statewide in a way that had not been seen since the early years of the twentieth century. More important, Hector seemed to promise a more mainstream approach, and he could well turn into a good political ally.

The Longoria incident, however, loomed as an even more important accomplishment for Mexican Americans. The incident represented the first major case of discrimination in Texas that had attracted national attention and united all the Mexican American and Mexican reformers and organizations in the state. It had also been a quick and decisive victory that sent two powerful messages to the state's two largest groups. First, it told the Anglo American community that Mexican Americans could unite, that their cause was just, and that there were many sympathizers outside of the barrio. It also communicated that there was no more unanimity among Anglo American politicians on the issue of discrimination in Texas. The second powerful message went to Mexican Americans. It declared that they could win if they stuck together, and that there had arisen another organization and a new leader ready to lead them forward. Just as important, the American creed of fair play was real, and Mexican Americans could best gain their rights by participating civically in their communities. Mexican Americans, or at least a good portion of them, had never been passive but they had never seemed so united and strong.

Hector did not leave a written record of his feelings on the Longoria incident, but it is not difficult to imagine how he must have felt.

He appreciated the idea of a victory. As a military man—he was still an officer in the Army Reserve—he saw victory as the outcome of a well-planned strategy combined with a passionate execution. While he understood that the fight for civil rights was often a war of attrition, he knew major victories were essential to keep morale high. The Forum had embarked on a number of campaigns, but it faced a daunting task in motivating Mexican Americans to chip away at the wall of segregation and discrimination over an extended period of time. The victory in the Longoria incident promised many more victories and possibly much quicker. It also assured Mexican Americans that they were not alone in their struggle. There were politicians and citizens who empathized with them and were willing to offer a helping hand. America was reaching out, possibly for the first time. It was acknowledging their sacrifice and loyalty in the great war. Hector saw in Mexican Americans a new valor and a new commitment to do something about their condition. Hector must have also seen the letters of praise from other reformers as an acknowledgment that they were stepping aside to allow him to take over the leadership of the struggle. Never one to refuse the limelight or leadership opportunities, Hector took over the mantle and did not release it for another two decades.

The Beginning of
a Protracted Struggle

The victory in the Longoria incident gave Hector much to rejoice but it in no way signaled the demise of segregation. No law had changed, no segregationist practice had ended, and those who discriminated were unrepentant. Yet, the Longoria incident had awakened many to the blatant discrimination that existed throughout the state. Mexican Americans who learned to accommodate and who pretended that things were "not that bad" were forced to look at their situation. Those who had a history of struggle against segregation but had been worn down, were reenergized. Victory in Felix's case reminded them that their fight was just. It also inspired the hope that a new organization would carry the fight to another level and possibly bring unity to all groups in the barrio.

In spite of Longoria's impressive funeral, segregation was still a way of life in Texas and most of the Southwest. Many Anglo Americans continued to feel superior, and every day one more Mexican American child accepted that he or she was inferior. The practice of segregation against Mexican Americans was anything but simple. Unlike segregation against African Americans, the brand used against Mexican Americans revealed nuances that changed according to region, employment, time, and expediency. Segregation as a form of social control was diluted in the urban areas by political machines that needed the Mexican vote to stay in power. *Patrones* in the rural areas did the same but they often combined it with a paternalism that allowed some Mexican Americans to assume some upward mobility in the middle ranks of the political or social ladder. These same Anglo American political bosses had a different relationship with the Tejano *patrones* in several of the counties that were overwhelmingly Mexican and Mexican American. Counties like Zapata, Webb, and Hidalgo had Mexican American political machines that kept Mexican Americans in power. But these *patrones* needed alliances with Anglo American bosses, who in turn were allied with state politicians, such as the governor or even the U.S. senators. Some of these Tejano leaders were supportive of organizations like LULAC and the American G.I. Forum. While they themselves did not face discrimination in their localities, they knew that loss of power meant they were just another Mexican. Their relationship with the economic elite in the county meant that they kept the same economic order as in other parts of Texas, but they tried to do so without blatant racism. At a time when Mexican American reformers were mostly concerned with traditional civil rights issues, the class structure in Texas was often ignored. Things would change later, but for the time being all Mexican American elites were on the same side.

While segregation provoked anger in Hector, he did not always understand the complexities of its implementation or its end result. For a deeper analysis, he relied on advisors and old friends. Gus García, old friend, LULAC reformer, and Forum legal advisor, proved to be the best legal mind in the battle to desegregate Texas. George I. Sánchez, Hector's former mentor at the University of Texas, was Gus García's counterpart in the sociopolitical arena of desegregation. Having already waged a decades-long struggle against segregation, Sánchez found renewed hope in the American G.I. Forum's militant advocacy against legal and de facto restrictions on Mexican Americans. He had fought the ideals of segregation in his home state of New Mexico, in the public schools in Texas, in federal governmental agencies during World War II, and in university departments, where liberal condescension combined with conservative scholarship to victimize Mexican Americans. He witnessed and participated in numerous reform activities, many of which were successful in the 1940s, but he also witnessed how Anglo American administrators, bureaucrats, and politicians simply found ways to circumvent the law. The militancy of the Forum and the tenacity of Hector seemed to Sánchez as the right formula for an all-out and final defeat of legal and de facto segregation.

The issue of segregation's constitutionality had come to the forefront with three events in the preceding two years. First, the Ninth Federal District Court in Los Angeles, California, had ruled in *Méndez et al. v. Westminster School District of Orange County* that the segregation of Mexican children by the Westminster School District was a violation of the equal protection clause of the Fourteenth Amendment. The decision came on February 26, 1946. Fourteen months later on April 14, 1947, Judge Paul J. McCormick's ruling was upheld by the Ninth Circuit Court. The decision marked the first time that a federal court had decided that segregation of Mexican children was unconstitutional. The court also acknowledged that integrated classrooms were more appropriate for learning English than separate ones. This, of course, undermined both Californian and Texan school officials' claims that the children had to be separated in order to learn the language. According to historian Guadalupe San Miguel, the ruling also established that separate but equal was simply not a reality because equality meant more than similar school facilities and equally equipped teachers.

The ruling by McCormick prompted the Texas attorney general, Price Daniel, to offer a legal opinion declaring that the separation of Mexican children based "solely on race" was forbidden by Texas law. The only exception was when children were separated in order to be immersed in English-language instruction, but this could only be done up until the third grade. Immediately, [Gus] García asked for clarification. He asked if racial origin or social background could be used in any manner to justify segregation. He also requested from the attorney general assurances that separation be based on scientific tests and that the separation would not mean inferior facilities or uncertified teachers. Daniel agreed and reiterated that "We meant that the law prohibits discrimination against or segregation of Latin Americans on account of race or descent and the law permits no subterfuge to accomplish such discrimination."

Daniel's opinion proved a major, although short-lived, victory for social reformers. Its importance lay in the fact that the state's top legal officer had discounted any legal basis for segregation that discriminated on the basis of race, national origin, or social condition. It also made it illegal to maintain separate facilities for more than the first three grades. These two aspects of the opinion made it significant because it was the first recognition that the state's school officials were discriminating against Mexican-origin students, and that beyond certain adaptations for English skill retention—which should be ameliorated by the third grade—the schools had the responsibility of integrating the students. Unfortunately for Mexican parents and their children, the attorney general chose not to provide guidelines to the school districts on how to accomplish the desegregation of the schools.

Even more devastating to his own opinion, Daniel failed to establish any coercive mechanism to pressure or punish school officials who resisted the opinion. The attorney general felt content to allow local school districts the latitude to resolve the problem of segregation in their schools as they saw fit. In this way, Daniel spoke out of both sides of his mouth. He could denounce segregation while allowing each locality the right to decide whether they believed they were segregating Mexican-origin students "solely on the basis" of race, national origin, or social condition. Within a short period of time, Mexican American reformers found out how ineffective the ruling really was. In challenging several school districts to desegregate on the basis of the attorney general's opinion, they found that none of the school officials agreed with their charges of segregation and they found state school officials supportive of those local decisions. In a study conducted by Sánchez and a University of Texas colleague, eight out of ten school districts investigated were found to engage in one form or another of segregating their Mexican students. They also found that most school officials simply ignored the legal opinion because they were under no threat to make changes.

It would take another lawsuit, this time in Texas, to add some teeth to the integration of Mexican children. One of the dilemmas of the California case, according to historian San Miguel, was that it failed to determine whether de facto segregation was as illegal as that which was de jure. In Texas there were no legal statutes that prescribed segregation; it had simply been a practice for as far back as anyone could remember. The *Méndez* case also did not clarify the responsibility of the state officials. If they were not enjoined to stop segregation, then the battle over separation of the races would have to be fought on a "school-by-school" basis. LULAC leaders sought to avoid this exhaustive and often disappointing effort by filing a lawsuit against several school districts in Central Texas. In the case of *Delgado v. Bastrop Independent School District*, filed in January 1948, LULAC lawyers argued that school officials were segregating school children contrary to the law. The case was based on two important points. First, the schools were violating both the state and federal constitutions by segregating Mexican children because of their race, and second, school officials had ignored repeated requests by parents to remedy the situation.

In June 1948, a federal judge ruled segregation as practiced in four Central Texas school districts to be unconstitutional. Judge Ben W. Rice declared that segregation violated the 14th Amendment to the U.S. Constitution. He ordered the schools to open all facilities to Mexican children and forbade school districts to use English-language knowledge as an excuse to separate Mexican children from other children. The only exception was in allowing first graders in separate classrooms for English instruction, but it had to be done within the same campus. He gave the school districts until September of the following year to comply or face loss of public funds, removal of accreditation, and contempt of court charges. More important for reformers, the judge made school officials liable for the establishment and maintenance of segregation in their districts. The ruling affected school districts in Portland, Mathis, Beeville, Aransas Pass, Kingsville, Robstown and Taft, all of them surrounding communities of Corpus Christi.

Hector reacted immediately to the decision, calling it "one of the foremost decisions in this state." He added that Mexican and Mexican American children would surely be better educated because of it, and the nation would be stronger for it. "People all over the world," he added with usual hyperbole, "and our Latin brothers in Mexico, Central America, and South America will now have greater faith in [the] true democratic United States of America." Mexican Americans, said Hector, had defended the nation in two wars and were ready to do it again, but this time they would do it feeling "equal." "It should teach

us to fight for our rights and demand our rights as long as we are entitled to them," García observed. The ruling, he declared, had restored
the people's dignity, thus allowing them to have hope for a better
future. "People without dignity," he added, "are people lost in a sea of
uncertainty."

Eight months later, however, state public school officials were still
recalcitrant. They did not budge unless specifically ordered, and even
then they found or (at least sought) ways to violate the spirit if not the
letter of the law. Mexican American reformers were again left to take
on each district one at a time or in small groups. Each effort took time
and resources that few individuals and organizations had. Sánchez,
sensing mounting frustration, decided to go for a grander scheme. On
April 14, 1949, he wrote Hector to invite him to be part of a "larger"
discussion on the "matter of segregation throughout the state." He first
praised Hector's effort on behalf of the case favorably decided by
Judge Rice. The veteran educator then expressed concern. Depending
on voluntary compliance, said Sánchez, would be like "pulling teeth."
He predicted that "in the last analysis, (Superintendent) Dr. [L. A.]
Woods and other state officials are going to move as little and as slowly as possible—because a forthright stand on the elimination of segregation is not politically wise for them at the present time." This political expediency would force reformers to keep "begging and cajoling"
to assure that any type of progress could be made. Expressing a defi-
ant attitude, Sánchez called for taking off the "kid gloves." After all, he
reasoned, the ruling gave the plaintiffs all the cards, and they would
"admit stupidity" by failing to move aggressively.

Sánchez called for a strategy to end segregation in the public
schools once and for all. He recommended a two-prong strategy by a
sponsor willing to raise "thousands of dollars" for legal costs, and
committed to getting the necessary facts on where segregation existed. "I think," he wrote Hector, "that the G.I. Forum would do well to
become that sponsor." He offered to serve as an unpaid consultant to
head the project. But he asked for a commitment to see the project
through if Hector and the Forum agreed to undertake the fundraising
and data collections. Hector took on that challenge to eliminate school
segregation once and for all. Unfortunately, the Forum never devel-

oped the financial capacity to "raise thousands of dollars" for the legal costs. Forum chapters always seemed to come through in an emergency and in times of crisis, but they simply did not raise enough to have a permanent office, staff, or a contingency fund for emerging legal matters. The organization lived from hand to mouth. There simply was not enough money in the barrio, and there were few outsiders willing to contribute. Unlike the NAACP, which had its dedicated white philanthropies, the Forum did not attract that kind of attention. In fact, not until the 1980s, when corporate America came to the rescue, was the Forum the recipient of much outside money.

The Forum, however, could help on the second part of the strategy. Forumeers went throughout those areas in which they had chapters and collected evidence of discrimination and segregation. The men and women who supported them became hypersensitive to acts of discrimination and prejudicial treatment. Most had lived under those conditions all their lives. While some had almost become used to it, the Longoria incident had reawakened them to it. Hector's aggressive condemnation of segregation and ill-treatment of Mexican Americans made it hard for the community not to be sensitive to its plight. Hector's approach, however, was not simply to follow the path set by others. He saw the importance of attacking school segregation through the courts, but there were other issues that mattered too. Segregation was everywhere: in the workplace, hospitals, city and county agencies, draft boards, theaters, swimming pools, and even in the minds of Mexicans and Mexican Americans in Texas. While LULAC had once fought all of these forms of exclusion—and still did periodically in the most severe cases—it had begun to concentrate on the schools. Hector wanted to attack discrimination on all fronts by challenging it in the courts through litigation, in the public arena through protests and rallies, and in every home in the barrio by getting Mexican Americans involved in mass numbers, even as he recruited the best and most tenacious among them based on the still-young Forum's growing list of successes.

Hector claimed that by the end of its first year of existence, the Forum had 3,000 members statewide, with a third of those in Corpus Christi. He could also claim several important victories. In response to veterans' medical needs, the Forum had been able to convince Congressman John Lyle to submit a bill for a 300-bed hospital for tuberculosis patients. They had gotten E. E. Mireles, a local educator, appointed to the local draft board. Numerous back-to-school drives had been initiated throughout the South Texas area. Hundreds of veterans had been convinced to go back to school, and thousands more had been encouraged to pay their poll taxes and register to vote. And of course, there had been the Longoria victory. In the process, Hector had reenergized the reform movement in Texas, which had floundered somewhat during World War II. Those who stayed on the home front had, for the most part, dedicated themselves to promoting support for the war effort and maintaining the few gains that Mexican Americans had made before the war years. Hector brought a vibrancy and tenacity that was clearly missing in reform activity in Texas.

Even more important for Hector, he had begun to define himself as one who sided with the underdog, the underprivileged, and the unheard. This was a position that few other reformers had been willing to assume. Many were liberal and defended the rights of their poor Mexican American compatriots, but they usually defined class conflict in the context of poor Mexican Americans living in the midst of enough wealth to provide for everyone. Rarely did they question or criticize the accumulation of resources by the few. While Hector spent most of his life fighting civil rights issues, he nonetheless continually affirmed his support for the masses of poor in the nation. On October 21, 1948, he wrote State Representative Roger Q. Evans to praise him for being a legislator "who represented the poor people of the state and not the rich, oil or industrial factors (sic) of the state." He would heap the same praise on Congressman Lyle and State Representative Rogers Kelley, who were moderates in a state of strong conservatives. Hector's defense of the poor was not ideological but philosophical. His parents had taught him respect for the poor, and his own poverty during his school years as well as the poverty he saw in Europe and Africa reminded him that being poor was not a choice for most. He also knew that starting life poor simply compounded every other problem in a person's existence. Poverty meant malnutrition, which led to poor school performance. That usually led to dropping out of school or learning little, which led in turn to underemployment or unemployment, which led finally to the cycle beginning again for the children.

It would be years before Hector became involved in job training, and he never did develop a good economic critique of the status quo, but Hector did attempt to tackle the problem of bleak futures by joining other reformers in getting Mexican American children back to school. The Forum's back-to-school drives had begun having success within their first year. Lazelle D. Alway, assistant secretary of the National Child Labor Committee was one to quickly point out the fruits of the drives. In a letter dated January 13, 1949, Alway told Hector that his committee had been impressed by the results. "Latest school figures show," he wrote Hector, "that there is quite an increase in the number of Latin American children in high school since the first six weeks school attendance report." The back-to-school drives were not originated by the Forum, but, rather, by LULAC. What made them such a success for the Forum was that by involving the veterans, they were able to assemble a core group that would consistently cajole even the most resistant parent, in ways LULAC had not been able to on its own.

Six days before Alway's letter, Hector had written a letter of his own to the editors of the *Edinburg Valley Review*, chiding city leaders for the low attendance of Mexican American children in their schools. He informed them that there were 1,475 Mexican American children not enrolled in school and another 1,332 who did not attend school regularly. "It is surprising that a city as progressive as Edinburg," he wrote, "with its good schools and college and its good spirit should tolerate such poor . . . attendance in its schools." Hector then pointed out the value of the back-to-school drives which had resulted in 1,100 children returning to school in Corpus Christi and 400 in Robstown.

The back-to-school drives were vintage Hector organizing campaigns. First, he contacted the Texas office of education for statistics on each of the state's school districts. He then selected the most flagrant areas in terms of low attendance and took a trip to the area to set up a committee of parents, Forum principals—if there were any—and other civic leaders. The committee then developed a campaign strategy that included ads in newspapers, signs all over town, radio spots, flyers, and a back-to-school rally when appropriate. That would be followed by house-to-house canvassing. This approach had worked rather well in Corpus Christi, where an eighteen-member committee had been organized. Hector and the Forum mounted this campaign following Judge Rice's outlawing segregation in several counties. Hector believed that parents had to respond immediately to the court's pronouncement. The committee enlisted social clubs, public officials, private firms, and citizens to promote the drive. The county attorney and justice of the peace promised to enforce truancy laws, while J. A. García, Hector's brother and a member of the school board, pledged to sign complaints against parents who refused to send their children to school. Spanish radio stations cooperated by stressing the importance of educating children, and also warned the parents of the consequences of not obeying the law. To assist children without adequate clothing or school supplies, the Forum organized dances, cakewalks, carnivals, and other activities to raise funds. The drive proved successful in Corpus Christi and several surrounding communities.

Hector, sensitive to some of the parents' skepticism, sought to convince them that education was worthy of sacrifice. Many of the children who did not attend school were part of the large migrant pool that resided in the state. The migrant worker families moved often and, when they were home, tended to have all members of the family work in order to meet their basic needs. Hector was sensitive to their economic limitations and need for every possible source of income, but he believed that the cycle of poverty could be broken only by children staying in school. He must have recalled his own family's sacrifice to keep the García children in school, when they could have helped with the finances as many of their friends had done. Eventually, Mexicans and Mexican Americans had to make the hard and long-term decision to sacrifice for the children's benefit. Quoting from a University of Texas publication entitled "Texas Born Spanish Name Students in Texas Universities," Hector told those in the school drives that "The Spanish-speaking people must, increasingly and to the fullest extent of their ability, assume responsibility for their own development." The creation of a professional class "would aid in the promotion of individual and group welfare."

Hector identified two other factors affecting school attendance.

One, directly related to segregation, was the horrible condition of the schools. The magazine *Border Trends* reported that where migrant children attended schools, the buildings were usually overcrowded and dilapidated. In one county, 800 students attended the Mexican school while only 250 Anglo American students attended the modern "regular" school. In the Mexican schools, students often had to use open privies, some of which were overflowing. Most county governments refused to provide more healthy facilities because they did not want to provide the 40 percent matching funds to fix the problem. Mexican and Mexican American students and parents found those physical deprivations very disturbing. They also felt humiliated by the segregation that often prevented them from participating in school activities. It was difficult to develop school pride or loyalty when teachers and administrators constantly made disparaging remarks.

Most Mexican American parents quickly understood that their children were seen as a burden to the school district. Even some of the more sensitive teachers revealed low expectations for the children. The situation in Texas reflected a very rigid class distinction. Middle-class Mexican American students, while often facing the same discrimination as poorer children, were assisted in succeeding by some Anglo American teachers who saw in them something that was "different." It was actually a triumph for a teacher to find one of those "likely-to-succeed" students who proved the stereotypes wrong, usually because he or she and their parents had decided to embrace Americanization wholeheartedly. But for those from working-class families, who had little discipline, few skills, and almost no knowledge of the language, not to mention hygiene problems, the doors were usually solidly closed. Some made it in spite of the obstacles, but so many more quickly learned that their only future lay in the fields, the canneries, or the unskilled jobs in the city. For them, their national-origin was a racial barrier that became more insurmountable as they grew older, poorer, and darker. By mid-century, the dichotomy within the race, between the poor dark and the middle-class lighter Mexican American was growing more noticeable. Both faced discrimination, had obstacles thrown their way, and suffered segregation; but for one group those were challenges to overcome and for the other group they were a reminder of how things were in Anglo Texas.

Compounding the dropout or no-show situation of the *mexicano* students was child labor. Hector quickly learned that no matter the threat or enticement to parents, most were still tempted to send their children to work, if the opportunity was there. There were simply too many parents who saw little value in sending their children to segregated schools from which they would drop out or graduate only to work in the fields. Even those who valued education often found themselves pressured by the growers to bring the whole family to the fields. In 1949, Hector estimated that there were at least 5,000 children working in the cotton fields in Texas. As was his nature, Hector did not want to simply count them. He wanted to know them and to understand how they felt about their situation. So he went to the fields to talk to children as they worked and to encourage their parents to take them out and send them to school. Child labor was against the law, although the law tended to be more lenient with children who worked in the fields. Most parents did not know the intricacies of the law, so Hector simply told them it was illegal. But he also contacted the employment service office of the federal government and the various school districts to protest and to get them to do all in their power to get the children into school.

For Hector, political segregation remained intertwined with the educational and public segregation that trapped *mexicanos* into a separate and unequal reality. Years of discrimination and discouragement had kept Spanish-speaking voters from the polls in most of the state, except in those border areas controlled by Mexican American political bosses. White primaries functioned in some counties, in others Texas Rangers and other law enforcement agents intimidated voters. Statewide, most primaries and local elections were held during the harvest season, when many Mexican migrant workers were out of town. But for Hector, the most insidious form of political segregation was the infamous poll tax, which forced citizens to pay for the right to vote. In 1949, only four states, all in the South, still had a poll tax. The three other states charged the fee to keep African Americans from voting. "It is my opinion," said Hector, "that Texas maintains this poll tax with the intent that the Mexican people become disheartened" and not vote.

Hector rejected the argument that fees from the poll tax were intended to support the public schools. "I say, if the state is interested in raising [funds] . . . let it pass laws raising taxes on the petroleum . . . and other industries . . . that gain their profits from exploiting the natural resources that belong to the people."

Hector called upon Texas to "modernize" and to become more democratic by allowing thousands of Mexican Americans to vote. The poll tax kept many honest, hardworking people from participating because of the cost. For those skeptics who believed that $1.75 was such a minimal cost, he reminded them that farmworkers and other unskilled laborers made barely three to four dollars a day. "They will not spend their money [on the poll tax] because they need it more to feed their malnourished children and their growing families." Hector made it clear to critics and skeptics that economics and not the level of civic commitment was the reason more Anglo Americans paid their poll tax. Paying $1.75 was a minuscule price to pay for participation in elections for those who had the money, but for the poor it was a fortune.

In describing the disparate situation, Hector sought to show that the situation in Texas was not just about discrimination. It was also about rich versus poor. In his mind, the monied interests in the state wanted to keep wages low and schools underfunded, in order to maintain a power monopoly for the rich. While this affected all of the state's residents, it hurt *mexicanos* even more, because their struggles with the economic system were compounded by the discrimination and hostility they received from both rich and poor Anglo Americans.

Hector understood that railing against the unfairness of the system did little good by itself. Mexican Americans had to pay the price to change things, and that meant paying their poll tax. That is why he had made paying the tax a requirement for membership in the American G.I. Forum. In a series of radio chats, which had now become a regular feature for Hector, he reminded the barrios that four years earlier the question of the poll tax had been placed before the voters. Although Mexican Americans numbered close to one million, they had less than 50,000 registered voters. It is likely that Hector was making "guesstimates," but he wanted Mexican Americans to understand the dilemma. Anglo American voters, according to Hector, would continue to support the poll tax as a way to keep barrios from gaining political power. Mexican Americans had to "awake" and begin paying their poll tax and running for office. He assured his radio audience that if half a million Mexican Americans paid their poll tax, the law would be changed in six months. He urged his listeners to pay the poll tax "right now" to be ready to vote against the poll tax the following year, when it would be up again for a vote. For Hector, the necessity of being ready to practice civic duty was part of the obligation of citizenship. Besides, there were other measures, which were of importance to the Mexican community. Two of them were obligatory automobile insurance and a move to make Texas a dry state.

In Hector's view, these laws were insensitive and directed toward Mexicans and Mexican Americans. Most *mexicanos* needed their cars to follow the crops, and the insurance payments were simply another burden that added to those of gasoline and maintenance, which were already significant for migrant workers. Failure to buy insurance meant no license plates, thus no cars, and for many, no work. Hector believed the law would be the ruin of many families. He again described the situation as one in which those with money would buy insurance and those without simply had to face life without a car. Hector was technically right, but he underestimated the ability of Mexicans and Mexican Americans to drive unregistered cars and to do so without a driver's license. Still, there were many who wanted to obey the law but saw insurance payments as another economic burden. Others simply believed that mandatory insurance was another way to tax the poor.

The discussion of Texas becoming a dry state would be a political exaggeration. While there were powerful, conservative religious forces pushing for the restriction, the possibility was remote. While Hector rarely drank, he knew that for many Mexicans and Mexican Americans their beer and alcohol was important. In warning the radio audience about the potential restrictions, he sheepishly told them, "If you want to protect your 'likes,' it is better to start buying your poll tax today and not tomorrow." Being that he well understood the problems that alcoholism caused in the barrio, Hector must have felt slightly uncomfortable promoting the payment of the poll tax as a way to save their addiction. But Hector faced a dilemma that other temperance reformers had

had in the past. Mexican Americans had been drinking for generations, and Catholicism had rarely promoted abstention, although it did recommend moderation. Hector's approach was to simply promote intelligent use of the habit; however, for the sake of more important political causes, he promoted its protection.

Hector reminded those who listened that there were an increasing number of Mexican Americans running for political office. "I am pleased by this," he told his listeners, "because I see the necessity of buying my poll tax and you [do] too." He also reminded Mexican Americans that if they had just turned twenty-one or were older than sixty, they would be exempt from paying the poll tax fee. Also, wives could pay for their husbands and husbands for their wives. But the payment had to be made by January 31. The year before, he reminded them, a cold freeze had caused many to stay at home and miss the deadline, thus barring them from voting for the rest of the year. Warning of dire consequences, however, was not the only way to get his people to pay their poll tax. Following a decades-old tradition, the Forum promoted raffles, dances, cakewalks, carnivals, and other activities in which the price of participation was the $1.75 the person needed to register to vote. While seemingly deceitful, Hector and the Forum realized that their efforts to get Mexican Americans to be civically minded would go for naught if they failed to meet the deadline out of forgetfulness or because of cost. Before becoming good voters, Mexican Americans first had to learn to pay their poll tax, register to vote, and then begin the process of understanding the issues and choosing the candidates.

The struggle for civil rights in Texas in the late 1940s and early 1950s confronted two major obstacles. The first and often most obvious obstacle was the institutionalized racism that served to limit the lives of most Mexican Americans. The other were hostile attitudes in barrios and rural communities where most Mexican Americans resided. Within them, the people had faced discrimination, poverty, and illiteracy for so long that they had found or created ways to survive as well as to resist the hostility of the outside world. In doing so, they had developed customs and habits to keep them outside of mainstream American society. They were then often reluctant to be as positive or enthusiastic about civic participation or social mobility as were most reformers. Had they believed things would change as easily as some reformers promised, they might have been more enthusiastic about getting involved, learning the language, and voting. But most had experienced disappointments too often in the past to believe that a new age was coming with this new burst of social reform activities. In spite of nearly fifty years of some form of reform activity, the barrios remained poor and segregated, and were disdained by mainstream Anglo American society.

This separation and destitution had created an attitude that reflected either an unwillingness by Mexican Americans to conform to American society or an ambivalence about their ability to adopt its ways. This circumstance made them even more suspect in the eyes of Anglo American politicians and educators. In a letter from Alfredo Guerrero, Jr. dated October 17, 1949, Hector received an appraisal of a school superintendent in San Marcos, a Central Texas community where Mexican Americans made up less than half the population. The superintendent was responding to pressures from the G.I. Forum to do more to integrate Mexican children in his schools and to participate in a back-to-school drive. He complained that parents did not teach their children to speak English, did not read nursery rhymes, or prepare them for school so that "it will not take us six years to teach them English in our Mexican school." Lack of cleanliness was another complaint. He accused Mexican children of carrying lice and of always having an "itch." And he called them clannish because they tended to congregate by themselves, away from the white children. "We want to help them, but they do not want to help themselves," Guerrero quoted him in the letter. The superintendent also added that children—and he was probably thinking of the parents too—had to be taught the principles of democracy: "Participate, mix, think, society will accept you when you are ready, not just because you are entitled to those rights. . . . They [Mexicans] will never attain our white level until such time they prepare themselves and accept responsibility in our community." Guerrero, head of the back-to-school drive and one of the Forum's leaders in San Marcos, admitted he was angered at the comments but acknowledged that the superintendent "was right in a lot of his points." He wanted Hector to provide him a way to rebut the criticism.

No letter exists with Hector's response, but it is likely that the Forum leader had pondered these points before and would do so in the future. He may have also wondered about Forum leaders, like Guerrero, who had a skewed view of their own people. The San Marcos Forum leader, like other reformers, often took a presentist approach to the problems of the barrio. While they acknowledged discrimination, illiteracy, and poverty, they were not as willing to accept that the consequences of such factors were not easy to overcome, or that it might take decades to reverse the damage done by them. Hector knew that parents could not teach their children English because they themselves did not know the language. Children went to school dirty because they came from homes with no running water, no soap, and no money to buy clean clothing. Children carried numerous diseases because—this was the case in San Marcos, according to Guerrero—there were no health facilities to treat the Mexican population. They stayed with their own because they were not wanted among the Anglo American children, many of whom were instructed by their parents to avoid Mexicans. As for not knowing the principles of democracy and participating in the civic affairs of their community, most had never experienced democracy firsthand because of white primaries, the poll tax, and because few candidates took them seriously.

Guerrero probably knew all of these things, but his frustration was high. Unable to make significant progress against Anglo American society, Guerrero and other reformers blamed their fellow citizens for being victims. "We have a lot of people in San Marcos who don't care [about] school," he wrote Hector. "They want their children as 'assets,' to make them work so that they can buy new cars and get drunk Saturday nights and brag about their not knowing how to read and write." Revealing a class bias, Guerrero further censured poor Mexican Americans for being dirty, having malnourished children, and for criticizing those who chose to learn the language and make something of themselves. In this last point, Guerrero failed to acknowledge the philosophical battle that had raged in the barrio for generations over whether to assimilate or remain ethnically identifiable.

Without a response, Hector refocused on the problems and set out to tackle them. Back-to-school drives were intended to convince parents that the sacrifice in sending their children to school was worth it. The drives also gathered money to provide clothing and supplies to students who lacked them. Hector made sanitation and health education a priority, plus he pushed for the building of new hospitals and clinics near the barrio. In the realm of citizenship, he pushed hard for repeal of the poll tax, even as he tried in the meantime to get Mexican Americans to pay the fee and to vote. A common feature of the Forum during election seasons was the candidate forum, in which people came to hear and question candidates. He also worked publicly for candidates he believed best served the community. In regards to those who opposed his brand of Americanization, there are few documents or letters attesting to any running battle with them. He simply believed that most Mexican Americans, if given information and hope, would opt to become civically minded.

Because economic instability was such an obstacle to civic engagement, few issues bothered Hector and other members of the American G.I. Forum more than the importation of contracted labor from Mexico through the Bracero Program. This contractual agreement between the two nations brought thousands of workers to the fields and canneries throughout the Southwest. The agreement meant that places like the Rio Grande Valley and South Texas always had more workers than needed; thus wages fell below livable levels for Mexican American farmworkers. It also meant that thousands of "wetbacks" were attracted to the area in the hopes that they too could find work amid the great movement and massive hiring occurring in the agricultural fields. Of course, growers had a chance to pick among native workers, legal foreign workers, and undocumented laborers. They usually opted for those who worked the cheapest. This constantly led to conflicts with the federal negotiators and agencies that brokered contracts with Mexico. Federal negotiators wanted workers to be paid at least 40 cents an hour as a wage, while Texas growers did not want to pay a penny more than 25 cents. In contrast, Hector and the Forum leaders wanted at least 75 cents an hour so that native workers would stay in the Valley and not travel to Oklahoma, Colorado, Minnesota, Arkansas, and Michigan to find a decent wage.

In a letter to Don Larsen of the U.S. Employment Service dated October 4, 1949, Hector informed him that the Forum opposed the importation of foreign labor. He estimated that more than 40,000 native-born Mexican Americans migrated out of the Valley because wages were too low and labor, both contracted and undocumented, was too abundant. "If counties like Hidalgo, Cameron, Nueces, and others would pay our citizens a reasonable and humane wage, there would not be this suffering migratory movement," wrote Hector. He added that as families moved to find a decent wage, they took thousands of children out of school, disrupting their education and condemning them to a future of hard work in the fields. But Hector was not only concerned with the native-born worker; he also sympathized with those who left their homes to come to *el norte* to find a job. The 25-cents-an-hour wage simply did not provide them enough to live on and to save any money to send or take home. This meant that they would have to continue to follow the crops and scrounge around for any job at any pay because they could not afford to go home. Eventually they would be deported with empty pockets.

Hector called on Larsen to send investigators to determine the effects that such low wages had on the children and families of poor Mexican Americans in the Valley and South Texas. Larsen would not be the only one to hear from Hector in a whirlwind of protests. The following day he wrote to Dean Acheson, secretary of state, to regretfully inform him that the International Labor Agreement "has hurt us severely." He told Acheson that Mexican Americans were already being hit hard by the demobilization of personnel at Army and Navy installations being pushed by the Truman administration. "We are suffering a great reduction in our income, greater numbers of unemployment, and a drastic lowering of our American standard of living," Hector told Acheson. He pleaded with the secretary of state to consider the circumstance of the people of the Valley before any further agreements were made. "It is indeed foolish to be importing foreign labor into areas that are being abandoned by our own citizens because of the low, inhumane wages there."

Hector pointed out to Acheson as he had to Larsen that enough labor existed, but growers refused to pay more than 25 cents an hour.

In fact, said Hector, thousands of contracted laborers had not been hired by Texas growers because the government had requested 40 cents an hour for them. Texas farmers had chosen to hire as many wetbacks as they could, but had even experienced trouble attracting workers who were waiting for the government to impose the higher wage. At the time, Texas growers were lobbying the federal government to negotiate an agreement in which the local growers would set the wage scale. Hector encouraged Acheson to have his department investigate before listening to the growers. He also suggested that the secretary of state make himself aware of reports by the Texas Good Neighbor Commission, the University of Texas, and the government's Office of Budget that confirmed much of what he had written.

Hector followed his letter to Acheson with one to the Texas Employment Commission on October 6. "We believe," said the letter, "that one of the primary objectives of the Texas Employment Commission . . . should . . . NOT . . . [be] furnishing 'cheap labor' to [these] 'slave bosses,' but should be to furnish them our own labor with humane and reasonable wages." Hector was willing to concede the importation of labor but only if the wages were at least 75 cents an hour. In his view, this wage scale would keep the workers home, and there would be little need for foreign workers. Anything that could keep the workers home was worth offering, although it is clear that Hector was in the beginning stages of formulating a view of the role of the foreign worker. In coming years, he would become less and less sensitive to the plight of the Mexican worker from down south, only to reverse himself years later as Mexican American reformers and activists became more aware of the strong interrelations of both labor forces. This insensitivity, it must be pointed out, never meant insensitivity to their conditions, once they resided here, legally or illegally.

For the time being, Hector continued to try to find a permanent barrier to the flow of foreign labor into Texas. Having already expressed his feelings to the federal and state agencies, he turned his focus to local Mexican American elites who supported the Bracero Program. Their families had lived in Texas for at least several generations and had survived the most negative aspects of Anglo American dominance of South Texas and the Rio Grande Valley. As elites they had made accommodations to Anglo Americans but had also secured concessions from the growers, merchants, and politicians who needed them as a buffer against the always potential backlash of the majority of Mexican-origin citizens of the region.

In some areas, these elites had control; in others, they shared power, but often they simply belonged to the dominant class. Some of them shared the same class antagonisms against the poor, illiterate Mexican and Mexican American workers. They stressed their difference in status, education, culture, and "whiteness." This difference allowed easy access to the Anglo American world of education and wealth. Their lives were not beyond the reaches of discrimination if they ventured out of their domain, but at home they were respected, admired, and sought after. Their presence always made racial discrimination and prejudices a complex reality for *mexicanos*, but it did harden class antagonisms.

Hector, having been born in the South Texas area where many of these elites lived, seems to have been initially ambivalent about them. Like other Mexican Americans, he admired their ability to survive and prosper amid a hostile Anglo American world. Their existence allowed Mexican Americans to believe that they too could be educated and wealthy, and provide leadership. They represented the best of the *mexicano* in the context of an agricultural capitalism that used and misused thousands of unskilled and semiliterate Mexicans and Mexican Americans. But like other Mexican Americans, Hector also shared a dislike for their politics and for their callousness toward the plight of their people. While some of those elite families produced reformers, and sometimes their governance eliminated blatant discrimination, overall they proved rather insensitive to the harsh conditions that their people faced in the fields and packing plants. They often used the same employment methods and paid the same low wages as Anglo-Americans, while segregating themselves from the working class.

Ironically, some of these elites supported racial uplift at the state level and might even join an organization like LULAC—rarely the G.I. Forum—but they were not interested in fundamentally challenging the status quo. Hector eventually became a strong critic of this type of Mexican American. Like Chicano activists to come, he considered some of them *vendidos*, or sellouts, but he never completely broke with them because they were often willing to accommodate him halfway. In fact, his own prominence gained him some grudging admiration from this class. He would have his enemies but few would be willing to challenge him in a public forum.

In pursuing a challenge to the Bracero Program, Hector saw these elites as potential allies. First, he reminded them of their high standing in the community, and second, he warned them that they were being used by their Anglo American neighbors. In a letter to Ignacio Garza, a politician in Brownsville, Hector presented his case as he did to other Mexican American elites, such as Valley growers—Guerra, Olivares, and Ávila—who were negotiating for a lower-wage scale for foreign workers. There was no doubt, Hector wrote, that their intentions were good, but by now they had seen that their neighbors were not as noble. "From the start I told you that the only thing they (growers) want is cheap labor. . . . I do not understand how you and the other members of the committee could tolerate such action." He reminded Garza that there had been an effort to legalize undocumented workers. Garza and others had explained that this was a "humanitarian effort," but in fact it was a ploy to get them as cheap labor. When the government did not budge in lowering the wage scale, the growers chose to have them deported instead of paying them the agreed amount. Thus, they encouraged more undocumented immigrants to come across the border.

Hector reminded Garza that nearly 50,000 migrant workers left the Valley each year to pick crops in other places that paid more. They joined 150,000 others from throughout the state. He asked Garza whether he believed that those thousands of migrant workers left the state because they wanted to go suffer somewhere else. "They don't do it out of choice, they do it out of necessity," wrote Hector. With them, he added, they took almost 75,000 children out of school. "Texas has no need of imported workers." He pleaded with Garza to help better the situation of Mexican Americans in the state:

> I wish you would go to West Texas, East Texas and other
> states and see our people working on the ground and under

the sun. I wish you'd visited our 40,000 tuberculosis patients
. . . or places in West Texas where they have us segregated in
the schools and don't serve us in restaurants.

As friends, Hector asked Garza and the others to consider the
effects of cheap labor. "It pains me," concluded Hector, "to see people like yourselves be manipulated by groups that take advantage of
your honesty and your position to pursue such inhumanitarian ends."
Hector then reiterated the high esteem that many Mexican Americans
had for them. This was not to be misused. Hector believed that most
people would listen to reason. He also took for granted that as people
of Mexican-origin, these elite growers would empathize with the poor
migrant farmworkers. Hector was continually disappointed, but chose
to see their callousness as an aberration rather than a typical attitude
of the rich Tejano class.

Hector's efforts did not immediately stop the growers' efforts to
lower the wages, but they did have an effect on the government agency
regulating the Bracero Program. In a letter to the Texas Employment
Commission, dated October 16, 1949, the director of the Bureau of
Employment Security declared that his agency would not recommend
the importation of Mexican agricultural workers to the Rio Grande Valley for less than 40 cents an hour. This was still less than the 75 cents
originally agreed upon, but more than what the growers demanded.
This was a partial victory for Hector and the Forum. First, their
activism had resulted in raised wages, and second, they had tainted the
image of the Rio Grande Valley growers who were, in the eyes of most
reformers, the worst employers in the state. Still, this was only a small
victory in a war that would last another fifteen years. The Immigration
and Naturalization Service had estimated that 76,000 Mexicans had
crossed the border seeking jobs in 1949. Thirty thousand had been
deported and 35,000 had been contracted. Another 10,000 had recently joined 40,000 native-born laborers presently in the Valley working
wherever they could. This still meant the displacement of thousands of
native-born workers.

Hector's almost nonstop crusading was remarkable even in a time
of reform. He seemed to have his hand in almost everything that hap-

pened in Texas, and it was natural that others would notice. On April 30, 1949, he was recognized as the "Outstanding Latin American of the Year" by the Alba Club, a student organization at the University of Texas. Hector's brother Xico was chairman of the invitation committee. The club had been founded by students from Laredo, Texas, but had gradually opened up to the best and the brightest Mexican American students attending the university. It set its mission as "dedicated to [solving the] problems of Spanish-speaking people of Texas." In making the selection, the club members recognized Hector's hand in almost all of the issues that affected Mexican Americans in Texas:

> We honor him for [his] efforts in the "back-to-school" drives . . . for his . . . protests against the segregation of Latin American children . . . for his interests . . . in demanding the civil rights of Latin Americans . . . for demanding . . . hospitals to care and treat the 30,000 to 40,000 tuberculosis patients in Texas . . . and for his many programs in the interest and well-being of the Spanish-speaking people in Texas.

In a letter to Hector announcing his selection, Cristóbal P. Aldrete, the club president who would himself one day become a well-known reformer, expressed a deeply felt admiration for him. Young Mexican Americans such as Aldrete seemed to have had a limited knowledge of past activism in the barrio. Possibly they were too young to remember the work of M. C. González, Alonso Perales, T. J. Canales, and others. It is also possible that Hector's more aggressive style was more suited to a new generation of Mexican American elites, who seemed impatient with the more diplomatic approach of an earlier generation. "When we see and recollect the inertia and the acquiescence to the status quo that used to prevail," Aldrete wrote Hector, "we cannot but see now a rosier picture in store for the future." Aldrete pointed out how the Forum had provided an avenue for young veterans to participate civically. Judging from the emotion-laden letter, it is certain that the establishment of Forum chapters were extremely important events in the local communities. They provided a voice and a place for discussing issues important to Mexican Americans. But they did so with an air of legitimacy. This was not just another organization in the barrio advocating for better treatment or complaining about segregation. This was an organization of veterans, many decorated for their actions in war, participating in civic responsibilities while also promoting self-help. For those young Mexican Americans who felt themselves more American than Mexican, the American G.I. Forum provided them a way to respond to the challenge of being American and Mexican. To the American challenge it responded that they were citizens, patriotic, and deserving of the fruits of victory. To the Mexican community, they could say that there was a way to fight discrimination, to better themselves without becoming "gringos" or self-haters. "We have . . . pride," wrote Aldrete, "at your . . . achievement and even now shed tears of joy as we . . . review memories of your organizing G.I. Forums in San Angelo and Del Rio."

This recognition must have been particularly special for Hector. He had graduated from the University of Texas as an obscure pre-med student. It was the state's major university, and the club had connections to particularly impressive social reformers, such as Carlos Castañeda, George I. Sánchez, and others. It was also the first recognition of his reform activities. There would be many more in his lifetime, but at this particular time, when most Mexican Americans were insignificant and often times invisible, Hector must have relished any kind of recognition. It was also most gratifying for Hector to see so many young college students who were concerned about their community. It probably crossed his mind that he himself had not been very involved in reform activity in his university years. Now, as the leading reformer in the state, a title just recently earned, he felt pride in the young men. Always conscious that each generation had to pick up the torch, he felt confident that his efforts were energizing young people all over the state to become involved. In a few years, several of those young club members would become part of the G.I. Forum's core leadership.

Sensing that the Forum needed to consolidate and coordinate its work and organize itself in an official convention, a meeting was called on September 24 of that year at the White Plaza Hotel in Corpus Christi. Thirty-four communities from throughout South Texas and the Rio Grande Valley sent four delegates each, and three towns sent representatives of the lady's auxiliary. Invitations were sent out to many prominent politicians, educators, and state officials. The records of the conference, however, seemed to indicate that few, if any, came.

Notes taken of the convention are sketchy and provide only a vague outline of the activities. They show that Hector called the meeting to order, but the notes do not provide any mention of opening remarks. It is hard to imagine him not making any comments, especially in the first ever meeting. But the minutes seem to indicate that Hector quickly passed the podium over to Gus García, LULAC's legal counsel and a member of the G.I. Forum. García spoke on the Delgado antisegregation case, which had been decided the year before and had started the Forum on the road to battling school segregation. He reiterated that the Texas constitution did not allow for the segregation of Mexican students, and added that the Delgado case had only confirmed that neither did the U.S. Constitution. For García and other antisegregation activists, it was important that Mexican Americans, unlike African Americans, had never been legally excluded from attending school with Anglo Americans. The practice of segregation had been de facto and not de jure.

George I. Sánchez was the next speaker, and he picked up the topic of segregation. He congratulated the Forum for providing the movement against segregation a strong boost. But he pointed out how much more needed to be done. The minutes-taker emphasized Sánchez's plug for political participation. If Mexican Americans registered to vote and voted, then they could "put someone in office that we can trust" and vote out those who supported segregation. There was simply no excuse, said Sánchez, to have "Latin American children" in separate schools.

After Sánchez's talk, the convention minutes note sketchy reports from various Forum chapters on segregation in their areas. There were forty-two reports; of those, twenty-one reported segregation fully entrenched, eighteen reported no segregation, and three reported uncertainty in the matter. The report, however, did not fully tell the story of segregation in Texas public school districts. Some were segregated by separate buildings, others by separate classrooms, and others by allowing "free choice," which often meant parents choosing the schools closest to home, thus continuing segregation. Still, the effects of the Delgado suit were evident by the attempt of some school districts to meet the letter if not the spirit of the desegregation ruling.

The afternoon session began with a discussion of several legislative bills and amendments to be voted on in the next election. Hector was particularly interested in having the delegates look closely at a pending raise for legislators and at an amendment to make changes in the poll tax. An amendment to end the poll tax would actually pass the legislature but be rejected the following spring by the voters. After a short discussion on the bills, the delegates heard from the president of the League of Women Voters, who admonished them to take a deeper interest in government and elected office. It became quite obvious that Hector wanted the Forum delegates to become more politically sophisticated. Registering voters but not providing them an education on the process meant many might not vote, or worse, they might be taken in by one of the numerous political machines in South Texas.

Speaker Ernest Meza of Corpus Christi made a motion to incorporate the American G.I. Forum as a fully chartered state organization. The motion passed and the delegates then structured the organization to have a state chairman, two vice chairmen (male and female), a treasurer, and a state secretary. They also voted to have a board of advisors consisting of seven members. They decided that the organization's headquarters would be in the city where the state chairman resided. This reflected the reality that the Forum had few funds to establish a permanent office with a staff. Whatever monies were raised went to the desegregation effort and other reform activities. After the structuring of the Forum, the delegates elected their leaders. Hector had opposition, but in the end was elected by acclamation.

Homer López of Kingsville was elected male vice chairman and Mary Sánchez beat out two other women for female vice chair, becoming the first female officer of a major Mexican American middle-class reform organization. In this area, the Forum was ahead of its time for traditional barrio organizations. Some early leftist groups, such as the Spanish Speaking Congress and the Asociación Nacional México-Americana, had elected women as national officers, but most organizations in Texas tended to be male dominated. With the leadership of the organization, the advisory board, as well as the ladies auxiliary, the Forum proved quite progressive for its time.

Apolonio Montemayor of Corpus Christi was elected treasurer, and Hector appointed Joe Zapata of Sinton as state secretary. The following were elected members of the advisory board: Julieta Santoy of Corpus Christi, Joe Cuevas of Robstown, Gabe García of Kingsville, Frank Chapa of Beeville, Frank Flores of Robstown, J. L. Saenz of McAllen, and Arturo Cantú of Robstown. Except for Saenz, all of the board members lived in close proximity to Hector. Interestingly, the board had a mixture of individuals formerly or even currently affiliated with LULAC and some newcomers to the social reform arena. Gus García, who served as temporary convention chairman, and George I. Sánchez were prominent members of LULAC. This fact revealed the shifting leadership of social reform in Texas from LULAC to the G.I. Forum. This shift also reflected the class "tensions" within LULAC, which was now almost completely dominated by professionals who were less apt to organize at the grassroots level and who preferred litigation and negotiation to protests and rallies. While LULAC continued to be active and to engage in major reform activities, it did not have the allegiance of working people.

After the speeches and discussions, resolutions were developed and presented to the membership for a vote. The resolution-making reflected the organizational mode of the Forum. In this it patterned itself after LULAC. Instead of some homegrown approach to organizing or operating, the American G.I. Forum simply chose to function like an American social club. Its leadership structure was rather bureaucratic, providing a position for those whom the organization deemed important. It followed Robert's Rules of Order, and its main convention activity was to motivate the membership and to pass resolutions. The convention delegates passed five resolutions that outlined their reformist agenda and Hector's priorities for the next several decades.

One of the resolutions condemned the concept of "free choice" in public education. "Free choice is an insult to our intelligence and a detriment to our children," declared the Forum delegates. They saw free choice as a way that school districts maintained segregation, as many Mexican American parents were likely to send their children to the nearest schools, usually the "Mexican schools," because of the proximity or to avoid conflict in the dominant Anglo American schools. School officials, in the guise of giving people a choice, would usually "convince" the parents to send their children to the Mexican schools because of safety issues or because, there, they could learn English without pressure. Forum leaders knew that many Mexican Americans were susceptible to this approach because they knew no better or because they did not want conflict with school officials and Anglo American parents.

The Forum delegates also voted to condemn the mistreatment and abuse of Mexican-origin people by the Immigration and Naturalization Service. The resolution called on the INS to be "more respectful of the rights of others and to modify their methods of questioning people of Spanish or Mexican origin." It also asked the INS to treat all people equally. If Mexican Americans were going to be asked to prove their citizenship, then other groups had to be asked to do the same. This was an attempt to stop the indiscriminate searches conducted against Mexican-origin individuals in the border area's factories, neighborhoods, and public streets. With the massive growth of immigration caused by the Bracero Program, the border patrol had become aggressive in its search for undocumented individuals. These searches promoted the view that all Mexican-origin people were "foreigners." If Mexican Americans accepted the searches without complaint, they weakened their claim to being "one hundred percent" American.

Another resolution called for the enforcement of truancy laws to offset the fact that an estimated 110,000 children of Mexican descent were not attending school. Forum leaders instructed the Texas Employment Commission not to permit the migration of families with children of school age. Interestingly, the Forum went on record opposing child labor but did not demand that the government take action against the agricultural industry. In this, it followed an old practice of putting pressure on the Mexican community to resolve its own problems. The resolution put most of the burden on the Mexican community. Thus, this resolution revealed the middle-class focus of some, including Hector, in the Forum. None of them depended on mobility and full-family participation for their livelihood. They could see the great value of children staying in school, but could not fully understand the impact that lack of mobility and a limited workforce had on the families. It would take a few more years for the Forum to aggressively work for a higher minimum wage. The other approach to ending child employment was to call for an end to imported workers who, the Forum leaders believed, depressed the wages in Texas for American-born migrant farmworkers.

The Forum delegates voted on a resolution opposing the practice of importing foreign labor for the harvesting of agricultural products. "Such practice," read the resolution, "is detrimental and injurious to the Latin American and Mexican population of Texas." The delegates chided government agencies for not consulting with local leaders, and for not having conclusive evidence that foreign workers were needed. This importation of foreign workers was displacing workers and depressing wages as employers preferred those willing to work for the lowest wages. Forum leaders were not yet exposed to the employers' trick of asking for more workers than needed, thus creating an oversupply, and then paying them lower wages than agreed. By having many workers with lower wages, they could also undermine the contractual agreement with Mexico that called for specific wages and a specific amount of time under contract.*

Finally, the Forum delegates voted to ask the federal government to withhold funds to school districts that still practiced segregation. They asked that the school districts meet the "spirit of the decision" reached in the Delgado case or not be eligible for federal aid. This

---

*Only one week after the convention, the *Corpus Christi Caller-Times* reported that agricultural leaders and representatives of the federal government were deadlocked over details of the Bracero Program. The stalemate revolved around four issues: 1) who would decide on the prevailing wage for each area; 2) the requirement that a labor contract must be for at least six months; 3) the requirement that a *bracero* must be guaranteed 75 percent of the contract period; and 4) that a bond of $25 for each worker be provided by the grower, to be forfeited in the event either party broke the contract. The growers wanted less regulation and less cost by reducing the contracted period and by withholding the $25 from the workers' salary. They also wanted, as mentioned before, a 25-cents-an-hour wage as the prevailing wage in the Valley. The Forum would eventually become more sophisticated in its analysis, but its main argument against importing *braceros* would never change.

coercive power was important since the Delgado decision had threatened punitive action, but the state educators and politicians had found ways to circumvent any kind of punishment. Also, the Delgado case had been interpreted as applying to some school districts but not all. Over the next several decades, Hector and other Forum leaders would find the law on their side but no enforcement agency willing to enforce the law. This continually frustrated Hector as well as George I. Sánchez and Gus García. The attempt to engage in a full-scale assault on segregation was ambitious and admirable, but in the late 1940s and early 1950s, it was doomed to provide only piecemeal victories that could be easily overturned by a change in the state's hierarchy or a recalcitrant school district. There simply were not enough state educators who were willing to take the Delgado decision to its logical conclusion.

When Hector and other reformers seemed to have brought Texas Superintendent of Education L. A. Woods to their side, however grudgingly, the state legislature transferred the decision-making authority from the popularly elected superintendent to a newly appointed Commissioner of Education. The same occurred in other areas. Illegal immigration did not cease, and growers continued to gain concessions from the government. The Truman administration, while often sympathetic to unions and working men, did not develop any particular sensitivity for the colored masses of the nation. Truman continued to see border issues as one of sovereignty and undocumented workers as part of the economic reality of the Southwest. Undocumented workers were abhorred but only after and in-between the harvest or planting seasons. Otherwise, they were a necessity. In Texas, Governor Beauford Jester, as a moderate progressive, sought changes in the poll tax and attempted to be more sensitive to the Mexican population, but his administration was cut short by his death, ending any possibility that Texas might move forward instead of lagging behind as most southern states did.

The political and social landscape for Hector was a geographic puzzle with numerous pitfalls and seemingly insurmountable barriers. He only had to look around his backyard to realize that whatever success he had was offset by what remained to be done, as well as by the reverses that were common. Without a state government willing to obey court decrees, victories were always tenuous. This took its toll on Hector personally. He became moody and preoccupied. The first three years after the war had flown by, and the Longoria victory, the founding of the Forum, his ascension to leadership had all been exhilarating; but, by the end of 1949, Hector must have seen that the struggle for Mexican American civil rights was going to be a protracted one.

The Fifties: Best of Times, Worst of Times

For reformers such as Hector, Sánchez, Idar, and others in LULAC and the Forum, the immediate postwar years, though difficult, were promising. The new nation—and it certainly was new to many of them—promised to be better for those who had been excluded in the past. The United States now represented the most powerful democracy in the world, and the propaganda seemed to indicate the nation was for everyone. The initial reform victories and the strong response that the Forum and other reform organizations garnered represented a groundswell of unprecedented support for change. Major reforms seemed possible in a way that had not been possible before. With economic growth and greater prominence in world affairs, the fifties were an optimistic time for many. Even the beginning of the Cold War initially meant to some reformers that the nation's leaders would do anything to prove that the American system was the most democratic and fairest in the world.

Texas, while still behind most of the northern states in many areas, had benefited greatly from the war's economic boom. By the middle of the 1950s, the petroleum industry had become the largest in the nation, and Texas agricultural expansion soared, second only to California's. Highway growth connected all parts of the state and made urban growth possible while leading to the decline of rural areas in terms of population and economic importance. The mobility, much of it job related, as well as the growth of agribusiness and petroleum, improved the state's per capita income to the point that Texans now made almost 90 percent of what the average American made. Even Mexican American income had expanded. Roughly 25 percent of all

Mexican Americans now found themselves in white-collar jobs. This number, no doubt, reflected a large number of Tejanos who were now established in communities where Mexican Americans predominated and had been there for several generations.

Still, there were communities, such as Laredo and Brownsville, where per capita income fell to just 50 percent of the national average. This kind of disparity also revealed itself in the educational arena, where thousands of veterans were attending college, finishing high school degrees, or receiving vocational training. The Forum had pushed hard to get school districts and the community colleges in the area to open vocational training programs or evening academic classes to veterans and had succeeded in rallying enough veterans to attend them; the Forum was so successful that there were often waiting lists for them. Yet, those pursuing their education amounted to a minuscule minority in the barrio. Most Mexican Americans still worked long hours for little pay and were usually too exhausted after the workday to attend night school. Most were even less able to reduce their workday to attend college full time.

Those who chose to further their education found themselves handicapped by the poor education of their public school years. And they had much to be concerned about in their children's education. The back-to-school drives were becoming successful in getting thousands of children to register and stay in school. The efforts to enforce truancy laws were not as successful, but they were nonetheless keeping more children away from the fields. Hector's and the Forum's vigilance of child labor in the fields was a constant thorn in the side of the growers and forced government agencies to continually send investigators into the fields. But in spite of these efforts, the educational system continued to fail Mexican American children. Being in school only meant that the best and the brightest, and those who had full parental commitment, benefited from attending school, and even they only benefited partially. Hector's "wonderful experience" in school hampered his ability to see the full effect of a discriminating public school system. The schools resisted integration throughout the 1950s, forcing the Forum to fight segregation piecemeal, despite Sánchez's "statewide" strategy.

Once forced to integrate, the schools developed classrooms, curriculums, and other methods to differentiate the instruction between the two groups. Even when the Forum could guarantee equal facilities and equal instruction, it could not do much about Anglo American teachers who saw Mexican American children as unteachable, filthy, and a corrupting influence. Hector no doubt had some grasp of the problems, but it would be another decade before he joined Chicano activists in demanding better curriculums, Mexican American teachers, and the firing of racist educators. Hector might well have moved in this direction earlier if it had not been for the retrenchment that occurred during most of the fifties. Not only did he and other Forum leaders fight the old injustices, but they had to tackle new ones. Poverty, always a constant for the nearly 300,000 farmworkers in the state, turned to destitution with the new hundreds of thousands of Mexican workers lured by agribusiness and the government through the Bracero Program. Overcrowded schools became more so with the baby boom among Mexican Americans and with the new immigrants who were choosing to stay rather than return to Mexico after the harvest. The social arena was made worse by several attempts at the state level to strengthen segregation and racial exclusion. These were officially focused on African Americans, but they solidified the prejudicial attitudes of those who discriminated against Mexican Americans.

Throughout the fifties, "No Mexicans Served" signs were found in cafes and restaurants around the state. Barbershops continued to be selective in whom they served, and public swimming pools still had a "Mexican and Negro" day, usually the day before the pools were drained. What made the fifties even more difficult was the emergence of a "new" American citizen. This new American was middle class, consumption-oriented, conformist in attitude, suburban in habitation, and as race-conscious as any of his or her predecessors had been. Yet, these new Americans did not need to resort to old prejudices—though they would when all else failed to keep the races separate—because they had their own prejudices. They did not resort to biological or religious justifications. Rather, they based their prejudices on the "failure" of minorities to "take advantage" of the opportunities of an abundant and democratic society.

In this worldview, Negroes and Mexicans were where they were because of their own actions. Octavio Romano, a Chicano anthropologist, classified this a decade later as the creation of the "ahistorical" Mexican. Mexican Americans, explained this new prejudice, were passive, clannish, unmotivated, and focused on "immediate gratification." They were content to work for someone else, to be told what to do and when to do it, and to be paid poor wages. Their children dropped out of school not because of prejudices or poverty but because their parents simply did not care enough to support them. Mexicans chose to speak Spanish and remain ignorant of the English language, thus disqualifying themselves from better jobs, and more importantly, from making friends with their Anglo American neighbors. One liberal social scientist characterized English-language deficiency as the most pervasive problem of Mexican Americans, and he blamed it on them.

It was in the decades of the forties and fifties that much of the denigrating social science literature to be attacked later by Chicano scholars and activists would be written. Academic authors tried to explain the Mexican American "problem," but they did so within the context of an affluent and democratic society that provided opportunities for all. They understood and noted that discrimination abounded, but in their minds they could not fully understand why Mexican Americans simply did not "bootstrap" their way out of poverty like the European immigrants had done in the past. Needless to say, there were still many "old Americans" who still had the old prejudices. In time, both old and new prejudices blended together to make the fifties a very difficult time for reform.

Hector did not have to read statistics, newspapers, or academic reports to understand the situation in which most Mexican Americans still found themselves. He could look around in Corpus Christi and surrounding communities and see the problems. This he did quite often. But Hector's reputation opened another window into the problems of the barrio, as people began to see him as resolver of all problems and thus reveal to him their own personal encounters with prejudices. They began to write to him from all over the state and even from outside the country. Most, unsure of how to resolve the problems of discrimination they faced, or certain that they had little power to make changes, were quickly drawn to him. They saw, or heard about, his dynamic personality and self-confidence and came to believe that he had the answers to their problems.

His successful back-to-school drives, the triumphant lawsuits, his radio programs, his American G.I. Forum, and the attention that politicians were paying him, all indicated to people that Texas now had a real leader. Affecting this view of him was the long tradition that Mexican Americans had of relying on advocates. Despite all the social reform groups in Texas in the past, most Mexican Americans usually depended on individuals to help them resolve their particular problems. Whether that person was the barrio politician, the Anglo American rancher, an elected official, or a social worker, Mexican Americans had come to depend on a person, not an agency or organization. This system did not work well in the collective sense, but it occasionally worked for the individual. *Caudillismo*, the strongman approach, also had a long history among Mexicans. While Hector sought to empower the barrios so that every man could be his own *caudillo*, his dominant personality seemed to always make him the man of the hour.

People wrote to praise him and to apprise him of their situation or that of their fellow countrymen. They did so believing they had a friend who listened. Some asked for assistance, others simply wrote to share the burden of being Mexican in a hostile land. Others sought to let him know that he had inspired them. Corporal José García, Jr., writing from Stuttgart, Germany on April 2, 1951, congratulated Hector for "trying to bring the true facts of our Constitution into our Mexican families back home." Like other Mexican Americans, the young soldier decried the assistance being provided foreign enemies to rebuild their homelands while Mexican Americans lived in poverty:

> How do you think I feel, sir; here I am helping preserve democracy, while my brother is in Korea and my younger brother is in the service in the states, still my dad doesn't even own a lot of land on which he can put his foot and says it's his own. As lots of Mexicans say, the only property I own is in the cemetery, and how true it is.

José explained that prejudices were just as rampant in the Army as they were back home. "A Mexican can't get ahead due to discrimination," said the young man, bemoaning the fact that he could not get into officer candidate school. He asked Hector for a reply and told him to "keep pitching."

A short time after the soldier's letter, Hector received one from a retired evangelist preacher who had heard him speak in Lamesa, Texas. E. B. González praised him for his work among children in San Antonio that had been highlighted in an article in *Look* magazine in February 1949. He described Hector as a man who "understood and practiced Christian charity." González then went on to describe to Hector several stalking incidents in which Anglo American neighbors and city officials had parked in front of his house and in the backyard. He saw this as a form of intimidation and felt his life was in danger. He was sure, he told Hector, that the stalking was in response to his religious teachings and his efforts to help his people. He asked for advice and then requested that justice be done in case something happened to him.

González cast Hector's work in religious terms and praised his mother for giving him birth and sacrificing herself to help him gain a profession and find his mission in life, a mission he described as one of healing "wounds and pains—a mission similar to that of Jesus Christ, the savior." While the letter might have seemed hyperbolic, it expressed a sentiment shared by many Mexican Americans, particularly the older ones. So completely shut off from Anglo American society around them, they seemed awestruck by Hector's ability to grace the pages of the large newspapers and the national magazines. His ability to come into town in a whirlwind, organize Forum chapters and back-to-school drives, and to castigate insensitive politicians and educators seemed surreal to many of them. In their own constructed past, Mexican American resistance to discrimination, poverty, and illiteracy was based on individual success stories and small victories. Mexican Americans usually became heroes in symbolic martyrdom. Glory came in tragic resistance. But Hector seemed able to take on the demons of prejudice, segregation, and racism and survive. In their minds, his heroic stature stood not so much on victories attained but courageous efforts made.

Given the almost mythical aura about him, it was natural that people came to him asking for assistance of all kinds. Benigno Martínez from Melvin, Texas, wrote Hector in 1953 requesting assistance in getting his U.S. citizenship. Because he had been bedridden for four years, Martínez needed Hector to investigate his case, seek references from a J. D. Morrow, and then provide him the details to facilitate the process. Herminia Vela Earhart sought help for her son Johnny, who had lost an arm and was unable to find work except picking cotton. The young man was attending college two days a week and worked as often as he could. Now a married man, he was in need of a job as a clerk for one of Hector's "friends." "He doesn't know I am writing this to you," penned the desperate mother. "If you can't help me, it's okay. I thank you anyway."

On November 16, 1953, Simón Vela wrote to complain that as a migrant worker traveling throughout the state, he constantly ran across signs that read "Whites Only" and "No Mexicans Served." He and his family had been denied service several times. He urged Hector to do something about this situation in the small rural communities in which migrant workers like himself worked or passed through. He admitted he feared to protest but was willing to help Hector fight this discrimination. He gave Hector his address and thanked him for the work to be done. Hector answered the letter five days later. This is one of only a fraction of the letters he was able to answer. There were simply too many requests and most were beyond his ability to fulfill. But Vela's complaint had a solution: organize a Forum chapter. "If you want to help yourself and your people," wrote Hector, "send the names of eight or ten war veterans that are interested in the G.I. Forum." Hector promised to get in touch with them and provide them the guidance and resources to get them organized. "If you organize, you can have the power to fight for your rights, but if only one of you wants to do it . . . you will do nothing."

Pilar Paez wrote to ask if the G.I. Forum could close down a restaurant that segregated its customers. Adam Saenz wanted to know if Hector could do something about a restaurant in Serling City that refused his family service. Saenz then advised Hector to tell "our *mexicanos* not to enter that café so they won't be humiliated," as were he and his family. He went on to tell him that all in his family were citizens and good Democrats. In a postscript, he told Hector that most restrooms in small town businesses were off limits to Mexicans.

In Asherton, several parents asked Hector to investigate the selection of the town's All District Girls Basketball Team. María Pacheco had led her team to a tournament title in Barksdale and in the process had outscored every girl in the event. But when the time came to select an all-star team, two of Pacheco's Anglo American teammates made the all-tournament team but she did not even receive an honorable mention. Most Mexican American parents and observers believed she had been left off the team because of discrimination. Asherton was a small rural community, and there was simply no one to articulate their concerns. Often these small communities were very difficult to organize because most people were afraid to protest their conditions for fear of losing their jobs. Also, Anglo American community leaders rarely negotiated or listened to complaints. The community, however, did have a Forum chapter and its members asked for Hector's assistance.

It is unclear what action he took locally, but Hector did write to Roy Williams, director of athletics of the Interscholastic League of Texas. In the letter, he expressed the people's concerns that discrimination had been the reason for leaving María off the team. "Certainly," he wrote, "we should compensate those that are honest and industrious and outstanding in spite of their racial origin, religious background or otherwise." He added that María had brought "victory and prestige" to her school but was not being recognized for it. "I don't believe . . . our minority group is entitled to any special considerations, but neither is the majority group." Hector sent a copy of the letter to the Good Neighbor Commission and to the governor's office. He ended by requesting an explanation. There is no record of response, and it is likely that no remedy followed. But for the people of Asherton, the articulation of the concern was a victory.

In the past, incidents like these had gone unprotested, or if protested locally, they were ignored outside the locality. But Hector took each issue and magnified it to represent the situation of all Mexican Americans. He was sure, as most Mexican Americans were, that there were hundreds of María Pachecos who were not being honored or recognized for their accomplishments. By making each local issue representative of the situation statewide, the Forum and Hector were giving voice to Mexican Americans across the state. Each case then allowed Hector to vicariously agitate and advocate for every Mexican American in every community in Texas. The vicarious reforms only served to enhance his reputation and make him even more indispensable to his community.

Still, in spite of his Herculean efforts to be in all places at all times and doing what was asked of him, Hector realized he needed help. This help, however, needed to be better trained, better educated, and more able to see issues clearly. The helpers Hector had in mind had to be professionals in order to be independent enough not to be intimidated, and they had to be skilled and confident enough to perform in the public arena. Local, hardworking, and loyal leaders were important to grassroots efforts, but for the organization to grow statewide and even nationally, the leaders had to be much more cosmopolitan. The fifties, then, became a decade of leadership building within the Forum to help handle the burden that Hector carried. This development of leadership proved to be one of Hector's greatest accomplishments, and is enough to have made him irreplaceable to the Mexican American community.

The individuals that he attracted to reform would all make names for themselves and advance the cause of Mexican American civil rights in a manner rarely seen before. Well-educated, ambitious, self-confident, and talented, they spread the Forum's gospel of organization, education, litigation, and civic participation. Unabashed patriots, they came to believe that the United States was squandering its greatness because it failed to utilize all of its citizens. Yet, these individuals also believed that Mexican Americans were *desperdiciando* or wasting their opportunities by refusing to embrace American ideals and culture. For the most part, they were proud of their heritage and loved their people, but they felt no hesitancy in criticizing their people and in confronting the nationalists in the barrio who distrusted American society. Unlike future Chicano activists who claimed to lead from behind or from amid the "masses," these new elites took center stage and called on people to follow them. They saw their military service, education, profession, intelligence, and sacrifice as the qualifying characteristics to lead. They believed themselves to be, and often were, the best and the brightest that the barrio could offer to American society.

This new elite came up two distinct paths. Some duplicated Hector's rags-to-prominence—rarely riches—journey, while others came from economically stable and even middle-class homes. Most, however, shared a common trait. They quickly distinguished themselves from their fellow students and other barrio youths because of their educational and professional goals, their work ethic, and their ability to navigate a hostile environment without acquiring the rancor and bitterness that many of their fellow youths did. In spite of all that went on around them, they had faith in American ideals and believed American society provided them a way to succeed. Like Hector, most were liked by their teachers, their military commanders, and important Anglo Americans. Because of their successes, like Hector, they saw more openings in society than their fellow Mexican Americans. Yet, this new leadership that would come together in the G.I. Forum would turn out to be more militant than any other middle-class leadership the barrios had ever known.

W.E.B. Du Bois had his Talented Tenth, and Hector had his *muchachos y muchachas*, young men and women, who caught his vision and followed his footsteps while enhancing his agenda. They followed him because they believed as he did, but even more so because he provided them a cause and an opportunity to distinguish themselves while helping their people. Some had interest in social reform from an early age; others, like Hector, developed it en route to their professional lives. Still others were attracted by the excitement of the cause and by Hector's personal charisma. Hector responded to their interest by finding them things to do and providing them the space and the opportunity to show their skills, talent, and leadership. Very little ideological training occurred. These individuals were overachievers who believed in the American Dream. They had been brought up to be civil, law-abiding, and disciplined. Like Hector, they had faith that the system would respond with the right kind of pressure. Thus, in their minds, what they needed was not ideology but opportunity.

There were hundreds of these individuals who came to join the Forum movement, but a few of them stayed with Hector most of their reform lives and had the greatest impact on the organization and Mexican American civil rights. Most of them merit their own biographies because without their stories it will be difficult to understand the decade of the fifties and early sixties. But the one common strand in all those biographies would have to be how these individuals interacted with Hector. He served, initially anyway, as their catalyst, their inspiration, and, for a number of them, their contrast. During their lifetimes, they would come to love him, respect him, tolerate him, fight with him, and even become his adversary. But in the long run, most all of them would remain his friends.

His most loyal and probably closest lieutenant was Ed Idar, Jr. of Laredo, Texas. Idar joined the Forum in Austin, where he was finishing school, when Hector made an organizing trip through the state capital. Idar was made chair of the local chapter and within two weeks had his first assignment to resolve a segregation issue in a nearby community. His success there started him on a lifelong journey of social reform. Idar proved crucial to Hector and the Forum. He brought to the organization two important skills. As a journalist—in training if not vocation—he wrote many of the most important Forum documents. His ability to critically analyze rulings—he would go on to become a lawyer—laws, political actions, and politicians' behavior proved important not only to Hector and the Forum but also future historians. Through Idar's words, a picture arises of an organizational philosophy that is militantly moderate and middle class, as well as a ferocious enemy of segregation, wetbacks, and discrimination.

Idar became the second state chairman in 1951 and set about strengthening the Forum's infrastructure, developing a monthly newsletter, and instituting a dues system to provide funds for the organization. A tough, often feisty individual, he served as Hector's enforcer and point man. Politicians, both conservative and liberal, came to fear and loathe him as his commitment to the Forum's vision made him an unrelenting critic. But he was also the Forum's most practical leader in that he rarely ever became involved in hyperbole and never promoted anything that was not based on sound reasoning or at least on the facts as he knew them. In this, he was often the most conservative and he would be one of the fiercest critics of Chicano activists and their radical visions.

If he trusted and depended most on Idar, Hector probably liked Tejano-turned New Mexican Vicente Ximenes the most and saw him as the most talented of the bunch. His letters to Ximenes were friendly and often less formal. Hector loved to joke that Forum women were lining up to marry him. More importantly, he believed Ximenes had all the characteristics and the background to be a Forum leader. Ximenes's military career might well have endeared him to Hector. He was a genuine warrior, having served as a bombardier in North Africa, where he earned the Distinguished Flying Cross. He stayed in the military until 1949, when he left to pursue an academic career. Like Hector, he rose to the rank of major, and like Hector, he had a burning desire to help his people. Unlike many New Mexican elites, who believed that there was no limit to how far a Mexican American could rise in their state, Ximenes understood that discrimination abounded and that opportunities were declining for people in the barrio. While *nuevo mexicanos* had been influential in their state, and had even held important political posts, most of the population was poor, badly educated, and segregated from mainstream society. Like George I. Sánchez, who wrote about New Mexican poverty, and Senator Dennis Chávez, who warned of the loss of political power by Mexican Americans in the state, Ximenes feared that things were getting worse rather than better.

It was during a fishing trip to Texas that Ximenes made his reacquaintance with Hector, whom he had met earlier. Stopping to chat, Ximenes became intrigued by the work of the Forum and Hector's tenacious and sustained campaigns to rally Mexican Americans to do something for themselves by going back to school, registering to vote, and protesting injustices. He also admired the way Hector forced politicians to take stands, some of which were unpopular with their Texas constituents. Ximenes never got to go fishing. So inspired by Hector's words, he cut his vacation short and returned to New Mexico to organize a local chapter of the Forum in Albuquerque. As tenacious as Hector, he did not stop there. He became the principal organizer outside of Texas and took the Forum message across the country, becoming one of the first national chairmen of the Forum.

There were others who heeded Hector's call. Chris Aldrete, the onetime president of the Alba Club at the University of Texas, would finish law school and join the ranks of the new Turks in the Forum. He played a pivotal role in the Forum's legal assault on segregated schools and other cases of public discrimination. He also became one of the few Forum leaders to enter politics when he served as county commissioner in Del Rio. Jimmy De Anda, later to become a federal judge, was another young attorney who became a lifelong friend and associate. He drove with Hector across state lines to organize Forum chapters and, as was customary for those who lived in Corpus Christi, he also accompanied Hector on his trips to patients' homes and to local gatherings. First as an organizer and then as a litigator, De Anda proved invaluable to the organization and to Hector personally.

Albert Peña, Jr. of San Antonio proved to be another valuable lawyer and organizer in the work of the Forum. More famous for his politics than his litigation, Peña was the most political of the bunch, getting elected to a county commissioner's seat in San Antonio and being the founder of several political coalitions. A rather independent individual, he nonetheless proved valuable in getting the Forum to become active in the political arena, even as it remained nonpartisan. Robert "Bob" Sánchez, an eventual law partner of Idar in South Texas, was another important ally in organizing Forum chapters and pursuing litigation to resolve issues of segregation and discrimination. His prominence in South Texas Mexican American circles helped the Forum retain credibility among more conservative Mexican Americans. He also helped Mexican Americans move up the ladder in Democratic Party politics.

These men, as well as numerous others, provided the Forum with a cadre of well-educated, highly motivated lawyers and leaders who responded quickly and unselfishly to Hector's requests. In fact, all of them had an anecdote or two to tell about being called by Hector unexpectedly to resolve a problem of discrimination. As mentioned earlier, Idar had been a member less than three weeks when he was called to settle a legal dispute, even though he had yet to finish law school. He did not have a car, and so he traveled by bus several times to the small community in question. He would also do organizing by bus until he got his own car. Peña remembered being called to go to Hondo, Texas, to resolve a segregation issue. A rather proud and independent man, Peña nonetheless remembers hopping in his car and going over to the little community and using all his persuasive powers to integrate the schools. Realizing that persuasion, strengthened by strong rhetoric and potential marches and protests, could be very effective, he rarely engaged in civil rights litigation. Still others saw their education and professional development interrupted every time Hector had an urge to get in his car and respond to a request for assistance, no matter the distance or the circumstance.

As the group of close associates grew, the Forum expanded quickly. As mentioned above, after his visit to Hector's home, Ximenes went and organized a Forum chapter in Albuquerque and then began branching out. In August 1952, Ximenes invited Hector to come to New Mexico to help him spread the message. Hector did so, traveling to several communities where he organized local chapters, and then he established a statewide organization. "The New Mexico Forum will always be grateful to Dr. Hector García," declared the New Mexico Forum newsletter. "He is one who will not restrict his area of operations to one place insofar as improvement of inter-racial relations is concerned." In November of the same year, Idar visited Pueblo, Colorado, to help strengthen a recently established chapter. The work then continued on in the Midwest, with a chapter established in Illinois in late 1953, although a statewide organization would not come there until 1957. Utah was organized in 1954, followed by Kansas and Nebraska in 1955. In 1956, three more states joined the Forum: California, Michigan, and Missouri. By 1957, Arizona, Indiana, and Wyoming joined Illinois in forming statewide Forum chapters.

It was in the formation of chapters throughout the country that several women stood out. Hector, probably more than any mainstream reformer of the immediate postwar years, committed himself to providing women an opportunity to participate for themselves in the struggle to liberate their people. Almost from the start, the American G.I. Forum allowed women to participate, hold office, and organize chapters. While the women had the Forum auxiliaries, this did not stop them from being officers of the organization itself or participating in policy-making. Initially, few were major players, but over time they did come to be a dominant force in the Forum.

Women—such as Molly Galván, who helped establish the Forum's national women's auxiliary; Nellie Navarro, who spearheaded the Forum organizing effort in Kansas; Dominga Coronado, who challenged segregation in small towns in Central Texas; Margarita Simón, whose *El Democrata* was a firm supporter and promoter of Forum activities in Austin; and Isabelle Telles, who helped her husband Louis run the national office in Albuquerque and provided administrative order to the national organization—were all important contributors to the Forum's early successes and development. There were hundreds of other local women who did everything from running meetings to selling raffle tickets to raise money. Their embrace of the Forum vision made it possible for the vision to expand and for chapters to appear throughout the country in large cities as well as in small communities where there were few Mexican Americans but many needs. In his book on the American G.I. Forum, Henry A. J. Ramos observes: "From its earliest days, the G.I. Forum was heavily influenced by the mothers, sisters, girlfriends, wives and daughters of the male Forumeers. Throughout the Forum's various stages of growth, they were incorporated wholeheartedly into the group's framework."

Hector proved sensitive to this firm commitment by the barrio's women, and he constantly sought to provide them a role in the organization. And it had to be a meaningful role. One time, he advised a Forum chapter that there were not any women or young people on their board and counseled its leaders to make the appropriate changes. While the fifties were a period in which reformers pointed to a modernizing trend in allowing female participation, few organizations, with the exception of some leftist ones, really provided them substantive participation. Hector had no qualms about allowing them full-range participation. One reason may have been that women quickly responded to his crusades. They wanted their children in school, wanted medical attention for the family, and well understood the burden of poor salaries. Having started his crusading in sanitation and back-to-school drives, his ability to rally women had been honed.

With this kind of active and supportive constituency, the Forum expanded its numbers quickly. Yet, despite the efforts to be meticulous and orderly in developing the Forum chapters, some of them were built on faith alone. Hector believed that if people were empowered, they would move on their own. Lacking resources, a national newsletter, and close association, these Forum chapters survived on sheer tenacity and commitment. It was not uncommon for Hector or one of his associates to arrive in a small town, gather up some interested people, elect the leadership, provide them rudimentary lessons on Forum bylaws and goals, and then bid them farewell. Hector understood that the key to organizing Forum chapters revolved around finding the right group of people, or even the right individual, who did not shirk from responsibility. The state of Utah was organized by one family that Hector met while traveling through the Southwest. This family was the last one to leave a company town on the way to find work. Hector, seeing no one else, appointed the man the head of the organizing effort in Utah and then bid the family goodbye. Two years later, a state chapter thrived in the Beehive state.

This kind of organizational effort spread quickly throughout small Mexican Americans communities in the Southwest and Midwest. California proved to be the most difficult state to organize because several Mexican American organizations already existed there that jealously guarded their terrain. Eventually, however, the idea of the American G.I. Forum proved captivating to many *californios*. The qualifications for membership were particularly appealing to working-class *mexicanos* across the United States. They had to have served in the military and have a desire to work for their people. They did not have to be particularly educated nor politically astute. For a community whose limitations often impeded them from participation in their own welfare, the Forum promised an opportunity to do something for themselves in ways that few organizations had done in the past. Possibly as important, the Forum offered an opportunity to "live out" their Americanism.

It is important to remember that in the years before the ethnic pride movements, Mexican Chambers of Commerce, Spanish-language television, or a "Hispanic market," success was measured by one's ability to integrate into American society. All that was "modern"—to use one of Hector's favorite terms—successful, smart, creative, and sophisticated was found outside the barrio. Immersed in the daily life of the barrio, these veterans proved hypersensitive to the failings of the Mexican community. This did not mean that Forumeers engaged in some form of self-hate. They only reasoned that the more affluent Anglo American society was doing better. Unwilling to be left out of what was happening on the outside, they sought a piece of the American pie. This distinguished them from those in the barrio who rejected American society, who were too unprepared for their own search, or who simply accepted things as they were. Americanism then, as historian Mario T. García has noted, became a distinguishing identity for those seeking to affirm their civic duty.

The Forum also attracted new middle-class members tired of the old, more conservative, status-conscious leadership of the mutual aid societies or civic clubs found in and outside of Texas. These organizational leaders had found their niche and learned to accommodate to American society. In doing so, they often became provincial—at least they seemed so to many of the younger veterans. They accepted their "place" but worked hard to build their own social and political hierarchy within. Having no place to go, they tenaciously fended off newcomers. The Forum, by contrast, offered an opportunity to newcomers, and leadership possibilities that promised to be merit-based. This, many believed, was the way it was in American society. While acutely conscious of discrimination against those not Anglo American, they nonetheless accepted that outside the barrio things worked fairly. Hector promoted that view. If Mexican Americans learned to participate and were given a chance, they would receive the benefits of an abundant society. Hector always emphasized the need to struggle against injustice, but the promise remained. That he succeeded in getting mainstream politicians to respond to his demands reaffirmed to his middle-class followers the reality of that promise. Justice simply had to be found. They firmly believed that with Hector leading the rush, they could break down the doors and enter a place where they all could be equal and share in the fruits of the greatest nation in the world.

Because of these beliefs, most reformers had strong faith in litigation. LULAC had shown the way with its early court challenges, and the new influx of lawyers to the Forum steered the organization in that direction. Joining LULAC lawyers, they challenged discrimination in school districts and in public places. Because most of the Forum lawyers were young, they served as assistants to the more experienced LULAC lawyers, but they nonetheless proved critical to the process of litigation. And they had one major case, the suit against the Driscoll School District in 1957, which Forumeers hailed as greater than the Delgado case in attacking segregation. Their suit forced the federal courts to rule that placing all Mexican Americans in the same classrooms and forcing them to spend four years in the first two grades was unconstitutional in that this arrangement was made on the basis of race rather than scientific evidence.

The Forum also took seriously its role as an investigating agency and as a fund raiser. Hector, not being a lawyer himself, concentrated on organizing people to fend for themselves, but litigation attracted him for two reasons. One, successful lawsuits forced a recalcitrant government to side with them because the judicial interpretations became the law of the land. Thus, it was easier to overcome—in theory, anyway—hundreds of discriminatory practices with one successful legal swoop. This did not actually happen, but what did happen was that it gave Forum activists more ammunition when they went in to negotiate with school districts and city officials who discriminated. Second, successful lawsuits helped reaffirm that Mexican Americans had the same rights as all other Americans. This proved important in the Forum's battle against those who challenged Mexican American civil rights or who saw them as existing beneath the law.

It proved just as important in convincing Mexican Americans that their best chance for a decent life was a commitment to American ideals. Mexico offered them nothing, and neither did their barrio nationalism. If they were to move ahead economically, socially, and civically, it would have to be by participating in American society. The importance of legal affirmations grew as the decade progressed because the affluence of the white population made the color gap more pronounced. Mexican Americans as well as African Americans could see the promises of the American Dream being fulfilled, but not on their side of town. Even as more Mexican Americans moved up to the middle class, more and more immigrants came, and more and more Mexican Americans dropped out of school or simply did not attend; and the bottom of society grew at an alarming rate.

In an open letter to Forum members in 1952 titled "Lest We Forget and Try to Rest on Our Laurels," Hector reminded them that in spite of the Forum's successes, many things remained to be done. Many Forumeers had acquired the benefits of an abundant society, but most other Mexican Americans had not. "Lest we forget because you and I are college graduates; lest we forget because we have brand-new cars; lest we forget because we have a nice home; let me remind you of the following statistical data," wrote Hector. He then rolled off a list of problems of most Mexican Americans in Texas: 3.5 median years of schooling; 250,000-plus with no schooling at all; an annual average income of $980; 35.2 percent of Mexican housing was dilapidated; 47.9 percent of Mexican-American homes lacked running water; 67.2 had no inside flushing toilets; and 43.3 percent lived in overcrowded conditions. "And lets not forget," concluded Hector, "that this poor *raza* is our blood and they are our brothers [and sisters] and our parents."

The urgency of the task called for major victories. Litigation seemed to promise those victories. In the case of Pete Hernández, it did. This case might not have been the best one for challenging discrimination, but it turned out to be exactly the kind of victory needed to advance reform in Texas and also to change some philosophical leanings of Mexican American reformers. Hernández was a cotton picker charged with murdering a fellow Mexican in Jackson County. Gus García, writing in a pamphlet "A Cotton Picker Finds Justice" compiled by Rubén Munguía, admitted taking the case because he could not say no to a tearful mother, certain that her son would not get a fair hearing in that predominantly rural community. The twenty-six-year-old farmworker faced a hostile Anglo American community that feared a "criminal element" in the masses of workers that came north to pick their crops. He also confronted an angry Mexican American community which loved and respected the man he killed.

It did not take García long to figure out that he did not have much of a chance of winning. By his own admission, the prosecution presented an almost perfect case. Unable to crack their case, he made three important decisions. First, he argued that Hernández could not receive a fair trial because he was not being judged by a jury of his peers. Second, he asked famed LULAC attorney John J. Herrera for assistance. Herrera brought with him Forum attorney James De Anda. The two attorneys helped in preparing the case and even served as witnesses to the exclusion of Mexican Americans in Jackson County. The third important decision was to bring on board Carlos Cadena, a St. Mary's University professor of law and possibly the greatest Mexican American legal mind of his time. The four attorneys basically argued three points: no Mexican American had been called to serve as a juror in Jackson County in 25 years; there were Mexican Americans qualified to serve; and discrimination and segregation in Jackson County was so common that Mexican Americans were actually treated as a "race, class or group apart from other persons."

In his account, García implied that he developed the three-part challenge on his own. Still others would claim that Cadena had developed the strategy. But in a letter to Hector, dated July 23, 1970, George I. Sánchez took credit for developing the "class apart" theory. This theory argued that the 14th Amendment to the Constitution protected citizens against discrimination not only on the basis of "race [and] creed, but also on the basis of recognition and differential treatment as a recognized 'class apart.'" He first taught this argument, wrote Sánchez, at a time when Cadena was a student of his. The theory had not been used before, said Sánchez, since it could not be tested successfully in a Texas court insofar as the state's supreme court had ruled that Mexicans were "white." Sánchez went on to add:

> . . . the lawyers in the pre-Courts of Criminal Appeal case of Pete Hernández did not raise the "class apart" issue. They argued other technicalities, on which the Court over-ruled them. Carlos and I, then . . . decided that Pete's case was ideal . . . so Carlos and I outlined the brief, Carlos put it in legal lingo, and the G.I. Forum and others made it possible to send lawyers to Washington. Gus argued Carlos' law and my fac-

tual findings brilliantly . . . no one except Carlos and I, with the eloquent assistance by Gus can be credited with master-minding it.

Gus García was rarely one to give anyone credit, although he did praise Cadena for his contribution and would call him the "best brain of my generation," but there is no mention of Sánchez by him in the pamphlet.

By his own admission, García tried "every trick in the book . . . to goad [the prosecution] into some ruling, word, or action" that would make appeal much easier. But with the guilty verdict came the real-ization that money had ran out. Still, the lawyers appealed the case to the Texas Court of Criminal Appeals, but were rejected once and then again on rehearing. Despite many misgivings, García, Herrera, and Cadena filed a Writ of Certiorari with the U.S. Supreme Court on Jan-uary 19, 1953. The application, according to García, was typewritten because there was no money for printing.

Little hope was given to actually getting a hearing, as this case competed against hundreds of others. But on October 12, 1954, "El Día de la Raza," the Supreme Court agreed to hear the case. The ela-tion proved short-lived when the plaintiffs were soon notified that they had to come up with a substantial sum to cover court costs. The Forum, however, was able to tap the San Antonio LULAC Council No. 2 educational fund. Another $1,236.95 came from the American G.I. Forum itself, according to a news release. That was on top of another $1,500 that Hector claimed in an open letter to Texas citizens to have been raised by the Forum for the case. The money from the Forum included contributions from three Chicago organizations and one individual. In raising the money, the Forum continued to play the part that Sánchez had outlined for it in his grand strategy against seg-regation and discrimination.

Cadena initiated the preliminary arguments at the Supreme Court hearing by stating that Hernández had been convicted by a jury not of his peers, in a county where Mexican Americans had not been called to jury duty in twenty-five years. He emphasized that there were Mex-ican Americans qualified to serve, but discrimination and segregation were so commonplace in that area that Mexican Americans came to be actually treated as a class or group apart from all other persons. García followed this argument, declaring that "practice," and not legal structures, was the main culprit in excluding Mexican Americans from jury duty. The jury selection system in Texas was actually fair and nondiscriminating, said García, but county officials did blatantly and continually discriminate.

Cadena's and García's arguments presented to the Earl Warren Court, which was then debating *Brown v. Topeka Board of Education,* another view of American prejudices. While African American lawyers argued that legal structures created unequal treatment, LULAC and Forum lawyers blasted de facto discrimination as just as debilitating. They called upon the Court to take a more nuanced look at discrimination and attack it at its core. It is interesting to compare the resources of both groups as they tried to gain the Court's ear. While NAACP lawyers could count on legal supporters from throughout the nation, and a budget of many thousands of dollars, García and his team could count on no more than $3,500. Practically the whole team stayed in the same hotel room and shared each other's meager resources in order to eat. Like most other Mexican American reform activities, this proved to be a shoestring operation, but a successful one.

On May 3, 1954 *before* its historic *Brown* decision was reached, the Supreme Court ruled that exclusion of Mexican Americans from jury service because of their ancestry or national origin violated the Fourteenth Amendment. It made it clear that the Amendment "is not directed solely against a discrimination due to a two classes theory, that is based upon differences between whites and blacks." Judge Warren added that the county's inability to find qualified Mexican American jurors in the last twenty-five years "taxes our credibility." It was obvious that Mexican Americans had been excluded because they were seen as different. "The results," added Warren, "bespeak discrimination, whether or not it was a conscious decision on the part of any individual commissioner."

The judgment was a tremendous victory because it allowed Mexican Americans to claim a constitutional victory that had nothing to do with the black civil rights movement. In fact, the ruling reaffirmed that all ethnic groups in the nation were assured equality before the law and were protected against discrimination because of their ancestry or national origin. The immediate effect of the ruling was two-fold. Hernández received a new trial, in which he was again convicted, and all pending indictments against persons of Mexican descent were void in Jackson County and nationally pending an investigation of jury selection procedures. It must be noted that they were void on paper. No record exists on how many cases were immediately affected by the ruling.

More importantly, the ruling allowed social reformers to advocate for Mexican Americans as a distinct group. For years, they had simply used their status as "white" as a basis for their civil rights arguments. Even Hector urged his fellow Forumeers to put "white" when classifying themselves. After the ruling, Carlos Cadena called on Mexican Americans to identify themselves with other minority groups, instead "of attempting to build a cultural fence around themselves and [living] in a vacuum." The decision by the Supreme Court affirmed what reformers had been arguing for decades, that Mexican Americans were protected by the Constitution. But it further argued that they did not receive protection because of their ability to assimilate into Anglo American society but rather because of their citizenship and residency. They could now claim special protections when their ethnicity became an issue. This had never been the case before.

Hector and the G.I. Forum leaders quickly recognized the importance of the victory and they staged a magnificent banquet at the Plaza Hotel in Corpus Christi. More than 350 people turned out to honor the lawyers and to hail the court ruling. Most of the major social reformers in Texas attended. The *Brown vs. Topeka Board of Education* decision, which struck down "separate-but-equal" as the law of the land, would overshadow the victory later that same year. But for those in attendance, the ruling had finally vindicated their efforts. It had also imprinted their presence on the Constitution and made them "real" citizens of the nation. The euphoria hid the fact that only a few more victories would come in the 1950s and that the struggle would eventually create tensions among a number of the reformers. These tensions came as the struggle for Mexican American civil rights became more complex and the toll on the reformers became greater.

Even before the Hernández case was settled, Ed Idar had complained to Carlos Cadena that Gus García had neglected the case. In a letter dated October 27, 1953, Idar told him, "I would personally feel much better if Gus were not to participate. . . . Sánchez and I have discussed this at length, but fail to find a way to keep him from it since it was originally his case." The Forum leader was particularly incensed because Gus García owed the Forum money for services he had never rendered. Over time, Gus broke with the Forum on a number of issues and on organizational strategy. It was probably too much to expect that an independent maverick like Gus would continue to take orders from any organization. Although he proved important to both LULAC and the G.I. Forum in their struggles, in the end he was too much his own person.

Gus, in most ways, represented both an older generation and a more recent assimilationist-focused generation. He often chided his own people for not working hard enough to pull themselves out of their situation. He often lamented that reformers were expected to keep "pulling Mexican chestnuts out of the fire for 'the people.'" Yet, often these people were not only forgetful and ungrateful but sadistic in wanting the reformers to sacrifice everything for them. Gus saw Mexican American problems as similar to those of earlier immigrant groups, with the exception that close proximity to the mother country compounded the situation a bit more. Mexican Americans had to get educated and stop worrying about whether they were served in private restaurants or allowed into exclusive sororities. Eventually, if they had money, they would resolve most of their social problems. He also cautioned Mexican Americans not to place reformers on a pedestal.

Gus was also not beyond admiring the kind of Anglo Americans who were anything but popular with many working-class Mexican Americans. In trying to explain the comment before the Supreme Court that Sam Houston was "only a wetback from Tennessee," he made it clear to readers of the Hernández pamphlet that he in fact admired the Texas hero, along with the other famous Texan, Jim Bowie. He admired them for being brave, reckless raconteurs and for not having notions of racial superiority. Most of his heroes tended to be Anglo Americans and Europeans. Ironically, Gus's greatest legal success helped usher in a new view among Mexican American reformers, which placed greater emphasis on ethnicity and less on whiteness. Gus would go along part of the way, but eventually he resented the sacrifices he had to make. An alcoholic, he died a broken man on a park bench in San Antonio.

Another conflict that broke the ranks of reformers and divided the past leadership from the newer one revolved around the problem of the undocumented worker or "wetback." By the mid-1950s, the Forum had made stopping illegal immigration as well as ending the Bracero Program one of its top priorities. Anyone or any action that assisted them in their position was quickly hailed. One report hailed as truthful in its assessment of the situation of the undocumented was "The Wetback in the Lower Rio Grande," written by Lyle Saunders of the University of Texas and Olen Leonard of Vanderbilt University, under the auspices of Sánchez. The report was devastating in its presentation of area growers, politicians, and government agencies. Not only were statistics highlighted that revealed discrimination against wetbacks and native farmworkers, but it also revealed the attitudes of unnamed area leaders toward people of Mexican origin. Those fighting against illegal workers could hardly have designed a better report to advance their cause. Unfortunately for Hector and the Forum, the report authors included three interviews that demeaned all persons of Mexican descent. The venomous words were so offensive to some reformers that they questioned their inclusion. Two well-known reformers, J. T. Canales and Alonso Perales, were particularly bothered by the inclusion of the comments. They were also incensed by the anonymous nature of the comments, which made it difficult to confront their owners. When the Forum endorsed the report, both reformers made their feelings known to Hector, Sánchez, and Idar.

The Forum, led by state chairman Ed Idar, defended the report while condemning the prejudicial views of those interviewed. In letters to both Canales and Perales during the period between December 1951 through January 1952, Idar insisted that the authors were only trying to do their best in portraying the views of many Anglo Americans in the Rio Grande Valley. While the comments made Idar's blood "boil," they proved the point that the Forum had been trying to make for years: Anglo Americans in the Valley were insensitive to the concerns of the Mexican-origin population. The anonymity given the interviewees, wrote Idar, was intended to give the authors access to people who otherwise might be unwilling to talk for the public record. Idar compared the authors' refusal to reveal sources to the privileged conversations between lawyers and physicians or their clients. But the two older reformers rejected that comparison, saying that such practices were simply a way to make an author's views known while allowing someone else to express them. Perales and Canales, while not particularly accusing the authors of racism, did believe that the views were simply so offensive that they damaged an otherwise valuable report. Canales, in a letter to both Hector and Idar, dated April 29, 1952, quoted the Chancellor of the University of Texas, James P. Hart, as saying "the beneficial effect of the pamphlet is, in my opinion, practically destroyed by the very unwise inclusion of the anonymous statements reflecting upon Latin Americans."

Sánchez, who took the brunt of the criticism, reacted angrily to the comments of those who questioned his involvement in the pamphlet's production. He threatened to sue a Valley Spanish-language paper, *La Verdad*, for libel. He also sought to marginalize Perales, calling him a "pathetic figure, a psycho-neurotic with delusions of grandeur." Sánchez rarely measured his words, and insulting Perales that way ensured a permanent split. Hector tried to stay out of the fray. He did not enjoy schisms within the ranks and was particularly distressed to see the conflict between Perales and Sánchez, both of whom were good friends of his and whom he saw as mentors. The open conflict, he believed, caused "the enemies of our people . . . to delight." In a letter to the editor of *La Prensa*, dated December 13, 1951, he called on the two men to drop their differences. The people were "suffering," said Hector, and the conflict took time and energy away from reform. "I do not intend to take sides nor to say who is good or bad," he wrote.

For Hector, the two men were "our . . . geniuses." More importantly, he saw the conflict over Mexican American civil rights as too daunting to afford a schism between two such popular leaders. Hector also revealed a characteristic that would be reflective of him throughout his life with a few exceptions. He did not like to become embroiled in public fights with his own people, and he rarely criticized other prominent reformers publicly. He chose to stick to issues. No one, however, is totally consistent, and he allowed himself a criticism of some of the lesser-known reformers who criticized the report. There is no lengthy defense of the report or a rebuttal to the critics of the Forum's support of it. It is quite possible that Hector was taken by surprise by the intensity of the debate over the report. It was also obvious to him that he was not the only one now who spoke for the Forum. Sánchez, who seemed to slip in and out of the organization, and Idar, who wrote most of the published statements for the Forum, were engaging in public debate on Forum positions. Neither requested his permission nor his position. They assumed he supported their positions and they were partly right. Hector, while confident of his abilities, normally acquiesced to "experts" or to those who invested the time to study an issue. During this period of time, Hector had to share the reformer's limelight with others, and for a short period his leadership position seemed to be challenged.

The report might have caused controversy, but over time that report was forgotten. Few Mexican American reformers or scholars would come back to it. But another report, this one by the Forum, would come to haunt Hector and his lieutenants for a long time. The report—more a pamphlet than an actual report—was titled *What Price—Wetback?*, written mostly by Idar. In it, the Forum attempted to provide a much more emotional and graphic view of the problems that "wetbacks" confronted, and the ones they created for people who lived on the border. The pamphlet was actually a joint project of the Forum and the Texas State Federation of Labor. Its main purpose was to garner sympathy for those displaced by Mexican workers and to put pressure on the state and federal governments to do something about illegal workers.

While most Mexican American reformers understood the problems of the undocumented worker and were acutely aware of the effect they had on Mexican American farmworkers, few had made the problems the focus of their efforts. There was danger in singling out the "wetbacks" because it would entangle them in cultural and social issues that had few solutions. To identify the "wetbacks" as problems was an invitation to increase the animosity of many Anglo Americans toward all Mexican-origin people. But to try to resolve the problems of Tejano farm laborers without dealing with the undocumented workers and the ones in the Bracero Program was unrealistic. Thus, many complained about the situation but few proposed any solutions.

The Forum leadership, particularly Hector and Idar, sought a different approach. While the report from Saunders and Leonard had been a tremendous coup for them, they felt that some would not read the report because it was lengthy and full of statistics. What was needed was a publication that took the citizens of Texas into the fields, labor camps, and communities where undocumented and legal immigrants lived and worked. Hector had proved extremely successful in taking this approach with his report on the migrant camps in Mathis, Texas. The pictures of poor laboring Mexicans and their children living under extreme situations had provided him a moral foundation for attacking the situation of farmworkers in Texas. It had also rallied many Mexican Americans to join the Forum. Hector and Idar probably expected that this kind of pamphlet might do the same while focusing even more scrutiny on the issue of the undocumented worker.

Idar, the journalist and most prolific writer in the Forum leadership, undertook the project. There was no one better than he at analyzing the situation or creating vivid pictures. He wrote well, pulling no punches, but tried hard to be objective. However, Idar may well have been the worse choice. He was legalistic, a stickler for the rules, and a person who fought discrimination and prejudices because they were constitutionally wrong and not because they were necessarily morally wrong. He was calculating but he also came across as cold and insensitive. When he undertook the project, he did so to prove a point and to make a case for legal change. He did not set out to promote the welfare of the people on whom he was reporting, although it is obvious that he cared for them and that the Forum did not usually differentiate between people when it came to helping them with their immediate problems. But it was typical of Idar to avoid sentimentality and to try to deal with only the "facts," as he understood them.

Untrained in the subtleties of working-class Mexican culture, Idar quickly fell into the trap of using stereotypes. He used the term "Guanajuato Joe," to describe those in the area he surveyed because many were from that state in Mexico. And he described Mexican undocumented workers as accepting mistreatment "stoicly and philosophically." He made them look like beasts of burden—just like the growers saw them—who cared only about their immediate situation. "[The Mexican wetback] understands only his way of life: to work, to suffer, and to pray to the *Virgen de Guadalupe* for a better life in the hereafter." He then categorized them into types. Apart from the stoic beast of burden, there was the *pachuco*, a category of Mexican workers, which could be further subdivided into the criminal and the one seeking jobs in the city. The word *pachuco* was charged and negative in the barrio. To call some of the Mexican workers *pachucos* simply reenforced their image as undesirables to many Anglo Americans and Mexican Americans on the border.

Idar understood that he was writing for two audiences and, that there would be a third one listening in. The first audience consisted of the political and community leaders in Texas. The second audience was comprised of those bureaucrats and politicians who made treaties with Mexico. The third audience was made up of the general population of Anglos and Mexican Americans in the state. He chose to address the first two because they seemed the only ones capable of remedying the situation. To the first one, he sought to portray a situation out of control. The illegal border crossings were rampant, crime rose during the harvest season, and diseased workers from Mexico threatened epidemics among American citizens. To the second constituency, he emphasized that the Bracero Program and the lax border vigilance was benefiting Mexico but not the United States.

He painted a picture of the hardworking, professional but overwhelmed Border Patrolmen doing their best to stem the tide of wetbacks; they were handicapped by dishonest growers and politicians who favored agricultural interests. He constructed an image of border businesses suffering because millions of dollars were going south instead of being spent in the local economies. He described the squalid living conditions of the Mexican immigrant workers in the underbelly of a prosperous nation. And he provided a subtle picture of a southern nation willing to accept the exploitation of its citizens in order to get American dollars, and to provide a safety valve for duplicitous Mexican political leaders to manage their growing population. Using all kinds of images, including that of prison camps in Nazi Germany, he provided the readers enough material to horrify them into pursuing change.

Unfortunately, the pamphlet had a different impact from the expected on Idar's target constituencies and even within them. There were nuances within the various reactions, but suffice it to say that the pamphlet did not have the intended results. The Bracero Program remained in place for almost another decade. Undocumented workers continued to be hired by Texas farmers and they continued to displace native workers. But the exposé did have unintended consequences. Wetback roundups became more frequent and nativist sentiments grew. In fact, the pamphlet may have added fire to what came to be known as "Operation Wetback," an INS effort to deport millions of Mexican undocumented workers during the 1950s. In his book on the topic, historian Juan García argues that the Forum assisted the Border Patrol in identifying those without legal documents in numerous communities of the Southwest.

Even among Mexican Americans, there were those who took note of the filth, disease, and criminality of the wetback. Instead of provoking sympathy from those outside the barrio, the pamphlet reaffirmed many of the stereotypes and hardened some of their feelings toward Mexicans. Mexican Americans, in particular, blamed undocumented workers for the rise in crime and the burden they placed on the schools; they were an embarrassment to those who were legal in the country. It was not uncommon for some Mexican Americans to use the derogatory term "wetback" or *mojado* to describe their neighbors born in Mexico.

Within the Forum and among Mexican American reformers and the population in general there were conflictive reactions. Several Forum leaders took issue with Idar doing the report without telling them. Others, still smarting from the earlier report, were uncomfortable with the depiction of the undocumented and with the sympathetic treatment of the Border Patrol. Again, the Forum leadership had to defend its support of a report that demeaned the image of the Mexican as it attempted to solve the problems of the Mexican American. This time, Canales and Perales were not prominent as critics, but there were others, such as Salvador Paz of *La Verdad*, who accused Forum leaders of taking food from the mouths of hungry people by pushing for massive deportations. Hector must have felt the sting of the criticism because he sought to avoid public comment and to stay away from Forum meetings that attempted to resolve the split within the Forum chapters. In a letter some months after the controversy had erupted, Idar told Hector that some people were suspicious that he was avoiding the issue by not attending several meetings intended to deal with the subject of the pamphlet. Idar also implied that Hector might have privately instructed several individuals to criticize the report. There is no evidence of that, but the accusations seem to imply that Hector had some misgivings about Idar's product.

For Hector and the Forum, the pamphlet was to have another unintended effect. It placed them, in the view of future Chicano scholars, on the side of the "gringo" enemy. According to this view, Forum leaders had committed several grievous mistakes. First, they had created a division between Mexicans and Mexican Americans rather than seeking to unite them. This, Chicano intellectuals believed, was always the way Anglo Americans kept the Spanish-surnamed population powerless. Second, they had characterized Mexican workers as dirty, illiterate, irreverent, and law-breaking. In doing this, they showed little sympathy for them as human beings. This kept Mexican Americans marginalized in the eyes of the public and made them unworthy of sympathy and respect.

Looking at Border Patrolmen as quiet, unsung heroes simply rewrote a history of abuse, arrogance, and insensitivity. Few in the barrio saw them as such. In the minds of most Mexican Americans, there was little difference between INS agents and the much hated Texas Rangers. Hector probably understood this better than Idar and for that reason distanced himself from the report. But his inevitable connection to it would make him a target of Mexican nationalists and Chicano activists. It also revealed a weakness. He did not always think through his actions. He jumped into so many "good sounding" campaigns that he rarely evaluated them in a more profound way. He trusted his friends and co-reformers because he had brought them into the struggle. Besides, other than commitment to *la raza*, he rarely asked for anything else, except loyalty to him.

Shortly before this time of conflict within the Forum, Hector had his own first ugly encounter with discrimination. Interestingly, in spite of the difficult task of fighting the growers of the state, the public school officials, and the insensitive politicians, small acts of discrimination came to be seen as particularly offensive to Forum leaders and Hector in particular. These discriminating acts seemed to say that no matter what state politicians or federal bureaucrats decided, Mexicans would still remain unwelcome in Anglo American public space. Refusal of service continued to humiliate Mexican Americans throughout the state. Three students from Laredo Junior College attending a cattle exhibit in San Angelo, Texas, were denied service at the Loma Linda Café. All three were veterans of World War II and were there as guests of the exhibit. Nine high school students from Mission High School were refused service in New Braunfels because they were Mexicans. Isaac Borjas, a veteran of 42 months of active duty, was humiliated in front of friends when the owner of the Ideal Sandwich Shop refused to serve him even water for being of "Latin American extraction." Mr. and Mrs. Paez met the same fate in Refugio, while Tomás Cantú, owner of the Distinguished Flying Cross for bravery in combat, could not buy a home on the Anglo American side of town in Corpus Christi.

The softening of some state and national politicians did not change the attitudes of some in their constituency who swore that Mexican Americans were not going to have the same mobility and accessibility to services that white people did. The barrier—at times invisible and other times very visible—was to be maintained to preserve the social status quo. Mexicans wanting service in Anglo establishments were seeking to violate a private space that had always been off-limits to them. To allow them to violate this space meant the mixing of the races and affirmed that Mexicans were equal to Anglo Americans. For many white Texans, it was enough that the two groups interacted on the job. That was tolerated because the political and economic reality demanded it, but taking this interaction into the social arena threatened to unravel a world most had known all their lives.

Urban centers were accommodating to the new reality, but smaller communities defended their social barriers with tenacity. Class, education, and prominence were no exception. Hector, who had never acknowledged acts of discrimination against his person or his family, would find that some Anglo Americans were willing to resist all intrusions. On February 19, 1950, while he spoke to school officials in Gonzalez, Texas, about segregation, his wife Wanda and their daughter went to eat at the local Manhattan Café, accompanied by Tito Díaz and his wife. Mrs. Díaz served as the president of the local ladies auxiliary, while Tito was an active member of the Forum. Upon entering the restaurant, they were quickly told that no Latin Americans or Mexicans were served in the establishment. Wanda was shocked. An aristocratic looking woman of white complexion, she had never experienced discrimination herself. But with a Mexican American couple alongside, she was mistaken for a Mexican.

It is ironic that her and Hector's introduction to discrimination at the personal level came in Gonzalez, Texas. While few people knew it back then, the small rural community had already found its place in Mexican American history. It would take another two decades before folklorist Américo Paredes made the community and surrounding area famous with his book, *With a Pistol in His Hand*. The book told the story of Gregorio Cortez, who became the target of the largest manhunt in Texas of the early 20th century. Cortez was accused of stealing a horse and in an ensuing argument with the local sheriff, his brother was killed and he killed the sheriff. Realizing he would find no justice, he fled and led a posse of volunteers, Texas Rangers, and U.S. Cavalry on a wild chase all the way to the border, where he was finally captured. During the chase, his family was imprisoned, several friends physically assaulted, and the Mexican community terrorized. Accused of killing another man, he was eventually exonerated of the killings but convicted of stealing a get-away horse. Sentenced to life imprisonment, he would serve more than ten years before he was pardoned. He died a broken man shortly after being released.

The chase, capture, and subsequent trial of Cortez had attracted the interest of Mexicans and Mexican Americans in Texas. Most followed the event, secretly hoping that he would escape into Mexico. *Corridos*, or ballads, were composed in his honor as the Tejanos saw him as a hero. He had defended his family from the kind of intrusion that had become a daily occurrence in communities like Gonzalez. He had stood his ground, unwilling to be humiliated. Cortez demonstrated the *machismo* and pride that ran through the blood of most Mexicans who had had enough. The fact that he could outride and outshoot any Texan and that he could avoid capture for days only enhanced his image. In the end, he was captured because he hesitated leaving his family behind. Ironically, it took betrayal by another Mexican to finally capture him.

In many ways, Gonzalez forty years later had changed only in small increments. Mexican Americans were still segregated, powerless, and discriminated against in public places. It was then no surprise that Wanda, her daughter, and their friends would still be seen as were Cortez and his family decades earlier. Hector, as would be expected, felt outrage at the incident. "Consider insult personal," he wrote in a memo to the Forum membership. The refusal of service always meant humiliation no matter the circumstances, but it proved particularly shameful to Hector because he never expected his family or himself to experience it. In spite of his haranguing against segregation, discrimination, and Anglo American insensitivity, Hector always felt he and his family were beyond reach. He fought against mistreatment of his people because he cared but also because it was wrong. But deep inside, Hector often allowed himself to think that it could not happen to someone as educated, articulate, and middle-class as he. It is as if he thought that he could will himself not to be discriminated.

The experience in Gonzalez brought to Hector the tenacious attachment that many Anglo Texans had to their feelings of superiority. The thought that a major civil rights victory or several court cases won would change attitudes across the state quickly dissipated in Hector's mind. Whatever victories came would be localized successes. The state had to be changed one locality at a time: one restaurant, one theater, one swimming pool, one bus station, one real estate agent, one policeman at a time. This must have been a daunting thought to Hector, but it is not likely that he spent much time on it. He immediately responded. He wrote the governor, the Good Neighbor Commission, several congressmen, and Senator Johnson. He also spoke to several others on the phone, hoping to use the issue of discrimination against his family as a way to discuss discrimination in the schools, in the selling of real estate, and in public facilities. Although he protested energetically the humiliation to his family, he tied the personal issue to segregation and other forms of prejudices against Mexicans in general.

As expected, the politicians responded but their responses revealed varying degrees of outrage. Senator Johnson and Representative Lloyd Bentsen were the most lukewarm in their reaction. "I realize your concern in this matter must be very great," wrote Johnson, but he added that he was powerless to "dictate the sentiments and actions of another individual." He hoped that education would change attitudes. Bentsen expressed regret that places like Gonzalez existed, but added that events like those were not common in his district. "You know my feelings toward citizens of Latin American descent and that I have done whatever I can to further the progress of our people," said Bentsen. He then referred the incident to Congressman John Lyle, in whose district the incident occurred. Lyle responded with a much more emotional tone. He wrote Hector that he was "deeply grieved" and offered his apologies on "behalf of those who were responsible." Lyle also promised to write to Gonzalez officials to protest and to ensure that this would not happen again. The congressman, however, revealed a discomfort with the publicity and the fact that Hector had written to federal officials. "We can never solve our problems by bringing the federal government down [here]," wrote Lyle. "We can solve our own problems at home."

Two state legislators were even more outraged. Marion Storm, secretary-treasurer of the legislature's Social & Legislative Conference declared that those who "believe in democracy are more than indignant." He assured Hector that he would investigate the possibility that the legislature could respond in some way. Rogers Kelley, an ally in the Longoria case also expressed indignation. "I want to do everything possible," said Kelley, "not only . . . to rectify this un-American act, but also . . . to prevent the occurrence of . . . similar acts in the future." He then promised, like Storm, to see if the legislature could respond in one form or another. All must have known, despite their outrage, that little could be done to rectify the situation.

The reality was that no law existed to punish anyone who denied service in a public establishment. Refusal of service occurred daily in Texas, and few paid any attention to it. Even if politicians cared to do so, they found it difficult to promote legislation that infringed on someone's right to do as he or she wished on their private property. In Hector's case they responded with outrage because he represented a potentially powerful adversary and few politicians wanted to incur his anger. No doubt that there were those bothered by the incident, but even more discomforting was the bad publicity for the state. Responding to Hector's familial encounter with discrimination was in a way much less complicated than actually trying to change traditions or pass new laws. In a typical states' rights mentality, Anglo Texan politicians hoped to change attitudes through simple evolution. Over time, they reasoned, the two groups would learn to live together but do so without changing Texan customs or tradition. In this they revealed how little they understood Hector. He simply did not believe that time could ever change anything.

The decade of the 1950s would prove to be the best of times and the worst of times. There were victories, such as the Driscoll case and the Hernández ruling, as well as the recruitment of many new Forum leaders. But there was also the reality of entrenched segregation, of thousands of undocumented workers, of the fiasco of the reports on the "wetbacks," and the first encounter with personal discrimination. Even as he moved forward in his efforts to end the mistreatment of his people, Hector kept confronting a retrenchment of attitudes that made him keenly aware that the light at the end of the tunnel was still far off.

Unity as Politics
but No Unity in Politics

By the late 1950s litigation slowed and there were few reform campaigns that brought any possibility of much change for the barrios. Since much of the discrimination against Mexican Americans was based on prejudices, rather than de jure policy, most challenges to it had to take a piecemeal approach, which required the kind of funding that few organizations had. But while one door seemed half open and stuck, another seemed ready to open more widely. Since the mid-fifties a number of Mexican Americans had been elected to office in Texas. The two most prominent were Raymond Telles, mayor of El Paso, and Henry B. González, state senator. Their elections were historic. There had not been a Mexican American mayor of a major Texas city since the Tejano hero Juan Seguín had been mayor of San Antonio in the nineteenth century. And no Mexican American had ever been elected state senator in the twentieth century. Having won election in a surprising fashion, Telles and González represented the possibility that this arena was opening up to Mexican Americans.

For Hector, politics always played an important part in social reform. One of his first campaigns had been to register Mexican Americans to vote, and in the late 1940s, he lent his name to candidates running for local elections. Already in 1949, Hector had been identified as someone who could deliver thousands of votes with his endorsement. Robert N. Jones, an engineer with the Texas Railroad Commission, wrote L.B.J. to offer an assessment of Hector's "political potentialities." Reflecting on the statewide elections held in November of that year, Jones credited the election of Neal Marriott to the state school board to Hector. "I do not intend to belittle the efforts of the candidate," wrote Jones, "nonetheless, I give Dr. García's endorsement and active campaigning credit for 95 percent of these [Corpus Christi] votes." He also made Hector the person responsible for the approval of eight out of ten state constitutional amendments in Nueces County, which were soundly defeated statewide.

Jones described Hector's hectic electoral effort in the weeks preceding the election. Hector had sent out two thousand letters that included marked ballots and a letter titled "El Voto de Honor," or the vote of honor, in which he endorsed candidates and amendments and encouraged Mexican Americans to go out to vote. He had gone on the radio and then personally urged Forum leaders and members to go out and vote. "He is always getting around to a great number of gatherings and dances all over South Texas," wrote Jones. "Lots of people make speeches, yes, but Dr. García has the universal admiration of these people down here. They believe in him. Everybody swears by him." The writer also gave Hector credit for the affirmative vote on the tuberculosis hospital in the county. In the past, he continued, Hector helped firemen get a pay raise and had helped elect a Mexican American to the school board.

"Senator, here is a man who cannot be ignored," said Jones. "Here is a man who was dissatisfied with the old fogies in the LULACs and in sixteen months has organized an outfit which puts LULAC to shame." Jones wanted the senator to harness Hector's power. Having married a Mexican American, Jones saw his children's happiness "tied up" with the well-being of Mexicans in Texas. "I believe that thousands of devoted people see in Dr. García a savior, no less. . . . García is destined to carry a lot of weight in South Texas . . . and I just wanted you to know," ended Jones. "P.S. He likes you."

The letter revealed that there were already those watching to see if Hector had political aspirations. Jones took him at his word that he did not. But there was no doubt that while Hector did not seek elected office, he did have an interest in the political arena. Mexican American reformers of the past had not had much luck in politics. A few, like J. T. Canales, who became a state representative, and LULAC co-founder M. C. González, who ran for the school board, did make a foray into the electoral arena, but most others stayed away. For one, they could rarely muster up a majority of voters, and usually the price seemed too steep to pay. Mexican American candidates could win if they lived in those few South Texas and Rio Grande Valley areas where their large population was favorable to them. But even there, most reformers were too liberal for the political bosses that governed. Most Mexican American and Anglo American bosses did not want much change in the status quo.

Mexican American reformers tried hard to rally their fellow citizens to register to vote and to vote for those candidates, usually Anglo Americans, who showed interest in helping the barrios. Always, it seemed that they had to choose the lesser of two evils. Aside from some of the political bosses, few Anglo American candidates promised much to the barrios and delivered even less. Consequently, few Mexican Americans bothered to participate, and this made it difficult for reformers to have much success in getting their people to the polls. Hector's initial success in getting people to register to vote hinged on his ability to convince Mexican American veterans that they actually could have an impact. But lacking any candidate who actually committed himself to ideas and platforms to assist the community, Hector initially devised another strategy. He pushed for the election of veterans to public office.

It is hard to know for certain, but Hector seems to have believed that Anglo American candidates who were veterans would be sensitive to other veterans not of their race. The idea of the "common experience" of World War II still carried a strong influence on Hector. In 1950, he supported Jack Pedigo for district judge. In an open letter entitled *Una súplica a nuestra gente en un punto de honor* (a plea to our people on a point of honor), he called on the people of Corpus Christi to vote for Pedigo because "he was a soldier, he fought, he suffered and was [highly] decorated." Pedigo, continued Hector, understood the problems of Mexican American veterans because he had fought alongside them. His opponent, to the contrary, had never fought in the great war. The legal-size letter presented no platform, no promises, no history of past commitments by Pedigo, only references to his "heroism." Said Hector, "If a man offers his life for his country, then we must offer him a position of honor. In honor of our heroic soldiers, vote for Jack Pedigo."

It is hard to imagine what a man's military record had to do with a judgeship in Corpus Christi. After all, many Anglo Texans who discriminated against Mexicans had also served, and some had also been highly decorated. But in Hector's view, participation in the war had exposed men to experiences that made them better citizens, more open-minded, and less color conscious. Most Texans had served in units with numerous Mexican American soldiers. They had witnessed their bravery and their commitment. And they had come back to live among them. More importantly, in Hector's mind, most American soldiers had fought for democracy, against tyranny and against subjugation of people who were seen as different. How could someone with that experience not be sensitive to the needs of other veterans?

That reasoning seems rather naive today but, in the early days of Hector's political life, it made sense to him. There were few liberal politicians in the state and even fewer in South Texas or the Rio Grande Valley. Populist politicians who might seem progressive tended to be—as were most southern populists—racists. Thus, the only option seemed to support moderate politicians who shared a common experience with Mexican Americans, especially if that experience was not completely asymmetric in detriment to Mexican Americans. Hector believed that most Anglo Americans were willing to accept the heroism of their neighbors, especially if they had been neighbors in the foxholes and on the beachheads. Rather than just naiveté, it reflected the few options available. Hector never sought elected office and only a few Forum leaders ever sought office, almost none of them statewide. This meant that Hector had no one to look to for political leadership. So he grabbed at whatever legitimate opportunity he could to promote electoral principles in the barrio. He understood that eventually the candidates would come, but first the constituency had to be developed.

The few Mexican Americans to be elected in the 1950s were still to come when Hector first entered the political arena. Only New Mexico, with its congressmen and one U.S. senator; Arizona with its Tucson-based public officials; and California with city councilman Edward Roybal, could claim a foot in the electoral door. Hector, thus, had to find crevices in the political landscape. The few Mexican

American political bosses in South Texas and the Rio Grande Valley were simply not good models to emulate, although they did show that Mexican Americans could organize well enough to win public office. In fact, these Mexican American political machines were a rather interesting phenomenon in Texas politics. While they tended to be just as corrupt and power-possessive as the Anglo American political machines, they did defuse public discrimination. While they were anything but liberal, some of these individuals came to support LULAC and the Forum's efforts to fight discrimination. Eventually reformers and bosses would part ways, but in the early years after the war, there was some effort to unite in fighting discrimination. Hector, conscious that he needed all the help he could muster, rarely engaged in open conflict with them.

In partisan politics, Hector chose to be a Democrat. It was an easy choice for two major reasons. One, everyone in Texas was a Democrat. Political leanings were unimportant in Texas, as they were in the rest of the South. The Democratic Party was the only game in town. Second, Mexican Americans everywhere, except in some communities in New Mexico and Arizona, had been Democrats since the turn of the century. The Democratic Party had consolidated its hold on Mexican Americans with the New Deal. While Roosevelt's programs were only marginally effective in combating Mexican American joblessness and poverty, they were an effort to do something, and this proved important because no effort had been made in the past to attack poverty in the barrio. Scholars such as George I. Sánchez and Carlos Castañeda and politicians such as Dennis Chávez had been deeply involved in New Deal programs and had become great proponents of government intervention in dealing with barrio poverty.

Once Hector became part of the Democratic coalition that survived the Depression and the war, he remained a faithful Democrat to the end of his life. Even his commitment to veterans did not make him vote Republican. When numerous Democrats, including some Mexican American reformers, joined the Eisenhower bandwagon, Hector remained a committed Democrat. He attended the 1952 and 1956 state party conventions and cast his votes for Adlai Stevenson. He also worked for Lyndon Johnson's campaign as he, like many other committed Democrats, tried to keep the Democratic Party strong in the midst of eight years of a Republican administration. But Hector did not simply play the part of a loyal Democrat. He believed that his support and that of other Mexican Americans needed to be compensated.

Hector believed that compensation began with inclusion. After one successful campaign season, he wrote Sam Rayburn, a fellow Texan and Speaker of the House of Representatives, to congratulate him and to make a recommendation. "I would like to recommend that some Texas Democrats of Mexican-origin be sent to the National Democratic Convention this year," he wrote on May 11, 1956. "I sincerely believe that this recognition from your part and . . . Johnson's part would keep the majority of our people in the Democratic Party in the years to come." Hector did not want the Mexican American vote to be taken for granted. He understood that many politicians still saw the Mexican American vote as did the political bosses: one to be manipulated. He also complained to Rayburn that Governor Allan Shivers had never taken a Mexican American delegate to the national convention.

Besides Johnson, Hector also supported a newcomer who proved to be a real power broker in Texas politics and both a friend and foe of the Forum. In 1957, Ralph Yarborough, the leader of the Texas liberal wing of the Democratic Party, became the junior senator through a special election to replace Price Daniel, who had defeated him for the governorship the year before. Hector, in what became customary fashion, sent out thousands of copies of an open letter to voters urging them to support Yarborough. Two points were stressed. Yarborough's victory would allow Democrats to retain the senate by one vote, and the Texas judge was a personal friend. He was also a liberal who had not betrayed the Democrats by supporting Eisenhower.

Hector's efforts, which included getting-out-the-vote rallies and tenacious personal campaigning did not go unnoticed. On April 29, 1957, twenty-seven days after the election, the newly elected senator wrote him a personal note. "I have found no fancy way to say this, but am going to rely on the simple plain and old-fashioned phrase— 'thank you; from the bottom of my heart, thank you.'" Yarborough promised to write him often and asked Hector to contribute advice freely. "By your labors of these long hard years, you have given new hope to Texas and new luster to her name," wrote Yarborough.

Responding on May 7, Hector called Yarborough a "gentleman, a good Christian, and a good friend." Then he quickly confided that he had a matter to discuss with the senator or a designated member of his staff. "It does not involve anything personal or any difficulty or scandal," wrote Hector mysteriously. "I believe we should get our heads together . . . [and see if] we can assure your continued popularity with our people." Hector never divulged the matter in the letter and there is no other letter to specifically indicate the "matter." But it is reasonable to assume that he was asking Yarborough, as he had also asked Johnson, to be more inclusive of Mexican Americans.

This inclusion proved multifaceted. Hector had already mentioned one aspect of it to Rayburn. He wanted Mexican Americans to be selected as delegates to the national convention. Since Mexican Americans voted almost exclusively for Democrats, the designation of delegates was one way to compensate the barrios for that support. It was a way to get the concerns and the voice of Mexican Americans into the national dialogue. It was also a way to get Mexican Americans to become committed to the electoral process. If they saw the workings of the national party and if they felt they had a voice within that process, they would come back more committed to getting their own people involved.

The inclusion also pertained to being an important part of the audience for national political leaders. Hector wanted national Democrats to come speak at Forum conventions. Almost a year to the day he helped elect him senator, Hector asked Yarborough for assistance in getting Adlai Stevenson to speak at the Forum convention. He reminded him of their friendship and asked him to do all that he could to help secure Stevenson for the convention. But Hector also reminded him that Mexican Americans had yet to be fully convinced that the Democrats were their party. "I have been severely criticized because I have always been faithful to the Democratic Party and yet it has been pointed out to me," wrote Hector, "that they have never given us the proper recognition or help." It was understandable, continued Hector, that the state Democrats were not sensitive to the needs of his constituency, but he could not understand why the national Democrats behaved the same way. "It has been pointed out that perhaps we should invite a Republican figure, in case we are turned down, and we shall see what the Republicans have to offer us." Hector admitted that it was something he did not want to contemplate, but the Forum had now expanded to fourteen states and there were Republican Forumeers who were exerting "some pressure on me. Please give your prompt attention to this S.O.S from an old friend," ended Hector.

Hector would be disappointed, as he was two years earlier when J. Edgar Hoover had excused himself from attendance, and even earlier in 1952, when most politicians stayed away. Still, Hector was not one to be easily discouraged. He knew that his work in the electoral arena would eventually pay off. It did over time, as both Republican and Democratic leaders came to speak at Forum conventions. But in the 1950s, the Forum still seemed just another organization of Mexican Americans, of which there had always been many, most lasting only a few years. LULAC had been the exception, but its influence in national politics still remained in the future. Hector understood this, but he also knew that politicians always asked for favors, and the best time to seek reciprocation was shortly after the favor was given. With elections coming every two years and moderates, liberals, and conservatives fighting hard for every vote in Texas, the Forum had to move aggressively. Even if they did not come the first time, the invitation had been given, and the next time they asked for favors, the politicians would remember they owed one.

While Hector moved aggressively to make accommodations with state and national politicians—at least those that resided in Texas—he did not soften his approach to condemning that which he saw as wrong. Hector wanted friends but rarely at the expense of his crusades. Even those politicians whom he needed were not beyond his ire when they did something he did not approve. Johnson proved to be one of his closest political allies, but even he came in for some strong criticism when he took a different side. At the 1952 Forum convention, Hector rallied the delegates to pass a strongly worded resolution condemning the U.S. senator for voting against new appropriations for the Immigration and Naturalization Service. Hector, as reflected in the wetback pamphlet, wanted a stronger Border Patrol presence as one step toward resolving the problems caused by illegal immigration. He continued to be critical of Johnson on the issue of the Bracero Program, even while he remained a faithful supporter until the end of the Texan's political career.

Accommodating while at the same time being critical of political figures reflected Hector's belief that politicians had to be held accountable for their actions. He did not hesitate to praise or to make a commitment to a politician. But that politician had to be right on the issues. While Hector had little patience with those with whom he disagreed, he had the ability to keep the anger and frustration within parameters. There were too many issues to lose his contacts over one particular issue. He often raised his voice, walked out of meetings, and acted highly critical, but he always came back and negotiated. He did so because he needed to have politicians willing to listen to his demands and requests. Hector understood that what made him successful and different from some of the reformers of the past was his ability to get politicians to listen and to act. It did not mean getting everything he wanted, but it meant getting attention and being able to negotiate. Few Mexican American reformers could claim that kind of leverage.

Having the leverage meant using it to keep it. Hector used it as often as he could. He constantly pushed politicians to take stands against segregation and discrimination. But he used wisdom by providing a situation in which politicians could benefit by doing the right thing. While often calling upon them to do the "right thing," he was acutely conscious of the fact that as politicians they often did things that were convenient or safe. That is one reason why Hector worked hard to register Mexican Americans to vote and to get them to exercise that right. If Mexican Americans became an important electoral constituency, then politicians would respond to their needs, because in this case doing the right thing meant getting votes. Hector saw this as a practical approach to American politics. It did not mean an abandonment of his idealism; it simply meant an accommodation to a reality. This reality was particularly harsh in Texas.

By the end of the 1950s, Hector had decided to challenge another part of that harsh reality. The last decade had seen the rise of numerous young new militants committed to reform. They shared a belief in the "American way of life" and had some of the same ethnocentric beliefs in America's greatness. They yearned for leadership opportunities. Reform was a way for them to experience that leadership, but it was not the only way. Many of them, less inclined toward reform, aspired to leadership in a larger arena that had remained closed to them. Other than New Mexico, Tucson, Arizona, and the lower Rio Grande Valley, there were few areas where Mexican Americans could fulfill those aspirations. Government positions and electoral offices were closed to most except the most tenacious. Hector understood this. He also realized that the Forum leadership had changed. There were more professionals in the leadership and in the membership. And while many of the problems of the barrio affected them, they were less likely to be hampered as much by them than their working-class neighbors. They thus sought opportunities to exert their talents.

Hector understood that Mexican Americans were likely to be served better by their own. Thus, he attached a new item to his reform agenda. He first publicly aired this new demand at the national Democratic Party convention in Los Angeles in July 1960. Unable to attend the convention because only one Mexican American was chosen as a delegate from Texas, he wrote a statement to be read at the platform hearings of the Democratic National Committee Nationalities Division, which handled the concerns of nonwhite Democrats. In it he underscored the dismal representation that Mexican Americans had in the Democratic Party and how this influenced their appointments in state and county party positions, and in state and county jobs. Hector accused the Democrats as well as the Republicans of engaging in a "selective exclusion" that kept Mexican Americans unable to participate fully in the electoral arena. It also kept them from leadership positions in the one international arena where they could be of assistance. Foreign service positions in Latin America were simply unavailable to Mexican Americans even though, in Hector's opinion, they were more qualified than those foreign service officers or political appointments that understood neither the language nor the customs of the region.

Hector argued that the government was "unable . . . to sell democracy" to Latin America because it failed to utilize the "Latin American." In his view, Mexican Americans were committed to democracy and were better fitted than Anglo Americans to promote that ideal to their brothers in Central and South America. He also implied that Latin American governments and leaders were watching to see how some of their countrymen were treated and what opportunities they received before they were ready to embrace American democracy. Hector also set the use of Mexican Americans in government in the context of the Cold War. The United States could only win the ideological war occurring in Latin America by becoming inclusive and allowing everyone the same opportunities. He called on John F. Kennedy, the apparent nominee, to "use [the] vast number of loyal citizens" of Latin American descent to promote democracy.

Foreign service was not, however, the only place where Mexican Americans and other Latinos could be of service to the nation. "We definitely want judges of Latin American origin," wrote Hector. This request underscored the fact that reform in the barrio constantly hinged on judicial decisions. Mexican Americans had engaged in litigation for over a decade and oftentimes had found themselves at a disadvantage. Even when courts ruled in their favor, the judges rarely provided coercive mechanisms for enforcing the new interpretation. Often their rulings were so limited in jurisdictional parameters that they had little impact on others who broke the same rules in other places. The request also reflected the reality that many Mexican Americans came before the bench for all kinds of problems.

The statement dealt with two other issues. One paragraph was included to demand an end to the Bracero Program. Calling it the "greatest shame" the nation faced, Hector questioned the federal government's willingness to protect foreign workers while allowing native workers to be exploited. In this point Hector knew he stood almost alone. Growers and grocers as well as many consumers were reluctant to support a ban on foreign and undocumented workers because of a danger of higher costs and prices.

The final point of the statement expressed strong support for a civil rights plank in the party platform. Hector was particularly concerned with the issue of police brutality. To him, police brutality was the ultimate form of discrimination and the most insidious. He questioned whether juries, which heard brutality cases, were concerned with justice and not just in acquitting law enforcement officers. Throughout its history, Texas had been a hostile place for Mexican Americans who found themselves on the wrong side of the law. While African Americans suffered from lynch mobs, Mexican Americans suffered "discreet" killings by law enforcement officers.

Hector called on the Democratic Party to support a law making it mandatory that law enforcement agents take an oath in which they swore that they harbored no prejudices against Mexican Americans. He also called for questioning potential jurors about their feelings toward minority groups, something that would eventually become standard in police brutality cases. Hector believed that the United States had much to prove to the world about its treatment of its citizens of Latin origin. Allowing them participation in government, adopting a civil rights plank, ending the Bracero Program, and eliminating police brutality would be a resounding message to the world that the United States was indeed a democracy. "Today more than ever we must prove to the world that we believe in the equality of man. Today we must convince our minority groups . . . and their brothers in other countries that their abuse and exploitation is a thing of the past," wrote Hector. He ended his statement declaring that the country had to be saved from Communism.

This last point seemed more than anything a reiteration of the loyalty of the Forum members during this tense phase of the Cold War. In the decade of the 1950s, the Forum had been invited to participate in anticommunist conferences in Mexico and had even sought clarification from the FBI on the status of groups with whom they were invited to associate. But despite this short forage into red-baiting, the Forum was more concerned about the civil rights of its people than about world Communism. As middle-class Americans, Forumeers accepted much of the government propaganda about world Communism, and had the same anxieties about losing their "economic system," but overall they proved to be rather limited partners in the fight against the Soviet threat.

What is clear about this message is that Hector and the Forum leaders were embarking on a middle-class crusade and shifting away slightly from more traditional working-class issues, such as dual wages, job discrimination, unsanitary working conditions, lack of collective bargaining, unsuitable housing, and health issues. This shift revealed that the middle class, although still small, was growing at a faster rate than ever before. It also reflected the class focus of most civil rights advocates, whether black, brown, or white. Civil rights spoke to inclusion and participation in the American economic system and not fundamental change. If Hector's militancy was leading toward something more radical—and that is not likely—the political climate of 1960 diverted any such change.

The following month in Wichita, Texas, at the national Forum convention, Hector continued to push his new agenda. Civil rights, political appointments, and migrant farmworkers again became the major topics of concern. The delegates passed three resolutions. The first praised the sit-ins occurring throughout the South for being done in an "orderly and mannerly fashion." After studying African American civil rights activities and the nation's mood, Forum members decided to support the assertive but nonviolent action. In their own minds, the Forum had itself engaged in nonviolent action to change the schools, desegregate public space, and win over politicians. They had organized rallies, boycotts, and publicity marches. Now they seemed ready to take more direct action.

The second resolution picked up on the discussion of political appointments. Again, using the rhetoric of the Cold War, Forum delegates offered their own as a way to check Communism in the countries to the South. It affirmed that Mexican Americans understood "the culture and heritage of the people in Latin America." They spoke the language, understood the history, and sympathized with the people. Considering the difficult struggle being waged in Latin America, they called on the U.S. State Department to "seriously consider" appointing Mexican Americans and other Spanish-speaking individuals to diplomatic posts throughout the southern hemisphere and even in the State Department.

Hector and other Forum leaders might have seemed quite naive to have asked for those diplomatic posts, considering few of their members had any foreign service experience, and few were really as "immersed" in the Latin American culture and history as the resolution implied. But the intent to change the public dialogue on Mexican Americans was vintage Hector. In order to be seen as full-fledged citizens, Mexican Americans had to be seen as willing and capable of participating in all aspects of American life. Hector knew that Mexican American middle-class veterans were extremely loyal, and American ideals were sacrosanct to them. Having Mexican Americans serve in these capacities allowed them upward mobility and would appease any concerns Anglo Americans had about their Americanism. Finally, it was a way to build a cadre of nationally prominent Mexican Americans who could present the issues of the barrio to a larger audience.

Hector's expanded agenda might have ended at the Forum convention. Surely, his statement to the National Democratic Party convention, which turned out to be a telegram to Albert Peña, Jr. to be shared with others, had attracted few supporters and almost no discussion. Mexican Americans and other Latinos were still invisible to most national politicians. Civil rights remained a black-and-white issue, despite the fact that the Los Angeles convention had attracted one of the largest contingencies of Latino delegates. But 1960 was an election year, and the Democratic Party, after eight years out of office, needed all the help it could muster.

By the time the Forum met in August for their convention, the Kennedy presidential campaign had mapped out a strategy to attract Mexican American support for its candidate. Robert Kennedy had met with Edward Roybal, Dennis Chávez, and Henry B. González at the convention to discuss the campaign among Mexican Americans. The discussion had been initiated by the three Mexican American politicians who wanted a more active role for their communities. While nothing was formalized, Robert Kennedy quickly seized on the idea to expand the work of the nationalities division of the party, which was in charge of getting minority communities involved in Democratic Party activities. Kennedy quickly assigned Carlos McCormick, a young aide to the campaign and a member of the G.I. Forum, to head the effort.

Before heading to the Forum convention, McCormick had numerous discussions with Mexican American leaders, particularly in

Texas, who suggested that for any campaign to be successful among Mexican Americans, the Forum and Hector had to be involved. Thus, McCormick quickly called for a meeting of Forum leaders to convene the day after the convention ended. There, he proposed setting up campaign units known as Viva Kennedy Clubs. The name came from Republican Latinos who had attempted to establish a Viva Nixon effort, but the Republican candidate had discarded the notion of an ethnic slant to his campaign. According to Ed Idar, the Forum leaders "jumped" at the chance to become part of the national campaign and to do it according to their own rules and style. As in the meeting at the national convention, no specifics were worked out. The Forum leaders, like Mexican American leaders across the country, were rather independent, and McCormick may have chosen simply to excite them rather than tell them what to do.

Peña, who by now had become a well-known politician in Texas, demanded total freedom from the state Democratic Party machinery. He did not trust the conservative party officials and he knew that being under them would de-emphasize the effort that Mexican Americans made in the campaign. He also asked McCormick for assurance that Mexican Americans would be considered for political appointments. By then, political appointments had become a major theme for the Forum and other Mexican American leaders. Robert Kennedy agreed to the "request," and Peña became the state organizer for the Viva Kennedy Clubs, while Idar became the first to organize a club in Texas.

McCormick, a small-time Forum leader in Washington, D.C. where he was studying law, became the national coordinator and quickly appointed several national co-chairmen, Hector being one of them. While Hector brought the most impressive credentials as an organizer and campaigner to the Viva Kennedy organization, his function would be more of an inspirational voice than that of a club organizer or campaigner. Hector saw his main responsibility in creating an image of the campaign that would rally Mexican Americans to the polls in great numbers. He sought to do this by promoting two important points. One, John F. Kennedy was a friend of the community and a personal friend of the reformers themselves. Second, the Viva Kennedy Clubs and the Mexican American voter were crucial, if not the most important ingredients, to a Kennedy victory.

The first point hinged on personalizing the campaign so that Mexican American voters could feel that Kennedy was actually a friend, someone who consulted frequently with leaders of the community and who felt their concerns personally. This effort reflected the reality that most Mexican Americans voted for Anglo American politicians not because they promoted a sensitive agenda or had proved to be supportive of community issues, but because they were "friends" or at least "friendly." Mexican Americans had come to develop a habit of choosing the least hostile of the candidates. Lack of hostility and in this case an invitation to join a new Democratic Party crusade was something to build on for Hector. In an undated letter to club members, Hector declared "John Kennedy and . . . Johnson beg us for our help." It was a call from friends and not just politicians.

Other Viva Kennedy Club leaders followed Hector's lead in promoting the "great friend." Talking to a crowd in Fresno, California, Senator Chávez loudly proclaimed that "Jack Kennedy has more humanity in his little finger than Nixon has in his whole body." Henry B. González would tell a Midwestern crowd of Latinos that the Kennedys were "men of vision; sensitive . . . and understanding of the problems confronting Hispanic peoples everywhere." In the minds of the Viva Kennedy Club leaders, there was no hierarchy between the nominee and themselves. The promotion of friendship by the club spokesmen served to define them as leaders of their community. Their connection to the possible next president of the United States was meant to distinguish them from other leaders in the barrio. As the people saw them rub elbows with the major figures in the Democratic Party, their status rose. The Viva Kennedy effort also helped nationalize the leadership of the Mexican American community. With Roybal traveling to the Midwest, Chávez to Arizona and Texas, González to the Midwest, and Hector anywhere he could, Mexican Americans across the country got to see the best and the brightest. There were others, such as Hank López of California, Raúl Castro of Arizona, Peña of Texas, and still others who became part of this nationalized leadership.

This leadership sought to enhance the role of the community even as their own roles were enhanced. Everywhere they went, they promoted the idea that the Mexican American and other Latino—they called it Latin American—votes could well determine the outcome of the election. "Never has there been such an important recognition," said an undated letter written by Hector and three others. "Thus, we have to be faithful to our leaders and our responsibility." There was in this pitch a subtle middle-class focus that indicated the shift in priorities. While they sought to empower the community, these leaders—Hector included—sought to magnify their own role as leaders. This was evident in their constant reference to what was basically a non-existent friendship with the candidate. The fact is that few of the Viva Kennedy leaders had ever personally met the candidate or had much interaction with his staff. But in personalizing this relationship, they gave greater importance to the Mexican American vote.

The tenacity and seriousness with which they approached the "house-to-house, building-by-building" campaign paid off for the Viva Kennedy leaders. The slim victory by JFK over Nixon brought jubilation. McCormick credited Kennedy's victory to "the overwhelmingly one-sided votes in precincts inhabited by persons of Mexican or Puerto Rican descent." Days after the election, Hector congratulated Albert Peña, the Texas state coordinator, for "assuring a great victory for the Kennedy-Johnson ticket." Others outside the leadership also credited the effort for the win. Said the *Press*, an independent Democratic Party journal, "Senator Kennedy [should] be thankful that the big turnout of Latin American voters in San Antonio, Laredo, Corpus Christi, and El Paso enabled him to offset losses sustained in Dallas, Houston, and [other] parts of . . . Texas." Kennedy himself sent a telegram praising the "magnificent job turned in by the national Viva Kennedy Clubs." But Robert Kennedy went even further when he told a reporter in Mexico City that it had been the "votes of Mexican Americans and other Latin Americans in the United States that [had] elected" his brother. Kennedy then added that this meant that the new administration was going to be paying more attention to the nations of the South.

For Hector and the other leaders, this signaled an opening for more inclusion of Mexican Americans in the new administration. On November 18, Hector broached the subject with Kennedy in a congratulatory letter. "I sincerely hope that we are given an opportunity to serve under your administration," he told Kennedy. When he wrote the letter, Hector believed that the Kennedy administration had a moral obligation to include Mexican Americans on the basis of their assistance and their loyalty to the United States. While placing it in the context of a humble request, he was simply reminding the president-elect of the commitment he had made. Manuel Avila, a Forum sympathizer, had written to a mutual friend of his and Hector that "he [JFK] can't deny us those things which we need and want." In a short time, Hector began sending resumes and recommendations to the president-elect's staff.

By January, 1961 it became evident to Hector that the presidential transition team had contacted almost no Mexican Americans to seek advice or to interview for a possible appointment. Sensing he had to do something quickly, he wrote the president-elect on January 11 and "respectfully" recommended former Forum national president and now college professor Vicente Ximenes to be assistant secretary of state for Latin America. "This will . . . help us to feel that we can be useful to our country both in time of peace and in time of war," wrote Hector. He reminded Kennedy that Mexican Americans had been loyal and that promises had been made before and during the election.

There would be other recommendations not only from Hector but from Roybal in California, Chávez in New Mexico, and from politicians in Arizona. There would also be criticism. Roybal lambasted the administration for not selecting Mexican Americans for any major positions, and Chávez publicly chided Texas Senator Ralph Yarborough on the Senate floor for failing to support E. D. Salinas of Laredo, Texas, for the federal bench. Salinas, as it turns out, became the focus of Hector's lobbying efforts for more Mexican American participation in the federal bureaucracy. He was as good a nomination as any that Mexican American leaders could make.

In fact, Salinas had been seen as a shoo-in just before the election. The Texas Bar Association had supported his candidacy, so did the governor, the Texas congressional delegation, and even Eisenhower's Secretary of the Treasury Robert Anderson, who had been a law classmate of Salinas. Salinas came from a well-connected family in Laredo, was a graduate of the University of Texas Law School, had been a special assistant to the American ambassador to Uruguay during the war, and had served as president general of LULAC in 1939 and 1940. He had also been one of the first Mexican Americans to be elected to the state bench in Texas. Few Mexican American candidates for appointment could compare their credentials to Salinas. That he was an active member of Viva Kennedy only endeared him more to Hector and other reformers.

Salinas seemed the most capable and qualified to replace Judge James V. Allred who had died in 1959. Allred had gained the favor of most reformers because of his "humane" treatment of Mexican Americans who came before his court. In a judicial system often seen as hostile to Mexican Americans, Allred's courtroom was an "island of civility and fairness in a sea of discrimination, segregation, and violence." Ed Idar, now a practicing attorney, described Salinas's style as the closest to approaching Allred's judicial attitude. "With the number of *raza* that are involved in civil [and] criminal litigation in the . . . Federal District Court for the Southern District of Texas, it is of the utmost importance that we try to get a man appointed who understands the general situation of our people," he told Hector in a letter dated October 26, 1959.

Hector considered Salinas a friend and a fellow crusader. Though he came from an elite family, from a community often considered a bit too conservative and accommodating for most reformers, Salinas had a good reputation among Mexican American liberals. Hector liked him because of his support of Forum activities and because he represented—despite his age—the new wave of Mexican American professionals who were committed to the barrios and avoided the elitism of the old LULAC members. Hector considered his appointment "the most vital single action" that the administration could undertake to repay the community for its support. "Never has the Spanish-speaking population of the Southwest been so united behind one single aspiration (sic) as they are in this case," wrote Hector in a letter cosigned by Henry B. González, Albert Peña, and El Paso Mayor Raymond Telles. Hector and his fellow reformers argued that the appointment did not amount to patronage but rather recognition for Mexican

Americans, whom they considered to be "the last major ethnic group that still has to fight to attain first-class citizenship."

Hector well understood that while Mexican American problems were not seen as acute by many, there was no doubt that their problems were the least attended to. Mexican Americans were still invisible to most people. Despite a major Supreme Court case, a massive roundup of "illegal aliens" known as Operation Wetback, and numerous movies on the big screen depicting border problems, most Americans ignored the concerns of Mexican Americans, and that was no different among politicians. Kennedy would respond twice during this period that he intended to "use" the Latin American in his administration, but only because he was pressed by the media which had gotten ahold of the discontent among Mexican Americans. Hector felt certain that this was a critical period in the evolution of Mexican American influence.

In the multi-signer letter, Hector warned the president that dire consequences lay ahead for the Democratic Party and his administration if he failed to respond positively to the support of the Viva Kennedy Clubs. The letter stated that a prominent Democrat threatened to quit the party and politics altogether if no appointments came. The letter did not designate the "devoted Democrat" who would withdraw, but it is likely that the administration understood that it was Hector. "While this may sound overly emotional," said the letter, "it is but a means of stating how deeply we look upon this [Salinas' appointment] as a matter of principle and justice, which goes to the very root of the attainment of first-class citizenship in every respect by the ethnic group we represent."

No one in the Viva Kennedy campaign had made a greater commitment to the Kennedy image than Hector. In personalizing the campaign and making it a crusade for a "friend," Hector had in fact raised the bar of expectation to a new and much higher level. With the number of positions diminishing, it became crucial that Kennedy respond to the one appointment that Mexican American leaders had defined as the most important. For Hector it was a matter of pride and a test of his influence both in Texas and with the new administration. If he could not deliver a federal judgeship in his own backyard, especially after all the promises of "rewards," his credibility would suffer not only among his people but also among state politicians.

In the end, the forceful lobbying and harsh criticism led to the appointment of a Mexican American to the federal bench. Unfortunately for Hector, it was not Salinas but another state judge, Raymond Garza, a friend of those close to Vice President Johnson. It is likely that no Mexican American would have occupied the post if not for Hector's and the other's tenacious lobbying effort, but it is also likely that this same effort led to the selecting of another "more moderate" Mexican American. Both Johnson and Yarborough disliked Salinas. And they particularly disliked the intense lobbying and criticism.

Yarborough had privately denounced Salinas and the Forum for "lobbying" for a federal judgeship, which in his view was completely inappropriate. His reluctance to commit to Salinas early had forced Hector and a few others to fly to Washington, D.C. to personally meet with the senator. But after intense words, Hector stormed out of the office. Idar, in a private memo, accused Yarborough of courting conservative support for future races, including another one for governor.

In a letter to his friend Manuel Ávila, Jr., dated July 22, 1961, Hector complained that Democrats were simply not responding nor were they interested in the concerns of Mexican American leaders. "They want us to help them," wrote Hector, "but they don't want to give us a break. *Estos desgraciados no nos quieren dar ni agua"* (Those bastards don't even want to give us water). The reference to not getting even water from the Democrats exhibited a growing frustration in Hector that the winners were not playing fair. After all, Mexican American reformers had done their part. They had campaigned hard, put out their own resources, and delivered the vote. All they had asked in return was recognition and an opportunity to serve the nation. Now, the national party seemed no different than the state party, which constantly broke its promises and ignored the needs of the barrios.

Had Hector not set the bar so high, he might have realized how effective the Viva Kennedy leaders had been. Never before had an administration considered a Mexican American or any other Latino for a federal appointment. Eventually, there would be several Latinos appointed in the Kennedy administration. Forumeer Raymond Telles, mayor of El Paso, would become ambassador to Costa Rica. Raúl Castro of Arizona would also become an ambassador, and a number of Puerto Ricans also came into the administration in the area of foreign service. Others would follow in lesser posts, but the process had begun. No future administration would ever again exclude Latinos—particularly Mexican Americans—from its federal appointee lists. Hector's tenacious effort and his strong criticism had galvanized support for Mexican Americans serving at the highest levels of government. His efforts made it nearly impossible for the Kennedys and future administrations to ignore that there was a pool of willing volunteers to serve the federal government.

Hector had wanted more. After all, in his own mind Mexican Americans were not only willing but they were ready to assume a larger role in American society. In the decade of the fifties, he witnessed a tremendous rise in Mexican Americans who had the education, training, and life experience to merit federal appointment. Besides this emerging talent, he saw a community ready to assume its rightful place in society. Unfortunately, Hector's evolving view hampered his ability to see the hard reality of Mexican Americans in the political appointment process. Those who eventually did get appointments never returned to the barrios nor did they provide the kind of political leverage that had been expected of them. Most returned to make money and live in political obscurity. Others would remain in the federal bureaucracy but never in policy-making positions.

In most cases, their ineffectiveness resulted from the fact that they had circumvented the traditional process of getting appointed. They were not close to the president or his advisors, they were not well-known outside their communities, they were not vote-getters nor fund raisers, and they usually brought no expertise or skills to their posts. Thus, many were appointees because of political expediency, and they were not seen as an integral part of the administration. Their inability to take advantage of their appointments resulted, in part, from the fact that they did not bring an ideological or deep-rooted philosophical view of the world to their posts. It is fair to say that few had distinguishing careers in the federal bureaucracy and almost none of them used the experience as a stepping-stone for a more significant career outside the government.

This crop of Mexican American leaders was simply not prepared to politic at the national or international level. They were naive about politics at those levels. Their philosophy of patriotism might serve to endear them to national politicians, but these same politicians never saw them as indispensable. Since they brought no constituency, they brought nothing to the bargaining table. The elected officials, with the exception of Raúl Castro and Raymond Telles, who feared tough re-election bids, chose not to take appointments when asked. They probably understood better than Hector and those who sought the appointments that these assignments were not likely to be important policy-making positions and that they would lead nowhere politically. Hector, who never sought elected office or political appointments, saw the appointments as a way to serve the nation and a way for his people to make a commitment to American ideals and policies. Rather than naiveté this view reflected Hector's commitment to serving his country. Service to country was a selfless act whose reward was personal satisfaction and heightened patriotism.

Hector's anger might have been more severe had he not himself been appointed as a member of a negotiating team that went to Jamaica to sign a mutual defense treaty. Amid the debate over appointments, Hector was hesitant to accept the assignment, fearing that his appointment would affect that of others. He did not want to be seen as taking someone else's more permanent appointment nor of being "bought off" to quiet his criticism. His chiding of the Kennedy administration had encouraged a loud and sustained protest from many Mexican Americans.

The South Texas Spanish-language newspaper *El Quijote* had categorized Kennedy's few Mexican American appointees as "grains of sand in the desert of federal employment." It also charged that Kennedy had placed his *consentidos* (favorites) in strategic foreign services posts throughout Latin America. Most lacked the knowledge of the language, culture, and "idiosyncrasies" of the region, said the newspaper editors. They also claimed that Hector's appointment was an effort to cover up the administration's dismal appointment record. José Alvarado, who had replaced Idar as the editor of the Forum's

News Bulletin, called Hector's trip to Jamaica a "junket" intended to defuse Mexican American criticism. "One still hears about the good doctor who spent his free time visiting and encouraging the humble people of that country, assuring them of our friendship and interest," wrote Alvarado, "but this was merely a junket."

Hector must have cringed at Alvarado's words. More distressing to Hector might have been Alvarado's veiled attack on some reformers' gullibility. Said the Chicago-based Forum leader, "Our traditions have led us to believe that if someone says he will do a thing, it can be dismissed as accomplished. Our patience and courtesy have been interpreted as ignorance and weakness." The frustration in Alvarado's words resulted from an inability to wrestle from the Kennedy administration any significant appointment. This was after the most significant electoral campaign ever waged by the nation's Latino population. If Mexican Americans could not collect after such a successful effort, what could be expected in other, calmer times?

Whatever Hector thought of Alvarado's words, he did not let it ruin his own appointment. Hector rarely asked things for himself, but he appreciated those he did receive. Being appointed to represent the United States in a mutual defense negotiation was something in which any veteran would be proud to participate, especially someone as patriotic as Hector. He marveled at the leadership of his nation and at the intricacies of foreign service. On February 11, 1961, at the signing of two project agreements between the West Indies and the United States, he told the press:

> We read newspaper accounts of the operations of this program and its accomplishments; our press is filled with the debates of Congress on the annual appropriations to carry the program forward; but it is not often that [a] United States private citizen has a chance to participate in this way in its actual operation.

Hector, caught up in the joy of the moment, declared to the press, "the joint programs . . . manifest . . . the interest of the people of the United States to help this new nation." He could not feel more proud of his country.

With that sense of conviction that his country represented all that was good and decent in a world confronting Soviet hegemony and rising leftist revolutions throughout the Third World, Hector set out to be a representative of American goodwill. He visited hospitals, clinics, and neighborhoods and spoke to anyone willing to listen. His message, as alluded to by the editors of *El Quijote*, was that the United States was a friend, one interested in the welfare of less fortunate nations. He quickly made a positive impression on the officials of the West Indies who must have marveled that a person of color was representing the world's most powerful nation.

"I am overwhelmed with your kindness . . . and for all the very nice things you said about your visit to our hospitals," wrote George Gemmill Smith, administrator of the general hospital in Port-of-Spain. "Due largely to the charm of your presence, the time went very quickly, and afterwards I seemed to have told you very little, but perhaps you will come again." In a letter from the Ministry of Health, another West Indian wrote, "My wife and I . . . remember you with considerable affection and were moved by the spirit of sincerity and genuine humanism that you radiated. You are a worthy ambassador of your president, your people and your great country."

In the West Indies, away from the pressure of organizing and the battles over appointments, Hector reverted back to that young Army officer who reached out to people who suffered and who yearned for a better life. He charmed those surprised that a representative of the most powerful nation in the world could be so humble, so genuinely concerned, and so caring about their circumstances. One month after his return, he wrote to his friend Manuel Ávila, Jr. to tell him that the agreement had been a success. "I learned a lot up there," wrote Hector. "I am certainly glad to have received this appointment." He also confided in Ávila his belief that the lack of a national political organization hurt Mexican Americans' chances at getting appointments. "If it had not been for the GI Forum, we would not have received such an honor (appointment)," said Hector. Mexican Americans, in his view, had been slow to organize.

It is interesting to conjecture as to whether Hector had any second thoughts about his activism. Having been honored with the appointment, he must have thought for a moment what a life of service to the country would have been like. While he saw his own activism as important for the country, it did take its toll, and many viewed the work as being demeaning to the nation because it exposed some harsh realities. To be an American whose service was to the nation and not a group within it must have been an exciting possibility for someone like Hector. But if he thought about it, he did not spend much time on it. As soon as he was back in Washington, D.C. he joined Peña and Virgilio Roel in a meeting with Senator Yarborough to lobby on Salinas' behalf. The tumultuous meeting with the Texas senator quickly brought Hector back to reality. Yarborough's stubborn refusal to support the Laredo native enraged Hector and he walked out on his former political ally.

A still fuming Hector received a letter in mid-March from Carlos McCormick inviting him to a meeting in Phoenix, Arizona, to discuss the organization of a national political group. Some of the Viva Kennedy Club leaders and members had contacted the former club national director about keeping the organization together or creating something similar. Never had there been such a united political effort by Mexican Americans. They had been exhilarated by the experience and the new comradery with reformers, activists, and politicians from other states. Many had also enjoyed traveling to other Mexican American communities and being treated with such friendliness and respect.

Just as important as the positive experience, the disappointing effort to get Mexican Americans appointed to federal jobs had reenforced their need to stick together. This group of Mexican American elites like Roybal, González, Peña, Castro, Chávez, Alvarado, and many others knew they had to retain unity in their ranks. In fact, unity became a quasi-ideology that revealed their inability to go beyond traditional American political ideals. They believed that if they stuck together, they could accomplish much. This was based on the assumption that most Mexican Americans faced the same problems and that most Anglo Americans had the same types of prejudices. What they did not immediately deal with was their own personal philosophies. Thus, they arrived in Phoenix excited by the prospects.

The Texas group came better prepared than any other state delegation. The meeting in Phoenix opened on March 26, but the Texas
reformers had met earlier in the month to establish the Mexican Americans for Political Action (MAPA) organization. Peña was named state
chair and Hector national organizer. The meeting attracted many of
the most prominent reformers in the state and brought together
numerous groups that had worked in the barrios for years. MAPA
attempted to do what no other organization had done: provide unity to
various groups. It brought local and regional *políticos* together with
organizational leaders and lone-wolf reformers. Their differences set
aside, they came to fulfill Hector's vision of a powerful movement of
Mexican Americans who would take their social reform agenda and
transfer it into a political agenda.

For many Mexican American reformers, and Hector in particular,
social reform had gone as far as it could. Now, Mexican Americans
had to become political. They not only had to register and vote, but
they had to participate in choosing candidates, promoting platforms,
and even running for office. The gap between the social reform liberal and the barrio politician had to be bridged. Interaction between the
two during the Viva Kennedy Clubs campaign had created the expectation that they could work together. This unity had potential to meet
the needs of both groups. Middle-class reformers could acquire recognition for their efforts, patronage for their votes, political appointments for their loyalty, and legislation to end segregation. Working-
class leaders could expect government efforts to end police brutality,
poor housing, high unemployment, and discrimination in public facilities. This unity had the makings of a dual-class strategy. This dual
strategy had become the only option because of the demise of most of
the more militant working-class organizations in the barrio. Political
reformism became the philosophy of the G.I. Generation.

The meeting in Phoenix opened with a strong condemnation of
national politicians and particularly of the Kennedy administration.
Roybal, in justifying the meeting, declared, "We find no consolation
[in Kennedy's actions] and for that reason we must do something
about it." Roybal told the gathered delegates that there would probably be no more appointments, and Mexican Americans needed to start

thinking about developing greater influence through political involvement. Hector expanded on Roybal's condemnation, accusing national politicians of being in "collusion" to keep Mexican Americans "down." Having forgotten the exhilaration of his "junket," he pointed to McCormick and told the club director that he had been used by new politicians who quickly reverted to the old ways of promising and not delivering.

While Hector had been as nationalistic as the other Mexican American reformers in favoring Mexican Americans for appointments, he called on the delegates to unite with other Spanish-speaking reformers. Geographic dispersion and different national origins, said Hector, must not keep them apart. In calling for this Pan-Hispanism, Hector was acknowledging a lesson that some Mexican American reformers had learned in the national campaign. Those who had traveled to the East Coast and the Midwest saw that Mexicans and Mexican Americans shared space with other groups, most commonly Puerto Ricans, but also Cubans and other Latin Americans. Places like Chicago, Gary (Indiana), New York, Miami, and even Los Angeles had large numbers of non-Mexican Latinos, and many of them experienced the same problems of discrimination and segregation. More important, most had been willing to put their differences aside to work in Viva Kennedy Clubs, and had accepted Mexican American leadership in the effort.

The rest of the morning session of the gathering was spent on delegates denouncing national politicians, discriminatory practices, and even their own fellow reformers. Gene Marín of Arizona argued that too many reformers were vying for "the same people, for the same monies, [and] for the same effort." They needed to work together. Lino López of Colorado called the development of a national organization the most critical decision facing the Spanish-speaking. If they did not do so, they would be "failing . . . five to six million Americans." Hector told the delegates that strong opposition existed to organizing Mexican Americans, but failure to do so meant "the *raza* will perish." The delegates ended the session with little discussion of ideology, goals, or political strategy, only with a reaffirmation of discontent.

Electing officers, developing an organizational structure, and selecting a name took up the afternoon session of the gathering. The structure turned out to be top-heavy with a national president, four vice presidents, a secretary, treasurer, executive secretary, and a board consisting of two delegates from each state. Hector was selected president and Roybal vice president. They were the most prominent of the reformers who attended and they had also developed a national reputation, both through their organizations and through their leadership in the Kennedy campaign. They represented the largest states with the most Mexican Americans. And they represented the two largest branches of Mexican American leadership, the political and the grassroots.

The choosing of a name proved to be harder. The effort revealed two challenges that eventually and quite immediately tore the organization apart. First, Mexican Americans had been segregated not only from their Anglo American neighbors but also their own people in other states. While they often experienced many of the same prejudices, their geographic dispersion, their different regions of origin in Mexico, and the varying degrees of hostility and discrimination they felt had given each a particular experience. That experience led to the choosing of their name and their identity. In Colorado, they were Spanish American; in New Mexico, Hispanos; in Texas, Latin Americans; in California, Mexican Americans; and in other places they might be Latinos, Spanish-speakers, or Americans of Mexican descent. They all avoided using the term "Mexican" by itself.

Hector had noticed even before the meeting that many resented any name associated with their national origin. In a letter to Manuel Ávila, Jr., one day before the meeting, he wrote, "I am surprised more and more that people resent the name Mexican-American. You know how I stand on this thing, but they are getting completely away. They don't want to use the word Mexican at all. It is a little confusing to me." Hector still carried the influence of his father, who had taught him to be proud of his heritage. Having resisted being called "Spaniard" as a young boy by those who wanted to distinguish him from other working-class and darker classmates, he now resisted those who called for avoiding any kind of ethnic label.

Eventually the organization chose the name Political Association of Spanish-Speaking Organizations (PASO). They would reaffirm the name in Las Vegas the following 28th and 29th of April but only after another furious debate on the name and the term Mexican. By then, however, there were signs that the organization would not last. It did not. No other national meeting followed the one in Las Vegas. In that one, Roybal joined González, Peña, and Chávez as a no-show. Mexican American fragmentation in politics, goals, and leaders overshadowed their common oppression. Leaders from California had already formed their own statewide Mexican Americans for Political Action (MAPA) and several other states did the same. Others simply refused to change their name.

Hector was furious and disappointed but not surprised. In a letter to McCormick, two weeks before the first meeting, he had criticized this kind of splintering. "Our *raza* always thinks of their individual problems first," he wrote. "They believe [that] what they do with themselves is [more] important to them than what they do for the people, and this is wrong." Following his rule not to criticize publicly or fight with them, Hector did not react publicly to the immediate collapse of the organization. But on September 18, he wrote Ávila to tell him that PASO, which the Texas delegation had chosen to continue, was not attracting too many people. "Sometimes I feel like giving up knowing well that we need organizations . . . badly, but people are not even willing to contribute one dollar to get it moving." He added that the "Negroes seem to be doing alright" and so were other groups, but "why in the Lord's name we cannot organize our people, Manuel, I do not know. Sometimes they don't even respect us or thank us for our work."

Hector was reacting as many reformers before him had done and many more would do after him. He spent much of his time trying to organize people to fight for their rights, but there seemed to be so little help. And so few people took the ball and ran. The opposition was too entrenched, the community too unsophisticated, the day too short, and the normal demands of family and work too much. He now had a growing family, a thriving business that he was neglecting, and his health was a problem. By now he had faced two heart attacks and he was beginning to feel tired.

Before the end of the letter, however, Hector had gotten his reformer's second wind. "I hope that this letter does not sound too despondent, because I am not despondent," said Hector. "I am just fighting mad again and when I get mad, I get down to do more work and more work every day." And this he did with a tenacity that rivaled that which he had exhibited during the Kennedy campaign. By July 10, he was declaring to all PASO members outside of Texas that the state chapter was not supporting the Democratic Party's candidate for the Senate. In an open letter to the PASO membership entitled "PASO Takes First Gigantic Step towards Its Grass Roots Movement and Local Organization," Hector told members and others who would listen that, "We had to prove to the Democratic machinery that they could not win without our work and help." Hector called on Mexican Americans not to support the Democratic nominee. The shift of support away from the Democrats caused the election of John Tower, the first Republican elected to the Senate in Texas in the twentieth century. "This took guts," said Hector, "but we proved [Democrats needed our votes]."

The nine-thousand vote victory would surely have been overcome by a strong PASO endorsement. At least that was the feeling of the PASO leadership. The Forum's newsletter promoted this view by proclaiming that an endorsement of the Democratic candidate by Hector would have meant thirty thousand votes in Corpus Christi alone. For Hector this was the first and last time he supported a Republican. This exception occurred because PASO wanted to send a message to the Democratic Party and the state's politicians that Mexican Americans were now ready to play hardball politics. They were not to be taken for granted. And no longer were they willing to come into alliances without specific guarantees. The Viva Kennedy Club experiences had taught them to depend on themselves and not to take "assurances" at face value.

The story of PASO is best told in this author's *Viva Kennedy* and in a master's thesis by Roberto Cuéllar. It suffices here to underscore several important points of this organization's successes and failures. PASO would change the nature of Texas politics, ushering in an era that eventually pushed—with the help of his poor health—Hector aside. It would also reflect the things that Hector wanted for his people. Even more than the G.I. Forum, PASO addressed the need for political change in Texas and across the Southwest. But its experience revealed how difficult it was to accomplish that change. It also underscored where the goals of Mexican Americans and political liberals parted ways.

PASO, established to fight conservative Democrats in Texas, ended up challenging liberals for the leadership of the progressive effort in Texas. Mexican American reformers, particularly Sánchez and Idar, but also Peña, Hector, and others, came to see many liberals as simply another group of Anglo Texans unwilling to accept *raza* as equal partners. They saw this when Henry B. González ran for Lyndon Johnson's vacated Senate seat and Texas liberals supported one of their own, despite their own organization having voted González as the "liberal voice" in the race. Liberal icon Ralph Yarborough also failed to support their efforts in ending the Bracero Program in order to appease the powerful growers' lobby. They also took issue with the liberal's *Texas Observer* magazine's failure to provide them coverage and support their candidates.

Ultimately, liberals took issue with PASO and Hector's view that Mexican Americans had to look after their own interests instead of simply allowing their political stands to be influenced by the conservative-liberal split in Texas politics. For a short, two-year period, PASO leaders led by Hector and Peña—who became the prime leaders of the organization—sought to forge their own agenda and on their own terms. PASO adopted an article by George I. Sánchez entitled "The American of Mexican Descent." In it Sánchez expressed the generations-old frustration that Mexican Americans were simply forgotten by society. He reiterated many of the concerns stated in the Texas Viva Kennedy statement, which itself reiterated much of what Hector had said in his statement to the Democratic Party national convention and to the American G.I. Forum members in Wichita two years earlier.

But Sánchez added something that Hector believed in but had never said publicly. The University of Texas educator declared, "Only *mexicanos* can speak for *mexicanos*." He would later explain to the *Texas Observer* editors that he did not intend to cause a storm of protest among liberals nor did he mean to create discrimination in reverse. But he did not back down. "I may be wrong in saying that only the *mexicano* can speak for the *mexicano*. Up to now there hasn't been any evidence that the contrary is so. . . . I can't help but take a completely cynical, pessimistic view of Anglo politics and Anglo politicians," said Sánchez. Five months later, in a letter to Idar, he would tell the Forum leader, "I personally no longer give a damn what the liberals think."

Sánchez, like Hector, had a strong strain of nationalism, but despite himself, he was also an avowed liberal. His liberalism was also more deeply rooted philosophically than that of Hector. Hector seemed to see liberalism as the one political ideology more conducive to getting Mexican Americans out of their problems. He also saw liberals as more inclusive, thus more likely to be allies than foes. But Hector's brand of liberalism was simply anything to the left of Texas conservatives. His brand revolved more around humanitarianism than political ideology. It then became much easier to see PASO alliances in terms of immediate goals rather than fundamental principles.

PASO's first major conflict—which signaled the demise of the Viva Kennedy Club unity—came over the gubernatorial election of 1962. Three candidates sought the organization's support during its first convention in San Antonio on February, 1962. The three were Price Daniel, the incumbent; Don Yarborough, the liberal challenger; and John Connally, Johnson's former assistant. Because of Johnson's backing, Connally had been seen as one of the stronger candidates, but he quickly disappointed the PASO delegates, despite fierce lobbying by Carlos McCormick, who had been sent by Johnson to be Connally's point man. The convention delegates then divided themselves between the governor and the liberal challenger, and in doing so revealed both their priorities and their ideological bent.

Some delegates, led by Peña, Hector, and Idar wanted to pick a candidate that would win but who also would recognize that he needed their help. Ideology played second fiddle to winning. Years later, Idar remembered that they "had always supported liberals and they lost." The PASO leaders decided that it was time to change their approach. "We needed," said Idar, "to try to get what we wanted instead of just supporting liberals." In their view, alliances with martyrs had brought little to Mexican Americans. Even when they won, most liberals tended to concentrate on labor issues and African American-focused civil rights activities. Mexican Americans were supposed to be supportive because "liberal government" was good for them, not because there were any particular promises made. Hector and others still fumed over the fact that few liberals had really given their full support to issues relevant to Mexican Americans.

Other delegates, led by Idar's law partner Bob Sánchez, Leo J. Leo, Ramiro Cassas, and other Rio Grande Valley reformers favored supporting the most liberal candidate. In this they were supported by George I. Sánchez and labor leader Paul Montemayor. "Principles rather than petty patronage must dictate our political choices," said Sánchez. In his view, Yarborough was "our kind," as he told Idar on the first night of the convention. Yarborough himself had lobbied the Rio Grande Valley politicians and had gotten their endorsement even before the convention. This was contrary to the request made by Idar to all delegates to come with an open mind and without endorsing anyone until the convention made its choice.

Yet, despite the talk of seeking unity in a candidate, the convention quickly turned into a wheeling and dealing session. Hector led a group of "six or seven" delegates that included Peña and Idar in a late evening discussion on the merit of the candidates. They decided that Price Daniel should receive the convention's nod. Idar remembered them believing that Yarborough could not win, especially since the governor had won his first reelection by almost a million votes. Daniel had also been very sympathetic to their demands and made the promise to start making appointments even before the election. Yarborough, on the other hand, seemed overly confident that he had the delegates in his pocket and he made what some considered typically liberal "sweeping generalities" that did not focus on the local issues.

The decision by what was the top leadership of PASO created a rift at the convention. Sánchez walked out but not before accusing Peña, Hector, Idar, and others of selling out. He and others attacked

Daniel for being a "revolving hypocrite" whose years in office had been characterized by mediocrity and indifference. They also charged that "change" did not come by simply reelecting incumbents who supported the status quo. Yarborough himself entered the fracas by telling the delegates that they could win with "real Democrats," and not by compromising their principles. In the liberals' view, PASO had to join the nationwide liberal movement that they believed Kennedy had launched. Civil rights had begun to pick up steam and liberals in Texas and nationally were making a concentrated effort to take control of American politics. The young Turks, led by New Deal populist Sánchez saw PASO as the new liberal organization in Texas.

Hector and the other veterans of years of social reform saw little value in martyrdom. They wanted results. They felt that although Daniel was the incumbent and the favorite, the liberal challenge had made him conscious of the need to find favor among Mexican American reformers. They also believed that while their candidate was not the most liberal, their own politics were liberal and liberalism would grow in Texas only through the growth of PASO. There simply were not enough Anglo American liberals in Texas for liberalism to flourish. More important, these reformers believed that Mexican Americans had suffered enough as a supportive constituency and now they needed to demand equal political space. Going with the liberal would be making no change at all.

In the end, Hector's supporters won the day. Daniel was named the convention's candidate with a vote of 51 to 41, with Connally receiving almost no votes. Immediately, Hector, Peña, and others sought to bring unity to the delegates. But the Yarborough delegates would have none of that. In leaving the convention before the vote, Sánchez lashed out at Hector and others. "I was, and still am," he told a reporter, " under the conviction that if we are to operate successfully in the interest of our people, we are going to have to operate simply, sincerely, and unequivocally as a moral force." Leo J. Leo went further in his condemnation, accusing Hector of selling out for political appointments. He reminded Hector that the good doctor had constantly criticized those who sold themselves for "*un pedazo de tortilla, barbacoa, o por una miserable chamba* (for a piece of tortilla, barbecue, or an insignificant job)." He warned that Daniel had never been a friend and never would be. "You did wrong," said Leo, "in using the tremendous . . . influence that you have . . . to turn the convention for a man that has never been our friend."

Hector must have wondered if the conflict had been worth it when Daniel went down to defeat in the primaries. A hurried PASO endorsement of Yarborough simply made things worse when the liberal candidate lost to Connally in a runoff. An endorsement of Connally against the Republican candidate—to save face and to try to salvage a relationship with Johnson's man—fell apart when Connally refused to agree to any demands from PASO. In the end, he swept the governorship easily and reinstated Johnson as the top power in the state. Hector and the other PASO leaders were stunned. In a few short months, PASO had gone down in defeat twice and been rebuffed by the new power broker in Texas. More importantly, the new unity had quickly dissipated in recriminations and personal name-calling. Hector, seen as the leader of a progressive movement to end segregation and to empower Mexican Americans politically, was now the target of criticism by some of his old friends and some of the new reformers. As always, Hector did not respond publicly to the attacks, but privately he fumed that upstarts with few victories in their pockets and old-timers, who had been wallowing in near obscurity before he came along, were now assuming they knew much better.

Hector believed that Mexican Americans had to confront the reality of the political landscape. Being defeated one more time with one more liberal held no promise. They had to be part of the game, part of the dialogue, and they had to be valued. Now, with two defeats and one major rebuff, PASO struggled to maintain some dignity. A *San Antonio Express* newspaper columnist had proclaimed that PASO "obviously doesn't speak for very many Spanish-speaking people." In ridiculing a PASO meeting to reconsider the Connally endorsement, the editorial writer asked, "In what telephone booth will you meet?" For Hector, who depended on legitimacy to negotiate with state politicians and to gain media attention, the year 1962 bordered on disaster. But 1963 would simply get worse.

Trying to save face and establish a foothold in politics, PASO became involved in local politics in Crystal City, a rural community in a region known as the Winter Garden, about two hundred miles west of Corpus Christi. There, an Anglo American resident, disgusted with the tax evaluation of his property, had helped launch a voter registration campaign among Mexican Americans. His aim was to frighten the entrenched city councilmen and mayor, but the effect was an excited Mexican American electorate. The local Teamster's Union became involved when two of its members became leaders in the drive. Initially, the union saw this as a good recruiting opportunity, but soon decided to move to the background because of the racial tensions that were aroused. Moses Falcón, a union member, then called Peña to get assistance from PASO. For Peña and his assistant Albert Fuentes, Crystal City provided an opportunity for the organization to become fully involved in empowering Mexican Americans in the political process.

What made Crystal City such a good test case was the fact that Mexican Americans were the overwhelming majority, the elections were nonpartisan, and all seats for the city government were up, meaning that Mexican Americans could really score a major political victory. PASO quickly sent one of their members to act as an advisor to the five, only slightly educated Mexican American candidates chosen to run for office. The Teamsters sent one of their agents to act as a legal advisor. The Anglo Americans realized only too late what was happening. Before they knew it, the majority of registered citizens were Mexican American, there was a well-advised slate of candidates, and major rallies were being held in the Mexican side of town. At those rallies were organizers and reformers from outside the locality. Peña, a rousing speaker, was there calling on all Mexican Americans to go to the polls and bring democracy to Crystal City.

Hector did not get involved in the Crystal City campaign. The Winter Garden was almost two hundred miles from Corpus Christi, and few in the media paid any attention until almost the end of the campaign. Hector had reintegrated himself into Forum business, still smarting from the gubernatorial fiasco. Probably just as important in keeping him on the sidelines was Peña's assumption of the leadership role among many younger reformers. Peña was a fiery speaker with tremendous energy. Like the Hector of old, he traveled everywhere, gave orders, made speeches, and assumed command. As a county commissioner and head of the liberal coalition in San Antonio, he seemed poised to take over the leadership of the reform movement in Texas. More importantly, there were those who felt that Peña's style was more in keeping with the new militancy of the civil rights movement.

This militancy received a major boost when the five Mexican American candidates swept the city elections. In a direct confrontation between Mexican American and Anglo American candidates, the barrio had won. This had never happened in Texas before. It had been a particularly ugly racial confrontation and Anglo Americans had used every trick they could, including calling in the Texas Rangers, but Mexican Americans had stood firmly united. PASO's executive secretary, Fuentes, declared, "The Mexicans have learned all South Texans are equal." Peña added that five Mexican American candidates stood as "a beacon to all others like them, struggling in the morass of discrimination and equality. For the first time in South Texas the true majority [rules]."

The victory in Crystal City sent shock waves throughout the state. The one thing that many Anglo Americans feared had come about. A Mexican American majority had finally taken control, and there were over twenty counties in Texas where that same outcome could occur. For Peña and Fuentes and other younger reformers, the victory sent a message that no PASO-supported Anglo American's victory could duplicate. Emboldened, PASO sent a spokesperson to Washington, D.C. to speak in support of President Kennedy's civil rights legislation. PASO chapters redoubled their organizing efforts and others prepared to make similar electoral challenges. One such effort, in Mathis, Texas, succeeded two years later.

There were, however, those who did not share the enthusiasm of Peña and Fuentes over the Crystal City victory. These were individuals bothered by the "quality" of the candidates. They could well have predicted, and some did, that the candidates would fight among themselves, make some terrible mistakes, and eventually be disgraced in the eyes of the public. Martin García, the PASO representative to the Crystal City candidates, believed that the new city officials were simply unprepared to govern. He lamented the fact that PASO offered them little advice after the victory. "We did not teach them to be politicians," García would tell the *Dallas Morning News*. But there was little that PASO could do since the organization itself had no political platform and no mechanism for training new politicians. Most PASO reformers had learned politics on their own or from the mentoring of older activists. Also, PASO depended on its members having an education and keeping abreast of what was happening around them. The Crystal City candidates were simply working-class people who had been asked to step up in a historic moment.

There were others bothered by the infusion of the "race" issue in the campaign, which had the potential of causing a backlash from the Anglo American majority in the state. It was a battle they knew they could not win. More importantly, it was a battle they did not want to fight. All their lives they had sought integration, an opportunity to be considered just plain Americans. Loyalty, patriotism, dignity, and morality were the kinds of characteristics that Mexican American reformers had sought to emphasize to the larger community. A flare-up of racial tensions only exacerbated the already present tensions. "One Crystal City is all we need and we don't want to repeat it if we can help it," Forum leader Bob Sánchez told a reporter. "When a man is elected to office for what he is, no distinction on race or anything else, I will be the first to ask that PASO be disbanded," he added.

Hector fell among those dissatisfied with the Crystal City election. There is no public record on his feelings about the candidates or on racial tensions, but he did write a friend to tell him that he objected to the "teamsters . . . money and their manpower . . . in Crystal City." Hector had never developed alliances outside the barrio, especially not with any organization that had more resources and members than the Forum. He liked the Forum's independence and preferred what some might categorize as a more "nationalistic" approach. Like George I. Sánchez, he believed that only "*mexicanos* [could] speak for *mexicanos*." His alliances with major Anglo American politicians bespoke any kind of racial hostilities. He simply feared that Mexican Americans would be overwhelmed by a major organization like the Teamsters.

The fact that the Teamsters were engaged in a major conflict with the Kennedy administration over corruption and ties to organized crime did not help matters any. Hector, always someone who kept things above ground and sought to be honest in all his dealings, had a hard time dealing with the Teamsters' reputation. And yet, the Forum had cordial relations with the Teamsters Union. Only a short time after Crystal City, the San Antonio chapter of the Forum honored Ray Shafer, Texas Teamster president, for his "outstanding effort on behalf of democracy and for being a 'great American.'" Hector, already seeing his leadership in the reform movement being challenged by Peña and others, did not relish the existence of another major player like the Teamsters.

Hector and others took the fight to the PASO convention floor in San Antonio that following June, 1963. As the national organizer of PASO, he called on the delegates to sever their ties with the national union, reminding them that Mexican Americans had always maintained themselves self-sufficient in their efforts. "We have won our battles [before] with our own money, our own talent, and our own guts," he told the delegates. He asked them whether PASO would let leadership of the reform movement be taken over by the Teamsters. In this reproach he gained some valuable assistance. William Bonilla, a longtime LULAC leader, joined the chorus of protest. "It is my opinion," said Bonilla, "that PASO . . . should fight its own battle freely and independently." He then castigated the Teamsters for "unlawful tactics." Carlos McCormick joined the fracas by also calling for independence from outside groups. His comments caused the *Texas Observer* to ask whether he had been sent by Robert F. Kennedy to assess the relationship between the two groups.

The convention conflict became heated as Peña, Fuentes, and others rebuffed Hector's call. They ridiculed the notion that PASO could go at it alone in trying to change Texas politics. Peña and Fuentes also denied profusely that PASO had received any money from the Teamsters, declaring that the relationship was based on a mutual desire to see Texas become more liberal. Sánchez, still frustrated over the gubernatorial campaign and with what he considered Hector's "accommodationist" views, publicly questioned the doctor's commitment to real reform. He was followed by a number of other delegates who denounced Hector's stand. Peña remembered years later that Sánchez had danced in the aisle as Hector got hammered.

A distraught Hector declared, "I cannot be a member of any organization that has Ray Shafer as one of its members," and stormed out of the convention. Soon after that, the majority of delegates declared their support of the Crystal City effort, but not before voting to bar any "outside interference" in PASO's work. This would not appease Hector, and he basically kept going until he was out of the organization. Rather than try to fix the situation, as he had done in the past when conflicts arose, he added fuel to the fire by reporting to Robert F. Kennedy what had occurred in the convention. Placing his own twist on the discussions, he accused the Teamsters of trying to take over PASO, and Peña of trying to embarrass Congressman Henry B. González. In Hector's view, the Peña faction was contemplating a challenge to González because of his lone-wolf approach. "I put up a good fight, but in the end I had to walk out," wrote Hector. In the letter, Hector created an exaggerated and almost sinister view of those in opposition. Worse for the little unity that was still left, he shifted allegiance. Rather than try to work with PASO leaders or resolve the conflicts, he told Attorney General Robert F. Kennedy that he and McCormick were "awaiting any suggestions that you might give." In putting himself under marching orders from the Kennedys, he violated his own go-at-it-alone creed and reversed his decades-long battle to do away with the asymmetric relationship between Mexican American reformers and Anglo American politicians. From this moment on, every time Mexican American leaders came into conflict, they would call upon Anglo American politicians to help them battle their enemies in the barrio.

The rash decision to abandon his practice of not engaging in public fights with friends and fellow reformers would turn out to be one of the greatest failings in Hector's legacy. For years, he had maintained the attitude that fights among reformers only benefited the opposition and caused great divisions among the Mexican American population. Throughout the past fifteen years, he had looked past the criticism and the challenges to maintain unity within the ranks. He had even accepted that the development of new leadership meant occasional misunderstandings. But the conflicts in PASO seem to have pushed him over the edge. In a private letter to a pastor friend, Sánchez accused Hector of being irrational and "virtually incoherent." Some form of this criticism got to Hector, as well as other criticism by some whom he considered friends in the struggle.

Hector took profound offense at the criticism and seems to have made an important shift in his reform activities. He remained nationalistic and grounded in the grassroots, and he even regained the friendship of Sánchez and others who disagreed with him at the PASO convention. But Hector never again became a partisan of Mexican American political organizations like PASO. He also moved away from purely political agendas. He continued to support candidates and lend his name to Mexican American candidates with whom he agreed, but he remained independent of any ties that demanded loyalty to agendas with which he disagreed.

Like Idar before him, Hector seems to have concluded that Mexican Americans were not ready for organizations like PASO. Without doubt he knew the talent existed, but the circumstances seemed to always place Mexican Americans in a combative mood. The leadership of the community had worked independently for so long that few in it knew how to work collectively. The Forum had worked because he had organized it, trained it, and led it for a number of years. But even there, there were conflicts within the leadership. Younger or newer officers seemed oblivious of the past and disrespectful of those who had made social reform a lifelong crusade. They seemed too anxious to lead and to make decisions without paying the price that it took to become leaders.

Hector could easily point out that much of what had been accomplished had been due to the Forum's work. The Viva Kennedy Clubs spread like wildfire because hundreds of Forum chapters and their leaders simply changed hats and became club members. The young turks that were now moving in another direction had come into reform and prominence because of the Forum or because of Hector's tutoring. No other reformer could claim the kind of influence he had had in the last fifteen years. In his mind, LULAC had grown stale and only recently was making a comeback. And people like Sánchez had been rabble-rousing for years but had never been able to develop an organization like the Forum. It had only taken a few years for Hector to assume the leadership of the reform movement, while others had been at it for much longer. Given the nature of Mexican American politics, Hector decided that calling in the IOUs might be the best way to go. Surely, it could not be any worse than coalescing with a group as divisive as PASO.

Early picture of Hector with parents and some of his siblings. *Left to right:* (first row) Hector, Antonio, Faustina with Cuitlahuac on her lap, José, Emilia and Cleotilde. Second row: Cuahutemoc and Dalia. (Latter daughter named after her). Courtesy García Papers, Special Collections & Archives, Bell Library, Texas A&M University-Corpus Christi.

José García when he was a teacher at the Colegio Normal de Tamaulipas in Ciudad Victoria, Mexico. Courtesy García Papers, Special Collections & Archives, Bell Library, Texas A&M University-Corpus Christi.

Hector P. García in a borrowed suit for his graduation from the University of Texas, Galveston Medical School in 1940. Courtesy García Papers, Special Collections & Archives, Bell Library, Texas A&M University-Corpus Christi.

Hector (*2nd from right*) as a second lieutenant in the Civilian Military Training Corp at Camp Bullis in the summer of 1935. Companions unidentified. Courtesy García Papers, Special Collections & Archives, Bell Library, Texas A&M University-Corpus Christi.

Hector as a young military doctor during World War II. Courtesy García Papers, Special Collections & Archives, Bell Library, Texas A&M University-Corpus Christi.

Hector (*far right*) with several indigent patients in North Africa during World War II. Courtesy García Papers, Special Collections & Archives, Bell Library, Texas A&M University-Corpus Christi.

Wanda and Hector pose for a picture on the way to a friend's wedding in 1948. Courtesy García Papers, Special Collections & Archives, Bell Library, Texas A&M University-Corpus Christi.

Picture of Hector and family taken by photographer of the *Forum News Bulletin* in January 1959. *Left to right:* Adriana, Hector, Jr., Wanda, Hector and Wanda Daisy. Missing is the smallest child, Susana Patricia. Courtesy García Papers, Special Collections & Archives, Bell Library, Texas A&M University-Corpus Christi.

Pete Hernández (*center*) with two of his attorneys, Gustavo García (*left*) and John J. Herrera (*right*), during the case that provided Mexican Americans protection under the 14th Amendment to the Constitution. Courtesy García Papers, Special Collections & Archives, Bell Library, Texas A&M University-Corpus Christi.

Mother's Day celebration activity in the barrio co-sponsored by the Forum. *Left to right:* Saba González, Rosa González, Mr. & Mrs. Cecil Burney, Hector and unidentified participants. Courtesy García Papers, Special Collections & Archives, Bell Library, Texas A&M University-Corpus Christi.

Robert F. Kennedy featured speaker at the American G.I. Forum national convention in Chicago, in 1963. *Left to right:* Hector, James De Anda, Kennedy and José Alvarado. Courtesy García Papers, Special Collections & Archives, Bell Library, Texas A&M University-Corpus Christi.

Hector testifying before the Texas Advisory Commission to the U.S. Commission on Civil Rights in 1965. Here he made his controversial statement that "Texas is not worth fighting for." Courtesy García Papers, Special Collections & Archives, Bell Library, Texas A&M University-Corpus Christi.

Hector visits President Lyndon B. Johnson in the White House in
1967 during a discussion of a White House Conference on Mexican
Americans. Courtesy García Papers, Special Collections & Archives,
Texas A&M University-Corpus Christi.

Group of students accompany Hector during a "sit-in" protesting the Corpus Christi School District's refusal to provide transportation to Mexican American students involved in school desegregation. Courtesy García Papers, Special Collections & Archives, Texas A&M University-Corpus Christi.

Ronald Reagan congratulates Hector P. García after conferring upon him the Presidential Medal of Freedom for his civil rights activities. It was a bittersweet moment for Hector. Courtesy García Papers, Special Collections & Archives, Texas A&M University-Corpus Christi.

Hector lays wreath on Felix Longoria's tomb during a ceremony on March 28, 1989. Unidentified individual stands next to Hector. Courtesy García Papers, Special Collections & Archives, Texas A&M University-Corpus Christi.

From the Halls of
D.C. to the Barrios of Aztlán

The difference in strategy among PASO leaders led to conflict, but more important it revealed that the reformers were drifting apart. Friends were fighting with friends and this was causing division within the movement." Idar's assessment was apt as he explained in a letter to Bob Sánchez on June 18, 1963: "All that PASO has done is ruin friendships and tarnish leaders." In his mind, Mexican Americans were simply not ready to engage in the kind of partisan politics that would allow them to play hardball. There simply was not enough unity or ideological consistency among the reformers. There was, however, an abundance of independence and feelings too sensitive to make the kind of compromises necessary to forge a strong organization.

The PASO debacle also revealed that many reformers, including Hector, had expected wholesale victories. They believed that this short-term unity had brought together the best that the barrio had to offer. Since most members were veterans of small but significant victories, bringing them together meant the potential for major successes. But few of the leaders in PASO, with the exception of Peña, were elected officials with a track record of successful political campaigns. There were also few state and national politicians who were committed to Mexican American reform or who felt a great dependence on barrio votes. The tremendous success of the Viva Kennedy clubs had given Mexican American reformers a false sense of strength, and unity lasted only until the reality of their weaknesses became apparent.

It is likely that Hector was taken aback by the quick demise of the organization and by how little was accomplished. In all fairness to PASO, the organization's impact would eventually be felt in the rise of the Chicano Movement. More research needs to be done on PASO to assess its legacy, but it is easy to see why in its immediate aftermath there was little optimism. The organization continued for several more years, and Hector again befriended its leaders, but it would not be an important part of his agenda. Hector decided to continue with his Forum activities, but he also decided that he now had a friend in the White House—Lyndon Johnson,—a real friend who had been there from the very beginning and was a fellow Texan.

The tall Texan had been Hector's choice for president before the Democrats had selected the senator from Massachusetts. Yet, Peña and other liberal Mexican American reformers had strong doubts about Johnson as a favorite-son choice from Texas from the beginning. In 1959, Peña had told the state Democrats that a Johnson favorite-son candidacy was premature. "I believe first we must decide what we stand for; and then we must fit our selection of favorite son to a strong liberal platform." But Hector, ever grateful for Johnson's intervention in the Longoria case and his subsequent assistance in minor situations, had jumped on Johnson's bandwagon early. Not only did he support the Texas senator, but he also set out to win over other Mexican American reformers not only in Texas but across the country.

At his own expense, Hector undertook a trip through the Southwest to poll Mexican American leaders on their presidential choices and to convince them to support Johnson. What he found disappointed him. Johnson had relied on party leaders to promote his candidacy while Kennedy's grassroots organization had captured the masses. He also found that most Mexican American leaders favored Kennedy. Others were horrified with Hector's support of Johnson. Most considered the Texan another southern bigot. Most did not remember his support of Roosevelt's New Deal and understood little of his Machiavellian work with Mexican American reformers in Texas. They simply saw him as either a member of the southern bloc or an opportunist who ran the U.S. Senate with an iron hand. Hector changed only a few minds, but he did write Johnson a very frank report telling him that he was in trouble with Mexican American liberals.

During the fall campaign, Hector emphasized his continuing, strong support for Johnson. But the relationship between the two men was anything but neatly reciprocal. As evidenced earlier, Johnson had not been as committed to Hector as Hector had been to him. In fact, their relationship had seen its ups and downs throughout the 1950s. Johnson had failed to support the ban on the Bracero Program, had voted against expanding the Border Patrol, and had established his own Mexican American alliances to counter the Forum and Hector's influence. But he had remained courteous enough and was there when Hector's crusades coincided with his own political actions. Johnson liked Hector, but the new president's loyalties were always first to his own political motives.

Hector's commitment to Johnson troubled some of his own friends and would also disturb future activists. But Hector understood that in Johnson's Machiavellian politics, room existed for Mexican American concerns. Maybe he foresaw what few others could: Johnson was a true New Dealer who had simply been biding his time to come out of the closet when he could do so expediently. It is also likely that Johnson's moderate-to-liberal political orientation paralleled that of Hector. Both believed in an active government, in civil rights, in a strong foreign policy, and in political patronage. They were both self-made men with domineering fathers and aristocratic wives, and both believed that they were *called* to do great things. Both also saw their leadership being challenged by younger, less experienced men.

Each was attractive to the other, but in different ways. For Hector, the relationship was one of friends, of fellow travelers in the work of civil rights. While never developing too many close, intimate friendships, Hector had the ability to develop intense "distant" relationships, which he fashioned in his own image. Hector thought for both himself and the person he sought to befriend. Hector could easily go from talking politics to talking about private issues. For example, in a letter dated May 7, 1957, Hector asked Johnson's advice on a professional matter. He wanted to construct an office building in which he could house his office, a pharmacy, three rental units, a dental office, and a meeting hall for the Forum. Hector could try to secure a loan but admitted some concern that he might not get the credit. "In case I am not able to secure this loan," asked Hector, "couldn't I get some help because being (sic) that I am a veteran, and if not then what do you suggest I do." Johnson, never having worked much in the world out-side politics had no good advice to give. He also did not see relation-ships in intimate terms. All was political.

Johnson saw his relationship with Hector through a political lense. But Johnson also made politics personal, and thus he could befriend Hector while avoiding a total commitment to the Mexican American reform agenda. His experience with Mexican Americans in Texas provided him a perspective that few politicians elsewhere had. His work with them in Cotulla as a schoolteacher, and his political alliances with their power brokers and *políticos* in South Texas and the Rio Grande Valley allowed him to feel at ease among them most of the time. The fact that he saw them as a supportive constituency, rather than a powerful interest group, allowed him to pick and choose their issues. He understood that most of them had nowhere else to go in Texas. Few politicians supported their issues, and the more liberal Texans had a tendency to be overly condescending. And if reformers hated anything, it was either outright disdain or condescension. They could put up with some form of paternalism, because they understood the asymmetric relationship in Texas politics, but they always assumed that one could speak frankly to one's political godfather. Condescension, however, did not imply any kind of relationship, except one of subservience.

Johnson offered political companionship. It was not outright friendship nor alliance, but it was a relationship explicitly supportive when agreement on the issues could be reached. This meant that Mex-ican Americans had to search for the points of commonality and sim-ply ignore the differences. But this difference did not need to be kept in private. Mexican American reformers, with Hector being the chief one among them, did not hesitate to criticize the former majority leader. And the vice president did not hesitate to ignore their pleas when disagreement prevailed on the issues. This was particularly true of Hector's demands. The Texas doctor filled up his file cabinets with requests, both personal and political, that kept Johnson abreast of what concerned Mexican American leaders. More importantly, Hec-tor's letters, pleas, and demands allowed Johnson to feel connected with the one community of reformers that stood by him the longest.

Hector's attachment to Johnson would be rewarded in a manner that the Kennedy administration could never have done. He was not their type. For Johnson, Hector represented Mexican American reform. Sánchez and Peña never trusted or liked Johnson, and Alonso and Canales never developed strong ties to him. The other young Mexican American turks simply could not deliver the votes. They were also more political and, in Johnson's view, more likely to favor the Kennedy-type liberals instead of the practical liberalism that he espoused. In Texas, he could count on two very loyal supporters, Hector and Congressman González.

When Johnson came into office, Hector believed that he now had a friend and ally in the White House. After all, the vice president had invited him and Cleotilde to the ranch for a barbecue and a visit. The Kennedys had rarely invited him to the White House. Also, Hector understood that Johnson had much more liberalism in him when he knew that he was in control. Hector, more than most Mexican American reformers, believed that New Deal sentiments ran in Johnson's blood. But it was Johnson's experience living with Mexican Americans and teaching them that seemed to endear him to Hector. One of Johnson's assistants believed that the president did remember and cherished the experience. "He would use [the Cotulla experience] in a stump speech or when he was trying to persuade a member of Congress . . . trying to sell the war on poverty or . . . talk about the importance of education . . . or the imperatives of democracy," said presidential assistant Bill Moyers years later.

This war on poverty and his public commitment to making things better for all Americans resounded with Hector. When Johnson called on a University of Michigan audience to "join in the battle to give every citizen the full equality which God enjoins and the law requires," Hector responded with an offer of help. "We can be of great help to you," he wrote the president. "We have a lot of qualified, experienced men . . . in approximately twenty states." Other Forum leaders offered to meet with administration officials to provide advice and to point out where current programs were deficient because they only concentrated on African Americans. The Forum also had hopes of getting funding for a new job training program, as it sought to expand its agenda beyond organizing chapters and protesting injustices. This was, for many, a way in which the organization was undertaking a "spirit" of cooperation with the government and taking social reform one step further by providing skills for upward mobility.

One of the first fruits of this new relationship with the administration turned out to be the repeal of the Bracero Program. While Kennedy had spoken against the program and sought its demise, it was Johnson who followed through on this promise. Johnson, in the view of Forum leaders, had stopped being a Texan and become the president of *all* the United States. He did not need, some believed, to curry the favor of conservatives. In Idar's view, the president "went all out" to end the program. In December 1963, Congress, which had withstood pressure from Mexican Americans, liberals, and some unions, succumbed to the new added pressure of the administration and voted to end the labor agreement with Mexico.

According to historian Julie Pycior, Mexican American leaders felt included in national policy-making discussions as never before. They believed they had an impact in shifting concerns over civil rights and discrimination from a strict focus on African Americans to other minorities, particularly Mexican Americans. Almost immediately they saw a greater access to employment in the government with this administration than under Kennedy's. In a matter of one year, from June 1964 to June 1965, nearly 2,000 Mexican Americans found jobs in the federal workforce. They also helped create the Community Relations Service Board of the Department of Justice to help in the fight against law enforcement brutality. This was a historic first for Mexican Americans. Never in the past had Mexican Americans been the focus nor the impetus for the establishment of a major federal agency.

Before Mexican American leaders were able to completely define their new agenda with the administration, however, they had to guarantee its existence. The first full year of the Johnson administration focused on the reelection of the president. Trying to ride the success of the Viva Kennedy clubs, Mexican American leaders suggested a Viva Johnson extension of the campaign. The president agreed and brought Vicente Ximenes from Ecuador, where he was on assignment for the State Department, to head the Viva Johnson campaign. In all, about 300 clubs were formed and millions of pieces of literature were disseminated in both English and Spanish. This effort, unlike the one in 1960, had full access to the major campaign, had paid staff positions, and had a large budget.

Yet, the Viva Johnson campaign proved to be less an opportunity to promote Mexican American issues than the Viva Kennedy effort. No statement came out about Mexican American concerns as there had been during the Kennedy campaign. Being tied to and regulated by the national campaign organization, the Viva Johnson leaders were not in a position to establish their own agenda. This did not mean that leaders like Hector were not enthusiastic nor that they did not promote some of their own issues. It simply meant that they were now under obligation to follow the major campaign's lead and to avoid those issues that might cause problems for the president. While Johnson might have been seen as the "American president" and not the Texan senator by some Mexican Americans, the president still felt beholden to his conservative friends. Johnson, confident of victory, nevertheless worked hard to maintain his coalition of liberals and Southern conservatives intact. For him, politics revolved around political coalitions, and governing required keeping several different constituencies happy.

The victory in November heartened Hector. He congratulated the president and told him that he was destined to be a great president, the Mexican American's president. Other exuberant supporters like Ximenes wanted to keep the Viva Johnson organization much in the way that earlier leaders had wanted to maintain the Viva Kennedy clubs. But the administration had other ideas. It quickly dismantled the clubs and sent Ximenes back to the State Department. In time, Mexican American leaders came to realize what many in Johnson's staff knew: the president liked to help ethnic Americans as long as he could keep them at a distance. In this, he mirrored many other Texans and southerners whose racial views might be tolerant but who still shared some of their countrymen's discomfort with those different from them.

Johnson's personal ambivalence toward close contact with Mexican Americans did not, however, restrain him from seeking to include them in his administration and in the federal bureaucracy. He definitely wanted to have them in government jobs and he wanted them included in the War on Poverty. He also sought to include them in the rhetorical discussion on civil rights. When he introduced the voting rights bill to Congress in March 1965, after state troopers had attacked a march led by the Rev. Martin Luther King in Selma, he again referred to Cotulla: "It never occurred to me in my fondest dreams that I might have a chance to help the [Cotulla youth and others like them]. But now I have that chance."

The Great Society legislation and the programs that came out of the War on Poverty created the kind of opening in government that no Mexican American reformer had ever experienced before. Lupe Anguiano, a women's advocate and a young reformer at the time, saw those days as exciting. For her and others, especially those who were too young to remember the struggles of the past, these were the best of times. Government seemed to offer them an opportunity to work for their communities. They found many federal officials conscious, if not completely sensitive, to the needs of the barrios across the nation. With the development of Community Action Programs, which allowed citizen input into federal poverty programs, Mexican American leaders in the government believed that the nation was finally listening. More important for them, the Johnson administration was institutionalizing reform, and the Mexican Americans were getting paid for the very thing they wanted to do with their lives.

As Mexican American reformers participated in the War on Poverty programs, they became conscious of just how many agencies had an effect on their lives and those of many others in the barrio. Given their enthusiasm for full participation, they became highly sensitive to their absence from numerous federal agencies and commissions. Having been brought into the national arena outside the traditional process, where paying the price politically or economically was the norm, they saw no deficiencies in their experience, knowledge, or political capital. Thus, they demanded the same consideration for appointments to government jobs as other, more integrated groups did.

Mexican American leaders also became hypersensitive as to "who" got the appointments. LULAC National President Alfred Hernández accused Hector and the Forum of engaging in a "one-way dialogue" with the administration. Every group sought inclusion even though many had never spent the time nurturing the relationship with Johnson that Hector had. Some had supported John Kennedy over Johnson and were even now more partial to Robert F. Kennedy than the president. Still, they believed that inclusion had nothing to do with politics and everything to do with the fact that they represented a Mexican American constituency in their area. They thus demanded government posts for their followers.

Hector, a more experienced veteran of the appointment wars, was sensitive to the demands. He continued to believe that the administration had an obligation to include Mexican Americans in government and in the agencies that affected the lives of most Mexican Americans. Along with others, Hector wrote an undated letter titled "Personal" to Johnson, accusing his administration of ignoring Mexican Americans in making federal appointments and in allocating resources. These leaders were conscious of what had been done but their gratitude was tempered by the obvious disparity between what their community received and what African Americans obtained from the federal government. They realized that there were few advocates nationally who had the same commitment to their issues as the seemingly hundreds, maybe thousands of white Americans who spoke, legislated, and promoted issues on behalf of African Americans.

There were some Mexican American leaders such as Félix Tijerina of LULAC, who were prejudiced against "negroes." But not all concerns with the black-brown disparity had their basis on racial feelings. There were many Mexican Americans who believed that the nation had tunnel vision when it came to civil rights and the War on Poverty. In the eyes of men like Hector, Mexican Americans were suffering just as badly as African Americans. While lynching did not present a problem for Mexican Americans as it did for African Americans, police brutality still did. Segregation continued to hamper their education, and the statistics on diseases in the barrio as well as those on housing, sanitation, and employment were just as bad if not worse in some areas. Lack of representation compounded the problems. Slightly naive about what it took to eliminate poverty, discrimination, and illiteracy, some of these leaders, Hector included, believed that the problems of African Americans were on their way to being solved.

Hector must have also realized that the political landscape did not look as promising. Johnson, who would serve another four years, had proved to be the only politician with any kind of commitment to Mexican American issues. Vice President Hubert Humphrey also had a good civil rights record, and Robert F. Kennedy seemed to be making a commitment to listen. But beyond those elected officials, there were few others who showed any understanding or sensitivity to the plight of the Mexican American community. Texas conservative politicians, headed by John Connally, seemed to have retrenched in their attitudes, and liberals like Ralph Yarborough only wanted Mexican Americans as a supportive constituency. Mexican Americans, thus, had to move quickly to consolidate their position and to become a permanent fixture in government and in civil rights circles.

While some Mexican American leaders talked of coalitions with African Americans there were few effective alliances. Hector had called for an alliance with African Americans during the early PASO years, but even he did not make inroads in that direction. The reality was that Hector, probably still the most significant Mexican American reformer of the time, never developed close relationships with African American leaders. While he did meet a number of African American civil rights leaders during his trips to Washington, D.C. and during a number of conferences and gatherings, he formed no special relationships with them. He would never really know Martin Luther King nor would he participate in some of the major civil rights events of the 1960s.

It is hard to explain why Hector did not befriend African American civil rights leaders. There is no document or personal remembrance that indicates that he held prejudices against them. He sympathized with those in South Texas who suffered segregation and who were discriminated against by his own people. And as mentioned above, he had even called for coalitions with them. The reasons for this lack of relationships may have been twofold. One, Hector saw the African American civil rights movement as much more advanced and sophisticated than the one being waged in the barrio. As with the case of the Teamsters, he feared co-optation and the loss of the leadership of the movement. This co-optation would maintain a simple black-white dichotomy in federal policy-making. Second, Hector as well as some of the older reformers were concerned with the more militant nature of some black civil rights leaders. As late as 1967, the Forum was still passing resolutions that denounced civil disobedience as a legitimate form of protest.

Hector sat on the fine line between respectable and dignified protest and civil disobedience. His own rhetoric had often been confrontational and his actions had often bordered on disobedience. He was not shy about challenging those policies and laws that he deemed unfair or morally reprehensible, and he had already praised the sit-ins occurring in the South. But Hector always seemed more comfortable when *he* was doing the "militating." It was not just a matter of being the leader; he wanted control. But he wanted that control because he felt that only he knew how far to go. He did not trust others to know how to agitate aggressively without crossing the line of propriety. In his mind, when he called his country unfair and unjust, it was within a context that already assumed that this was the most democratic and fairest nation in the world. Calling on his homeland to be kinder and more inclusive was part of the process of making America greater. He believed others simply threw out accusations and demeaned the nation without first having made a commitment to love it like he did.

Most Mexican American reformers were simply asking for a bigger piece of the pie. They feared, as did Hector, that the slices were going fast and Mexican Americans were in danger of losing their share. Their participation in government now provided them a sense of urgency as program monies and positions were either going to African Americans or to Anglo Americans committed to the issues of the ghetto and not the barrio. Sensing that potential loss of place at the poverty-fighting table, they angrily demanded to be included, consulted, and appointed. They also demanded to be heard. Thus, Hector and others urged the president to call a White House conference on Mexican American issues. This had already been done for African Americans.

Johnson reacted angrily to assertions that he had ignored Mexican Americans in his policies and appointments. During the election his campaign staff, led by Ximenes, had proudly pointed out his achievements in including Mexican Americans in the government and in the War on Poverty programs. No president in history could claim so many appointments and so many programs dedicated to the betterment of the barrios. Frustrated, he scribbled on the letter from Hector and others that the allegations were not true. He even mockingly designated Hector as a presidential assistant. Still, always the politician, he agreed to meet with Mexican American leaders at the White House, but only a few, and he made sure to avoid calling the meeting a White House conference.

On May 26, 1966, Hector led a delegation of leaders from the Forum, LULAC, and MAPA (of California) to the White House. But before doing so, these leaders met with others not invited in order to prepare an agenda. Those not included in the White House meeting wanted Hector and the other organization leaders to "demand" the president's attention to Mexican American problems. Hector, uncomfortable with the tone of the more militant members, told them, "No, you don't call them demands." Seeing a historic opportunity to speak to the president in his own residence, he believed that much could be accomplished if they spoke assertively but with respect. After all, this was a friend in the White House. More importantly, Hector knew that one did not speak to this Texas giant with disrespect. He would not tolerate it; he had shown more than once that he could be quite vindictive. No, Johnson had to be praised and then be asked for help. He wanted always to feel that his actions came from the bounty of his heart and not because of demands from his constituency.

At the White House meeting, the Mexican American leader praised the president for his actions, but complained that some of the federal agencies exhibited a profound indifference to their concerns. They did not hire Mexican Americans, did not earmark monies for barrio issues, and did not return the calls of Mexican American leaders. Hector and others also brought out the fact that the president had not called a White House conference on their problems. They believed that if federal agency heads and congressional leaders saw the president committed to Mexican American issues they would adjust their policies. Believing that having someone close to the administration could voice their concerns, the leaders called for the appointment of a

Mexican American presidential assistant. Hector added one more request on behalf of the Forum and LULAC. He requested funding for their joint training program SER—Jobs for Progress.

Johnson, who met the leaders after they had spoken to cabinet members, agreed to all the requests except the one for a presidential adviser. He believed that giving Mexican Americans a presidential assistant would set a precedent that would have the White House "inundated with ethnics." After granting their wishes in the style of a godfather, he wined and dined the representatives, showed them several films that highlighted his achievements, and then gave them a tour of the White House. The tour, according to one presidential aide, had the delegates wide-eyed and almost high schoolish in their excitement. They shouted "Viva Johnson" several times and oohed and aahed as the president explained the significance of the different rooms and had them sit on the presidential bed.

Having fought for years to have American society listen to their concerns, they were overwhelmed by the presidential reception. For Hector, this was exactly what he had hoped for when he began working in the barrio and organizing Forum chapters throughout the state. He wanted attention from the highest levels. Mexican Americans deserved all that other Americans were guaranteed, and now a sitting president spoke of responding to their needs. Kennedy had promised but barely delivered anything. Hector also understood that much of the Kennedy "promise" had been constructed by the Viva Kennedy leaders. It was they who took his moderate liberal platform and turned it into a commitment to resolving Mexican American poverty. In Hector's view, Johnson not only said the right words, he also gave the orders for the promises to be carried out.

Still disconnected from other interest groups and political alliances, the Mexican American leaders saw themselves being treated as a high priority. On the other hand, they did not really understand where exactly they fit into the War on Poverty. They also failed to understand that Johnson could be so accommodating even as he was only partially sold on their participation. This could be seen in the Community Action Programs, which for Mexican American reformers represented the best of the social agenda. Johnson accepted them but only if the people humbly participated, praised his administration, and then let the local officials actually run the program. Johnson had a great belief in elected officials, in America's great status quo. He believed they would act sensibly and would serve as a balance to the wild expectations of the barrio people. In true American fashion, Johnson wanted to help but only in an orderly, moderate way. Unfortunately for Johnson, there was too much anger and frustration in the barrio. New grassroots activists were emerging who were not inclined to let their "gratitude" hamper their demands.

Johnson's staff kept the idea of a White House conference moving despite the president's misgivings. They invited a group of Mexican American leaders, expanding on the number entertained at the White House, for a preplanning meeting to discuss details for a larger meeting. One week before this meeting took place, the leaders of PASO, MAPA, LULAC, the G.I. Forum, and CSO met in Albuquerque to prepare their agenda. In it, they called for greater inclusion in the government, an EEOC commissioner, a minimum wage and collective bargaining rights law for farm laborers, and the participation of more women in government. Here, Hector hoped to coalesce all the requests and demands into a workable agenda. He also wanted a person liked and respected by the administration to present the arguments. While this might have seemed like an effort to have himself appointed as the spokesperson, it was also consistent with Hector's experience in organizing. People might gather to discuss issues and they might protest together, but the articulation of the demands and the solutions were best left to one voice.

Other leaders who hoped to share their demands balked at one representative, especially since they viewed Hector as too friendly to the administration. These new, independent, and talented individuals believed that their organizations had something important and unique to say. In a characteristic style of too many Mexicans talking all at once, they all demanded equal access and equal time. The problem that PASO had confronted only a few years earlier seemed to have returned to haunt this effort. Hector wanted to eliminate the problem before it became divisive and disruptive, but he quickly understood that he did not carry the influence he once did. This new generation of leaders suffered from the problems that most preceding generations had. They knew little history—there was no one to teach them—and so they believed they had invented the civil rights movement when they joined it. This was something that José Angel Gutiérrez would say of his own generation of Chicano activists years later. The attitude in both generations developed because things were moving so fast that few leaders could consolidate their power or influence, and new opportunities to advocate were creating new leaders constantly.

At the preplanning meeting, the government officials and the Mexican American representatives agreed to schedule a White House conference for 1967. They expected to convene some 500 to 1000 people from communities throughout the country to discuss education, health, housing, poverty, the military, and women's issues, among other topics. This would be an airing of grievances unparalleled in the history of Mexican American reform. There were those, however, who felt uncomfortable with the idea. Governor John Connally quickly made his displeasure known, calling the potential meeting a "useless exercise." For conservatives like the Texas governor, most of the grievances were known but few could be corrected without disrupting the social order. Having poor people complain about their limitations was like leopards complaining about their spots; nothing could be done about them without changing the animal. And many Texans liked their Mexicans the way they were.

Hector knew that Connally had a great influence on the president. They were friends who had worked together for years. Connally was governor because of Johnson's intervention, and Connally kept conservatives on the president's bandwagon, even when many felt uncomfortable with the administration's liberal programs. Hector tried to meet with Johnson to counter the governor's influence, but the president had already had a change of heart. Seeing the rising tide of expectations and the conflict it was creating for him among his conservative allies, Johnson decided to distance himself from the coming conflict. He told his domestic advisor, Joseph Califano, "We'd better get away from this." Johnson had seen the humble, grateful Cotulla-like Mexican American leaders become just as demanding and loud as the African American civil rights leaders he dealt with constantly.

Having them come together in what he referred to as a "Mexican meeting" was asking for problems. He decided to cancel the White House conference but left open the possibility of a meeting somewhere else.

Hoping to counter the bad publicity and ill feelings of those who wanted the conference, he ordered staff and agency heads to make a greater effort at hiring Mexican Americans for entry-level and mid-level positions in the federal bureaucracy. He also ordered a sustained effort to try to "sell" his achievements to the Mexican American community by publishing literature extolling the administration's programs that were helping Mexican Americans in one form or another. He also had his lieutenants speak to anyone who listened about the president's commitment to the Mexican American community.

Johnson also moved to support legislation that showcased his commitment. One such piece of legislation was bilingual education. Mexican American educators, led by George I. Sánchez, believed that children who used their native language to learn content were also the ones most likely to learn English. In this view they were supported by the National Education Association, which confirmed in a report that children whose language was ignored tended to do worse in the classroom. To remedy the situation, Texas Senator Ralph Yarborough submitted a bill to establish bilingual education programs in every school where needed. Almost immediately, most Mexican American reformers rallied around the proposal. They liked the idea of having their former language and their culture recognized. American legislators were accepting the fact that Mexican Americans could bring something to the educational table. Spanish was no longer an impediment but rather a resource.

Sánchez quickly called on the educational establishment to avoid making bilingual education a remedial course. He wanted a mastery of both languages. Hector agreed and called on business people and educators to see Spanish-language skill acquisition as a preparation for the future; he foresaw that most business in the United States would be conducted in both languages. Hector knew from past experience how effective he had been because of his ability to speak both languages. He had also witnessed other reformers and organizers struggle in their efforts because they had not mastered one or the other language. Not speaking Spanish well was one way to turn off people in the barrio.

Unfortunately for both Hector and Sánchez, the execution of bilingual education became a controversial and divisive issue, even among Mexican American educators. Few educators and policy-makers supported the scholarly approach. They simply could not envision another language competing with English in the classroom. Many, like Armando Rodríguez of the Department of Health, Education and Welfare, wanted to use Spanish as simply a way to get students to be proficient in English. He feared, like many others, that bilingual education had the potential of creating a backlash from Anglo Americans who did not want another national language. Hector and Sánchez fought hard to create a more expansive view, but they soon found that they were not in a position to make much headway on the issue.

By February 1967, Mexican American leaders had decided that if Johnson did not call for a conference, they would do their own calling. They decided that Cinco de Mayo, or May 5th, would be an appropriated time to convene. Quite conscious that the symbolic date in Mexican history—a day of victory over a conquering foreign army—was known to most Mexicans and Mexican Americans in the country, they wanted to send a strong message: this army of ragtag volunteers was aiming to have its own victory. This time MAPA called for the meeting. Johnson continued to resist, as his own anxiety grew over Mexican Americans uniting to criticize his administration. He told his advisors to "keep this trash out of the White House."

By 1968, another dilemma besides Johnson's suspicion interfered with Mexican American leaders' efforts to get the demanded attention. The war in Vietnam had begun to push all other issues off the front pages and out of the attention of Congress and many administration policy-makers. Hector saw this quite clearly and bemoaned the fact that civil rights no longer held center stage. The shift in administration focus to a foreign land threatened to narrow the Mexican American community's recent opening to national politics. Funding for social programs, he believed, would quickly decrease. Yet, while Hector and others saw the critical shift, they were hesitant to criticize the administration's war policy. Few sought to engage in the ongoing debate over the conflict in Southeast Asia. Many, like Congressman González, felt a loyalty to the president. Hector felt that the military had provided opportunities that other American institutions had not. He still believed that the war in Vietnam—and by now it had turned from a police action to a war—allowed Mexican Americans to again display their loyalty, courage, and abilities.

The Forum seemed unable, however, to provide more than a patriotic interpretation of the war that was killing a disproportionate number of Mexican Americans. While some concern had been expressed during the Korean conflict over disproportionate casualty numbers, most Mexican American organizations had stayed loyal to the effort. The Forum sought to do the same during this war. The membership passed several resolutions supporting the war and even staged rallies in support. Hector, as he had done during the Korean conflict, led other Forum leaders in welcoming home the bodies of dead Mexican American soldiers, often providing a color guard, a flag, and a wreath for the grieving family. Hector also managed to get permission to sponsor a trip to Vietnam by a group of Mexican American entertainers to provide some homegrown music to the Latino soldiers. Hector lost himself so much in the details of being loyal that he failed initially to ponder the more philosophical questions being asked by college students and a few brave politicians. Hector, whose war experience had been the "Great War," seemed not able to find a good enough reason to question this war.

Even those who felt uneasy about the war in Vietnam chose to work around the conflict rather than openly criticize the president. Some promoted the military academies as a way to avoid the conflict or at least the ground war. Others encouraged Mexican American young men to seek college deferments. After all, Anglo American youth were getting them in large numbers. This, of course, was a solution for very few Mexican Americans because so few of them qualified to go to college and even fewer had the money to pay for tuition. The Vietnam War, almost across the board, was soon to be a working-class war with the lowest rung of society providing most of the ground troops.

But eventually, opposition to the war became a legitimate option for reformers in the barrio. Bert Corona was one of the firstChicano critics of administration policy in Vietnam, but eventually most of the MAPA chapters in California went on record as opposing the war. Albert Peña, who had, according to historian Julie Pycior, led his neighborhood buddies to the recruiting station at the beginning of World War II, became one of the first Tejano reformers to oppose the war. State Senator Joe Bernal of San Antonio did it in more dramatic fashion when he declared his opposition to the war during a speech to an American G.I. Forum convention. No one applauded, he remembered later. But he also remembered that Hector said nothing and continued to retain cordial relations with the state senator.

For Hector, the contentious debates over the war brought grief and discomfort. Grief came because as a proud veteran, he had served his country loyally and had never questioned his nation's foreign policy. But grief also came from the fact that thousands of young Mexican Americans were coming home in body bags, and so little seemed to be accomplished. While many Mexican Americans still came back proud of having served, many others came back disillusioned and bitter. Unlike veterans of past wars, they were not interested in joining mainstream organizations that supported the war effort.

Hector felt uncomfortable about the divisions among Mexican American leaders. Differences of opinion on the war might have been less divisive had the war not pushed civil rights from the public's attention. He was also uncomfortable with the new leaders arising in the barrio and with the changing attitudes of some of the old-timers like Peña. They had taken to protesting, marching, walking out, and criticizing the Democratic Party publicly. Hector had done all of that before and would do so again, but Hector always believed that his timing was better and that his reasoning was more sophisticated and mature. Most others, he believed, were either following the "negroes'" lead or were hotheads that did not understand protocol.

Hector believed that Johnson may have been an imperfect civil libertarian, but his administration had opened the doors to the White House as no other had done before. Mexican Americans were still too weak politically to force the changes themselves. They needed access to the president and his closest advisors. In that arena they could advocate, be adamant in their demands, and even walk out, but always with the understanding that the spat was between friends. Criticism of the war effort threatened to unravel the relationship between the president and Mexican American leaders. This bond had taken a long time to develop. Hector had staked his reputation on Johnson and he was determined to remain loyal to the end. He knew it was a gamble, but he believed there was still more to be had from his fellow Texan.

This turned out to be the case. Johnson appointed Hector to the National Advisory Council on Economic Opportunity. The move sought to bring the president's top supporters into a position where they could defend the administration's record. Hector quickly moved to get the president to appoint a Mexican American as Office of Equal Opportunity (OEO) commissioner. He suggested Vicente Ximenes, and the president concurred, but went further by creating an Interagency Committee on Mexican American Affairs and making Ximenes the chairman. This new agency included all the cabinet members that dealt with domestic issues as well as the head of OEO, Sergeant Shriver. Hector was delighted by the president's move. Not only were Mexican Americans becoming an integral part of the federal bureaucracy, they were now being placed in leadership positions. Also, not even African Americans had their own agency. It was truly a coup of immense proportions.

Yet in spite of the appointment of Ximenes and the long list of "benefits" that Mexican Americans had received from the administration, pressure continued to build for the convening of a conference. Two reasons seemed to emerge as the catalyst for the conference. First, Mexican American leaders worried that the new militants in the barrio seemed ready to upstage the more moderate leadership. These new firebrands continually pointed to things not done and played on the frustrations of those whose expectations had been awakened. This frustration threatened to undermine traditional Mexican American civil rights efforts and to create a class conflict in the barrios. Hector and others were not blind to the worldwide feelings of revolution, and they understood that many in the barrio would dispute their claims of progress.

These new militants attracted the lowest rung of barrio society as well as the angriest students on campus. The impressive list of the administration's War on Poverty programs seemed to have had no impact on the rising anger. For despite all that had been done, much more was needed. More importantly, the new attention on the barrio—and it was immense in comparison to the past—only served to highlight continuing disparities and to increase expectations. Most Chicano activists who emerged in the barrios had no historical recollection of the ongoing struggle. Their view was that Mexican Americans had never done enough and that their leaders had stood with hat in hand, pleading and begging but never demanding. They had, in this view of the world, simply worked for their own benefit. Just as white youth were delegitimizing their own leaders because of the war in Vietnam, Chicano activists were seeking to undermine the Mexican Americans leadership. And just as Mexican American reformers were reaching the apex of their relationship with the federal government, the barrios were exploding.

The second reason for the need for a conference was that it represented legitimacy for Mexican American reform, allowing it an equal footing in the civil rights movement. This last reason resulted from the perception of most Mexican American leaders that the nation and even most of the federal bureaucracy saw African Americans as the only players at the time. In spite of major reform efforts in the Southwest, the Supreme Court ruling on Hernández, Johnson's more inclusive programs, and growing media attention, most Americans knew little and cared even less about Mexican Americans. Mexican American leaders also worried that if they did not build a national constituency, the attention paid their communities would not outlive the Johnson administration.

The pressure on Johnson to respond eventually paid off and Cabinet Committee Hearings on Mexican American Affairs were finally called for October 27–28, 1967, in El Paso, Texas. But before the hearing even convened, controversy arose over those who were not invited and those who chose not to attend. George I. Sánchez declined the invitation because the meeting had been scheduled outside of the nation's capital. He called it a "consolation prize" at most. César Chávez felt the administration had no commitment to collective bargaining for farmworkers and chose not to participate. Bert Corona chose to boycott the meeting, and so did Ernesto Galarza. Rodolfo "Corky" Gonzales, an important national Forum leader but now an emerging Chicano leader, also did not attend. Many believed he had been excluded, but Ximenes would claim later that he had invited him; however, the Colorado leader had refused to attend. Peña chose not to go but was convinced to present his views at the conference. Other leaders also boycotted.

Ximenes tried to put the administration's best foot forward. He knew that many would be watching closely as Mexican Americans convened and conducted a national meeting with such significance. It was an attempt to epitomize what his generation believed could be done. He brought together some of the best young minds of this generation, who now worked with the poverty programs and other federal agencies, and he allowed them an opportunity to shine as they elaborated the government's efforts to alleviate suffering in the barrio. Coming to hear them and to give them an earful were representatives of organizations from throughout the country who had identified problems and believed they had the right proposals for immediate and specific action. This action point ranged from calls for specific, localized programs to a domestic Marshall Plan, proposed by Peña.

Inside the conference, the delegates listened to not only their own but also to Vice President Hubert H. Humphrey, who wooed them with the administration's pledge to continue to do more. The cheers inside served to drown out the voices of those on the outside that were protesting not only the delegate list but the fact that meaningful issues were not being addressed. Before the conference itself, Chicano leaders led by Ernesto Galarza and Bert Corona had convened to discuss the merits of the conference. They had decided to have their own conference in El Paso, to protest the official one. There, MAYO (the Mexican American Youth Organization), a new group based in Texas, had taken a leading role in developing an opposition. The opposition conference organizers represented a new nationalist rhetoric sentiment that castigated Hector and his entire generation of Mexican American reformers for being "Tío Tacos" or turncoats. Gonzales, now increasingly a voice for disenchanted Chicano youth and community members, had earlier called on his colleagues in the Forum and other middle-class organizations to "live among the people" and to "hear what they're saying." Too many reformers, he felt, had moved away from the barrio and had little in common with the people for whom they advocated. "I'm an agitator and a troublemaker," he had told them. "They didn't buy me when they put me on this job [national board of the Community Action Programs]." For those inside the conference, the protesters outside were the barbarians at the gates, ready to take over the Mexican American civil rights movement and take it the way of the Black Power movement.

While there was sympathy among some of the delegates for the concerns of the more militant Chicanos, most were convinced that by working within the system they were finally getting the attention and the opportunity to make some headway. This optimism would come to a shattering halt when the president arrived. Once there, he made two strategic and almost unforgivable mistakes. First, he brought along Governor Connally and introduced him to the delegates as a friend of the administration. Connally had only recently called this type of conference a "useless exercise," and refused to meet at the capitol building with farmworkers who had marched to Austin to seek collective bargaining rights. If there was anyone who Texas delegates did not want to see, it was this Johnson friend.

Johnson had come to El Paso, moreover, not specifically for the conference but to meet with the president of Mexico to turn over *El Chamizal*, a piece of land that had belonged to Mexico but had become U.S. territory when the Rio Grande River deviated slightly from its course. Under normal circumstances, Mexican American leaders would almost certain applauded the border adjustment; but on this occasion they were more concerned with their own issues than those of Mexico. After speaking to the delegates and promising more action, the president cancelled the conference in order for the delegates to attend the ceremonies welcoming the Mexican president.

The cancellation came as a shocking surprise to Ximenes and the other conference organizers. To the disbelieving delegates, it was another instance of Anglo American condescension. They were outraged that the president had come not to inspire them but to put them in their place. Again, it was obvious to many that the administration had limited regard for their views. While Johnson had done more for their communities than any other, he still saw their concerns as secondary. A large number of delegates chose to walk out and join those on the outside. Their middle-class anger now joined the working-class fury of the opposition protesters. Gonzales described the defectors as "well-meaning, confused middle-class Chicanos who knew they were being had."

Hector had not attended the conference. At the time, he was serving as an alternate ambassador to the United Nations. In fact, the day before the convening of the meeting in El Paso, Hector had spoken in Spanish during one of the United Nation's assemblies. In the speech, he praised Latin American countries that earlier in the year had signed a treaty forbidding the construction and deployment of nuclear weapons, making the region one of the first nuclear-weapons-free zones in the world. He praised the Latin American delegates for their vision and their commitment, and assured them of American efforts to do the same in other areas. The speech, the first one ever given by an American in Spanish, was applauded and praised by the Latin American delegates as well as the ambassadors from Canada and Greece. Arthur J. Goldberg, U.S. Ambassador to the United Nations, sent Hector a note commenting on the response from other delegations and adding, "I want you to know that in undertaking this in behalf of the delegation, you did a service for all of us."

Again, as in Jamaica, Hector had represented his nation with pride and hope. He was proud to have been asked to render such important service for his country. And he held out hope that his actions would reaffirm to the nation that Mexican Americans could represent the United States well. This was the second time that Johnson had appointed Hector to represent the United States in the international arena. In 1964, he had been designated Special Ambassador to represent the president in the inauguration ceremonies of new Venezuelan President Raúl Leoni. During that time, he praised both Kennedy and Johnson for their "use of Spanish-speaking citizens in Latin America." "It is encouraging," he added, "to all of us to be given the opportunity to serve our country." As he did in Jamaica, Hector also spent his time trying to create goodwill toward the United States among average Venezuelans. He traveled throughout Caracas, visited clinics and hospitals, inspected projects assisted by American aid, and toured slums. He noted that his "impressions were very favorable."

During that trip as an alternate ambassador, Hector again revealed the contradictions that were an integral part of his politics. Before Venezuela, he had denounced President Kennedy's appointments, and after Venezuela, he had denounced Johnson's appointment record. Only shortly before going to the United Nations, he had joined a number of other Mexican American leaders in criticizing the president for being negligent in integrating Mexican Americans into his administration. But in Jamaica, Venezuela, and now the United Nations, he basked in the recognition that came from being a "Spanish-speaking" representative of the United States. He also spoke as if this were a common occurrence and as if the two administrations had done it out of the goodness of their heart. Yet, the reality was that both administrations had simply found it easier to appoint Hector to temporary assignments than o integrate him or others into the administration.

Since Hector tended to see the world according to his own experiences, he saw his appointments as the reality of Mexican American integration into the higher levels of the federal government. But he only had this vision when he was "on assignment" for the nation. Back home, in the reality of the barrio, he understood that both administrations had done much less than what his praise had indicated. Hector never seemed able to bridge the gap that separated the loyal patriot from the social critic. He dichotomized his world to be able to be both a harsh critic and a beneficiary of the fruits of a powerful nation. In doing so, he undermined a consistent and profound view of his own country. This myopic vision was aggravated by Hector's lack of a global vision. While trained in ancient history and the veteran of several trips outside the country through military service and diplomacy, he still saw most of the world through the eyes of American ethnocentricity.

He rarely sought to understand what others believed. While on diplomatic assignment, he tended to focus on the disparity between the nations he visited and the United States. He also sought out American projects in the various countries to justify American foreign policy. He did not talk to opposition leaders, did not read opposition literature, and did not question American actions. Only in the case of Mexico was he concerned about that country's perceptions. But this was limited to trying to prove to Mexicans that Mexican Americans were respected in this nation and that they did have a voice. Once, in trying to pursue appointments for his fellow crusaders, he warned that Mexicans would not believe "America had a democracy" if more Mexican Americans were not appointed.

Hector tended to accept American borders or boundaries, whether they were geographical, political, cultural, or ideological. That is why he could comfortably mingle with diplomats in foreign capitals and proclaim American compassion and American greatness, and then come back and be a harsh critic of American domestic policy. Although the American G.I. Forum based its identity on its members' foreign policy endeavors—going to war—it really only discussed and analyzed domestic issues. As former soldiers, the members simply took for granted that American foreign policy was fair and right. They tended to see the Cold War in terms of conflict and propaganda and not in terms of the larger moral questions being debated by the two superpowers. Lacking anyone who could provide them an assessment of American foreign policy, they simply assumed what they did not know did not really concern them.

Hector's lack of global vision robbed him of a comparative angle and so he lacked the ability to place his people's problems within a wider context. The revolutions going around him, the debates on the distribution of wealth, the rising tide of nationalism, and American response to the yearnings of the Third World simply did not concern Hector. No doubt, he thought of some of these issues, because they were all around him, but he did not articulate a vision. Neither did he attempt to use those discussions as a basis for a new domestic strategy. This would eventually hamper his organizing efforts and would cause his stock to fall as Chicanos began calling for a new approach to activism.

When Hector returned to the states, many Mexican American reformers were disillusioned. The debacle at the El Paso meeting had shaken the little faith they had had in Johnson and had made them vulnerable to the Chicano Movement leaders' criticism that they were simply "worn out race horses . . . still listening to the bugle of the past and still dancing to the tune of the power structure for their daily bread." New organizations had arisen in the barrio, and they had served notice by early 1968 that they were the new leaders in the barrio. While they were scathing in their attack on "gringo America," they were just as virulent about the Mexican American leadership. Corky Gonzales, once the president of the National Citizen's Committee for Community Relations and a former member of the Colorado Forum, led the attack on middle-class reformers. In describing one of the last meetings of Forum leaders he attended, he declared,

> They shadow boxed, growled ferociously, pledged undying brotherhood, grinned, fawned over each other and strutted like gladiators. Only there was one thing wrong: they never finish in the winner's circle.

José Angel Gutiérrez, founder of MAYO and later the La Raza Unida Party of Texas, characterized the old reformers as Mexicans with hats in their hands always begging for crumbs. Reies López Tijerina, head of the Alianza Federal de Pueblos Libres of New Mexico, would characterize many of them as traitors to their culture and their land.

The rhetoric disturbed Hector. It was disrespectful, inciting, and immature. But more worrisome was the fact that it was having an impact on the tone of the civil rights struggle. There were Forum members who were swayed by the more militant words. In a Denver seminar sponsored by the Colorado Forum chapter, one Forum leader declared, "If there is violence, the indifference that exists in this community is what will cause violence, not the Mexican American . . . but the insensitive white man who sits in front of his TV set watching Tom Mix shoot *bandidos*." Peña, Corona, and Galarza were blasting away at the politics as usual of the administration and challenging their colleagues to take a stronger stand.

Academicians such as Américo Paredes, Rudy Acuña, Juan Gómez-Quiñones, and others began writing about culture and history that provided a different perspective. So did young faculty members and graduate students who wrote what came to be known as Chicano history. They were quick to reject Carlos Castañeda's "complementary history." They tended to agree with sociologist Ralph Guzmán, who stated after a four-year study, "We found really not much wrong with our people, but a heck of a lot wrong with American society." Or with poet Alurista, who wrote, "Nothing has intrinsic value in AmeriKKKa, but everything does have pecuniary value. Human beings are as disposable as dirty diapers or last year's car."

The Chicano Movement activists, born out of frustration and anger, and nurtured on the working-class rebellion that had always existed in the barrio, sought to challenge and prove illegitimate the world that Hector and others had created. They rejected the American Dream and opted for a spiritual-political homeland called Aztlán, after the mythical birthplace of the Aztecs. They politicized education and culture, and they challenged the protocol of activism by exchanging civility, appropriateness, restraint, and discipline for militancy, loudness, belligerency, and coarseness. More importantly, they cast the blame on Anglo America for most of the problems in the barrio. "The problem is not us. The problems is white society," declared Gutiérrez, the Raza Unida Party leader. Anthropologist Octavio Romano would put it in more academic terms, but he said the same thing when he accused Anglo American social scientists of creating "ahistorical" Mexican Americans. "Contrary to the ahistorical views . . . Mexican Americans . . . have not . . . wallowed passively in some teleological treadmill, awaiting the emergence of an acculturated third generation before joining in the historical process."

The Chicano Movement challenge proved hard for Hector and his companions of the Mexican American generation. Their world seemed to be turning upside down. Hector had fought for twenty years to open doors, attract attention, and build a more civically-minded community. He had served his country well in war, in diplomatic assignments, and in his civic duties. And he had constructed a view of the American Dream that was inclusive of his people. He believed, as others of his generation, that things were changing, although admittedly there still lay ahead a long, hard road. He must have realized that his own militancy and harsh criticism had contributed to this alienation. While he and others promoted their Americanism, even as they criticized American society, more and more people were listening only to the charges of insensitivity. Particularly mindful of the charges were working-class Mexican Americans, who had always seemed suspicious of the middle-class reformers. Within the lower depths of the barrio were people rarely touched by the social programs or even the civil rights campaigns. There were also those who simply did not buy the American Dream.

Hector knew this, but he had managed in the past to alleviate suspicions or to provide hope. After all, working-class *mexicanos* were the core supporters of his early organizing efforts. They had accepted him into their homes, their dance halls, and their churches. Police brutality, segregation, discrimination in public facilities, health issues, employment, and other issues to which he had dedicated his life were really working-class issues. His efforts had always been directed toward the most vulnerable and the most needy. To see a movement that claimed to speak for the less fortunate and that excluded him was simply not acceptable to Hector. He had been there when most of the Chicano activists had not yet reached puberty. He also felt betrayed by those whom he had taught and brought into activism. These "old fools" as Congressman González would refer to them, had lost faith and abandoned ship just as land was being sighted. They were giving up the fight just as victory was becoming more possible.

Hector did not then understand that Chicano activists were not the only ones living an illusion. Mexican American reformers were seeing a lot of movement, they were being heard, and programs were being funded. They confused this with fundamental changes in the barrio. Though much of what they had accomplished had provided a foundation, it had not really changed the situation in the barrios. When they began their fight against segregation, most Mexican Americans were either attending Mexican schools or they were contained within an Anglo American public school system where they were usually still the minority. By the time of the Chicano Movement, whole schools were now Mexicanized and segregated from the other schools. Mexican American students might have been attending in larger numbers, but their education remained poor, and many continued to drop out in large numbers. Inclusion now meant being the target of Anglo American faculty committees anxious to de-Mexicanize them and to control them. The racism of exclusion gave way to the racism of control.

In politics, exclusion gave way to a partial inclusion but that coincided with the rise of condescension and paternalism toward those willing to participate. As Mexican Americans participated, the more they came into contact with the feelings and attitudes of many who felt uncomfortable with them. They confronted the reality that many did not want to see them or hear them. They also realized that, with a few exceptions, most of their electoral races turned into battles of racial bloc voting. While most Mexican Americans voted for their own kind, there were still a significant number who voted for Anglo American candidates because that is what they had been doing for years. Some of these voters had the feeling that Mexican Americans still could not compete with their Anglo American counterparts. On the other hand, there were few Anglo Americans willing to vote for a Mexican American. Henry B. González proved the exception to the rule, but he had achieved this distinction by publicly disavowing any ethnic angle.

Stereotypes in the media and in advertising continued, and academicians kept writing condescending material that continued to blame Mexican Americans for their problems. All of this Hector and other reformers had fought for almost two decades now. Yet, while they continued to see these problems, the fact that many of these leaders had gained a certain amount of respect among politicians and elected officials and even from some in the business community meant that they often experienced less arduous prejudice. It seemed, as Texas State Senator Joe Bernal would say, that there was a "friendly atmosphere for change." But working-class Mexican Americans rarely felt anything "friendly."

Hector understood this frustration better than any other Mexican American reformer of his time. In this, he shared the strong feelings of most Chicano activists that American society simply did not do enough for the working people of the barrios. In a hearing of the Texas Advisory Committee to the U.S. Commission on Civil Rights in April of 1966, he disavowed any allegiance to the state of Texas. "Texas is not worth fighting for," he angrily declared. "We are sick and tired of being abused by the power structure." When asked to define the "power structure," his answer might have delighted Chicano activists, if they had taken time to listen. He described the power structure as a conglomerate of business, industry, newspapers, Anglo Protestants, ranchers, and farmers. These were the entities that most Chicano activists and most working-class *mexicanos* would point the finger at as the culprits for the barrios' condition. Hector knew that Mexican Americans were frustrated and wanted very much to abandon the language of propriety and civility, something he often did himself.

In that same meeting, Hector accused Anglo ranchers of seeking aid for "hungry cows but not for the people." This was in reference to the refusal of Texas counties to participate in the federal surplus food program. He also charged the Southwestern Bell Telephone Company of not wanting to hire Mexican Americans, no matter their qualifications. "We have tried . . . but we are not qualified. We are too young or too old, too radical or too conservative." He warned the advisory committee that Mexican Americans were going to start demonstrating if things did not change soon. "In the view of some," declared Hector, "I am a radical. I am a radical in that I am for equality."

The outburst infuriated many. Anglo Americans responded immediately, but so did some Mexican Americans who felt that Hector had betrayed their confidence in him. After hearing it so often from Hector and others like him, they believed that this nation—meaning Texas for them—was "worth fighting for." Said one college student from nearby Kingsville, "If this is what the G.I. Forum is going to stand for, count me out of your organization, Dr. García." Hometown fellow reformer Tony Bonilla would add to the criticism and declare that he was "proud to be a Texan"; he resented anyone who would divide the state. Still there were others who came to his defense and ridiculed anyone who thought Hector to be unpatriotic. Said Rudolph Garza, Jr., a professor at the University of Texas, "I can't condemn 20 years of unselfish devotion and deprivation in the relentless quest for a better Texas."

This "relentless quest" had made Hector a hero to many, and they were not willing to abandon him despite the rise of a new militancy. While they might look favorably at some of the new nationalist rhetoric and the boldness of the new leaders, they trusted Hector and knew he was on their side. Hector tried hard to nurture that view. He kept a constant pressure on Johnson to do more, and he continued to criticize local officials for not doing enough to push forward Mexican American civil rights. His testimony to the Texas Advisory Commission would be followed by a letter to the president requesting that a Mexican American be appointed to the Civil Rights Section of the Attorney General's department.

> The problems of the Mexican American will multiply and become more demanding unless we have Mexican Americans in your Administration that will understand our problems and will look for solutions and will be heard by you. The feeling nationally is that we are being ignored and treated poorly by your Administration.

Johnson would respond to this request almost two years later, on November 14, 1968, when he appointed Hector to the U.S. Commission on Civil Rights. Hector would serve in that capacity until October 1969, when the new president, Richard M. Nixon, submitted the name of Manuel Ruiz, Jr., to the Senate for confirmation.

Hector knew as early as January 23 that he would not serve a full term. On that day Nixon removed his name from consideration for Senate approval. Nonetheless, Hector used his time on the commission effectively. Through it, he tried to bring the issue of Mexican American discrimination into the forefront, pushing for and getting the commission to hold hearings on Mexican Americans, something it had never done before. He also used his position to take on issues and individuals. Two things occupied his mind. One was finding a way to turn back the tide of militant Chicanismo and the other was to strike a blow at retrenched bigotry. As a member of the commission, he attended protests and rallies but did so as a representative of the federal government. He hoped that this would convey to Mexican Americans that the government was on their side and that all they needed was faith in American institutions. He sought to intimidate those who opposed civil rights by presenting the power of the government in support of changing society. As would be the case, he came to be disliked and despised by both sides.

One incident that proved pivotal in Hector's attempt to co-opt the emerging Chicano Movement in Texas occurred in the border town of Del Rio. There, the county commissioners voted to terminate the Vista & Minority Mobilization Programs on March 10, 1969. The action came because county officials believed that the Vista workers were actually recruiting residents into the Chicano Movement. In this they were partly right. MAYO, Texas' first major Chicano Movement organization, had infiltrated the Vista programs and had gotten its members jobs in the program. With what one leader described as "a job, telephone, office and a constituency," MAYO set out to organize the community. Yet, despite this activity, the Vista volunteers were doing exactly what the Community Action Programs were supposed to do. They got the residents to participate in the execution of poverty programs in their locale.

Val Verde County officials had been some of the most resistant to providing services to their Mexican American constituency. They were also particularly resistant to Mexican American residents telling them what they must do. The organizing of Mexican Americans in any kind of grouping presented a future challenge to most of the elected officials. Already, they had turned back a PASO challenge earlier and they feared more would come, once the Mexican American residents got organized. Governor Preston Smith felt the same way and therefore he asked the national office to terminate the program in Val Verde and to dismiss all program personnel. "The abdication of respect for law and order, disruption of the democratic process, and provocation of disunity among our citizens," he wrote, "shall not be tolerated by my office." The national office complied with the request.

The county commissioners had also passed a resolution—later found unconstitutional—prohibiting marches and demonstrations against the legal authorities. Hector, who had long engaged in a feud with the county for not permitting a food stamp program or the establishment of other social services, quickly called for an investigation of the county commissioners' actions. He also called on the National Advisory Council on Economic Opportunity not to permit the governor's action. The county commissioners had given no "legal reason," said Hector, for the removal of the program and the dismissal of the Vista workers. They had also not sought public input and had made the decision in private consultation with the governor. The governor had acted without a "sincere and thorough investigation." To allow the governor to get away with his action, wrote Hector, would establish a precedent that would allow other governors to do the same with any social program they disliked. He added:

> If we permit a county commissioners court, which is "not a true representative of the people," to pass and adopt meaningless resolutions and then use these resolutions to destroy the representatives and helpers of the poor, then we do not have a representative type of government and government becomes oppressive.

Hector was particularly galled by the gerrymandered county precincts in Val Verde. In his letter to the federal agencies overseeing the poverty programs, he claimed that the three Anglo Americans on the commissioners' court represented about 6 percent of the county's population, while the fourth commissioner, a Mexican American, represented nearly 94 percent of the county's citizenry.

This type of situation was rampant in South Texas and the Rio Grande Valley. To allow the state leaders to determine the use and removal of poverty programs would simply add to their ability to repress their Mexican American constituencies. Politically powerless in the state, they sought redress from the federal government. "If we cannot receive the help of the Federal Government, then there is no recourse for the Mexican American since he has already been a victim of state government exploitation and abuse for over 133 years," said Hector. "The basic freedoms and guarantees of democracy are on trial not only for us, the Mexican Americans, but for all Americans."

The controversy in Del Rio climaxed with a large rally in which most of the major social reform and activist organizations in Texas participated. The march and the rally ended with "The San Felipe Del Rio Mexican American Manifesto to the Nation" being tacked onto the courthouse door. This document reviewed the people's grievances and indicted the city's and county's actions. But the manifesto went beyond local complaints. In the fashion of numerous manifestoes that would appear during the Chicano Movement, it expanded the grievances beyond local social needs. Applying a militantly radical historical filter, it accused the "Anglo Establishment" of stealing "our land," resenting the use of Spanish, practicing racism, criminalizing Mexican American youth, caricaturing "our ancestors," and inflicting "legal violence."

The document also engaged in cultural definition as it spoke of "something invincible in our people" that had sustained Mexican Americans through years of oppression. "It is such an experience of cultural survival that has led us to the recovery of the [magnificence] of La Raza . . . . La Raza is the affirmation of the most basic ingredient of our personality, the brownhood of our Aztec and Mayan heritage," read the document. It changed the rhetoric of reform in Texas from that of requests, pleas, and justifications to one of demands. "On this day," continued the document, "we serve notice on Del Rio and the nation that . . . we are willing to lay down our lives to preserve the culture and language of our ancestors." Conscious of Hector's participation, the document writers did remind those who listened that "thousands of our Mexican American brothers have gallantly fought and died in defense of American freedoms enjoyed by us more in hope than in reality."

Hector would agree with much of what had been said even as he found the tone a bit more militant than usual. Even the call for a cultural rejuvenation was not foreign to him. After all, his father had named several of his siblings after famous Indian leaders in Mexico. The term "la raza" had already begun to creep into the rhetoric of Mexican American reformers, and Hector himself had used it in some of his speeches and press releases. There was in this situation a tension that both inspired and alarmed Hector. Never before had so many young people become involved in their own civil rights. They were articulate, thoughtful, and unafraid to confront the usually intimidating elected officials and their personal bodyguards, the sheriffs, highway patrolmen, and Texas Rangers. That they were not ashamed of their heritage and language surely pleased Hector. Their "redefinition" of the rhetoric of civil rights, however, bothered him. In fact, it must have dawned on him that this new rhetoric was not really about civil rights but about nation-building. While they had interjected "our beloved country" in speaking of the United States, he sensed that not all of the young people there expressed love for their country.

Hector's way to meet this new challenge was to revert back to the organizer and the fighter. Over the next several years he would seek to balance the new rhetoric in the barrio by participating in those rallies, marches, and protests in which there was a cross-section of the community. He would also make it a point to lecture these young radicals. José Angel Gutiérrez, the chief competitor for the hearts of Mexican Americans disgusted with Texas justice, remembered years later "Hector arriving in his big Cadillac" to lecture him and others about civil rights. Over time, Hector would not be welcomed and he stopped going, worried about potential violence and the fact that some Anglo Americans were more than willing to accuse him of guilt by association. In fact, that is what had happened shortly after the Del Rio march, when several Anglo American writers complained to the Civil Rights Commission over his participation. Some had even called for his prosecution because he was "a federal worker." Of course, his appointment did not mean federal employment, and so there was no case against him. Also, most of the commission members admired him, and he had the support of the president.

Along with his organizing and his speaking out, Hector burrowed into his work with the commission. He convinced the Civil Rights Commission to hold hearings in the Southwest to investigate the discrimination and violence that Mexican Americans confronted. This action turned out to be historic, as never had the commission taken time to look into Mexican American civil rights. For Hector it promised to officially record the situation of Mexican Americans in the Southwest. This would be a significant action that would have a lasting effect on civil rights in the barrio. Hector's efforts in this connection paralleled those in which he had gotten government agencies and state universities to document the conditions in which Mexican Americans lived and worked and the consequences these had on their health and social well-being.

The Commission's hearings brought hundreds to testify about the treatment they faced, and about the failure of state agencies and elected officials to respond to their needs. The experience of Mexican Americans in the judicial system, in poverty programs, in schools, and in the public arena were exposed in numerous communities in which hearings were held. As a member of the Commission, he asked hard questions of elected officials, poverty program directors, and law enforcement personnel. He also asked open-ended questions of the complainants in order to provide them the forum to speak openly about their grievances. This forum provided many Mexican Americans a first time-ever hint that their government cared and that their concerns were legitimate. This is exactly what Hector wanted. It was, in his mind, the surest way to counterbalance the rising nationalism of the angry barrio youth and the disillusioned older militants.

Unfortunately for Hector, while the report would carry his name, he would not be on the Commission when it came out. On October 8, 1969, President Nixon, ignoring requests and pleas from both Mexican Americans and Anglo Americans to keep Hector, replaced him with Manuel Ruiz, Jr., a Republican who belonged to the MAPA organization in California. From the beginning, the Nixon administration had wanted Hector out of the Commission, but had delayed replacing him because of pressure from Mexican American elected officials and Anglo American sympathizers. But after Hector helped lead the Commission to unanimously protest Nixon's school desegregation policies in a public statement, the administration decided to move. Thus ended Hector's last assignment with the federal government. Twenty-two years after he became involved in social reform, Hector found himself with little influence in the federal government and challenged for the leadership of the civil rights movement in Texas from both the moderate center and the left.

Lifelong Pursuit of Justice

[McGovern] should have turned . . . to men like you—men who are established in the best sense: deeply patriotic, but determined foes of imperialist adventures—and unnecessary killing; grateful, participating members of the good life of economic and social success who are dedicated to the eradication of poverty and prejudice and afflictions.

—Bill Clinton, 1972

Hector's removal from the Civil Rights Commission ended much of his involvement in national politics. He never again had such influence nor would he work with another president as closely as he did with Johnson. The Republican presidents who served for five of the next six terms rarely invited him to advise them or to participate in any official capacity. And even the lone Democratic president, Jimmy Carter, did not develop a close relationship with Hector. This proved to be a difficult time for Hector. As a lifelong Democrat, he did not find it attractive to accommodate to conservative Republicans like Nixon, Ford, Reagan, and Bush. Only once in his life had he supported a Republican, and that was shortly after the establishment of PASO, when he wanted the Democrats to know they could not take the Mexican American vote for granted.

The Kennedy campaign had created a negative image of Nixon, and the California Republican did not do much in office to dispel that image in Hector's eyes. Like many other moderates and liberals, Hector had seen with dismay the rightward shift of the American populace. The backlash against liberal social programs and government intervention in the solution of poverty left social reformers like Hector out in the cold. At the same time, American middle-class reformers like Hector were being challenged on the left. Young activists of all colors were categorizing the nation's leaders and even the nation's values as illegitimate. Government, attacked on all sides and besieged by the war in Vietnam, by racial riots in the major cities, and by major deficits, moved away from its activist posture of the 1960s. This left reformers like Hector without a valuable ally at the national level.

The Nixon administration did, however, seek to portray itself as sensitive to the poor and the racial minorities. Seeking acceptance or at least tolerance among more moderate sectors of the American populace, the Nixon administration institutionalized some of the social programs of the Johnson era but with a more limited social agenda. It extended the food stamp program and expanded some of the assistance programs to women and dependent children. But as was the case with most social welfare agendas of the Republican administrations in the twentieth century, there was much more smoke than fire. By his second year, Nixon's staff proudly announced that only 300 counties in the whole country did not have a food stamp program. Ninety-three of those were in Texas. Hector, looking in from the outside for the first time in nearly a decade, quickly responded to that announcement with his own take on the situation. In a letter to the president, published in the *Forumeer* in January 1969 and entitled, "Nixon Misled on Food Stamps Says Dr. García," Hector satirically thanked the president for "your great interest in the hungry and poor," but pointed out that someone had misled him about the extent of the distribution of the food stamp program. Only ten counties in Texas had a food stamp program, said Hector, and the state had 244 counties. He also informed the president that the administration's own Agriculture Department revealed discomfort in taking credit for the expansion of the total number of food stamp programs in the nation.

Hector advised the president to check with his own people to avoid embarrassment when the truth came out. "I have marked this letter personal," wrote Hector, "because this is a serious matter and this is your 'responsibility' as you said at the White House Conference on Food, Nutrition and Health." Hector requested a response, but none came. He ended his letter again with satirical praise: "I wish to thank you for your interest in the poor and the hungry once again and I know that your intentions are sincere and good, but somebody, Mr. President, has failed you." Hector followed with another letter on January 30, 1971. This time he protested the petition of a "stay order" from the Justice Department to keep food programs from being established in 89 counties in Texas. This petition came after a Texas judge had ordered the programs be set up in counties with neither a food stamp nor a commodity program.

The Nixon administration played a twofold game. The president sounded the call for more aid to the poor, while his departments sought ways to cut funds, eliminate programs, and resist the expansion of others. Hector saw through it, but he still sought to maintain some form of relationship with the White House. "It is evident to me that they (Agriculture and Justice Departments) either do not want to feed the poor or they do not wish to obey your orders. Which?" asked Hector. Nixon again failed to respond. Over time, there would be few people that Hector came to loathe more than Richard Nixon. In his view, the man represented a return to a past when government did not take responsibility for the welfare of its minority citizens. Hector had believed, or possibly hoped, that the Kennedy and Johnson administrations had created an irreversible safety net.

Hector continued to write the president and speak out against his policies when provided the opportunity, but mostly he became involved in a host of local and regional issues across the country. In late 1969, Hector led the charge in demanding the ouster of California Superior Court Judge Gerald S. Chargin who suggested to a 17-year-old that he commit suicide. The Mexican American youth had been accused of committing incest with his sister. Declaring that "maybe Hitler was right," the judge called the boy an animal and told him and his family that people like him needed to be eliminated from society. He then suggested the suicide.

Hector found the judge's statement especially abhorrent because it reflected the worse kind of racism that people argued did not exist anymore. He demanded that the judge be disciplined and removed from the bench. But one year later, the state legislature, which had the power to impeach him, and the Judicial Qualifications Committee failed to censor the judge, and he was in fact seeking reelection. In a rally in San Jose, California, Hector told a crowd of 1,000, "We don't have a democracy here! The legislators in this county have refused to take a position. They are not representing you." He added that the judicial reviewers were, " a white-washed, racist committee," and then shouted to the crowd, "If it's not so, let them prove it."

This kind of rhetoric from Hector was not necessarily uncommon, but those who had followed the Forum over the years might have found its scathing nature a bit more than they were used to. But the rhetoric only reflected both the frustrations of Hector and his belief that the times were demanding greater militancy. At the rally, he stood among a number of more militant organizational leaders who had begun to lose faith in the system. He also found that those in the crowd wanted action now. They were younger and more frustrated than the crowds that usually attended a Forum rally. They also did not believe in the "system" in the way that Hector did. His involvement was an attempt to show them that those who still "had faith" in the United States were there in the streets with them. In the streets was where Hector had founded his movement and the place in which he felt most comfortable. It was also a place in which few others of his generation were comfortable in this time of corporate negotiations and government social advocacy.

The California issue evolved at the same time that the Forum undertook a national boycott of the Coors Beer distributors. This boycott had begun in Denver in 1968, when union workers accused the family-owned company of discriminating against minorities in wages, hiring, and promotion. Hector jumped into the fracas because Adolph Coors, owner of Coors Beer, was a major contributor to right-wing causes and one of the forces behind the conservative movement spreading throughout the political spectrum. The battle with Coors took almost a decade to resolve and would be one on which the Forum and Chicano activists agreed. As will be discussed later, this issue and its resolution would have major consequences for the Forum and other traditional civil rights organizations. The victory would turn out to be costly to Hector's style of social reform.

While battling discrimination and racism throughout the country and state of Texas, Hector was also busy fighting segregation at home. In the summer of 1970, he testified in a lawsuit that alleged that the Corpus Christi school district segregated children along ethnic lines. Instead of simply dealing with the issue at hand, Hector engaged the court in a historical odyssey that outlined his work in trying to desegregate schools, hospitals, residential areas, and other public entities. He pointed out that less than 10 percent of the schoolteachers in the city were Mexican Americans, despite the fact that the majority of the students were. He also spoke eloquently about segregation in the political arena and pointed out that no Mexican American had ever served as mayor of the city and only one Mexican American had served on the city council. "We have been held down by massive resistance," Hector told the judge.

When the judge asked if progress had been made, Hector replied, "Yes, we have made progress. I can't deny it. But it has been made by force—all the way." Some saw his reference to the political anemia of the community as an example of "sour grapes" because Mexican Americans were not voting in high numbers, but Hector meant to reiterate that Mexican Americans were being kept out of their place in society. After all, Mexican American children were being "pushed" out of school, they were not finding good jobs, and they were confronting major problems in social acceptance. Given that situation, it was difficult for them to participate actively in their community. Without this participation, they had no voice in the way government functioned, and thus the cycle remained unbroken. Without a voice they found no reason to participate, and without participation they were guaranteed no voice.

Besides fighting discrimination at home, Hector undertook to re-energize the American G.I. Forum. Elected national chairman in the summer of 1969, he decided the organization had to build new chapters and to reactivate older ones. This was a constant challenge. Most Forum chapters rose because of an issue or a particular need. Once that need was met or once the Forum members realized they could not win, the chapter usually floundered for a while and then became inactive. One reason was that most Forum members were working-class

Mexican Americans who had little time beyond their jobs and personal lives. They also usually depended on one of the more articulate members of the national organization to advocate for them. As Forum leaders became involved in national issues, they had less time to become involved in local issues, and thus ignored the strategy that had made the Forum effective.

It became evident to Hector that another dilemma confronted the Forum. The organization confronted a problem in keeping the former leadership intact. Many were simply going on with their lives, trying to gain an economic stability that had eluded them when they had engaged wholeheartedly in the Forum's organizing efforts. There were others who heeded the call to government work and found themselves unable to continue their organizing efforts because they were either forbidden by their jobs or because they might jeopardize their upward mobility. Here, Hector saw some of the same challenges that LULAC had faced when some of its leaders began to feel accepted in mainstream circles and consequently lost interest in being the "outsiders." Ironically, as the Forum faced conservative tendencies, LULAC became more liberal in the late 1970s.

Hector faced another challenge in rejuvenating the Forum chapters. Some of the newer Forum leaders were much more militant in their approach than the old guard had been. They tended to associate much more frequently with Chicano activists. They were also more into protests and rallies than into quiet negotiating. They used harsher rhetoric and became more involved in issues of identity and culture than the Forum leaders of the past. Since the Forum had never developed a nationalist culture or a rhetoric of liberation, these new leaders tended to be more loyal to the activism of the organization than to the organization itself. Some came and went depending on how far they could move the Forum.

During an organizing trip to the Pacific Northwest in 1970, Hector told Forum members that the organization had to broaden its scope to deal with the improvement of the social, economic, and political conditions of the "entire Mexican American population in the United States." He told anyone that listened that the Forum "can be the organizational voice for a great many people [who have no one] to speak for them." Hector saw an opportunity to rejuvenate the Forum in times of crisis. The Forum had the track record, it had the leadership, and it had the "right" philosophy. The Forum now had to speak with a stronger voice, become more political and more disciplined. But while Hector heard the call for a more sustained effort, others were less in tune.

The conservative shift at the White House and to some extent in Congress led to a decrease in federal funding for numerous social programs, particularly those that were not directly administered by the government. Programs established by groups such as LULAC and the American G.I. Forum saw their funds cut or reduced, and foundations seemed hesitant to provide funding for social reform. Even the Forum, which had depended on its membership dues and fund raisers, was affected by this shift. By the early 1970s, the Forum leadership began to sense a need to develop ties with corporate America.

The tie-in to corporate America began at the end of the Coors boycott in 1979, when the American G.I. Forum and LULAC, as well as other Latino organizations, extracted millions of dollars to train Latinos in managerial jobs, to provide money for leadership development, and a host of other projects for the two organizations. Coors' contribution spurred other beer-makers and distributors to donate to both organizations. These contributions signaled that the Forum had become one of the forerunners of the "corporate accountability movement" that began in the mid-to-late 1960s. This movement meant to make American businesses a part of the solution of poverty and discrimination. Businesses were asked to provide affirmative action programs, to be accountable for whom they hired, and to contribute funds to offset the reduction of government spending on social programs.

Initially, corporations resisted this wholesale demand for funds by community and national organizations that in the past had been seen as antibusiness. But within a short time, corporate boards saw the tremendous possibilities for expanding their markets and creating goodwill among many grassroots organizations. They soon saw corporate contributions as a way to head off future consumer boycotts as well as negative publicity. For community and national grassroots groups, corporate funding meant the ability to maintain their structures in the wake of government spending reductions. It also meant being able to enter the American mainstream, which was what most organizations wanted. Corporate funding for organizations, such as the Forum, LULAC, the National Council of La Raza, the Mexican American Legal Defense and Educational Fund, and a host of others, meant extravagant national conventions, scholarships, salaries, and legitimacy. For the Forum, it was also a way to influence corporate America into becoming more committed to providing jobs for Mexican Americans.

The chumming up to business had its consequences for Hispanic organizations. Over time, most became much more conservative and less confrontational. The Forum would be no different. After a rejuvenated decade of the 1970s, the Forum elected its first "moderate" Republican as its national president. José Cano, Texas Forum chairman, came to office seeking to navigate the organization into the new, conservative times. A supporter of Ronald Reagan, he was able to develop a more cordial relationship for the Forum with the Reagan White House than any other Hispanic organization. In fact, this kind of flirtation with the traditional "enemy" would have the consequences of maintaining funding for Forum programs and getting President Reagan to publicly announce support for bilingual education, something he had vowed to do away with during the campaign.

The Forum's friendliness with the "enemy" made Hector uncomfortable. The new Forum was organizationally self-serving, and its actions were inconsistent with the actions of the early founders and leaders. Republican leaders were becoming a large part of the staple of convention speakers, and the Forum national leadership was using Forum offices as a stepping-stone to Corporate America and the Republican federal bureaucracy. Unable to attend the 1981 national convention in Dallas due to illness, Hector sent a passionate statement to the membership. In the statement that was reproduced in the convention brochure, he reiterated the Forum's commitment to civil rights and to serving as the voice of a voiceless community.

I hope the organization continues to work for the poor, the uneducated, the elderly and the suffering. During this year and other years to come, [government] programs for the poor will be cut. I foresee more suffering, more hunger and less education for our people. I foresee efforts to completely eliminate bilingual education. We must not permit this to happen.

Hector's strong stand forced Cano to moderate his once strong endorsement of the Reagan economic plan. Unfortunately, Hector's frail health did not allow him to pursue the liberalization of the Forum.

By the late 1970s and early 1980s, Hector had begun a long bout with several serious illnesses that badly debilitated him. He suffered several heart attacks and by the 1980s had developed stomach cancer. Years of constant movement with an accompanying disregard for good nourishment, exercise, and rest had left Hector a frail shell of his former self. The once tall, athletic, and gregarious former military man and social reformer had been reduced to a short, skinny, weak physician who could only see a few patients at a time. Attendance at out-of-city Forum events became infrequent and he left all organizing efforts by the 1980s.

Two deaths in his family contributed to his declining health. Although they occurred years apart, they were significant losses. In the early 1960s, he lost his young son, Hector, when the young man was visiting relatives in Mexico. He had fallen down some stairs and ruptured a spleen. As his only son and the one most likely to follow in his footsteps, Hector Jr. was the love of his life. His death had Hector wondering for weeks and months whether he had a reason to live. Six years later, in 1969, he lost his brother, Antonio, to suicide. The once brilliant doctor and LULAC activist had been charged with Medicare fraud. Rather than face a possible conviction and public humiliation, he shot himself at his home. As was customary, Hector left little written record of his feelings. But he did confide to friends that there were times that he "felt he could not go on."

Hector had faced tragedy before. Even before he left for the Army, he had lost his youngest sister and one of his younger brothers, both of whom died suddenly and unexpected. His mother's death would follow shortly after the young man had died, as she never got over losing two children in their youth. Faustina, as mentioned before, had been Hector's great friend and confidant. Without her at home, Hector would rarely venture back. Her absence probably made it easier for the siblings to grow apart. At the time, Hector had simply done what he would always do: work harder and focus on his dreams. The death of his son only made him more committed. It would be the same with his brother's death. Hector knew no other way to deal with tragedy. But in doing so, he only pushed back the inevitable time of reckoning, when he would have to evaluate the joys and tragedies of his life.

These tragedies affected his entire outlook. No one could go through so much tragedy without being scarred. The response caused a further alienation from his family. Rather than face tragedy with family support, Hector tended to suffer alone. It is possible that Hector gained some of his empathy for his people from these deaths. Hector understood that in the barrio tragedies occurred often. The death of his two younger siblings may well have been classic barrio deaths. In the barrio, children are prone to diseases and accidents.

Combining tragedy with illness finally slowed Hector. His weak heart, his bouts with his liver, and his stomach cancer took their toll, and by the 1980s, he was forced to cut back on his activities. He continued to participate in Forum conventions but leadership was no longer an option. His frail body could not take much strain, and his politics were respectfully ignored. The new Forum leaders were either into the corporate world or they were government employees whose agenda did not involve much organizing at the grassroots level. Periodically, a local Forum chapter protested some unfair practice or city ordinance, but for the most part Forum chapters served as fund-raising units for scholarships or Mexican American social-cultural clubs. By the late 1980s, the organization had stopped attracting new leaders with an ability to rally people or who could negotiate with federal officials. Being able to put together conventions and maintain funding for its primary programs SER—Jobs for Progress and the Veterans Outreach Program—became the most important functions of the American G.I. Forum. By the mid-1980s few people considered the Forum much of a civil rights organization.

For the next decade, Hector became an icon in the Mexican American reformist community and among Anglo American politicians friendly to the Mexican American community. In what became almost an avalanche of ceremonial recognition, Hector received every conceivable award that could be given to a man for charitable service. For more than a decade, the Forum held a founder's banquet in which dignitaries, politicians, elected officials, and Forum leaders bestowed praise and plaques on Hector. The feisty old warrior became the recipient of goodwill and politically-smart recognition from the Mexican American community. Even President Ronald Reagan, a man he disliked almost as much as Nixon, recognized Hector's achievements by presenting him with the Presidential Medal of Freedom in 1984. Gilbert Cásares remembered Hector feeling the occasion to be bittersweet. He was proud of the award and thankful to the president, but he had wanted so much for it to have been a Democratic president who recognized his work.

Hector, nonetheless, accepted this award and many others with dignified enthusiasm, always pointing out that any recognition he received was to be shared with the Forum. Within a short time, he began to see himself as an open history book on the life of his people, even to the extent of developing a video presentation that showed the viewer all the awards and plaques he had ever received. He also lined a wall with pictures of his family and then retold the story of the Mexican American through their pictures and his awards. In the process, Hector developed a history in which all of his family members became an integral part of the struggle and in which most of Mexican American history was connected to his activism. Hector was again trying to create the family image that he had yearned for when he was a young medical doctor going off to war. Few in his family, with the exception of Cleotilde and Antonio, had ever really done much in the struggle for Mexican American civil rights, but Hector saw to it that they got their few minutes in the limelight. This was Hector's only way of overcoming the gap that seemed to separate the family members, whose search for the better life had taken them their separate ways.

This almost pathetic video underscored some of the personal tragedies in Hector's life. He had an idyllic view of the American middle-class family, with its nice home, educated parents, high-achieving children, and the warm and friendly familial reunions. Success and some semblance of affluence were also an important part. Yet, the García clan never really developed into that kind of family. José's harsh discipline and his children's search for educational, economic, and, in Hector's case, social recognition actually left little space and much less time for familial bonding. Familial pride and long-ago familial love brought them together in times of crisis, but the rest of the time they lived their lives apart. Only Cleotilde, deeply involved in social reform within her own right, developed a close relationship with Hector. He came to depend on her not only in their shared activism, but as a trusted physician who cared for his patients when he fulfilled government assignments or organized Forum chapters.

This lack of close familial ties would haunt his own nuclear family. Wanda, ever the loyal, loving wife, would lament the lack of time for family activities. Close family friends whispered that she "disliked" the Forum and many of its members. They took too much time, they drained the family's resources, and they seemed ever dependent on Hector. They also stole Hector's recreational moments, when he often chose to play dominoes with his beloved Forumeers, rather than spend time with his daughters. Family vacations became more and more infrequent as Forum activities became more intense. Although Hector was a charmer with the ladies, he never quite knew how to treat an aristocratic wife and three "normal" daughters. Wanda proved too loyal to demean her husband's reputation, but she did privately admit that her life had been consumed by his activism. The dashing young man with the big dreams and unlimited potential had changed within three years of their marriage. She admired his selflessness, his courage, his compassion, and his "victories," but she longed for a dutiful husband and a stay-at-home father. His quick temper made discussions short, and his reluctance to tell her of his trials within the Forum often made their conversations shallow. Without doubt, his financial sacrifices caused worries that she and her daughters felt should have been unnecessary. She would rarely visit her relatives in Italy and her home, while nice, was not what it could have been. She rarely complained, but learned to live her role so he could live his.

It is doubtful that a more dutiful husband could have accomplished what Hector did in his lifetime. He stood out precisely because he put all his talents, time, and energy into social reform and not into making money, becoming a famous physician, or reading to his children. Helping those around him and making sure Mexican Americans gained their rights became his lifelong obsession. This obsession fed both his desire to serve and his ego. He gave up financial security and professional recognition to be a leader to his people. He loved their praise, their dependence on him, and their loyalty. Being around them, serving as their children's *padrino*, treating their ailments, defending their rights, and calling them to accountability provided him all the avenues necessary for personal fulfillment. In this manner, his obsessions and even his ego proved to be positive, if not for his family, at least for his community.

There would be many social reformers during his time, but few ever acquired, nurtured, or retained as much love and adulation of his people. While others engaged in reform because they wanted to prove something about their people, because they were liberal, or because Anglo American racism angered them, Hector became involved because he loved people and loved to serve them. People noticed that of him quite early in his life. In a letter to Nixon, a former army commander of Hector and at that time the president of a textile fiber company commented on how "remarkable [a] medical officer" he was. "In every country in which we served," wrote Charles E. Rodgers, "Dr. Hector P. García selflessly and voluntarily would work with the local, impoverished natives with the zeal of a missionary."

When he came back from the war, Hector had undertaken health education crusades even before his own medical practice was firmly established. This was at a time before he even considered dedicating himself to social reform. His travels through the barrio with a loudspeaker and his time on the radio to teach mothers how to take care of their children revealed his concern for those who struggled with poverty, disease, and disillusionment. His medical services at extremely low prices or free to those who could not pay, cost him financial security and never allowed him to buy his own building and establish the pharmacy he always wanted. His personal visits to the barrio to treat people continued even at a time when most other physicians only left their offices to visit their patients in the hospital.

He also expressed love for his people by feeling comfortable around them. Many a young person in the barrios and rural communities of South Texas could proudly declare that Hector had been his or her godfather, or that he had been there at their wedding or christening. And many a parent could remember a serious and pained Hector being there to receive their son's body when it arrived from Korea or Vietnam. He always had time to arrange a color guard, to present them with an American flag, and to provide words of comfort that made them feel that their son had not died in vain. And he continued to do that even when the wars had become unpopular and most politicians and reformers sought to distance themselves from American foreign policy.

Many a young Mexican American professional could attest to the interest that Hector had had in them. He found them jobs, provided them a challenge, and taught them to be leaders in their own community. While Hector could be envious, overbearing, and sometimes rude to them, he never took conflicts personally and he would soon come around with a new bit of information or advice. When they were starting out, he showed a tremendous amount of confidence and trust in them. He gave them duties and then he held them accountable. That would prove a great training process that few would have gotten in the outside world. Many owed their federal appointments, ambassadorships, and professions to him. He rarely asked anything in return, except that they remember where they came from. A former Mexican American Texas state attorney general remembered Hector as the first person he visited to talk about his aspirations. "The best advice he gave me was: 'Make sure you never forget where you came from,'" said Dan Morales. "[He] lived his life according to that philosophy."

When others tired or decided that it was time to concentrate on their finances or professional development, Hector continued in the grassroots trenches. One time, an exhausted Ed Idar told Hector he was going to give it up. Hector expressed his sympathies and his best wishes, but he also told Idar that reform required sacrifice and, if the civil rights attorney wanted "compensation" for his efforts, he was very mistaken. Unlike Gus García, who lamented the peoples' constant requests for help, Hector was not burdened by it. One either gave his life to reform selflessly or one did not get involved. Idar would never talk about leaving again. For Hector there was simply no turning on and off one's role as the people's servant. Social reform was not a profession, a hobby, or a "phase" in one's life; it was a lifelong, "relentless pursuit of justice."

This tenacity, however, did not come without a guiding vision. Hector did not leave behind any major philosophical writings, and his letters are not likely to contribute to any expansive discussion of political theory. Even for those studying organizing techniques, his writings will provide very little fruit. Hector simply did not formulate or construct any scientifically based or philosophically coherent set of principles. But Hector did have an enduring vision of what his people had contributed to American society and what they lacked in order to continue to contribute. The vision was shortsighted as it seemed to begin only after World War II. Yet for Hector, Mexican American history had for all practical purposes begun at that time. Confronted by a ruthless Japanese attack on Pearl Harbor, Mexican Americans had to decide whether they were on the side of democracy and would be brave and enlist, or whether they would hightail it to Mexico. While some did return to Mexico, most could not even if they wanted to, as they were American citizens and their families resided on the U.S. side of the border. But once that decision had been made, Hector believed that the process of Americanization had begun. Thrown together with Anglo Americans, they interacted—many for the first time—with them, ate with them, slept in the same barracks, and learned war alongside them.

In the process of this interaction, many Mexican Americans learned that they were equal to Anglo Americans in some things and even superior to some of them in others. For the first time, Mexican Americans were given a fair chance to compete and to learn, and most proved equal to the task. Once the experience proved positive to many, it was a simple matter for many of them to desire that same equality on the outside. Hector also believed that most Mexican Americans had expanded their horizons, as he had. For those educated or lucky enough, officer commissions became available, along with jobs in intelligence, administration, and medicine. Others got experience in driving large trucks, guiding tanks, flying planes, and operating large equipment. They saw towns, cities, and historical sites not seen by their predecessors in the barrio. They traveled far from their homes and felt important. Many matured and found they were either good at some necessary skill or that they were natural leaders. More importantly, they were feeling this way in an Anglo American world, and this was something thoroughly new for most of them.

Without doubt, this idyllic view of military life obscured some of the realities. Many Mexican Americans came into the military with limited English proficiency and few useable war skills. These then went directly into infantry units and combat. Many never received a promotion, and some did not get their medals or only received lesser ones because they could not speak the language or were not seen as citizens. Before combat, many still faced discrimination in enlisted men's clubs, USOs, and in some of the communities in which they were stationed. It would also be decades before the military recog nized their contributions as a group to the war effort.

Still, in Hector's mind, the experience had created a "historical space" in the American narrative for the Mexican American. Hector believed that Mexican Americans had always lacked a unifying experience on which to build a strong civil rights movement. He knew that they had worked the fields, built the railroads, and agitated for reform, but they had done it without the unifying experience that World War II gave them. In this, Hector showed that he could only see history as he experienced it. José Angel Gutiérrez called this "inventing the movement at the moment of joining it." Hector's vision always remained a personal one, and so did his history.

This vision of history made it possible for Hector to believe that the qualities of ingenuity, hard work, loyalty, maturity, and leadership that Mexican Americans exhibited in war were there to be utilized in the civilian world. Because he surrounded himself with war veterans, all willing to share their war experience and anxious to prove their "machismo" in the home front war, Hector's imagined history became all he really knew. Taking this shared history, he made it come alive as he marched to battle against segregated schoolhouses, discriminating restaurants, hostile elected officials, and insensitive national politicians. With his leadership, he found "his men" more than capable in the social and political battlefield. More important, this activity of a select number of veterans in small communities or hotel convention sites, created a compact world in which Hector's words and beliefs became prophetic. Mexican Americans were reacting and acting as he believed they could and would. It was only when he began to interact in a larger arena that he became frustrated and temporarily disillusioned.

The frustration and disillusionment came in short spurts because as a war veteran and a medical doctor, he understood that bad moments often preceded the victory or the cure. He simply worked harder and called on his followers to do likewise. Rather than quit or become angry with his people, he chose to refocus on the enemy and to reenergize his troops. The lesson he learned in the CMTC, when he forgot to feed and water the mules before himself, he never forgot. Hector never again neglected those in his command or those that followed his lead. They were too important to the cause. For that reason, Hector worked to rejuvenate and reorganize the Forum chapters at a time when most national Forum leaders were more interested in negotiating with presidents and getting funds from corporations.

While Hector loved the convention life and the trappings of political wheeling and dealing, he never neglected the loyal membership in the small communities or the isolated barrios of the nation he loved so dearly. In this, he shared a conviction more like that of the Chicano activists who disliked him and the old union and *mutualista* organizers he had supplanted. Unlike many contemporary reformers who established organizations and rallied people to a cause, Hector felt a brotherhood with the membership that allowed him to be patient with them—even as he was intolerant of some of their failings. His association with them was not limited to the official but extended to the personal. That he tended to the health needs of many of those who followed him only made this relationship closer, even if asymmetric.

This type of "commander's" approach created difficulties. The most obvious was that he always wanted to be in charge. Mexican

American reformers in the past had never held together because they had no historical hierarchy and they often forgot their beginnings. While they idolized their heroes at the moment, they quickly discarded them. Hector wanted to make sure that Forum members knew who the founder was and that he would always be the guiding light. This proved possible in the early years, but increasingly more difficult with the rise of new leaders in the Forum. They found it difficult to tolerate his constant takeover of meetings, his relentless private criticism, his organizing Forum chapters on his own, and the public role he played as "spokesman" for the Forum. His quick temper was legendary and often a subject of letters between Forum leaders. Vicente Ximenes, one of his favorite young leaders, once even called him a tyrant. Idar threatened to resign, and others simply left the organization or chose to stay out of his way.

Chicano activists remembered him as a "finger pointer" who constantly chastised them during rallies and protests. They found it easy to criticize him because of the fancy Cadillac he drove, his propensity to reduce Chicano history to participation in World War II, and his habit of dropping names of the important individuals he knew. In one instance, one of the Chicano newspapers castigated him for coming to a rally of the La Raza Unida Party candidate for governor with his signs supporting the Democratic Party's own candidate. The newspaper questioned his leadership status among his raza and accused him of being a sellout. Chicano activists particularly disliked him because his rhetoric could often be scathing and militant, but his solutions were, in their minds, simply more "liberal hogwash." They accused him of having his generation's distrust of younger leaders and their unwillingness to step aside.

Those who looked beyond the annoying aspects of Hector saw a much more complex man. Yes, he could dress down grown men with such harshness that he made them cry. But he also attracted such loyalty that they would often take time from their jobs or schooling to travel with him, organizing chapters or simply visiting patients. Gilbert Cásares remembered, with a chuckle, the times he helped Hector push his old car home when it gave out after repeated use, or the times they spent on the road going to conventions or to investigate yet another case of discrimination. Men, remembered Cásares, would run away from Hector because they knew his assignments meant getting home at one or two in the morning. But once he found them, they responded with complete devotion.

Hector had an almost incomparable ability to call Mexican Americans to action because he could define the issues for his generation in a way that few had done before. People came to believe that Hector not only "knew" the issues, he understood them in a broader context. Chicano intellectuals would accuse him of "simplistic analysis," but they failed to understand that most working-class Mexican Americans shared many of Hector's views. They could not call on Aztec history, Vasconcelos' cosmic race theories, or Marxist ideology to define their problems. They simply knew that they were being discriminated against, their children were segregated, and they had bad housing and low-paying jobs. Hector understood those problems at their most basic level: Mexican Americans were simply not treated as American citizens. Like them, he saw poverty amid abundance, illiteracy within an educated society, and limited rights despite a constitutional republic. He spent little time philosophizing about race issues or lamenting the loss of Mexico's territory to Manifest Destiny, or even about where Mexican American activism fit within the revolution of the Third World, a concern many Chicano activists and other older intellectuals had.

Hector was too much a product of an Enlightenment ethos that developed in South Texas with the arrival of Mexican exiles like his father. Theirs was a very Western viewpoint. As positivists, anti-positivists, liberals, and even leftists, they tended to have a modernist view of the world. Despite the presence of anarchists and syndicalists in the area during the early years of the Mexican Revolution, they did not have an impact on the educated classes, nor on those who would become the barrio's best and brightest.

What Hector wanted for Mexican Americans everywhere, however, was anything but simplistic. He did not just want integration, as some have argued. Being like the "gringos," another charge made, was not a goal. Nor was it simply middle-class respectability. Hector did want Mexican Americans to integrate the schools and the public arena. He respected American ideals and he sought respectability for his people. But those were simply part of a larger goal of making Mexican Americans good citizens, while constructing an American society that was fair, color-blind, democratic, and equal for everyone. On assignment for his government in foreign lands, Hector promoted a vision of the United States that bespoke the image of "a city on the hill." He believed that the nation's government had a direct responsibility to assure that all its citizens had health care, jobs, decent housing, good schooling, and opportunities. Yet, all these benefits and rights of citizenship did not have to come at a cost of losing one's culture or history. Hector felt at home with his people and believed all Americans could do so too.

Hector had been raised to be a professional with independent means. His father had taught him to be a good citizen and his mother to be charitable. But Hector combined both teachings and went beyond the admonition. While he did become a professional, he never attained the kind of economic independence that his other siblings did. From quite early, he chose service over economic rewards. Others might have sought both, but Hector committed too many hours and too many of his resources to his people to ever find a balance. Helping others help themselves was too daunting a task to combine it with becoming affluent.

His father taught him pride in who he was. Hector never forgot that, but he did not let his racial pride become more important than his humanity. As a medical student, he had volunteered to serve not only his community but also poor African Americans and any poor white willing to be treated by a "Mexican doctor." While in the North Africa campaign, he had selflessly worked many extra hours to provide indigent care to those affected by war. It was not simply charity. It was not doing something with his extra time. He had committed himself to that effort just as he had to his regular medical routine with the soldiers. As an Army surgeon, he treated his patients, black, white, or brown, with equal attention and concern. There was no race or ethnicity when Hector undertook helping others. He was clearly color-blind.

Hector retained that outlook throughout his life. His health crusades were for anyone who cared to be helped. He targeted them to the lowest rung of society, and in South Texas that was always a racially mixed group. As a member of the city's civil defense team, Hector scoured the city to help victims of the numerous hurricanes that hit his beloved Corpus Christi. His efforts to desegregate hospitals, schools, restaurants, and factories had African Americans as well as Mexican Americans in mind. At his death, the president of the local NAACP called him a "civil rights leader for all of the people," and greatly lamented the community's loss. In Hector's America, all were equal and all had the doors open for economic and political opportunity.

Hector rarely made foreign affairs his concern. He cared about American involvement overseas, but the domestic front was his main battleground. Yet, in seeking ambassadorships and foreign service appointments for his followers, he showed his concern for American interests overseas. He wanted his nation to be seen as democratic and freedom-loving. Making America a real "city on the hill" was a preoccupation. He constantly chastised national leaders for forsaking Mexican Americans at home while trying to sell American ideals abroad. He believed that if Latin American nations saw Mexican Americans in major foreign service posts, they were likely to believe in American benevolence. Always conscious of his fellow Latinos south of the border, he constantly reminded those who worked with him and those who listened to his protestations, that Mexico [and Latin America] was watching. He told both Kennedy and Johnson that the Bay of Pigs fiasco could have been avoided with a "highly" placed Latino in the State Department, and he admonished them that only Mexican Americans could save Latin America from Communism. The reality of having grown up poor and having faced discrimination, yet eventually succeeding, would provide Mexican Americans the tools to help their southern neighbors avoid the temptations of radical solutions. Revealing strains of ethnocentricity, he argued that Latin American countries respected Mexican Americans more than other Latinos. This came after one of the Puerto Rican appointees got pelted by vegetables during a visit to South America. This, of course, also revealed that in the early 1960s, Mexican Americans were the overwhelming majority of Latinos in the nation.

Still, he sought coalitions with other Latino groups. In the founding meeting of PASO, he called for an alliance with all Latino organizations and cautioned those there to see them as potential allies rather than as competitors. He followed this proposal by working to establish G.I. Forum chapters among Puerto Ricans. He also met with some of their leaders in a civil rights conference called by the Kennedys during the 1960 campaign. Ideas were shared but little came of the contact. Hector wanted some type of national coalition, but he did not pursue the issue because of pending issues in Texas. And as has been seen, Hector did not do well in coalitions. He had an agenda and he stayed mostly to it. He also revealed an uneasiness with the leadership of others.

This may be another reason that he never forged any significant ties to black organizations during the heyday of the civil rights movement. There is, in fact, very little discussion of black civil rights activities in his letters or correspondence to his friends and allies. The 1960 Forum national convention had approved of the sit-ins occurring in the South at the time, but little else had been said or done to forge any kind of ties. This would be the same with most Mexican American organizations, and even the Chicano militant groups had only minimal ties to Black Power groups. A historical divide, that continues into the new century, kept Mexican Americans and African Americans from coming together. Too often their interests have been pitted one against the other.

As noted before, coalitions with groups much more financially and politically endowed than the Forum were perceived as a threat to Mexican American issues. Becoming involved with the larger civil rights organizations threatened a loss of Mexican American identity. Losing identity was unacceptable to Hector. He cared too much for the problems that affected Mexican Americans. But he also cared about his own role within any coalition. It became quite obvious in PASO, and during the rise of numerous new leaders in Johnson's time, that Hector's approach was seen as archaic and that the young turks did not provide the respect he believed he merited. More than ego, he had a great dislike for reformers who did not pay proper respect to those who had come before. In his case, he had "won" the respect of the older reformers and had replaced them at the forefront without attacking them or undermining their status.

Hector's inability to gain the respect of a number of new leaders, his failure to create coalitions, and his unwillingness to accommodate either to the new Chicano activists or the new "moderates" in Mexican American reform put him out of sight and out of mind in the historical record by the early 1980s. Reformers still spoke of what he had "done for them" and how he was a "precursor," but they did not particularly consult him about issues. The Chicano activists, who by the early 1980s were getting careers in academia and federal and state governments, saw him as irrelevant. Or they tended to relegate him to the category of "middle-class *vendido*," which they had reserved as a historical abyss for those who had agitated for reform before the mid-1960s. It became more fashionable to write about *mutualistas*, union organizers, social bandits, revolutionaries, Aztec gods, and *Chicanismo*.

In doing this, Chicano historians created a time gap that has only recently begun to be bridged. This gap has distorted Mexican American history as well as Southwest and U.S. history. More tragically, it has undermined the study of traditional Mexican American civil rights by lumping it together with the study of nineteenth-century separatist struggles and late twentieth-century nationalist/leftist movements. These aforementioned struggles did have vestiges of traditional civil rights movements, but they were not integrationist in spirit, a fundamental principle of the major civil rights organizations and leaders. Recent years have seen efforts by Chicano power movement advocates to integrate into the larger rubric of civil rights, but that is more a political tactic than a historical reality. This does not demean those rights and benefits that cultural and power movements achieved, but these accomplishments should be placed in their own historical time and space and not lumped in with the civil rights movement.

Without Hector and his cohorts, Mexican American history loses not only an important historical space but important legacies and lessons. Hector's activities reflected important aspirations among Mexican Americans. These aspirations continue even today. Hector's frustrations over Anglo American recalcitrance never clouded his vision of what most Mexican Americans that he knew wanted. To downplay that history—as has been the case within Chicano studies—for the sake of presenting an alienated community in the throes of a nationalist or leftist struggle skews the historical record. True, Mexican Americans have struggled in many forms, and nationalism and some form of socialism have been a strain for over a century, but in the end, most Mexican Americans struggle for inclusion or participation in the abundance of the United States. No one represented that struggle better than Hector. His cross-generational and interclass movement reflected an effort by most sectors in the barrio to fight for their civil rights and their place in their native land.

Hector's reform efforts were not without their tensions and conflicts. While truly committed to attaining civil rights for his people, Hector revealed profound contradictions, as did most middle-class reformers. Hector fought hard for his people and recognized them as a group apart but, unlike Mexican activists of the past or Chicano activists contemporary to him, he never defined a cultural or political space for them. Other than the war, Mexican Americans in Hector's world occupied no historical space outside the American narrative. They simply did not exist as a people without American institutions, wars, or civil rights struggles. Thus, in Hector's movement there was no culture of resistance, no new rhetoric, no new philosophical foundations, and no politics beyond the usual.

He understood his people's poverty, but he could not articulate a solution other than more food stamp programs, more job training programs, and more sensitive hiring from corporations and government. He sought corrective measures for his people, but he assumed that most of the time all they needed was opportunity and less racism. At times it escaped him that many Mexican Americans had lived in such difficult situations and seen themselves in such inferior circumstances that they could not compete, even if given an opportunity. To admit to that meant admitting that American racism and disdain went beyond just closed doors and segregated facilities. Given his Horatio Algier personal success story, Hector never saw the need to create racial and ethnic pride beyond the most superficial manner. Cultural identity was not an issue for him. He was an American and he had Mexican ancestry. But his identity really came from his accomplishments and his personal achievements, as it did for most of his cohorts. While he empathized with those in the bottom rung, he never quite understood their anger, frustration, and feelings of inferiority.

Hector wanted to make his country more democratic and pluralistic, but he never engaged in or promoted a larger and more profound discussion on how to accomplish the task. This would have been acceptable from a lesser reformer, or someone satisfied to change the ills of his locality, but Hector was a national player who had the ear of many politicians and government officials and at least one president, something that few Mexican Americans could ever claim. He also had the faith of many of his people. Yet, during those times that he served in foreign policy assignments or as an advisor in domestic issues, Hector rarely articulated a position not already within the mainstream of American politics. He spoke too often as if democracy and pluralism could be accomplished without pain and without major discomfort to those who had little interest in Mexican Americans and other minorities.

In the end, Hector wanted his America to be the same even as it made major accommodations for his people. In this, he was hampered, as were many other middle-class reformers, by his inability to fully acknowledge American unfairness and injustice. Unlike Chicano radicals, Hector did not foster any great anger against his country. Because of this, he never sought radical change. Pursuing justice without pursuing fundamental change was not a contradiction to Hector. In fact, this is what made him so effective during his most active days of social reform. By ignoring the contradictions, he forged his way ahead, articulating the issues of concern, resolving those he could, and calling on both Mexican Americans and Anglo Americans to change the way they saw things. By having a profound confidence in the system, he could challenge so many of its assumptions and structures without having to find a replacement for the "American way."

Hector's life then is the quintessential American story, with its inherent contradictions as well as its successes. When he died at 84, on July 26, 1996, hundreds of old veterans, reformers, and politicians came to bid good-bye to an American hero. There were many others who had been affected in one way or another who came to say thank you. They brought their children to get a glimpse of their past. The funeral attendance may have paled in comparison to the one for César Chávez or even fellow Corpus Christi native Selena, but those who came understood that someone important to them and their history had died. Many came to thank him for opening up American society, while others, less fortunate, came to mourn that they had lost a friend who never forsook them.

Hector would have been proud to see the viewing, the mass, the funeral procession, and his final goodbye. His friends and admirers in the Forum knew his favorite songs, and so numerous bands and choirs sang them: "Amazing Grace," "The Battle Hymn of the Republic," "America the Beautiful," and "The Star-Spangled Banner," the last sung by a Vietnam veteran. Flags adorned the church, the Selena Auditorium, and the entrance to the cemetery. An honor guard of the G.I. Forum accompanied his casket at the viewing, and a military funeral cadence provided the background to his entrance into the Corpus Christi Cathedral. Hundreds of cars made the six-mile trek to the cemetery, where amid his brothers, sisters, daughters, Wanda, and hundreds of his people, he was buried.

Bibliographical Note

As mentioned in the introduction, this biography is the first significant work done on the life of Hector P. García. Much of this work is thus based on primary sources. Still, there are several important works that deal with the organization he founded and with the important events in which he was involved. The first work done on the American G.I. Forum was written by Carl Allsup in *The American G.I. Forum: Origins and Evolution*, the most significant scholarly work on Hector's veterans' organization. Henry A. J. Ramos also does an excellent job of introducing the aims and goals of the Forum in his short, but well-written *"The American GI Forum, In Pursuit of the Dream, 1948–1983.* While much more needs to be done on the activities of the Forum, these two works provide a good foundation for understanding some of Hector's organizational efforts. Guadalupe San Miguel's *"Let All of Them Take Heed"* is still the best study of educational reform in Texas. While San Miguel gives LULAC more credit for educational reform in Texas—as well he should—his discussion of the topic includes the Forum and is yet to be surpassed. David Montejano's *Anglos and Mexicans in the Making of Texas, 1836–1986* provides what this author believes is the best discussion of segregation in Texas, as well as the best analysis of the economic changes that occurred in Texas during Hector's reform activities. To understand rural Texas politics and social parameters, Evans Anders' *Boss Rule in South Texas* is a must. Julie Pycior's *LBJ & Mexican Americans* is the only work done on Lyndon Baines Johnson's relationship with Mexican American reforms. It provides information on important meetings and offers the best analysis of what that relationship accomplished.

The author's *Viva Kennedy, Mexican Americans in Search of Camelot* provides a foundational discussion on the politics of Hector and his cohorts during the early 1960s. *Chicano Politics* by Juan Gómez-Quiñones's is the best work done on Mexican American political activity since the Southwest became part of the United States. Mario T. García's *Mexican Americans* was the first and is still the best discussion of the generational ethos of Mexican Americans from the 1930s to the 1960s. Several new biographies have also come out recently that deal with individuals that Hector knew well: *Mexican American Odyssey* by Tom Kreneck deals with LULAC president Félix Tijerina; *Knight without Armor* by Félix Almaraz is on Carlos E. Castañeda, one of Hector's mentors at the University of Texas; *Border Boss* by Gilberto Quezada is about Manuel Bravo, an important South Texas border boss who knew Hector; and *All Rise: Reynaldo G. Garza, the First Mexican American Federal Judge*, by Louise Ann Fisch, is about one Mexican American political elite who took a different route from that of Hector.

Understanding the Chicano Movement is critical to both understanding Hector's later years and to comprehending why he was left out of Mexican American history for so many years. Armando Navarro's *The Cristal Experiment: A Chicano Struggle for Community Control* is the best work on the two Crystal City Chicano revolts that would cause Hector much trouble and lead to the demise of PASO. The author's *Chicanismo, The Forging of a Militant Ethos among Mexican Americans* is currently the only work done on the ideals of the Chicano Movement. Readers would also benefit by reading José Angel Gutiérrez's *The Making of a Chicano Militant*, which is a view of Mexican American reform activities and politics from a nationalist radical perspective. The bibliography herein provides many other important works that help place Hector in his time and place.

To understand Hector, however, it is important to engage the large amount of material available in the Hector P. García Collection at Texas A&M University in Corpus Christi Special Collections. Unless otherwise noted, the documents, letters, pamphlets, political announcements, radio scripts, telegrams, and obscure magazine articles cited in this study are found in the collection. The only source of information on Hector's youth is found in the collection's oral interviews of Hector and his sister Cleotilde. In those interviews are also found the only discussion of Hector's time at the university, medical school, and military training. There are also several taped interviews done on Wanda, which tell a little bit about their courtship and her views of his social reform. There are also a few documents from the college and war years. Otherwise, there is little on Hector's early life.

Hector was probably one of the most meticulous collectors of primary sources of any Mexican American reformer. He not only kept that which he produced, but also numerous letters and memos that his friends and detractors wrote to each other. Hector was a prolific letter writer, although he did not necessarily follow through on any particular topic. He wrote much, but to many people and on many different topics. Thus, one can get a glimpse of his political character but not necessarily of his ideology. His political announcements or open letters to the Mexican American community can be mined for information on numerous topics relevant to the barrios of the fifties, sixties, and early seventies. There are also numerous reports, studies, and statistical data about Mexican Americans. Given the amount of material, there are numerous books still waiting to be written in those several hundred boxes. Researchers will be disappointed, however, over how little personal material is there.

Researchers would also benefit from the Dennis Chávez Collection at the University of New Mexico and the Edward R. Roybal Collections at UCLA and California State University, Los Angeles. The George I. Sánchez Collection at the University of Texas is also important. The University of Texas's Mexican American Collection also has several taped interviews of Ed Idar, Jr., and houses the League of United Latin American Citizens papers. This work only scratches the surface of the large amount of material available, but it does provide a framework for future work on Hector P. García.

Bibliography

Books

Adams, Michael C. C. *The Best War Ever: America and World War II.* Baltimore: Johns Hopkins University Press, 1994.

Allsup, Carl. *The American G.I. Forum: Origins and Evolution.* Austin: Center for Mexican American Studies, 1982.

Almaraz, Félix D. *Knight without Armor, Carlos Eduardo Castañeda 1896–1958.* College Station: Texas A&M University Press, 1999.

Anaya, Rudolfo A., and Francisco Lomelí, eds. *Aztlán: Essays on the Chicano Homeland.* Albuquerque: University of New Mexico Press, 1989.

Anders, Evan. *Boss Rule in South Texas: The Progressive Era.* Austin: University of Texas Press, 1982.

Arellano, Anselmo F., and Julian Josue, eds. *Arthur L. Campa and the Coronado Cuatro Centennial.* Las Vegas: Editorial Telerana, 1980.

Balderrama, Francisco E., and Raymond Rodríguez. *Decade of Betrayal: Mexican Repatriation in the 1930s.* Albuquerque: University of New Mexico Press, 1995.

Brands, H. W. *The Devil We Knew.* New York: Oxford University Press, 1993.

Castañeda, Carlos. *Our Catholic Heritage of Texas, 1519–1936.* Austin: Von Boeckmann-Jones, 1936.

Chafe, William H. *Civilities and Civil Rights.* Oxford: Oxford University Press, 1980.

Dolan, Jay P., and Allan Figueroa Deck, eds. *Hispanic Catholic Culture in the U.S.: Issues and Concerns.* Notre Dame: University of Notre Dame Press, 1994.

Ferber, Edna. *Giant*. Garden City: Doubleday & Company, Inc., 1952.

Fisch, Louise Ann. *All Rise: Reynaldo G. Garza, the First Mexican American Federal Judge*. College Station: Texas A&M University Press, 1996.

Foster, James C., ed. *American Labor in the Southwest: The First One Hundred Years*. Tucson: University of Arizona Press, 1982.

García, Ignacio M. *Chicanismo: The Forging of a Militant Ethos Among Mexican Americans*. Tucson: University of Arizona Press, 1997.

____. *United We Win: The Rise and Fall of La Raza Unida Party*. Tucson: Mexican American Studies & Research Center—The University of Arizona, 1989

____. *Viva Kennedy, Mexican Americans in Search of Camelot*. College Station: Texas A&M University Press, 2000.

García, Juan Ramón. *Operation Wetback: The Mass Deportation of Mexican Undocumented Workers in 1954*. Westport: Greenwood Press, 1980.

García, Mario T. *Mexican Americans: Leadership, Ideology, and Identity, 1930–1960*. New Haven: Yale University Press, 1989.

Gardner, Richard. *¡Grito! Reies Tijerina and the New Mexico Land Grant War of 1967*. Indianapolis: Bobbs-Merrill Company, Inc., 1970.

Gómez-Quiñones, Juan. *Chicano Politics: Reality & Promise 1940–1990*. Albuquerque: University of New Mexico Press, 1990.

Griswold del Castillo, Richard, and Arnoldo De León. *North to Aztlán: A History of Mexican Americans in the United States*. New York: Twayne Publishers, 1996.

Gutiérrez, José Angel. *The Making of a Chicano Militant*. Madison: The University of Wisconsin Press, 1998.

Jackson, Byran O., and Michael B. Preston, eds. *Racial and Ethnic Politics in California*. Berkeley: Institute of Governmental Studies Press, 1991.

Keller, Gary D., ed. *Chicano Cinema: Research, Reviews, and Resources*. Binghamton: Bilingual Review, 1985.

Kreneck, Thomas H. *Mexican American Odyssey: Felix Tijerina, Entrepeneur and Civil Leader, 1905–1965*. College Station: Texas

A&M University Press, 2001.

Lomitz-Alder, Claudio. *Exits from the Labyrinth: Culture and Ideology in Mexican National Space*. Berkeley: University of California Press, 1992.

Maciel, David R., and Isidro D. Ortiz. *Chicanas/Chicanos at the Crossroads*. Tucson: The University of Arizona Press, 1996.

Marín, Christine. *A Spokesman of the Mexican American Movement: Rodolfo "Corky" Gonzales and the Fight for Chicano Liberation, 1966–1972*. San Francisco: R and E Research Associates, Inc., 1977.

Márquez, Benjamín. *LULAC: The Evolution of a Mexican American Political Organization*. Austin: University of Texas Press, 1993.

Martínez, Oscar J. *Troublesome Border*. Tucson: University of Arizona Press, 1988.

Memorial Address Delivered in Congress. Washington, D.C.: U.S. Government Printing Office, 1963.

Montejano, David. *Anglos and Mexicans in the Making of Texas, 1836–1986*. Austin: The University of Texas Press, 1987.

_____. *Chicano Politics and Society in the Late Twentieth Century*. Austin: University of Texas Press, 1999.

Moore, Joan W. *Mexican Americans*. Englewood Cliffs: Prentice-Hall, 1976.

Munro, Edmonson S. *Los Manitos: A Study of Institutional Values*. New Orleans: Middle American Research Institute, 1957.

Navarro, Armando, *The Cristal Experiment: A Chicano Struggle for Community Control*. Madison: University of Wisconsin Press, 1998.

Noriega, Chon A., ed. *Chicanos and Film: Essays on Chicano Representation and Resistance*. New York: Garland Publishers, 1992.

Pycior, Julie Leininger. *LBJ & Mexican Americans, The Paradox of Power*. Austin: The University of Texas Press, 1997.

Quezada, J. Gilberto. *Border Boss*. College Station: Texas A&M University Press, 1999.

Ramos, Henry A. J. *The American GI Forum, in Pursuit of the Dream, 1948–1983*. Houston: Arte Público Press, 1998.

Rocard, Marcienne. *The Children of the Sun*. Tucson: University of Arizona Press, 1989.

Rosales, F. Arturo. *Chicano! The History of the Mexican American Civil Rights Movement*. Houston: Arte Público Press, 1996.

Ruiz, Vicki L. *Cannery Women, Cannery Lives: Mexican Women, Unionization, and the California Food Processing Industry*. Albuquerque: University of New Mexico Press, 1987.

Samora, Julian, ed. *La Raza: Forgotten Americans*. Notre Dame: University of Notre Dame Press, 1966.

San Miguel, Guadalupe, Jr. *"Let All of Them Take Heed."* Austin: University of Texas Press, 1987.

Sheridan, Thomas E. *Los Tucsonenses: The Mexican Community in Tucson, 1854–1941*. Tucson: University of Arizona Press, 1986.

Shockley, John Staples. *Chicano Revolt in a Texas Town*. Notre Dame: University of Notre Dame Press, 1974.

Valdés, Dennis Nodín. *Al Norte: Agricultural workers in the Great Lakes Region, 1917–1970*. Austin: University of Texas Press, 1991.

Vigil, Maurilio E. *Joseph Montoya, Democratic Senator from New Mexico*. Washington: Grossman Publishers, 1972.

Waxman, Chaim I., ed. *The End of Ideology Debate*. New York: Funk & Wagnalls, 1968.

Whitfield, Stephen J. *Culture of the Cold War*. Baltimore: Johns Hopkins University Press, 1991.

Articles, Dissertations, and Theses

"1971 Convention Resolutions." *Forumeer* Oct. 1971.

"5 Aliens Are Found Registered." *Corpus Christi Caller-Times* 19 Apr. 1966.

"A Giant Rouses." *Texas State AFL-CIO News*, undated news clip.

"A Hero's Return: Bigotry in Texas." *LULAC News* Jan. 1949.

"Adverse Publicity Ires Local Citizens." *Three Rivers' Paper* Feb. 1949.

"American G.I. Forum Asking Valley Quiz." *Corpus Christi Caller-Times* 5 May 1956.

"The American G.I. Forum" and "Wetbacks." *Border Trends* 8 (Sept. 1948).

"Announce Viva Kennedy Club in Cal City." *Advertiser* (East Chicago, Ind.) 27 Oct. 1960.

"Another Viewpoint: 'Peon Labor Not My Type'." *Daily Texan* 21 Oct. 1949.

"Arizona Viva Kennedy Officers, Board Members Listed by Leader." *Phoenix Republic* 5 Oct. 1960.

"Arlington Burial Arranged for Three Rivers Veteran." *Corpus Christi Caller-Times* 13 Jan. 1949.

Arrieta, Olivia. "The Alianza Hispano Americana in Arizona and New Mexico: The Development and Maintenance of a Multifunctional Ethnic Organization." *Renato Rosaldo Lecture Series Monograph* 7 (1991): 55–82.

"Attorneys At Corpus Christi." *Forum News Bulletin* Nov. 1954.

"Back Democrats." *Hammond Times* 16 Oct. 1960.

"Back To School." *Border Trends* 7 (Aug. 1948).

Baggarly, H. M., and Tulia Herald. "Other Voices: The Coors Family Heritage." *Hays County Citizens* 4 Sept. 1975.

Barnes, Bill. "García Hits Texas Law." *San Antonio Express News* 29 Oct. 1969.

Beene, Richard. "'I Don't Want to Live This Way All My Life'." *San Jose Mercury-News Focus* 24 Aug. 1969.

"The Best Newspaper in Texas" (*La Prensa*). *The Journal of Mexican American History* 4 (1974).

"Both Sides of the Catholic Issue." *U.S. News & World Report* 26 Sept. 1960: 74–81.

"Boycott Coors." *El Mestizo* 3 (Feb. through Mar. 1975).

Briegel, Kaye. "Alianza Hispano-Americana, 1894–1965: A Mexican American Fraternal Society." Diss. U of Southern California, 1974.

Broder, David S. "Mexicans Ask Jobs on Nixon Staff." *Washington Post* 22 Jan. 1969.

"Caller's Selections in Tuesday Election." *Corpus Christi Caller-Times* 31 Oct. 1976.

Cardenas, Leo. "MAYO Members Most Active of Activist Chicanos." *San Antonio Express News* 16 Apr. 1969.

Carpenter, Marj C. "'Two Spoonfuls of Beans . . .'" *Mercedes Enterprise* 15 Sept. 1982.

_____. "Two Generations Fought Malaria, Hurricanes." *Mercedes Enterprise* 15 Sept. 1982.

Carta Editorial 2 Oct. 1967.

"Carter Critics." *San Antonio Express News* 31 July 1977.

"Carter Should Find Posts for Hispanics." *Corpus Christi Caller-Times* 22 Jan. 1977.

Castañeda, Carlos E. "Why I Chose History." *The Americas* (Apr. 1952): 476–477.

Castillo, E. "Let Them Join NAACP, Writes E. Castillo." *Houston Post* 9 May 1957.

"Chicago Groups Contribute To Hernandez Case." *Forum News Bulletin* Feb. 1954.

"The Chicanos: America's Newest Angry Minority." *San Francisco Sunday Examiner & Chronicle* 2 Aug. 1970.

"Coors Boycott Continues." *Forumeer* Apr. 1970.

"Coors Boycott Sweeping East Coast." *Mi Tierra* 1 (Oct., no year available).

"Coors Guilty of Discrimination!!" *Forumeer* Sept. 1970.

"'Corky' Gonzales Says: Hispanos Should Die In T-A, Not Vietnam." *New Mexican* 13 July 1967.

"Corpus Christi Forum Welcomes State Inquiry." *Corpus Christi Caller-Times* 18 Feb. 1949.

Cortéz, R. A. "A Monthly Message From the . . . President General." *LULAC News* 4 (Jan. 1949).

Corwin, Miles. "Hispanic Leader Critical of Carter." *San Jose Mercury News* 18 Jan. 1980.

"Crystal City Mayor Rejects LULAC Bid." *Corpus Christi Caller-Times* 14 June 1963.

"Declaración Ante El Comite Investigador: El Padre del Héroe Niega Tener Dificultades Con la Viuda." *La Verdad* (Mar. 1949): 1.

"Del Rio Demonstration Shows Militant Spirit." *San Antonio Express News*, undated copy of the original article.

"Deny PASO, Teamster Tie." *Brownsville Herald* 10 June 1963.

Dinwoodie, D. H. "The Rise of the Mine-Mill Union in Southwestern Copper." In *American Labor in the Southwest: The First One Hundred Years*. James C. Foster, ed. Tucson: University of Arizona Press, 1982. 46–56.

Dodson, Anne. "Latin Swing To Nixon Is Predicted." *Corpus Christi*

Caller-Times 6 Nov. 1972.

"Dr. García & Family Visit Aradmac Base." *The Forumeer* Sept. 1971.

"Dr. García Gets U.N. Post." *Forumeer* Oct. 1967.

"Dr. García, Many Forumeers At Texas Rights Hearings." *Forumeer* Jan. 1969.

"Dr. García Speaks To U.S. Civil Right Com." *Forumeer* June 1970.

"Dr. García To Attend Meeting With Johnson." *Corpus Christi Caller-Times* 14 Aug. 1964.

"Dr. García's Statement To The Democratic National Committee." *Forum News Bulletin* July 1960.

"Dr. H. García Moves To Morgan Avenue." *The Sentinal* 11 June 1948.

"Dr. H. García To Close Office For Two Weeks." *Corpus Christi Caller-Times* 28 May 1948.

"Draft Boards Asked To Name Latin-Americans." *MCAllen Newspaper* 1 Oct. 1950.

Dunn, Si. "The Legacy Of Pvt. Longoria." *Scene* 6 Apr. 1975.

"Education." *Border Trends* June 1948.

Edwards, A. W. "Dr García's Comment on Texas Hit." *Corpus Christi Caller-Times* 19 Apr. 1966.

"El Señor José Alvarado Invitado de Honor a La Toma de Posesión del Señor Presidente John F. Kennedy." *El Anunciador* [Chicago, Ill.], 14 Jan. 1960.

Elam, Dick. "Helping Wetback Helps Us." *Daily Texan* 21 Oct. 1949.

Estrada, Ralph. "Ethnic Equity and Political Progress." *Alianza* 6 Sept. 1961.

Evans, Mary Alice. "Bilingualism Aid to U.S., Says García." *Corpus Christi Caller-Times* 8 July 1968.

"Ex-Servicemen Invited to Protest Meeting Here." *Corpus Christi Caller-Times* 26 Mar. 1948.

"Facts, Not Propaganda." *Valley Evening Monitor* 14 June 1949.

"Farm Workers." *Border Trends* June 1948.

Fleisher, Bob. "Clinic Dep't . . . ," undated article from the *Stars & Stripes* on Hector's aid to North Africa indigents.

"Forum Head Asks Armstrong to Quit." *Fort Worth Star-Telegram* 8 Feb. 1974.

"Forum Rejects Rioting As Means To Civil Rights." *Forumeer* Aug.

1967.

Freitag, Elroy. "Criticism of Mathis Countered." *Corpus Christi Caller-Times* 22 Apr. 1966.

"From the National Chairman." *Forumeer* Feb. 1974.

"Funeral For Pvt. Longoria Held at National Cemetery." *Corpus Christi Caller-Times* 17 Feb. 1949.

"Funeral Home Action Draws Forum Protest." *Corpus Christi Caller-Times* 11 Jan. 1949.

"G.I. Forum Continues National Coors Boycott." *Forumeer* Jan. 1972.

"G.I. Forum Declares 'War' On Coors, Frito-Lay." *Forumeer* Mar. 1971.

"G.I. Forum Forecast: No Mexican-American Riots." *Denver Post* 3 Aug. 1967.

"G.I. Forum Holds Austin Demonstration" (in support of Vietnam War). *Corpus Christi Caller-Times* 2 July 1966.

"The G.I. Generation." *Aztlán* 2 (Fall 1971): 145–50.

"García Active in Civic and Educational Fields." *Corpus Christi Caller-Times* 24 June 1971.

García, Cleotilde P. Biographical sketch, untitled, undated newspaper clip in *Corpus Christi Caller-Times*.

"García Grocery Carries On Tradition Begun in 1913." *Mercedes Enterprise* 15 Sept. 1982.

"García Has Earned Medal of Freedom." *Corpus Christi Caller-Times* 24 Feb. 1984.

García, Hector P. "Letters to the Editor on Children not in School." *Edinburg Valley Review* 7 Jan. 1949.

_____. "Nixon Misled On Food Stamps Says Dr. García." *Forumeer* Jan. 1969.

_____. "Take a Trip With a Migrant Family." *American Child* Jan. 1957.

García, Mario T. "In Search of History: Carlos E. Castañeda and the Mexican American Generation." In *Renato Rosaldo Lecture Series Monograph* 4 (1988): 1–20.

Garza, G. Rudolph, Jr. "Rights Fight Not Unpatriotic." *Corpus Christi Caller-Times* 28 Apr. 1966.

George, Ron. "'More of a Compromiser Than An Antagonist'—García is Remembered As the Martin Luther King, Jr. of Mexican-American History." *Corpus Christi Caller-Times* 27 July 1996.

Gilenson, Lewis W. "Texas' Forgotten People." *Look* 27 Mar. 1951.

González, Henry B. "Poll Tax Primer: The Behead Tax." *Texas Observer* 18 Oct. 1963.

"Government Jobs: Mexican-Americans Recruited." *Corpus Christi Caller-Times* 10 Oct. 1971.

Gray, J. F. "Letters to the Editor." *Corpus Christi Caller-Times* 12 Feb. 1949.

____. "The Lookout." *Corpus Christi Caller-Times* 12 Feb. 1949.

Groh, George. "Arlington Burial for Three Rivers Veteran Planned." *Corpus Christi Caller-Times* 12 Jan. 1949.

Hall, Martin. "Roybal's Candidacy and What It Means." *Frontier* June 1949.

"Health." *Border Texas* 6 (July 1948).

"Henry Barbosa González: Mexican American Political and Governmental Leader, Lawyer." In *Notable Latino Americans*. Matt S. Meier, ed. Westport: Greenwood Press, 1997.

"Hernándcz Case Lawyers." *Forum News Bulletin* Nov. 1954.

"Hispanics Challenge Carter on Rights." *Fort Worth Star-Telegram* 24 May 1978.

Hogan, George. "Valley Farmers Hopeful of Bracero Settlement." *Corpus Christi Caller-Times* 4 Oct. 1949.

"Honor Roll (of the University of Texas, class of 1936)." *Daily Texan* (Spring 1936).

"Hospital Segregation." *Border Trends* 7 Aug. 1948.

"Humphrey Wows 'Em!" *Forumeer* Nov. 1967.

Ibáñez, Armando P. "Dr. Hector García: Social, Political Reform His Forte." *Corpus Christi Caller-Times* 23 Jan. 1983.

"The Incorrigible Texans." *El Fronterizo* 12 Nov. 1949.

"Insistimos En Que Debemos Tener Un Latinoamericano En El Draft Board." *Las Noticias* 21 Sept. 1950.

"Investigation of Longoria Case Called: Hearings on Racial Discrimination Are to Be Public." *Corpus Christi Caller-Times* 18 Feb. 1949.

Isaacs, Stephen. "Coors' Capital Connection: Heritage Foundation

Fuels His Conservative Drive." *Washington Post* 7 May 1975.

"It's Time For Citywide Tribute to Dr. García." *Corpus Christi Caller-Times* 27 Apr. 1985.

Jain, Bob. "G.I. Forum Hears LBJ Aide: Mexican-American Civic Role Told." *Denver Post* 4 Aug. 1967.

"Jim Wells Goes Strongly Demo, Two Boxes Out." *Corpus Christi Caller-Times* 9 Nov. 1960.

Johnson, Ed. "Texas' Latins Bid for Better Lot With Ballots." *Fort Worth Star-Telegram* 5 Apr. 1964.

"José Angel Gutiérrez: A Militant Exponent of the Chicanos." *Corpus Christi Caller-Times* 10 May 1970.

Kells, Michelle Hall. "Legacy of Resistance: Hector P. García, the Félix Longoria Incident, and the Construction of a Mexican American Civil Rights Rhetoric." Diss. Texas A&M University, 2002.

"The Kennedy Story." *U.S. News & World Report* 21 Nov. 1960: 46–55.

"Kennedy Wins Starr by Heavy Majority." *Corpus Christi Caller-Times* 9 Nov. 1960.

"Kennedy's Liberal Promises." *Time* 19 Sept. 1960: 23.

"Kennedy's Promises for the Future." *U.S. News & World Report* 21 Nov. 1960: 42.

"Latin Americans Organize Viva Kennedy Committee." *Dallas News* 5 Oct. 1960.

"Latin Group Split on Endorsement." *Texas Observer* 16 Feb. 1962: 1.

"Latinos en Varios Puestos Oficiales." *La Prensa* 14 Feb. 1961.

"Latins and Votes." *Texas Observer* 19 Jan. 1962: 1, 3.

Loory, Stuart H. "Nixon Answers Plea of Mexican Americans." *Los Angeles Times* 27 Feb. 1969.

———. "Voice of Mexican-Americans." *Los Angeles Times* 18 Mar. 1969.

"LULAC members laud Coors' hiring." *Corpus Christi Caller-Times* 2 Feb. 1976.

Mayorga, R. G. "Charges of Discrimination." *Corpus Christi Caller-Times* 28 Apr. 1966.

McCracken, Bob. "The Crow's Nest." *Corpus Christi Caller-Times* 6 Feb. 1949.

_____. "The Crow's Nest." *Corpus Christi Caller-Times* 19 Feb. 1949.

Mercedes Enterprise Centennial Edition. 15 Sept. 1982.

"Mexican-American Cheated By Nixon, Rep. Gonzalez Says." *LULAC Newsletter* 31 Dec. 1972.

"Mexican-Americans Irked With Nixon Since Election." *San Antonio Express News* 20 Feb. 1973.

"Mexican-Americans: Nixon Reported Gaining Support." *Corpus Christi Caller-Times* 26 Oct. 1972.

Milton, Chad. "Boycott of Coors May Be Expanded." *Golden Daily Transcript* 16 Mar. 1970.

"Minorities to Be on 'Team' in Carter Administration." *Corpus Christi Caller-Times* 30 Nov. 1976.

"Minority Hiring Leveling Off, Ex-White House Staffer Says." *Corpus Christi Caller-Times* 2 Sept. 1973.

Munguia, Ruben, compiler. *A Cotton Picker Finds Justice!—The Saga of the Hernández Case.* June 1954.

Nakkula, Al. "G.I. Forum Rejects Rioting As Means to Attain Rights." *Rocky Mountain News* 4 Aug. 1967.

"Name Two Local Spanish Speaking Men for Kennedy." *Calumet News* 12 Oct. 1960.

"National Demonstrations vs. Coors Set For Feb. 26th by G.I. Forum." *Forumeer* Jan. 1972.

Nelson, Georgia. "Dr. J. A. García, 59, Dead of Gun Wound." *Corpus Christi Caller-Times* 24 June 1971.

"New Hidalgo Unit Head Says Group Not Anti-PASO." *Corpus Christi Caller-Times* 14 June 1963.

"Nixon Policies Called Evasive." *Denver Post* 15 Mar. 1970.

"Nixon Steps Up Plans for Mexican-Americans." *Los Angeles Times* 27 Feb. 1969.

"Not Such A Rosy Picture." *Valley Evening Monitor* undated copy of article.

"One of the Foremost Decisions Rendered Recently: Dr. García." *Sentinel* 18 June 1948.

Pearson, Drew. "LBJ's Latin 'Fumbles'." *Corpus Christi Caller-Times* 19 Apr. 1966.

Peñalosa, Fernando. "Toward an Operational Definition of the Mexican American." *Aztlán* 1 (Spring, 1970): 1–12.

Pickering, David. "Jurors Indict Local Doctor J. A. García." *Corpus Christi Caller-Times* 26 Feb. 1971.

Pierson, John. "Señor Nixon Makes A Pitch for the Votes Of Mexican-Americans." *Wall Street Journal* 11 Apr. 1972.

"Political Summons in Bexar." *Texas Observer* 5 Oct. 1962: 1.

"Politics." *Border Texas* 6 (July 1948).

"'Radical' Defends School Vote." *Corpus Christi Caller-Times* 22 Apr. 1966.

"Raza Movement Goes to Laredo." *Corpus Christi Caller-Times* 16 May 1970.

"Record Registration in East Chicago." *Latin Times* 22 Oct. 1960.

"Rep. Tinsley Asks Report On Longoria Case Be Withdrawn." *Corpus Christi Caller-Times* 9 Apr. 1949.

"Rights Issue Disputed by Coors Co." *Corpus Christi Caller-Times* 20 Aug. 1969.

Rodríguez, Javier. "García To Receive Medal of Freedom." *Corpus Christi Caller-Times* 22 Feb. 1984.

———. "G.I. Forum Founder States Goal: 'Dignity For My People'." *Corpus Christi Caller-Times* 26 Feb. 1984.

Salazar, Rubén. "L.A. Lawyer Given Civil Rights Post." *Los Angeles Times* 9 Oct. 1969.

Salazar, Verónica. "Dedication Rewarded: Prominent Mexican-Americans." *San Antonio Express News* 6 Sept. 1973.

Salinas, Rigoberto, Sr. "Salinas Family Carries On Long Tradition of Service." *Mercedes Enterprise* 15 Sept. 1982.

Sánchez, George I. "Bilingualism and Mental Measure: A Word of Caution." *Journal of Applied Psychology* 18 Dec. (1934): 765–771.

Santillán, Richard, and Federico A. Subervi-Vélez. "Latino Participation in Republican Party Politics in California." In *Racial and Ethnic Politics in California.* Byran O. Jackson and Michael B. Preston, eds. Berkeley: Institute of Governmental Studies Press, 1991. 285–319.

"School Segregation." *Border Trends* (June 1948).

———. *Border Trends* 6 (July 1948).

"Sen. Chávez Charges of Spanish American Snub Brings Some Appointments." *Forum News Bulletin* Mar. 1961.

"Senator Kennedy Joins G.I. Forum." *Forum News Bulletin* May 1960.

"Senator Kennedy Sends Warm Message to G.I. Forum in Los Angeles." *Forum News Bulletin* Sept. 1959.

Simpson, Peggy. "Minority Leaders Hit Nixon Administration." *Corpus Christi Caller-Times* 20 Feb. 1973.

"State to Fare Well, Sen. Chávez Asserts." *Albuquerque Tribune* 10 Nov. 1960.

"This Is John Fitzgerald Kennedy." *Newsweek* 23 June 1958: 29-34.

"Three Rivers C of C Brands Reburial Story 'Bad Publicity'." *Corpus Christi Caller- Times*, 14 Jan. 1949.

"Three Rivers Replies." *Corpus Christi Caller-Times* 20 Jan. 1949.

Toohey, John. "Court Petition Seeks Coors Hiring Records." *Denver Post* Oct. 1969.

"'Tragic Blot' Kelley Raps Three Rivers Case Report." *Corpus Christi Caller-Times* 8 Apr. 1949.

Trejo, Frank. "Forum to Demand Judge's Ouster." *San Antonio Express News* 29 Oct. 1969.

Underwood, Kathleen. Process and Politics: Multiracial Electoral Coalition Building and Representation in Los Angeles Ninth District, 1949-1962." Diss. U of California, 1992.

"U.S. Supreme Court Bans Discrimination In Jury Service." *Forum News Bulletin* May 1954.

Valdés, Dennis Nodín. "El pueblo mexicano en Detroit y Michigan: A Social History." Diss. Wayne State U, 1982.

"Valley Counties Solid for Demos." *Corpus Christi Caller-Times* 10 Nov. 1960.

Villalobos, Ramón. "Juárez Report: Mexican-Americans Feel Nixon Honeymoon Over." *El Paso Times* 9 May 1971.

"Viva Clubs Now Permanent, Choose Mexican Americans for Political Action Name." *Forum News Bulletin* Mar. 1961.

"Viva Kennedy Club" *Latin Times* 15 Oct. 1960.

"Viva Kennedy Club Is Planned." *Corpus Christi Caller-Times* 23 Sept. 1960.

"Viva Kennedy Clubs Host Senator González." *Latin Times* 29 Oct. 1960, 7.

"Viva Kennedy Leaders in Revolt." *Valley Morning Star* 28 June 1961.

"Viva Kennedy Movement in East Chicago." *Latin Times* 1 Oct. 1960, 1.

"Viva Kennedy Quarters Opened in East Chicago." *Hammond Times* 9 Oct. 1960.

"Vote or Suffer Consequences, Sen. Chávez Tells S.B. Group." *San Bernardino Sun* 9 Oct. 1960.

Wainwright, Jonathan M. "Why I Live In San Antonio." *Pageant Magazine* (June 1950).

"The Wetback Invasion." *Our Catholic Southwest* 18 (June 1951).

Wise, Bert. "Mexican-American Militancy Rises." *Washington Post* 1 Apr. 1969.

Wood, Jim. "Discrimination Here Charged: Unit on Civil Rights Ends Stormy Session." *Corpus Christi Caller-Times* 17 Apr. 1966.

"Yes to LULAC Plaza, no to Coors, G.I. Forum says." *Corpus Christi Caller-Times* 12 Nov. 1975.

Zaragoza, Ed. "Efforts to Divide State Resented." *Corpus Christi Caller-Times* 22 Apr. 1966.

Documents, Reports, Transcripts, and Interviews

Advertisement and information for the American G.I. Forum State Convention as issued by Hector P. García, Chairman. 15 Sept. 1949.

Announcement by Hector P. García regarding a meeting to protest the Felix Longoria incident. Undated.

Announcement by Hector P. García regarding vacancies in the U.S. Fifth Circuit Court of Appeals. 7 Dec. 1978.

Announcement by the American G.I. Forum of Colorado urging support for the Coors Beer Boycott by Chicanos. Undated.

Announcement encouraging the boycott of Coors Beer (in Spanish). Undated.

Announcement of a meeting in Corpus Christi, Texas to organize classes of reading and writing as well as classes for becoming citizens. Undated.

Announcement of a meeting to all Mexican Americans (in Spanish). 30 June 1949.

Announcement of a meeting to discuss a resolution adopted by Leaders of the Latin American Citizenry of the Rio Grande Valley. Undated.

Announcement of a protest meeting held by the American G.I. Forum about the Longoria situation (in Spanish). 11 Jan. 1949.

Advertisement of the Adolph Coors Company in *Corpus Christi Caller-Times* regarding its hiring record of minorities and females. 18 Sept. 1977.

Advertisement of the Concerned Citizens of South Texas appearing in *Corpus Christi Caller-Times*. 4 June 1976.

Announcement of the death of José G. García. 11 Aug. 1957.

Announcement of the 1980 Señor Internacional Award. Undated.

Announcement supporting a stay-in-school drive, calling attention to fines that can be assessed to parents that take their children out of school prematurely (in Spanish). Undated.

Announcements by the American G.I. Forum concerning the Hernández case and a new political party. 3 Jan. 1955.

Bank deposit slip for the Hernández Fund. 2 Jan. 1954.

Biographical data of R. P. Sánchez containing important highlights of his life. Undated.

Biography on Xico García. Undated.

Call to Action for all Spanish-surnamed persons of the U.S. given by José A. Gutiérrez. 16 May 1977.

Certificate from the U.S. president, appointing Hector P. García to the National Advisory Council on Economic Opportunity. 4 Mar. 1967.

Certificate from the United States Commission on Civil Rights to Hector P. García for his service on the Texas State Advisory Committee. 30 June 1980.

Certificate of Baptism by the Parrish of Our Madam Rosario en Llera, Tamps. for Hector P. García. 18 Nov. 1959.

Certificate of Capacity to the grade of First Lieutenant, Infantry Reserve, from the Officers' Reserve Corps of the Army of the United States, issued to Hector P. García. 1 Nov. 1937.

Certificate of internship to Creighton Memorial Saint Joseph's Hospital, given to Hector P. García. Undated.

Certificate of marriage of the municipality of Victoria City, Tamaulipas, (Mexico), of José G. García and Faustina Perez. 29 Dec. 1910.

Certificate of Merit from the European Theater of Operations of the United States Army, awarded to Captain Hector P. García. Undated.

Certificate of military training from the Citizens' Military Training Camps issued to Hector P. García. 14 July 1932.

Certificate of military training from the Citizens' Military Training Camps issued to Hector P. García. 19 July 1933.

Certificate of service from the Army of the United States given to Captain Hector P. García. 1 Mar. 1946.

Civil Action Complaint filed in the U.S. District Court, District of Colorado, by the Equal Employment Opportunity Commission against the Adolph Coors Company. Undated.

Comparison and analysis of the presidential appointments made by Presidents Kennedy, Johnson, and Nixon. Typewritten and untitled. 1972.

Death certificate from José G. García by the Catholic Saint Mother Church. 12 Aug. 1957.

Description of the aims and purposes of the American G.I. Forum. 1948.

Document certifying the award of the Bronze Medal to Hector P. García. 20 Sept. 1945.

Document certifying the award of the Star for Meritorious Service unit plaque to the 591st Engineer Boat Regiment. 16 Aug. 1945.

Document of the promotion to the rank of Major, given to Hector P. García. 3 Jan. 1947.

Draft statement regarding agreement between the U.S. and the West Indies. Undated.

Fact sheet issued by the American G.I. Forum regarding the Coors Beer Boycott. Undated.

Facts sheets (2) issued by the Coors Company about its Mexican American Employees. Undated.

Felix Longoria Miscellaneous Tape. Sound cassette, reproduced in written form.

Felix Longoria Texas Legislation Committee Report to the Speaker and Members of the House of Representatives, headed by Chairman Cecil Storey. 14 Jan. 1949.

García, Cleotilde P., Interview by Tom Kreneck, (17 Feb. 1994, 22 Feb. 1994, 8 Mar. 1994, 17 Mar. 1994, 28 Mar. 1994, 4 May 1994), Corpus Christi, Texas. Hector P. García Collection.

García, Hector P. Interview by Tom Kreneck, (18 Feb. 1991, 4 June 1991, 16 July 1991, 23 July 1991), Corpus Christi, Texas. Hector P. García collection.

García, Hector P. Interview by unknown author. Undated.

García, Wanda F. Interview by Tom Kreneck, 22 May 1997–18 Aug. 1999, Corpus Christi, Texas, Oral History Collection, Texas A&M University in Corpus Christi.

Information release of a meeting by the Southwest Council of La Raza, announcing a protest of the actions of the U.S. Commission on Civil Rights and Texas Council of Churches. 6 Feb. 1969.

Interview of Hector P. García, as sent to Mario Eugenio Escamilla. 15 Jan. 1975.

Interview of Hector P. García by the Good Neighbor Commission. 12 May 1950.

Invitation to a "scholarship ceremony" regarding matters of education, sent to the public of Corpus Christi by the American G.I. Forum. 17 Aug. 1949.

Invitation to the forty-ninth annual commencement of the University of Texas Medical Branch, with the class role and class officers index. Held 31 May 1940.

List of Precinct Chairmen elected at the Democratic Primary Election in 1948. Undated.

Listing of Presidential Hispanic Personnel Appointments and White House Staff. 23 June 1978.

Majority Report of the Committee Pursuant to H. S. R., NO. 68. Prepared by Cecil Storey, Chairman. *House Journal*, 1420–1423, 7 Apr. 1949.

Manuscript of a conference with Lyndon B. Johnson and other state leaders regarding the future of the Naval Base of Corpus Christi,

Texas. 27 Dec. 1958.

Map of Arlington National Cemetery, with the location of Felix Longoria's grave.

Memo by John B. Connally giving a summary of conversations with Mr. Paul J. Reveley of the State Department. 25 Feb. 1949.

Memorandum from Ed Idar, Jr., to Hector P. García. Undated.

Memorandum from John B. Connally regarding his involvement in the Felix Longoria case. 11 Jan. 1949.

Memorandum of José Antonio García. Undated.

Message by Hector P. García, Chairman of the American G.I. Forum of Texas, to members of the same organization. 1951.

Message from the State Chairman Ed Idar, Jr., to the Fourth Annual Convention of the American G.I. Forum of Texas. 1952.

Minority Report on the Longoria Investigation by Frank C. Oltorf. *House Journal.* Undated.

Minutes of a meeting of Corpus Christi's American G.I. Forum. 4 June 1948.

Minutes of a meeting of the American G.I. Forum. 19 Aug. 1948.

Minutes of a meeting of the American G.I. Forum of Nixon, Texas, regarding the protest of problems inherent in the Southward Latin American School. Undated.

Minutes of a meeting of the Board of Directors of the American G.I. Forum of Texas. 10 Jan. 1960.

Minutes of the American G.I. Forum of Texas' Board of Directors Meeting. 19 Feb. 1961.

Minutes of the American G.I. Forum of Texas' Board of Directors Meeting. 12 Nov. 1961.

Minutes of the American G.I. Officers and Advisory Board Meeting. 30 Oct. (no year available).

Narrative Report of the National Leadership Conference of the Viva Kennedy Clubs. 26 Mar. 1961.

Newsletter of the New Mexico division of the American G.I. Forum. 17 Nov. 1952.

Notes from an American G.I. Forum newsletter, including news of Hector P. García's heart attack. Undated.

Notes from the Mid-Year Conference of the American G.I. Forum of the U.S. 19 Feb. 1966.

Notes from the morning session of the American G.I. Forum Convention. 25 Sept. 1949.

Notes from the radio station KWBU in Corpus Christi, regarding a talk show given by Hector P. García. Between 1948–50.

Notes from the Viva Kennedy-Johnson Clubs meeting as submitted by Ed Idar, Jr. 5 Feb. 1961.

Notes on wetback pickers by Hector P. García. 24 July 1950.

Notice addressed to voters in the city of Corpus Christi, urging a vote for the People's Party. Undated.

Notice issued by the Adolph Coors Company in *El Chicano* announcing that LULAC no longer supports the Coors Beer Boycott. 30 Jan. 1975.

Notice of a boycott by the American G.I. Forum of Washington D.C. against Coors Beer. 5 Sept. 1975.

Notice regarding a meeting of the American G.I. Forum, sent by Hector P. García. 21 Feb. 1950.

Notice regarding the nomination of Hector P. García to the U.S. Circuit Judge Nominating Commission, the Western Fifth Circuit Panel. 3 May 1977.

Notice to all Spanish-speaking residents of Corpus Christi by Hector P. García, inviting all to come to a meeting discussing the possibility of building inexpensive rental houses. Undated.

Notice to members of the American G.I. Forum, regarding a mass protest against the termination of the Veterans Administration's contract with the U.S. Naval Hospital in Corpus Christi. Issued by Hector P. García. 21 Feb. 1950.

Occupational application for Hector P. García concerning his position as a Presidential Appointment on the U.S. Commission on Civil Rights. 7 Nov. 1968.

Office report of the Washington D.C. office of the American G.I. Forum recounting the actions of Congress concerning poverty and Mexican Americans. 11 June 1966.

Official Registry of Statements of the Court regarding the trial of a Mexican American youth in Santa Clara, California. 2 Sept. 1969.

Physical examination report of Hector P. Garcia, given on 27 Nov.

1940.

Press memorandum from the office of Governor Allan Shivers of Texas regarding the formation of the Council for the Study of Human Relations. 4 May 1950.

Press release by Hector P. García concerning his petitions for an investigation into allegations of discrimination in Val Verde County, Texas. 25 Mar. 1969.

Press release by the American G.I. Forum regarding the denial of letting boys of Mexican origin carry the flag of the United States 11 Feb. 1957.

Press release by the Southwest Council of La Raza protesting the actions of the U.S. Commission on Civil Rights and Texas Council of Churches. Undated.

Press release concerning the monetary contribution of the American G.I. Forum to the Hernández case. 1953.

Press release from the U.S. Department of Labor regarding its actions against recent violations of Federal Child Labor laws. 10 June 1957.

Press release issued by Hector P. García concerning the 1964 national and state elections (Texas). 29 Feb. 1964.

Press release issued by Hector P. García regarding the "height" requirement for police officers. 15 Jan. 1971.

Press release regarding favorable reactions to the use of Spanish-speaking citizens in foreign service missions to Latin America. 1964.

Proceedings from the 12th Annual Convention of the American G.I. Forum of Texas. 1–4 July 1960.

Program from the first annual convention of the American G.I. Forum. 24–25 Sept. 1949.

Protest statement of several Spanish-speaking parents concerning the proposed change of schools in the Marathon Independent School District of Texas. Undated.

Receipt for the Hernández Fund of $131.00. 2 Jan. 1954.

Recommendation for the promotion of rank of Hector P. García, issued to the Surgeon General. 28 July 1942.

Record of the allocation of financial support to José G. García. Undated.

Report by the Adolph Coors Company regarding its hiring record of minorities and females. Undated.

Report from the Washington D.C. office of the American G.I. Forum regarding the anatomy of a Presidential Statement on Equal Employment Opportunity and Civil Rights for Mexican Americans. Undated.

Report issued by the Carter administration regarding the administration's dealings with Hispanics. Undated.

Report made by Ed Idar, Jr. to Hector P. García regarding his findings on the "wet back situation" during a tour to South Texas. Undated.

Report of the President's Commission on Migratory Labor. Undated.

Report to the Good Neighbor Commission of a survey of Midland, Texas. Mar. 1951.

Report to the President of the United States by various Cabinet Secretaries regarding the progress of Mexican Americans. 9 June 1967.

Resolution by the American G.I. Forum of Texas recognizing the Veterans' Land Board of Texas for the long-term loans available to Texas veterans. Undated.

Resolution by the American G.I. Forum of Texas, requesting Congress to abolish the Poll Tax and any literacy tests in relation to voting. 28 Aug. 1950.

Resolution by the American G.I. Forum of Texas to show approval for the G.I. Bill for Veterans of the Korean War. Undated.

Resolution by the American G.I. Forum of Texas to urge local Congressmen and the Veterans Administration to locate a Veterans Hospital in Southwest Texas. Undated.

Resolution of the Bexar County Central Council of the American Legion, Inc., signed by R. H. Farley, Treasurer. 27 Jan. 1949.

Resolution passed by the American G.I. Forum of Texas concerning a push for the establishment of Kindergarten classes in Texas. 23 June 1957.

Resolution passed by The Northern Colorado Trades Council in support of the Coors Beer Boycott. Undated.

Resolutions passed by the American G.I. Forum of Texas in its Annual Convention in Corpus Christi, Texas. 26–27 Sept. 1949.

Resolutions passed by the Board of Directors of the American G.I. Forum of Texas. 9 Dec. 1951.

San Felipe Del Rio Mexican-American Manifesto To The Nation. 30

Mar. 1969.

Separation Qualification Record of the Army of the United States, of Hector P. García. Undated.

Seventy-five-year history of the faculty and staff of the University of Texas Medical Branch at Galveston, Appendix P: Graduates in Medicine 1892–1967.

Special Bulletin by the American G.I. Forum of Texas to all state and auxiliary leaders. 16 Jan. 1952.

Special Notice of the death of Hector P. García Jr., sent to the American G.I. Forum. 19 July 1962.

Special orders of a new assignment given to Hector P. Garcia, by the War Department 15 June 1942.

Statement by Carolina Longoria concerning her experiences in the Longoria case. The statement was certified by J. Guadalupe Trevino. 7 Mar. 1949.

Statement by George Groh concerning his involvement in the Felix Longoria situation, certified by Hector de Peña. 18 Feb. 1949.

Statement by Gladys Blucher, secretary to Hector P. García, regarding what she heard from García's conversation with Mr. Kennedy of the Rice Funeral Home on the telephone while she listened in. The statement was certified by Hector de Peña. 9 Feb. 1949.

Statement by Hector P. García for the President's Commission on Migratory Labor. 31 July 1950.

Statement by Hector P. García given to the United Nations regarding the Treaty for the Prohibition of Nuclear Weapons in Latin America. 26 Oct. 1967.

Statement by Hector P. García given to the United Nations regarding the Treaty for the Prohibition of Nuclear Weapons in Latin America. 26 Oct. 1967 (in Spanish).

Statement by Hector P. García on the occasion of the two-projects agreement between United States and West Indies. 11 Feb. 1961.

Statement by Hector P. García to a committee of Congressmen from Washington, D.C. regarding the needs of the Texas Naval Hospital in Corpus Christi, Texas. Undated.

Statement by Hector P. García to the state of Texas concerning his conversation with Mr. Kennedy of the Rice Funeral Home in Corpus Christi, Texas. 9 Feb. 1949.

Statement by Hector P. García, representing the American G.I. Forum. 28 Apr. 1976.

Statement by Hector P. García, to the President's Commission on Migratory Labor Hearings, occurring from 31 July to 1 Aug. 1950, regarding the health and welfare conditions among underprivileged migrant workers of Texas. Undated.

Statement by Hector P. García, to White House Officials on the plight of Mexican Americans. 28 Oct. 1966.

Statement by Juventino Ponce concerning racism he experienced in Three Rivers, Texas. Certified by Hector de Peña. 12 Mar. 1949.

Statement by Mrs. Beatrice Longoria regarding the burial of her husband, Felix Longoria. Certified by Hector de Peña. 9 Feb. 1949.

Statement by R. P. Sánchez regarding the Mexican Farm Labor Importation Program before the Senate Agriculture Subcommittee on General Legislation and Agriculture Research. 12–13 June 1961.

Statement by R. P. Sánchez, representing the American G.I. Forum, to E. C. Gathings relating to proposed legislation protecting domestic farm workers. 25 Mar. 1960.

Statement by Sara Moreno about the Félix Longoria burial situation. 18 Feb. 1949.

Statement issued by Guadalupe Longoria regarding her involvement in the Felix Longoria situation. Certified by Hector de Peña. 20 Feb. 1949.

Statement issued by leaders of the James Edmond Post No. 121 American Legion concerning the burial of Felix Longoria. 12 Jan. 1949.

Statement issued by Lyndon B. Johnson regarding the progress of his efforts of ensuring full opportunity for all Spanish-speaking Americans. 21 Feb. 1966.

Statement made to the Board of Directors of the Three Rivers Chamber of Commerce by Lupe Longoria regarding his son's burial case. Jan. 1949.

Statement of Hector P. García before the Education and Labor Committee of the U.S. House of Representatives. 28 May 1968.

Statement of Inspection on the area of Three Rivers. 21 Feb. 1949.

Statistics of the results of various elections for governor and other positions for the state of Texas. Compiled by Hector P. García. Apr. 1974.

Summary of Lyndon B. Johnson's lifetime record of personal concern and public assistance to Americans of Mexican or Spanish origin. Undated.

Table of contents in the "Vista Incident" in Del Rio, Texas. 25 Mar. 1969.

Testimony given before the Special Congressional Subcommittee on Hospital Facilities by Hector P. García relative to the closing of the Corpus Christi, Texas Naval Hospital. 22 Mar. 1950.

Texas State Board of Medical Examiners Certificate to practice medicine and surgery in the state of Texas, given to Hector P. García. 29 July 1940.

Transcript from a radio talk entitled "The Social, Economical, and Educational Aspects of the American G.I. Forum" delivered by Hector P. García in McAllen, Texas. 19 Aug. 1950.

Transcript of comments made by Hector P. García in a meeting discussing a meat boycott in Corpus Christi. Undated.

Transcript of Hector P. García's comments during the Equal Employment Opportunity Commission's hearings regarding the segregation of Mexican-Americans and Blacks in Texas. Undated.

True Copy of Act of Marriage, for Hector P. García and Wanda Fussillo, certified by Josephine D. Antonio. 23 June 1945.

U.S. Congress. House. Honoring Dr. Hector P. García, Recipient of Presidential Medal of Freedom. Report prepared by Solomon P. Ortiz. *Congressional Record*, 130, 36. 26 Mar. 1984.

U.S. Congress. House. Recognition of Dr. Hector P. García. Report prepared by Rep. Bill Richardson. *Congressional Record*. 20 July 1983.

U.S. Congress. Senate. Executive Reports of a Committee, United Nations, and Confirmations. *Congressional Record*, 113, 150. 22 Sept. 1967.

Unpublished manuscript on Felix Longoria Case by Patrick Carroll and Joe Frantz.

"What Price Wetbacks?" Pamphlet of the American G.I. Forum of Texas and the Texas State Federation of Labor (AFL). Austin, Texas.

Letters

Aanstoos, Ted, to Roy Williams, 13 Apr. 1951.

Acosta, Oscar Zeta, to Hector P. García. 7 Oct. 1969.

Adj. General, to Hector P. García. 15 June 1942.

_____, to Hector P. García. 14 July 1942.

Aldrete, Cristóbal P., to Hector P. García. 18 Apr. 1949.

_____, to Ed Idar, Jr. 27 Aug. 1953.

_____, to Hector P. García. 28 Sept. 1953.

_____, to Hector P. García. 28 July 1955.

Alexander, Ben O., to Hector P. García. 6 Feb. 1961.

Allison, Joe M., to the Commanding Officer of the 591st Engineer Boat Regiment. 29 July 1942.

Allsup, Carlos, to Hector P. García. 28 Mar. 1977.

Always, Lazelle D., to Hector P. García. 13 Jan. 1949.

_____, Lazelle D., to Hector P. García. 18 Sept. 1950.

American G.I. Forum of Texas form letter to the Senators, Representatives, and other leaders of Texas, 1949.

_____, to Sam Rayburn. 15 Oct. 1949.

Armendariz, Faustina, to Hector P. García. 14 Sept. 1967.

Ávila, Manuel Jr., to Hector P. García. 19 June 1961.

Baird, Allan, and Andris I. Cirkelis, form letter to supporters of the Coors Beer Boycott. 13 June 1975.

Bakshian, Aram, Jr., to Louis P. Telles. 11 May 1983.

Barnes, Bob, to Hector P. García. 2 June 1980.

Barrera, Nickolas S., to _The Houston Post_. 9 May 1957.

Barrera, Rudolph, to Price Daniel. 21 Nov. 1952.

Barry, Gordon J., to L. A. Woods. 18 Sept. 1949.

Barry, Ralph M., to First Lieutenant Hector P. García. 21 Feb. 1942.

Beaton, Carolyn W., to Hector P. García. 14 Jan. 1949.

Beckel, Bob, and Tom Henderson, to Hector P. García. 20 May 1980.

BeLieu, Kenneth E., to Joseph M. Montoya. 11 Mar. 1969.

Bentsen, Lloyd M., Jr., to Alexander J. Leo and Everett Sieger. 24 Feb. 1950.

_____, to Hector P. García. 11 Jan. 1949.

_____, to Hector P. García. 12 Jan. 1949.

_____, to Hector P. García. 8 Mar. 1950.

_____, to Hector P. García. 4 Aug. 1981.

_____, form letter to various individuals. 26 May 1983.

Berry, K. L., to Hector P. García. 19 July 1948.

Bird, Lady, to Hector P. García. 2 Apr. 1974.

Bland, Earl, to Hector P. García. 9 Nov. 1949.

Bond, Richard E., to Fenn Ellery. 19 July 1974.

Bone, to Hector P. García. 12 Dec. 1950.

_____, to Hector P. García. 6 Sept. 1964.

Bonnie (Bone), to José G. García. 23 Nov. 1943.

Borjas, Isaac P., form letter to various officials regarding recent acts of discrimination. 1950.

Brown, Newell, to John Young. 22 Mar. 1957.

Brown, William H. III, to Hector P. García. 4 Nov. 1970.

Bryan, L. W., Jr., to the National Commander of the American Legion. 18 May 1948.

Burnett, William H., to William K. Coors. 16 Mar. 1970.

Bush, George, to Hector P. García. 26 Mar. 1984.

Bustillos, Isabel, to Hector P. García. 8 Dec. 1952.

Califano, Joseph A., to Hector P. García. 24 May 1966.

Canales, J. T., to Alonso S. Perales. 12 Dec. 1951.

_____, to Ed Idar, Jr. 13 Jan. 1952.

_____, to Ed Idar, Jr. 18 Jan. 1952.

_____, to Ed Idar, Jr. 1 Dec. 1952.

_____, to Hector P. García and Ed Idar, Jr. 29 Apr. 1952.

_____, to J. A. García. 26 Jan. 1953.

Cannon, O. E., to Hector P. García. 14 Jan. 1949.

Cantú, Tomás, form letter to Veterans of Foreign Wars. 16 June 1948.

Carrizales, Jesse, to Hector P. García. 10 Nov. 1948.

Carroll, W. D., to Hector P. García. 5 July 1957.

Carter, Jimmy, to Hector P. García. 29 Apr. 1977.

_____, to Hector P. García. 15 Sept. 1980.

Cásares, Ralph C., to Hector P. García. 1 Mar. 1970.

Chacón, José A., to Hector P. García. 8 Apr. 1969.

Charlie, to Hector P. García. 1950 (no month or day given).

Chávez, César, to Hector P. García. 14 Oct. 1985.

Chávez, Dennis, to Bob Sánchez. 10 Aug. 1956.

Clinton, Bill, to Hector P. García. 1 Dec. 1972.

_____, to Hector P. García. 2 Oct. 1984.

Coney, Bill, to Hector P. García. 12 Feb. 1951.

Coney, William, to T. W. Kennedy. 11 Jan. 1949.

Congressional Hispanic Caucus, to Ronald Reagan. 12 July 1983.

Connally, Tom, to Hector P. García. 7 Oct. 1949.

_____, to Hector P. García. 12 Feb. 1950.

_____, to Hector P. García. 5 May 1950.

Contreras, Dan, to Allan Shivers. 10 Dec. 1950.

Coors, Joseph, form letter to the Committee for Survival of a Free Congress (CSFC) contributors. Undated.

Coors, William K., to Lawrence Amaya. 22 Apr. 1969.

_____, to Paul Gonzales. 5 Mar. 1970.

_____, to Paul Gonzales. 31 July 1973.

_____, to Tony E. Gallegos. 23 July 1974.

Coronado, G. E., form letter to various voters. 28 Mar. 1961.

Cortez, R. A., to Hector P. García. 13 Jan. 1949.

Cosa (Cleotilde P. García), to Neto (Hector P. García). 1 Feb. 1950.

_____, to Neto (Hector P. García). 23 Sept. 1950.

Crain, Ernest, and Earl Maxwell, to Hector P. García. 5 Oct. 1977.

Crozier, Harry Benge, to Milton D. Richardson. 15 Nov. 1951.

Dancy, Oscar C., to Hector P. García. 2 Jan. 1960.

_____, to Lyndon B. Johnson. 30 Dec. 1959.

_____, to Sam Rayburn. 2 Jan. 1960.

_____, to The Ford Foundation. 2 Jan. 1960.

_____, to The Rockefeller Foundation. 2 Jan. 1960.

_____, to Albert Peña Jr. 7 June 1963.

_____, to Lawrence P. O'Brien. 10 June 1963.

Daniel, Price, to Hector P. García. 11 Jan. 1949.

Davis, T. J., to First Lieutenant Hector P. García. 18 Sept. 1942.

De Anda, James, to Clifton C. Carter. 25 July 1962.

_____, to the Editor of *Corpus Christi Caller-Times*. 15 Aug. 1963.

Deaver, Michael K., to Hector P. García. 13 Feb. 1984.

DeLugo, Isaac S., B. Th., to Hector P. García. 26 Mar. 1949.

Douglas, Paul H., to Hector P. García. 9 June 1960.

DuPlessis, F. D., to Hector P. García. 16 Jan. 1951.

Dugger, Ronnie, to Hector P. García. 9 May 1957.

Duran, Ezequiel, form letter to all national and state officers and local chairmen of the American G.I. Forum. 30 Nov. 1971.

Edgar, H. L., to the Commanding General of the Eighth Corps Area. 15 July 1942.

Edgar, J. W., to Ed Idar, Jr. 13 Oct. 1950.

Egan, Michael J., to Hector P. García. 7 Apr. 1977.

Escobedo, M., to Hector P. García. 29 Jan. 1949.

Gallegos, Tony E., to Paul Gonzáles. 4 Dec. 1973.

_____, to William Coors. 22 Feb. 1974.

García, J. O., to Fando Longoria. 14 Jan. 1949.

García, Gus C., to George J. Garza and Hector P. García. 18 Oct. 1950.

_____, to Alonso S. Perales. 6 Dec. 1951.

_____, to John J. Herrera. 21 Jan. 1952.

_____, to Hector P. García. 8 June 1960.

_____, to Pete Hernández. 8 June 1960.

_____, to Ed Idar, Jr., 28 July 1960.

García, Hector P., form letter asking for contributions to the Hernández case. Undated.

_____, form letter to all friends interested in helping the poor. Undated.

_____, form letter to all state officials, board of advisors, presidents of Forums, presidents of Ladies Auxiliaries of the American G.I. Forum of Texas. Undated.

_____, form letter to Mexican American Veterans. Undated.

_____, form letter to news media in the Corpus Christi area and state of Texas. Undated.

_____, form letter to Spanish-speaking parents, truckers, and working-class. Undated.

_____, form letter to various organizations and their leaders located in Corpus Christi, Texas. Undated.

_____, form letter to various people regarding the presidential elections. Undated.

_____, form letter to veterans and their families. Undated.

_____, form letter to voters in support of Ralph Yarborough for U.S. Senator. Undated.

_____, to Allan Shivers. Undated.

_____, to J. W. Edger. Undated.

_____, to Joe Greenhill. 16 Feb. (no year given).

_____, to José Antonio García. Undated.

_____, to José G. and Faustina García. Undated.

_____, to Tom Connally. Undated.

_____, to Headquarters First Military Area. 16 Dec. 1941.

_____, to the Commanding General of the Eighth Corps Area. 25 Jan. 1942.

_____, to the Editor of *Corpus Christi Caller-Times*. Undated.

_____, to Headquarters First Military Area. 19 Feb. 1942.

_____, to the Office of the Executive at the Headquarters of the First Military Area. 19 Feb. 1942.

_____, to Douglas County Local Board Number 3. 18 Mar. 1942.

_____, to the Adjutant General at Headquarters Eighth Corps Area. 24 May 1942.

_____, to José G. and Faustina García. 8 July 1942.

_____, to José G. García (and siblings). 12 July 1942.

_____, to José G. García (and siblings). 18 July 1942.

_____, to José Antonio García (Tono). 29 Aug. 1942.

_____, to José G. García. 24 Oct. 1942.

_____, to José G. García. 26 Oct. 1942.

_____, to José Antonio García. 23 Dec. 1942.

_____, to José G. García. 23 Dec. 1942.

_____, to Adjutant General of Washington D. C. 22 Jan. 1943.

_____, to Bone. 1 Feb. 1943.

_____, to José G. García. 10 Feb. 1943.

_____, to José G. García. 12 Feb. 1943.

_____, to José G. García. 9 Apr. 1943.

_____, to José G. García. 22 July 1943.

_____, to José G. García. 24 July 1943.

_____, to José G. García. 31 July 1943.

_____, to José Antonio García. 2 Sept. 1943.

_____, to José G. García. 2 Sept. 1943.

_____, to José Antonio García. 21 Oct. 1943.

_____, to José G. García. 8 Nov. 1943.

_____, to José G. García. 11 Nov. 1943.

_____, to José G. García. 14 Nov. 1943.

_____, to José G. García. 12 Feb. 1945.

_____, to the Commanding Officer of the 2755 Engineer Combat Bn. 6 July 1945.

_____, to José G. García. 29 July 1945.

_____, to the Army concerning Hospitalization, Redeployment, or Discharge. 14 Sept. 1945.

_____, to Mrs. Ruth. 27 Sept. 1945.

_____, to John E. Lyle. 26 Mar. 1948.

_____, to the American Legion. 6 Apr. 1948.

_____, to a Veteran. 18 May 1948.

_____, to John E. Lyle. 18 June 1948.

_____, to Mr. Jones. 23 June 1948.

_____, to Tomas Sutherland. 13 July 1948.

_____, to José Cueva. 13 Aug. 1948.

_____, to José Cueva. 8 Sept. 1948.

_____, to Guadalupe Valdez, Jr. 14 Oct. 1948.

_____, to Roger Q. Evans. 21 Oct. 1948.

_____, to the LULAC Council No. 1. 22 Nov. 1948.

_____, to Lyndon B. Johnson. 10 Jan. 1949.

_____, to Alfredo Moreno. 13 Jan. 1949.

_____, to Thomas Sutherland. 31 Jan. 1949.

_____, to Salvador Álvarez. 9 Feb. 1949.

_____, to Mr. Sutherland. 8 Apr. 1949.

_____, to Pauline Kibbe. 16 Apr. 1949.

_____, form letter to various individuals. 21 Apr. 1949.

_____, to José Cueva. 21 Apr. 1949.

_____, to Frank Oltorf. 27 Apr. 1949.

_____, to Ignacio Garza. 7 May 1949.

_____, to Carlos García, Jr. 4 July 1949.

_____, form letter to various organizations. 5 July 1949.

_____, to Ed Idar, Jr. 5 July 1949.

_____, to Lyle Saunders. 8 July 1949.

_____, form letter to various delegates of the American G.I. Forum. 27 Sept. 1949.

_____, to Horace Caldwell. 27 Sept. 1949.

_____, form letter of thanks and commendation to individuals in the community. 29 Sept. 1949.

_____, to Don Larsen. 4 Oct. 1949.

_____, to Dean Acheson. 5 Oct. 1949.

_____, to the Texas Employment Commission. 6 Oct. 1949.

_____, to Ignacio Garza. 7 Oct. 1949.

_____, to Joaquín Govella. 10 Oct. 1949.

_____, form letter to members of the Corpus Christi American G.I. Forum. 19 Oct. 1949.

_____, to Allan T. Shivers. 22 Nov. 1949.

_____, to Mr. Mora. 3 Dec. 1949.

_____, to Allan T. Shivers. 4 Dec. 1949.

_____, to all auxiliaries and G.I. Forums of Texas. 7 Dec. 1949.

_____, to Julieta Santoy. 7 Dec. 1949.

_____, form letter to voters in the city of Corpus Christi. 10 Dec. 1949.

_____, form letter to all state officials of the American G.I. Forum regarding recent acts of discrimination. 1950.

_____, form letter to Spanish-speaking veterans of Texas. 12 Jan. 1950.

_____, to James W. Stroud. 27 Jan. 1950.

_____, form letter to all members and officers of the American G.I. Forums and their auxiliaries. 22 Mar. 1950.

_____, to Edna Ferber. 24 Apr. 1950.

_____, to Dennis Chávez. 29 Apr. 1950.

_____, to unidentified person. 4 Aug. 1950.

_____, form letter to all G.I. Forums, Ladies Auxiliaries and Jr. G.I. Forums. Sept. 1950.

_____, to Lyndon B. Johnson. 15 Oct. 1950.

_____, form letter to all American G.I. Forums and Ladies Auxiliaries of Texas. 20 Oct. 1950.

_____, to Lyndon B. Johnson. 20 Oct. 1950.

_____, to George Garza. 23 Oct. 1950.

_____, to Mrs. Arrendongo and Mr. Valles. 24 Oct. 1950.

_____, to Cesario Martínez. 25 Oct. 1950.

_____, to Allan T. Shivers. 28 Oct. 1950.

_____, to Professr Van Hecke. 31 Oct. 1950.

_____, to Claude Gilmer. 15 Nov. 1950.

_____, to the Editor of *Corpus Christi Caller-Times*. 25 Nov. 1950.

_____, to the Commanding Officer at Fort Hood, Texas. 1 Dec. 1950.

_____, to Lyndon B. Johnson. 15 Dec. 1950.

_____, to the Civil Rights Section of the U.S. Attorney General. 16 Dec. 1950.

_____, to Allan T. Shivers. 20 Dec. 1950.

_____, to Ireneo Medina and E. G. Aranda. 20 Dec. 1950.

_____, to the *National Guardian*. 31 Dec. 1950.

_____, form letter to all officers, District Chairmans, and members of the American G.I. Forum, Auxiliaries, and Jr. G.I. Forums. 5 Jan. 1951.

_____, to Ed Vela. 23 Jan. 1951.

_____, to Merle Griffin. 25 Jan. 1951.

_____, to Oscar C. Dancy. 7 Feb. 1951.

_____, to Longino Sánchez, Jr. 12 Feb. 1951.

_____, to Michael Michaelson. 15 Mar. 1951.

_____, to Lyndon B. Johnson. 21 Mar. 1951.

_____, to the Editors of *Look*. 21 Mar. 1951.

_____, to Roy Williams. 11 Apr. 1951.

_____, to Allan T. Shivers. 18 Apr. 1951.

_____, to J. W. Edger. 2 May 1951.

_____, to B. C. Davis. 30 May 1951.

_____, to the Chairman of the House Agricultural Committee. 5 Aug. 1951.

_____, to Evelyn Rice. 29 Aug. 1951.

_____, to the Editor of *La Prensa*. 13 Dec. 1951.

_____, form letter to all members and officers of the American G.I. Forum. 1952.

_____, to Gus C. García. 3 Jan. 1952.

_____, to Tom Connally. 27 Feb. 1952.

_____, to Lyndon B. Johnson. 18 Oct. 1952.

_____, to Anastacio Álvarez. 21 Dec. 1952.

_____, to Antonio Hernández. 21 Dec. 1952.

_____, to Inéz Yanez, Sr. 21 Dec. 1952.

_____, to J. T. Canales. 27 Jan. 1953.

_____, to Herbert Brownell. 15 Aug. 1953.

_____, to Jesse R. Espitia. 10 Nov. 1953.

_____, to Arthur Tafoya. 11 Nov. 1953.

_____, to Eloisa Alaniz. 11 Nov. 1953.

_____, to Joe Martínez. 11 Nov. 1953.

_____, to Isabel Ogas. 17 Nov. 1953.

_____, to Chris Aldrete. 18 Nov. 1953.

_____, to Simón S. Vela. 21 Nov. 1953.

_____, to Salvador Monroy. 25 Nov. 1953.

_____, to Samuel Cardinal Stritch. 13 Mar. 1954.

_____, to Maury Maverick, Jr. 1 June 1954.

_____, to Robert Jones. 8 Sept. 1954.

_____, to George I. Sánchez. 19 Mar. 1956.

_____, to Vicente Ximenes. 30 Apr. 1956.

_____, to Sam Rayburn. 11 May 1956.

_____, form letter to all members of the American G.I. Forum. 23 June 1956.

_____, to Lupita Martínez. 4 Sept. 1956.

_____, to Manuel Ávila, Jr. 4 Sept. 1956.

_____, to Gilbert A. Torrez. 10 Sept. 1956.

_____, to Vicente Ximenes. 10 Sept. 1956.

_____, to Vicente Ximenes. 15 Oct. 1956.

_____, to Vicente Jasso. 30 Oct. 1956.

_____, to Vicente Ximenes. 30 Oct. 1956.

_____, to Vicente Jasso. 12 Nov. 1956.

_____, to Vicente Ximenes. 12 Nov. 1956.

_____, to Vicente Ximenes. 19 Nov. 1956.

_____, to Vicente Ximenes. 21 Dec. 1956.

_____, to Vicente Ximenes. 11 Mar. 1957.

_____, to John E. Young. 12 Mar. 1957.

_____, to William D. O'Conner. 12 Mar. 1957.

_____, to Adán Saénz. 16 Mar. 1957.

_____, to Cristóbal Aldrete. 19 Mar. 1957.

_____, to George I. Sánchez. 19 Mar. 1957.

_____, to Richard Casillas. 19 Mar. 1957.

_____, to Vicente Ximenes. 19 Mar. 1957.

_____, to Abraham Kazen, Jr. 25 Mar. 1957.

_____, to Joseph Álvarado. 25 Mar. 1957.

_____, to Lionicio M. Parra. 25 Mar. 1957.

_____, to Ronnie Dugger. 10 Apr. 1957.

_____, to Joseph M. Montoya. 12 Apr. 1957.

_____, to Frank Paz. 13 Apr. 1957.

_____, to Ramona Morín. 13 Apr. 1957.

_____, to Henry Gonzáles. 15 Apr. 1957.

_____, to Manuel Velasco. 24 Apr. 1957.

_____, to Lyndon B. Johnson. 27 Apr. 1957.

_____, to Ed Idar, Jr. 7 May 1957.

_____, to Lyndon B. Johnson. 7 May 1957.

_____, to Ralph Yarborough. 7 May 1957.

_____, to Vicente Ximenes. 7 May 1957.

_____, to the Texas Law Enforcement Foundation. 15 May 1957.

_____, to James P. Mitchell. 27 May 1957.

_____, to Leonardo Hernández. 28 May 1957.

_____, to Lyndon B. Johnson. 28 May 1957.

_____, to Saul Grossman. 28 May 1957.

_____, to James P. Mitchell. 4 June 1957.

_____, to Mary Zamarripas. 4 June 1957.

_____, to Virgilio Roel. 10 June 1957.

_____, to Joe I. Lucero. 14 June 1957.

_____, to the Bureau of Vital Statistics. 15 June 1957.

_____, to Vicente Jasso. 15 June 1957.

_____, to Henry LeBlanc. 25 June 1957.

_____, to John J. Herrera. 25 June 1957.

_____, to the Editor of the *Dallas Morning News*. 28 June 1957.

_____, to Milton Plumb. 4 July 1957.

_____, to Ted Estrada. 21 Jan. 1958.

_____, to Ralph Yarborough. 17 Feb. 1958.

_____, to Ralph Yarborough. 1 Apr. 1958.

_____, to Lyndon B. Johnson. 12 Apr. 1959.

_____, form letter to all national, state, local officers and members of the American G.I. Forum. 3 May 1959.

_____, to Ed Idar, Jr. 6 Aug. 1959.

_____, form letter to unidentified persons regarding information on the education of non-English speaking preschoolers. 1960.

_____, to Lyndon B. Johnson. 3 Mar. 1960.

_____, to E. C. Gathings. 15 Apr. 1960.

_____, to John Young. 23 Apr. 1960.

_____, to John Young. 2 June 1960.

_____, to Pete Esquivel. 3 June 1960.

_____, to Lyndon B. Johnson. 17 June 1960.

_____, to John F. Kennedy. 2 Aug. 1960.

_____, to Joe Alvarado. 18 Jan. 1961.

_____, to Carlos McCormick. 18 Feb. 1961.

_____, to Roy Elizondo. 22 Feb. 1961.

_____, to Carlos McCormick. 24 Feb. 1961.

_____, to Hector Moreno. 25 Feb. 1961.

_____, to Manuel Ávila, Jr. 25 Feb. 1961.

_____, to Ben Alexander. 27 Feb. 1961.

_____, to Ted Butler. 27 Feb. 1961.

_____, to John Young. 5 Mar. 1961.

_____, to Manuel Ávila, Jr. 11 Mar. 1961.

_____, to F. L. Silva. 25 Mar. 1961.

_____, to Lino López. 25 Mar. 1961.

_____, to Manuel Ávila, Jr. 25 Mar. 1961.

_____, to Carlos McCormick. 4 Apr. 1961.

_____, to Jerry Holleman. 4 Apr. 1961.

_____, to Mike Cieplinski. 13 Apr. 1961.

_____, to John F. Kennedy. 26 Apr. 1961.

_____, to Manuel Ávila, Jr. 9 May 1961.

_____, to Teodoro Estrada. 9 May 1961.

_____, to Dennis Chávez. 9 June 1961.

_____, to Michael Cieplinsky. 12 June 1961.

_____, to Hector Arce. 23 June 1961.

_____, to Manuel Ávila, Jr. 22 July 1961.

_____, to Hesiquio Rodríguez. 2 Aug. 1961.

_____, to John F. Kennedy. 2 Aug. 1961.

_____, to Manuel Ávila, Jr. 28 Aug. 1961.

_____, to Teodoro R. Estrada. 30 Aug. 1961.

_____, to Manuel Ávila, Jr. 18 Sept. 1961.

_____, to Manuel Ávila, Jr. 19 Sept. 1961.

_____, to John F. Kennedy. 22 Sept. 1961.

_____, to Manuel Ávila, Jr. 27 Sept. 1961.

_____, to John F. Kennedy. 6 Oct. 1961.

_____, to Carlos McCormick. 10 Oct. 1961.

_____, to Manuel Ávila, Jr. 30 Oct. 1961.

_____, to John F. Kennedy. 22 Nov. 1961.

_____, to Carlos McCormick. 24 Nov. 1961.

_____, to Manuel Ávila, Jr. 28 Nov. 1961.

_____, to Carlos McCormick. 19 Dec. 1961.

_____, to Leo J. Leo. 24 Feb. 1962.

_____, to John F. Kennedy. 1 Mar. 1962.

_____, to Vicente Ximenes. 7 Mar. 1962.

_____, to Manuel Ávila, Jr. 14 Apr. 1962.

_____, to Lyndon B. Johnson. 31 July 1962.

_____, to Melchor Díaz Rubio. 31 July 1962.

_____, to Robert F. Kennedy. 31 July 1962.

_____, to Manuel Ávila, Jr. 1 Oct. 1962.

_____, to Lyndon B. Johnson. 20 Oct. 1962.

_____, to Manuel Ávila Jr. 20 Oct. 1962.

_____, to Rodolfo Loa Ramos. 19 Mar. 1963.

_____, to Carlos J. McCormick. 20 Mar. 1963.

_____, to Joe Alvarado. 20 Mar. 1963.

_____, to Robert F. Kennedy. 20 Mar. 1963.

_____, to Robert F. Kennedy. 13 June 1963.

_____, to Ralph Yarborough. 30 July 1963.

_____, to Lyndon B. Johnson. 10 June 1964.

_____, to Lyndon B. Johnson. 8 Sept. 1964.

_____, to Lyndon B. Johnson. 13 Jan. 1965.

_____, to Willard W. Wirtz. 13 Jan. 1965.

_____, to James Wright. 24 Feb. 1965.

_____, to Nicolas D. Katzenbach. 18 Jan. 1966.

_____, to John W. Macy, Jr. 24 Jan. 1966.

_____, to Luis Telles. 6 Sept. 1966.

_____, to Lyndon B. Johnson. 22 Sept. 1966.

_____, to John W. Macy, Jr. 28 Jan. 1967.

_____, to Mr. and Mrs. Edward H. Harte. 20 Sept. 1967.

_____, to Lyndon B. Johnson. 22 Sept. 1967.

_____, to Mr. and Mrs. Geronimo Ruíz. 6 Oct. 1967.

_____, to James De Anda. 12 Oct. 1967.

_____, form letter to all Representatives and Senators regarding a four-year university at Corpus Christi, Texas. 5 Apr. 1969.

_____, to George P. Schultz. 29 Nov. 1969.

_____, to Leon E. Panetta. 10 Dec. 1969.

_____, to Richard M. Nixon. 30 Jan. 1970.

_____, to Mr. Mahon. 17 Feb. 1970.

_____, to Mrs. Lyndon Johnson. 22 Jan. 1973.

_____, to Dolph Briscoe. 17 Sept. 1973.

_____, to J. Antonio García. 31 July 1974.

_____, to J. L. Pruett. 2 Aug. 1974.

_____, to the "Letters From Our Readers" section of _Corpus Christi Caller-Times_. 3 Nov. 1974.

_____, form letter to Mexican Americans of Texas. 1 Nov. 1975.

_____, form letter to minority groups regarding the Coors boycott. 11 Nov. 1975.

_____, to Jimmy Carter. 3 Nov. 1976.

_____, to Jimmy Carter. 4 Nov. 1976.

_____, J.A. Tony Canales, Cleo García, and Xico García to Jimmy Carter. 12 Nov. 1976.

_____, and J.A. "Tony" Canales, to Jimmy Carter. 22 Jan. 1977.

_____, to Jimmy Carter. 24 Jan. 1980.

_____, to Wilson Riles. 25 Jan. 1980.

_____, to William Bonilla. 7 Feb. 1980.

_____, to Bob Block. 8 Feb. 1980.

_____, to Ronald Reagan. 17 Feb. 1984.

_____, to Sarah Weddington. 28 Feb. 1980.

_____, to Walter Mondale. 3 Mar. 1980.

_____, to Bob Beckel. 11 June 1980.

_____, to the American G.I. Forum State Convention. 18 June 1980.

_____, to Jimmy Carter. 23 June 1978.

_____, to the Editor of _Corpus Christi Caller-Times_. 15 Oct. 1980.

_____, to Ronald Reagan. 17 Feb. 1984.

García, José G., to Captain Hector P. García. 1 Aug. 1945.

García, José, Jr., to Hector P. García. 2 Apr. 1951.

García, Xico, to Hector P. and Wanda García. 16 Apr. 1949.

_____, to Hector P. García. 12 Feb. 1950.

_____, to Hector P. García. 15 Nov. 1950.

_____, to Hector P. García. 23 Sept. 1950.

_____, to Hector P. García (confirming Hector's acceptance of the Alba "Man of the Year" award). Undated.

Garriga, M. S., to Hector P. García. 15 Jan. 1951.

Garza, José J., to the American G.I. Forum. 2 Aug. 1949.

Gates, Thomas S., Jr., to Lyndon B. Johnson. Undated.

Gay, E. A., to L. A. Woods. 16 Sept. 1949.

Gaytan, S. I., and S. D. Moreno, to Hector P. García. 29 Jan. 1949.

Geiger, Joe F., to Hector P. García. 29 Mar. 1948.

Geis, L.R., to Hector P. García. 30 Sept. 1969.

Glickstein, Howard A., to Hector P. García. 3 Jan. 1969.

_____, to Hector P. García. 14 Jan. 1969.

_____, to Hector P. García. 24 Jan. 1969.

_____, to Joel T. Broyhill. 16 Apr. 1969.

_____, to Junio López. 19 Sept. 1969.

Goldberg, Arthur J., to Hector P. García. 26 Oct. 1967.

Gonzáles, Arnold, to Hector P. García. 4 Aug. 1981.

González, E. B., to Hector P. García. 26 Apr. 1951.

González, Henry B., to Hector P. García. 17 Apr. 1957.

González, Joe (and others, as a petition), to the City Comission of Corpus Christi, Texas. 15 May 1941.

Gonzales, Paul, to W. K. Coors. 26 Feb. 1970.

_____, to William K. Coors. 3 July 1970.

Goodwin, Robert C., to Harry B. Crozier. 18 Oct. 1949.

A group of over a hundred veterans, to Lloyd M. Bentsen. 15 Mar. 1951.

Guerrero, Alfred Jr., to Hector García. 17 Oct. 1949.

Guerrero, Salvador, to Hector P. García. 7 May 1957.

Gutiérrez, José Angel, to Hector P. García. 6 Oct. 1976.

_____, to Hector P. García. 6 Oct. 1976.

_____, to Hector P. García. 16 May 1977.

Gutiérrez, Oscar E., to Richard M. Nixon. 24 Jan. 1969.

Hall, H. Boyd, to Hector P. García. 26 Sept. 1950.

Hannah, John A., to Richard M. Nixon. 23 Jan. 1969

Harte, Edward H., to Hector P. García. 18 Sept. 1967.

Harvin, E. L., to Hector P. García. 12 May 1949.

Hassett, William D., to Hector P. García. 15 May 1951.

Hernández, Albert, to Hector P. García. 5 May 1970.

Hernández, Antonio, to Hector P. García. 29 Nov. 1952.

Hernández, Heriberto, to Bob McCracken. 27 Sept. 1950.

Hernández, Rodolfo, to Hector P. García. 14 May 1980.

Herrera, John J., to Hector P. García. 16 June 1950.

_____, to Phil J. Montalbo. 14 June 1957.

Hinman, Geo. W., Jr., to the American G.I. Forum. 31 Jan. 1949.

Hodges, Gahl L., to Hector P. García. 14 Sept. 1983.

Holden, Emery L., to Hector P. García. 8 Mar. 1949.

Hoover, J. Edgar, to Hector P. García. 21 Mar. 1956.

_____, to Hector P. García. 27 Apr. 1959.

Howell, Leon P., to Hector P. García. 11 Jan. 1949.

Idar, Ed, Jr., form letter to all members of the Board of Directors of the American G.I. Forum. Undated.

_____, to Hector P. García. 27 Sept. 1950.

_____, to Brig. Gen. Paul Wakefield. 4 Oct. 1950.

_____, to J. W. Edgar. 8 Oct. 1950.

_____, to Hector P. García. 12 Nov. 1950.

_____, to Hector P. García. 14 Nov. 1950.

_____, to Harry B. Crozier. 20 Nov. 1951.

_____, to Maurice J. Tobin. 5 Dec. 1951.

_____, to Dick Gonzales. 4 Jan. 1952.

_____, to A. H. Cardenas. 12 Jan. 1952.

_____, to Richard Moreno. 12 Jan. 1952.

_____, to J. T. Canales. 15 Jan. 1952.

_____, to J. T. Canales. 22 Jan. 1952.

_____, to James E. Murray. 25 Jan. 1952.

_____, to Lloyd Bentsen. 3 Mar. 1952.

_____, to Hector P. García. 2 May 1952.

_____, to Ed Cazares. 31 Oct. 1952.

_____, to Lyndon B. Johnson. 21 Nov. 1952 (letter never sent).

_____, to Carlos Cadena. 4 Dec. 1952.

_____, to Gus C. García. 4 Dec. 1952.

_____, to J. T. Canales. 4 Dec. 1952.

_____, to Lyndon B. Johnson. 4 Dec. 1952.

_____, to Hector P. García. 24 Aug. 1953.

_____, to Hector P. García. 7 Sept. 1953.

_____, to Hector P. García. 16 Sept. 1953.

_____, to Leonelo Gonzales. 19 Oct. 1953.

_____, to Albert Armendariz. 27 Oct. 1953.

_____, to Carlos Cadena. 27 Oct. 1953.

_____, to Gilbert García. 4 Nov. 1953.

_____, to Albert Armendariz. 23 Nov. 1953.

_____, to Chris Aldrete. 23 Nov. 1953.

_____, to Hector P. García. 23 Nov. 1953.

_____, to Chris Aldrete. 25 Nov. 1953.

_____, to Carlos Cadena. 15 Feb. 1954.

_____, to Hector P. García. 23 Mar. 1954.

_____, to Apolonio Montemayor. 1 Sept. 1954.

_____, to Carlos C. Cadena. 21 Dec. 1954.

_____, to Hector P. García, 21 Dec. 1954.

_____, to Hector P. García. 8 July 1955.

_____, to Hector P. García. 25 July 1955.

_____, to G. I. Sánchez. 24 Sept. 1956.

_____, to Hector P. García. 19 Apr. 1957.

_____, to H. T. Manuel. 21 Nov. 1959.

_____, form letter to all state officers, directors, and local groups of the American G.I. Forum of Texas. 14 Jan. 1960.

_____, to Gus C. García. 26 July 1960.

_____, to George I. Sánchez. 1 Aug. 1960.

_____, to Gus C. García. 1 Aug. 1960.

_____, to James De Anda. 14 Feb. 1961.

_____, to George I. Sánchez. 17 May 1962.

_____, to R. P. Sánchez. 18 June 1963.

_____, to 5 officers of the American G.I. Forum. 3 Aug. 1955.

Jasso, Vicente B., to James De Anda. 25 July 1961.

Jenkins, E. L., to L. W. Bryan, Jr. 25 May 1948.

Jester, Beauford H., to Hector P. García. Undated.

Johnson, Louis, to Tom Connally. 15 Feb, 1950

Johnson, Lyndon B., to E. E. Mireles. 15 May 1941.

_____, to E. E. Mireles. 29 May 1941.

_____, to Hector P. García. 11 Jan. 1949.

_____, to Hector P. García. 10 Feb. 1949.

_____, to Frank Oltorf. 12 Mar. 1949.

_____, to Hector P. García. 5 Oct. 1949.

_____, to Hector P. García. 13 Oct. 1949.

_____, to Hector P. García. 28 Oct. 1949.

_____, to Hector P. García. 15 Feb. 1950.

_____, to Eucelia Lerma. 23 Feb. 1950.

_____, to Hector P. García. 24 Feb. 1950.

_____, to Hector P. García. 23 Mar. 1950.

_____, to Hector P. García. 5 May 1950.

_____, to Hector P. García. 19 Dec. 1950.

_____, to Ed Idar, Jr. 14 Nov. 1952.

_____, to Hector P. García. 11 Aug. 1953.

_____, to Hector P. García. 8 Mar. 1956.

_____, to Hector P. García. 14 Mar. 1956.

_____, to Hector P. García. 17 May 1956.

_____, to Hector P. García. 24 July 1956.

_____, to Hector P. García. 4 June 1957.

_____, to Thomas S. Gates, Jr. 26 Dec. 1958.

_____, to Frank X. Paz. 13 Aug. 1959.

_____, to Hector P. García. 25 Aug. 1960.

_____, to Hector P. García. 6 Oct. 1962.

_____, to Hector P. García. 31 Aug. 1965.

_____, to Hector P. García. 12 Feb. 1966.

_____, to Hector P. García. 29 Jan. 1968.

_____, to Hector P. García. 2 Nov. 1968.

Jones, E. N., to Hector P. García. 26 June 1948.

Jones, Robert N., to Lyndon B. Johnson. 13 Nov. 1949.

_____, to H. S. Truman. 1 July 1951.

Juraschek, Erwin A., to Hector P. García. 5 Dec. 1952.

Katzenbach, Nicolas D., to Hector P. García. 7 Mar. 1966.

Kazen, Abraham, Jr., to Hector P. García. 28 Nov. 1950.

Kelley, Rogers, to Hector P. García. 22 July 1948.

_____, to Hector P. García. 11 Jan. 1949.

_____, to Tom O. Inabinette. 19 Feb. 1949.

_____, to Hector P. García. 21 Apr. 1949.

_____, to Hector P. García. 23 Feb. 1950.

Kemp, W. T., to Captain Hector P. García. 17 Nov. 1943.

Kennedy, Edward M., to Hector P. García. 14 Apr. 1969.

_____, to Hector P. García. 5 May 1970.

Kennedy, John F., to Hector P. García. 28 Dec. 1959.

Kennedy, T. W., Jr., to Beatrice Longoria. 12 Jan. 1949.

Kerr, Walter K., to Hector P. García. 1 Sept. 1950.

_____, to Hector P. García. 15 Sept. 1950.

Kilgore, Joe M., to L. Alvarado. 22 June 1949.

Kozeletz, John F., to Joel T. Broyhill. 5 Apr. 1969.

Kraemer, Richard H., to Hector P. García. 6 Oct. 1977.

Larkin, T. B., to the Commanding Officer of the 591st Engineer Boat Regiment. 27 Oct. 1944.

LeBlanc, Henry, to Hector P. García. 11 Sept. 1956.

_____, to Hector P. García. 27 June 1957.

Leonard, Jerris, to Hector P. García. 13 Oct. 1969.

Longoria, Beatrice, to Mr. Kennedy. 14 Jan. 1949.

Longoria, Dolores (and 8 others), to Lyndon B. Johnson. 15 Jan. 1949.

López, L. M., to Hector P. García. 18 Dec. 1952.

Lyle, John E. Jr., to Hector P. García. 11 Jan. 1949.

_____, to Hector P. García. 23 June 1949.

_____, to Hector P. García. 8 Oct. 1949.

_____, to Hector P. García. 21 Feb. 1950.

_____, to Eudelia Lerma. 25 Feb. 1950.

Mackay, A. R., to Hector P. García. 10 Oct. 1949.

Martínez, Benigno, to Hector P. García. 31 Oct. 1953.

Massie, Glenn W., to Hector P. García. 11 Jan. 1949.

McCarthy, Edward R., to Captain Hector P. García. 22 Sept. 1945.

_____, to Commanding General of the Delta Base Section. 27 Sept. 1945.

McMullen, Hugh P., to Hector P. García. 9 May 1950.

Medina, Ireneo, and E. G. Aranda, to Hector P. García. 15 Dec. 1950.

Meiling, Richard L., to Hector P. García. 2 Mar. 1950.

Ministry of Health, Water, and Sanitation (from Trinidad), to Hector P. García. 13 Mar. 1961.

Mitchell, Maurice B., to Hector P. García. 11 Dec. 1969.

Mondale, Walter F., to Hector P. García. 13 Aug. 1969.

_____, to Hector P. García. 14 Aug. 1970.

Montgomery, J. K., to Hector P. García. 11 Jan. 1949.

Montoya, Joseph M., to Richard M. Nixon. 24 Apr. 1969.

Mora, Calixto, to Hector P. García. 21 Feb. 1950.

Morales, Dionicio, to Hector P. García. 1 Nov. 1956.

Morales, Hector T., to John Young. 1 Oct. 1975.

Moreno, Alfredo A., Jr., to Hector P. García. 14 Jan. 1949.

Morgan, Daniel C., Jr., to Hector P. García. 28 Mar. 1966.

Morgan, M. B., to Hector P. García. 5 Oct. 1949.

Moskowitz, Jack, to Hector P. García. 26 Feb. 1966.

Moya, Juan, to Hector P. García. 15 Jan. 1949.

Mrs. Frank X., to Hector P. García. 5 Dec. 1952.

Neumann, Thomas L., to Hector P. García. 30 June 1980.

Nixon, Richard M., to Hector P. García. 2 Dec. 1968.

North, David S., to Hector P. García. 11 Oct. 1966.

Obledo, Mario G., to Hector P. García. 17 Apr. 1980.

O'brien, Lawrence F., to Hector P. García. 2 Oct. 1965.

Oliver, E. J., to First Lieutenant Hector. P. García. 17 Feb. 1942.

Oltorf, Frank C., to Hector P. García. 2 May 1949.

Ortiz, David M., to Hector P. García. 15 Jan. 1949.

Padilla, Ivan, to Gordon Jones. 18 July 1977.

Páez, Pilar G., to Hector P., García. 9 Dec. 1952.

Palmer, W. B., to Hector P. García. 13 Dec. 1950.

Parker, David H., to Hector P. García. 10 Mar. 1949.

Patterson, C. C., Major, to Colonel Sylvan Lang. 12 Aug. 1939.

Penrose, Neville G., to John Ben Shepperd. 13 Dec. 1949.

Perales, Alonso S., to Hector P. García. 15 Mar. 1949.

_____, to Hector P. García. 15 Feb. 1951.

_____, to G. I. Sánchez. 3 Dec. 1951.

Plumb, Milton, to Hector P. García. 3 Jan. 1957.

Pope, Jack, to Hector P. García. 25 Feb. 1989.

Ramos, Rudy L. and Hector P. García, to John W. Macy, Jr. Undated.

Rayburn, Sam, to Hector P. García. Oct. 1952.

_____, to Hector P. García. 16 May 1956.

Reagan, Ronald, to Hector P. García. 17 June 1982.

Reed, Bevington, to Hector P. García. 20 Oct. 1970.

Reveley, Paul J., to Lyndon B. Johnson. 8 Mar. 1949.

Richardson, Bill, to Hector P. García. 27 July 1983.

Rivera, Natividad, to Hector P. García. 14 Jan. 1949.

Rodgers, Charles E., Jr., to Hector P. García. 21 Sept. 1967.

_____, to Richard M. Nixon. 6 Jan. 1971.

Rodríguez, Robert V., to Hector P. García. 23 Oct. 1963.

Rogers, William J., to Thomas S. Sutherland. 30 Sept. 1949.

_____, to Hector P. García. 9 Oct. 1950.

_____, to Hector P. García. 12 Dec. 1956.

_____, to Hector P. García. 10 June 1957.

Rosales, Ismael, to Robert Kennedy. 4 Oct. 1963.

Rosas, L. S., to Hector P. García. 21 May 1951.

Rountree, James T., to Richard M. Nixon. 29 Jan. 1969.

Royall, Kenneth C., to Hector P. García. 20 Jan. 1949.

Rucker, J. C., to First Lieutenant Hector P. García. 2 Feb. 1942.

Sáenz, Adán, to Hector P. García. 5 Nov. 1956.

Saénz, J. Luz, to Hector P. García. 16 May 1949.

_____, to Lyndon B. Johnson and four others. Nov. 1949.

_____, to Hector P. García. 1 Nov. 1949.

Sánchez, Frank L., to Hector P. García. 14 Jan. 1949.

Sánchez, George I., to Hector P. García. 11 Mar. 1949.

_____, to Hector P. García. 14 Apr. 1949.

_____, to Gus García. 23 Apr. 1949.

_____, to Robert E. Lucey. 24 July 1950.

_____, to Hector P. García. 10 Apr. 1951.

_____, to Alonso S. Perales. 5 Dec. 1951.

_____, to Hector P. García. 20 Dec. 1951.

_____, to Jack Danciger. 28 Oct. 1953.

_____, to Ed Idar, Jr. 7 June 1955.

_____, to Hector P. García. 7 Mar. 1957.

_____, to Ed Idar, Jr. 29 July 1960.

_____, to Hector P. García. 24 Apr. 1962.

_____, to Ed Idar, Jr. 16 May 1962.

_____, to Hector P. García. 27 May 1963.

_____, to William D. Bonilla. 17 June 1963.

_____, to Hector P. García. 23 July 1970.

Sánchez, Henry, to Joseph Juárez. 23 Nov. 1971.

Sánchez, R. P., to Hector P. García. 31 Jan. 1956.

_____, to Joe Borrego. 4 Apr. 1957.

_____, to Hector P. García. 6 Mar. 1958.

_____, to Xico and Yolanda García. 17 July 1958.

_____, to Joseph M. Montoya. 13 Apr. 1960.

_____, to Hector P. García. 10 Feb. 1969.

_____, to Hector P. García. 16 Aug. 1972.

Saunders, Lyle, to Hector P. García. 14 Mar. 1949.

Schondau, Marguerite, to Hector P. García. 11 Mar. 1957.

Scull, Chas. L., to Hector P. García. 16 Mar. 1951.

The Secretary of Defense, to Hector P. García. 11 Jan. 1949.

Shivers, Allan T., to Hector P. García. 10 Oct. 1949.

_____, to Hector P. García. 2 Dec. 1949.

Shulman, Stephen N., to Hector P. García. 24 Apr. 1967.

Smith, George Gemmill, to Hector P. García. 13 Mar. 1961.

Smith, Preston, to Hector P. García. 27 Mar. 1969.

Smith, R. E., to Hector P. García. 31 Oct. 1950.

Smith, Weldon A., to Hector P. García. 5 Apr. 1949.

Solis, G.R., to Ralph Yarborough. 17 June 1967.

_____, to Hector P. García. 30 June 1967.

State Headquarters of the Texas American G.I. Forum, to all Forum officers, and auxiliaries. 15 Jan. 1952.

Storm, María, to Hector P. García. 22 Feb. 1950.

Storm, Marion, to Hector P. García. 22 Feb. 1950.

Sutherland, Thomas S., to M. B. Morgan. 21 Sept. 1949.

Telles, Luis, to Lyndon B. Johnson. 30 Aug. 1966.

Torres, Esteban E., to Hector P. García. 16 Apr. 1980.

Torrez, Gilbert A., to Hector P. García. 9 Oct. 1956.

Tower, John, to Ronald Reagan. 27 May 1983.

Unnamed author from Washington, D. C., to Hector P. García. 29 Jan. 1949.

Untitled, undated memorandum to Hector P. García regarding his request for promotion. Likely source is the Army Reserves or the War Department.

VanCronkhite, John, to Hector P. García. 25 Apr. 1949.

Vásquez, Arturo, form letter to all forums and auxiliaries of the G.I. Forum of Texas. Dec. 1950.

Vaughan, Harry H., to Hector P. García. 12 Jan. 1949.

Vela, Simon S., to Hector P. García. 16 Nov. 1953.

Vela Earhart, Herminia, to Hector P. García. Undated.

Velasco, Manuel A., to L. P. Nava. 20 Mar. 1957.

Viera, Alex, form letter to members of the American G.I. Forum and Affirmative Action Team. 10 Nov. 1976.

Von Dohlen, Tim, to Hector P. García. 11 June 1980.

Watson, W. Marvin, to Hector P. García. 8 June 1967.

Weiler, William F., to the Commanding General of the Seventh Army. 31 May 1945.

Wellford, Harrison, to Hector P. García. 18 Apr. 1980.

Westerberg, George E., to Lawrence Amaya. 5 Aug. 1969.

Wheeler, John E., to Hector P. García. 3 Apr. 1957.

White, Mark, to Hector P. García. 18 June 1980.

Wise, J. B., Jr., to the Commanding General of the Seventh Corps Area. 21 July 1942.

Woodard, Jimmy O., to Hector P. García. 15 Oct. 1981.

Ximenes, Vicente, form letter to members of the National American G.I. Forum. Undated.

_____, to Hector P. García. Undated.

_____, to Hector P. García. 8 Sept. 1951.

_____, to C. W. Burrell. 30 Aug. 1956.

_____, to Hector P. García. 15 Oct. 1956.

_____, to Hector P. García. 19 Oct. 1956.

_____, to Frank X. Paz. 28 Oct. 1956.

_____, to Hector P. García. 3 Nov. 1956.

_____, to Manuel A. Velasco. 10 Nov. 1956.

_____, to Hector P. García. 14 Nov. 1956.

_____, to the City Editor of the *Albuquerque Journal*. 14 Nov. 1956.

_____, to Mrs. Frederic A. Groves. 21 Feb. 1957.

_____, to James de Anda. 11 June 1957.

_____, to Robert L. Shortley. 22 Mar. 1961.

_____, to Dominga Coronado. 11 Oct. 1967.

_____, to Hector P. García. 2 July 1970.

Ximenes, Waldo E., to the Mayor of San Angelo, Texas. 17 Mar. 1950.

Yarborough, Ralph, to Hector P. García. 29 Apr. 1957.

_____, to Hector P. García. 1 July 1957.

_____, to Lyndon B. Johnson. 13 July 1966.

_____, to G.R. Solis. 23 June 1967.

Young, John, to Hector P. García. 23 Mar. 1957.

Index

Acuña, Rudy, xxxii, 278
African Americans, 21–22, 260–261, 270, 271
agricultural capitalists(ism), 14
agricultural revolution, 105
Alba club, 163
Aldrete, Cristóbal P., 163–164, 184
Allred, James V., 226
Alurista, 278
Always, Lazelle D., 148
American dream (HPG), xviii–xix, xxvi–xxviii, xxix–xxx, 181, 189, 278
American Century, Hector's place in, xix–xx
American G.I. Forum, xvii; Albuquerque, 264; among Puerto Ricans, 309; call to "re-enlist", xxvi–xxvii; captivating idea, 187; child labor, 168; conservative shift, 295–296, 297; democratic, xxxi; democratic meetings, 117; exclusively Mexican American, 90; first

convention, 165–169; foreign labor, 169; founding of, 88; fundraising, 149; good issue for, 115; hail Hernández suit, 194; Hector at center of, xxxvi–xxxvii; job training, 255–256; national chair (HPG), 292–294; national entity, 101; not focused on ethnicity, xxii–xxiii; praiseworthy, 120; provided reform avenues, 164; recruitment, 97–99; school drives, 148; shifts agenda, xxxiii–xxxv; Viet Nam, 268; White House, 262–263; withhold funds, 170
American Legion, 93–94, 125; James Edmond Post, 121
Americanism, 96, 188
Americanization, 157; of Southwest, xxi; process of, xxx–xxxi, 6, 13–14
Anderson, Robert, 226
Anglo Americans: few advocates among, xxi; new politicians,

xxxi; segregation
appropriate, 13; sought out
Hector, xxxv; superiority
feelings, xx; views,
155–156; vigilante groups, 6
Anglo Texan: malevolence,
xx–xxi; Mexican interaction
with, 20
Anglo Society, assimilation into,
xx–xxi
Anguiano, Lupe, 258
Asherton, 179
Asociación Nacional México-
Americana, 167
attack discrimination (HPG),
146; bracero program,
157–160; philosophy,
147–148; rich vs. poor, 152;
Spanish speaking must,
149–150
anti-business bias (HPG), xxxv
attitude toward barrio (HPG),
xxiv–xxv; toward poor, xxxii
Ávila, Manuel, 225, 228, 232,
236
Aztlán, 278

back-to-school drives, Forum's,
148–150
battle for inclusion, xxvii–xxviii
barrio Americanism, xxi,
xxv–xxvi, 85–86
barrio politicians, xxix–xxx
barrios, change difficult in, xxx
Bentsen, Lloyd M., 116, 206

Bernal, Joe, 269, 280
bilingual education, 226–227
biography of one (HPG),
xxxv–xxxvi
birth/childhood (HPG), 1;
academic GPA, 22;
advantages, 20; Anglo
friends, 19; defends father,
9; ease with Anglos, 24;
enjoyed life, 8; move to
Texas, 2; grew up bilingual,
12; inspiring mother, 11;
knew few Mexicans, 18;
loved environment, 16–17;
no ugly encounters, 21–22;
precious, 25; prepared for
school, 15; tests father's
patience, 7
Bonilla, Tony, 281
Bonilla, William, 247
Border Patrol, 202, 215, 253
Borjas, Isaac, 203
bracero program, 152–159,
161–163, 168, 170, 174,
201, 216, 218–219, 253, 256
Bronze Medal, 73
*Brown v. Topeka Board of
Education*, 193

Cabinet Committee Hearings on
Mexican American Affairs,
271–274
Cadena, Carlos, 34, 191–195
Califano, Joseph, 265
Canales, J.T., 36, 163, 196–197,

201, 209
Cannon, O.E., 121
Cano, José, 295–296
Cantú, Arturo, 167
Cantú, Tomás, 203
Carter, Jimmy, 288
Cásares, Gilbert, 79, 98,
    110–111, 298, 306
Cassas, Ramiro, 241
Castañeda, Carlos, 35, 37, 212,
    278
Castro, Raúl, 223, 229, 230
caudillismo, 176
Chagrin, Gerald S., 290
Chapa, Frank, 167
Chávez, César, xvii, xix, xxxvi,
    272, 313
Chávez, Dennis, 212, 221, 223,
    225
chicano activists, xxxii, 161,
    165–166, 180, 183, 202,
    265, 271, 278–279,
    280–281, 304, 305–306,
    310. *See also* chicano
    nationalists
chicano movement,
    xxxiii–xxxiv, 38, 245, 252,
    278, 279–280, 283
chicano nationalists(ism),
    xxix–xxx, xxxi, 17
chicano scholars, xvii, 97, 175
child labor, in Texas, 151, 162
Citizens Military Training Corp
    (CMTC), 28; harsh training
    in, 53–54; Hector joins, 51;

"masquerading," 52
civil rights, 89, 219–220;
    black/white issue, 221; equal
    footing, 271; LBJ, 253;
    leaders, 226
Cold War, xxvi, 71, 172
communism, 219–220
Community Action Program,
    258, 263–264, 273
complex man (HPG),
    xxxvi–xxxvii
Coney, William, 116
Congress of Spanish-Speaking
    People, xxiii
Connally, John, 123–124, 240,
    242–243, 260, 265, 273
Constitution of 1917, 2
Coors, 291; boycott of, xxxv
Corona, Bert, 269, 272, 277
Coronado, Dominga, 186
corporate America, xxxv,
    294–295
Corpus Christi, 19, 69, 75, 77,
    79–80, 90–91, 103, 107,
    115, 149, 165, 175
Cortez, Gregorio, 204–205
Cortez, Raoul, 121
Cotulla, 122, 254
Crystal City, 244–248
CSO, 264
Cuevas, Joe, 167

Daniel, Price, 240–242; ruling
    on *Méndez*, weak legal

decision, 143
De Anda, James, 184, 191
death: in family (HPG), 296–297; of (HPG), xvii, 313
De la Fuente, Mike, 37–38
Del Rio, Texas, 283–286
Delgado v. Bastrop Independent School District, 144, 170, 189
Democratic Party, xxxvii, 184, 212, 219, 221, 223, 227, 269
Díaz, Juan, 128
Díaz, Tito, 204
discrimination: accommodation to, 155; awakened to, 140; Hector confronts, 203; Hector's view on, 156–157; in sports, 179; José's avoidance of, 35; middle class, 36; national attention, 138; of Mexican Americans, xxi–xxii; outraged, 205; racial, 16; rampant, 6; resilience of, xxii–xxiii; siblings remember, 22
diversity: Hector's first encounter, 46; in war, 71
draft boards, 96
Driscoll School Dristict, 189
Du Bois, W.E.B., 181

Earhart, Herminia Vela, 178
EEOC, 264
El Chamizal, 273

English-only, 13–14
ethnic politics, xxxi
Evans, Roger G., 147
exiliados, 10, 12

Falcón, Moses, 244
family ideals/conflicts (HPG), 55–57; chastises José, 60; status concerns, 61; *Tono v. José*, 62–65
fifties: best/worst, 207; denigrating literature, 175; leadership building, 180; "No Mexicans Served," 178; piecemeal battles, 173; retrenchment during, 174
Flores, Frank, 167
foreign service (HPG): ambassador, 274–276, 308; Jamaica, 230–233
forgotten people, xxii–xxiii
Forum leaders, 180–186; Hector's interaction with, 181–182, 305
Fuentes, Albert, 244–245
Fusillo, Wanda: accompanies Hector, 99; "call," 74; change, 102–103; faces discrimination, 204; family, 67; funeral (HPG), 313; Hector, 229–300; "long time," 75; marriage, 68–69; met Hector, 66; sees Hector change, 102–103

Galarza, Ernesto, 38, 272, 277
Galván, Molly, 186
García, Antonio (uncle), 2, 23
García, Antonio (Tono), 27,
    29–30, 32, 40, 62, 74, 75,
    149, 296, 299
García children, xix; education
    first, 31; enjoyed school, 17;
    financial difficulty, 39;
    tenacious in school, 15–16;
    were bilingual, 12
García, Cleotilde, 1, 15, 17,
    23–25, 75, 99, 299; close to
    Hector, 57; husband, 44; in
    college, 28
García, Cuauhtemoc, 12
García, Cuitlahuac (Bone), 12,
    63–64
García, Dalia, 296–297
García, Faustina, 1, 8–12, 297;
    death of, 45
García, Gabe, 167
García, Gustavo (Gus), 34;
    deeper analysis, 141;
    Delgado case, 165; forum
    legal advisor, 89; in
    Hernández case, 190–193;
    Longoria counsel, 136;
    philosophical views,
    195–196, 302; seeks
    clarification, 142
García, J.O., 121
García, José, 1–7, 9, 15, 25, 27,
    29–30, 32–33
García, José, Jr., 176–177

García, Martin, 245–246
García, Moisés, 4
García store, 4
García, Xicoteutactl (Xico), 12,
    31, 97, 99, 103, 163
Garza, Ignacio, 161–162
Garza, Rudolph, Jr., 281–282
Garza, Raymond, 228
Geiger, Joe E., 76, 90–92
G.I. Benefits, xii, 85
G.I. Generation, xii, xxi–xxii
global view (HPG), 276
Goebel, Della, 128
Goldberg, Arthur, Jr., 274
Gómez-Quiñones, Juan, 278
Gonzales, Rodolfo "Corky",
    272, 273, 274, 277
González, E.B., 177
González, Henry B., 208, 221,
    223, 226, 239, 248, 268, 280
González, Manuel, 36
González, M.C., 163, 209
Good Neighbor Commission,
    124, 129, 134–135, 159,
    179, 205
Gray, J.F., 134
Great Depression, 24–25, 27, 28,
    31, 42
Groh, George, 111–113
Guerrero, Alfredo, Jr., 155–157
Gutiérrez, José Angel, xxxvii,
    264, 277, 278, 286, 303–304
Guzmán, Ralph, 278

Hart, James P., 197
health (HPG), 295, 297; decline
of, xxvii; kidney infection,
75
health crusades (HPG): in
Africa, 65; in Galveston,
41–43
Hernández, Alfred, 258–259
Hernández, Pete, 190–193, 271
heroic stature (HPG), 176–178
Herrera, John J., 191–192
higher education (HPG): ahead
of others, 46; concentrated
on studies, 37–38; exciting,
30; graduation, 39;
internship, 45; junior
college, 27–29; medical
school, 39–44; medical
profession, 29; Mexican
American studies, 36;
opportunity, 33–35; to
Austin, 32; transforming
value of, 47–48; work, 31
Hinojosa-Smith, Rolando, 5, 8
honors (HPG): Alba club,
163–164
Hoover, J. Edgar, 215
Humphrey, Hubert H., 260, 272

Idar, Ed, Jr., 38; called to
resolve, 184–185;
complaints on Gus,
195–196; defends report,
196–197; end of bracero
program, 256; Hector

chastises, 302; joins Forum,
182–183; liberals, 241;
PASO, 251; supports
Salinas, 226; threatens
resignation, 305; Viva
Kennedy, 222; writes
wetback pamphlet, 198–201
immediate post-war years:
"American way," 74–75;
attacks VFW, 94;
compadre/godfather, 99;
critical juncture, 100; early
medical practice, 76–78;
education, 82–83; founding
of Forum, 88–89; health
crusades, 79–82; ideals of
democracy, 84–85; medical
practice, 101–102;
organizing efforts, 86–87;
promotes "whiteness,"
96–97; rallies local clubs,
95–96; two Hectors, 103;
veteran rights, 92–93;
visibility, 97
Immigration and Naturalization
Service, 168, 200
Interagency Committee on
Mexican American Affairs,
270

Jackson, Robert, 124
Jester, Beauford H., 115, 171
Jewish background (HPG), 2
Johnson, Lyndon B.,
"conferring," 115; Hector's

discrimination, 206;
informed of Longoria
incident, 113; political
opportunity, 123–134;
proposal, 117–118; Salinas
appointment, 228; two-fold
criteria, 125; White House,
252–277; wrote Beatrice,
112

Jones, Robert N., 208

Jornaleros of Waco, 121

Kelley, Rogers, 115, 137, 147,
206

Kennedy, John F., 218, 221–222,
223–224, 227, 245, 259, 263

Kennedy, Robert F., 221, 224,
247, 248, 259, 260, 267

Kennedy, Tom W., 107; appalled
at, 121; communal attitude,
137; exonerated by
legislature, 135; "not refused
it," 113; offers body
preparation, 109; re–affirms
refusal, 112; receives letter,
116; refuses chapel, 108;
speaks with Hector, 110;
statement of, 126–127;
waivering, 124

King, Martin Luther, 260

La Prensa, 10, 12

Larsen, Don, 158

Leo, Leo J., 241

letters from (HPG): Ávila, 228,

236, 237; congratulates JFK,
225; Forum convention,
295–296; Johnson, 259;
NACEO, 284; Nixon, 289;
to Forum, 190; to
McCormick, 232; to voters,
224

letters to (HPG): González, E.B.,
177; García, José, 176–177;
Martínez, Benigno/Earhart,
179; nationwide, 175; Vela,
Simón/Paez, Pilar/Saenz,
Adam, 178

liberals, 129, 175; conflict with
PASO, 239; few in S.T.,
211; left out, 288

Longoria, Alberto, 126, 127

Longoria, Beatrice: burial
arrangements, 107; chapel
rejection, 108; considers
burial sites, 117–118;
informed of death, 106;
legislative committee, 135;
misunderstanding, 125; must
accept, 129–130; rumored
conflict, 126–127

Longoria family, 126

Longoria, Felix: a concern of all,
119; affection for, 120;
Arlington Cemetery, 118;
birth/childhood, 105; burial
104; burial controversy, 134;
chapel rejection, 108; death,
106; funeral arrangements,
107; public record, 111;
rally for, 115, 117

Longoria, Guadalupe, 126, 127
Longoria, Guadalupe, Sr., 127,
130–131
Longoria incident (HPG):
challenges report on, 136;
fumes over rationalization,
129–130; Hector informed,
110; Hector's emergence in,
137; investigates T. R.,
131–133; organizes rally,
113; praised for, 136;
promised victories, 139;
reads LBJ telegram, 118;
receives support, 120–122;
seeks funds/support, 119;
telegrams of indignation,
115–116; victory in, 140
López, Hank, 223
López, Homer, 167
López, Lino, 235
LULAC, xxiii, xxxiv; Antonio
in, 62; approach of, 86;
Castañeda and, 35; funds
cut, 294; Hector joins,
79–80; hypersensitive on
appointments, 258; in
Mercedes, 17; litigation,
189; prejudices, 259;
Sánchez in, 34; stale, 249;
Tejano leaders, 141; veterans
in, 50; White House, 262
Lyle, John, 115, 147

MAPA (CA), 237, 262, 264, 267
MAPA (Texas), 234

Marín, Gene, 235
marriage (HPG): proposal, 68;
wedding, 69
Martínez, Benigno, 178
Maya, Juan, 121
Maya, Manuela, 121
MAYO, 272–273, 283
McCormick, Carlos, 221–222,
224, 233, 235, 247, 248
McCormick, Paul J., 142
McCraken, Bob, 124, 134–135
medal of freedom, 298
*Méndez et al v. Westminster
School District of Orange
County*: ends segregation,
142; responsibility of state,
143–144; short-lived victory,
142
Mercedes, 2–7; 10–13; 17–19;
23, 27, 32, 52, 64, 78
meritorious commendations, 65,
72–73
Mexicanism, xxxii
Mexican American elites,
160–161, 181
Mexican American experience,
xviii–xix
Mexican American history,
xxxiv–xxxv
Mexican American soldiers:
dispelled stereotypes, xx;
views on war, 50–51
Mexican elites, 16, 18, 20, 27,
32, 78
Mexican exiles, 9, 33. *See also*

exiliados
Mexican immigrants, 4, 7,
    11–12
Mexican o*rgullo*, xxii
Mexican refugees, 3
Mexican Revolution, xxi, 1, 3,
    9–10, 307
Mexico, 1, 3, 276
Meza, Ernest, 166
Middle class, 187, 190; issues,
    219–220; little challenge to,
    xxi; loyal, 221; Mexican, 1;
    reformism of, 17
military training. *See* CMTC
military experience
    (HPG):commissioned in
    reserves, 51; confident of
    victory, 58–59; convoy
    attacked, 57–58; enlistment,
    50; Germany, 69; idyllic,
    303; in reserves, 49; Italy,
    65; learned languages, 66;
    letters home, 55–58; MD
    questioned, 59; North
    Africa, 64; rank conflict,
    54–55; refiner's fire, 73;
    "stay home," 63; view of
    war, 70–72
minimum wage, 169
Mireles, E.E., 147
Montemayor, Apolonio, 167
Montgomery, J.K., 117
Morales, Dan, 301–302
Moreno, Sara: answers rumor,
    127; consults Hector,

109–110
Moyers, Bill, 255
multiculturalism, xxx
Munguía, Rubén, 190

NAACP, 193, 308
National Council of La Raza,
    295
nationalistic old-timers, xxix
nationwide crusading (HPG),
    185; with women, 185–187
Navarro, Nellie, 186
new generation of reformers, xx;
    middle class, 36; more
    pluralistic, xxxiv, 19–20;
    professional advocates, xxxii
Nixon, Richard, 224, 287,
    288–290

OEO, 270
old social reformer, xxxiv
old veterans, succumb to
    patriotism, xx
Oltorf, Frank, 137
Operation Wetback, 201, 227

Pan-Hispanism, 235
Paez, Pilar, 178
Pacheco, María, 179–180
Paredes, Américo, 204, 278
PASO, 237–250, 251–252, 260,
    264, 283, 310
Paz, Salvador, 202
Pearl Harbor, 49–50, 302

Pedigo, Jack, 210
Peña, Albert, Jr.: cabinet
    meetings, 272;
    congratulations, 224; Cyrstal
    City, 244–248; doubts about
    LBJ, 252; letter, 226–227;
    national convention, 221;
    stronger stand, 277; valuable
    organizer, 184; Viva
    Kennedy organizer, 222–223
Perales, Alonso, 36, 136–137; 163
Pete Hernández v. State of Texas,
    34, 190–193, 271
police brutality, 98, 219, 259, 279
political bosses, 212, 251
politics (HPG): appointments,
    217–218, 220–221, 212;
    compensation, 213;
    condemns LBJ, 215–216;
    Democrat, 212; inclusion of
    M.A., 214; important, 208;
    Kennedy appointments, 225,
    229–230; likes Yarborough,
    214; not ideological, xix;
    organizing national entity,
    233–237; supported
    veterans, 210–211; Viva
    Kennedy, 222–223; vote
    getter, 209
politics of identity, xxxi;
    ethnicity within,
    xxxiii–xxxiv
poll tax, 152–154, 166
Ponce, Juventino, 135
positivists, 2, 6

post-war boom, 172–173
post-war society, 70
Progressives, 6
prosperity, xxvi

quintessential American (HPG),
    xviii

racism, 36
Ramsey, S.F., 126
Rayburn, Sam, 213, 214
Reagan, Ronald, 29, 295
reform activities (HPG): became
    professional, xxxiii; out of
    his heart, xxi–xxiii; seemed
    radical, xxix
reformers: black militants, 261;
    challenged, 289; chicano
    activists, 271; chose lesser
    evil, 210; continually
    protested, 133–134;
    disillusioned, 276–277; faith
    in litigation, 188–189;
    litigators, 100; paternalistic,
    99; remembered Hector,
    310; saw themselves white,
    97; seek appointments,
    217–218; traditional civil
    rights, 141; Vietnam, 269
relations with LBJ (HPG),
    252–255, 262, 263, 269–270
Republican presidents, 288
Revely, Paul J., 123–124
rhetoric (HPG), 261
Rice, Ben W., 144–150

Rio Grande Valley, 3, 5–6, 13,
    16, 18, 23, 28, 45, 52, 80,
    105, 162
revoltosos, 3. *See also sediciosos*
Roberts, Lloyd, 66–67
Rodgers, Charles E., 300
Rodríguez, Armando, 267
Roel, Virgilio, 233
Romano, Octavio, 175–278
Roth, Abraham, 71–72
Roybal, Edward, Jr., 38, 211,
    221, 223, 225; condemns
    Kennedy, 235
Ruiz, Manuel, Jr., 287

Saenz, Adam, 178
Saenz, J.L., 167
Saldívar House, 38
Salinas, E.D., 225–228
Sánchez, George I., xvii; Alba
    club, 164; at UT, 34–35;
    attacks liberals, 239–240;
    bilingual education,
    266–267; cabinet hearings,
    271–272; "class apart"
    theory of, 191–192; defends
    wetback report, 197–198;
    distrusted LBJ, 255; Forum
    convention speech, 165–166;
    fought segregation, 141;
    grander legal scheme,
    145–146; New Deal, 212;
    splits with HPG, 241–242,
    247–249; writings, 37
Sánchez, Mary, 167

Sánchez, Robert "Bob", 184,
    241, 246, 251
Saunders, Lyle, 136, 196, 199
schools, 7, 13, 15; imaginary
    classlessness, 18
sediciosos, 5
segregation, xxvii–xxviii, 12;
    attention to, 14; cemeteries,
    114; condition of schools,
    150; Corpus Christi, 292; *de
    facto/de jure*, 143; during
    fifties, 174–175; education,
    259; free choice, 168; in
    Three Rivers, 131–133;
    more rigid, 105; persistence
    of, 140; political kind of,
    151–153; re-enforced
    inferiority, 82; Rio Grande
    Valley, 13
segregation battles (HPG): hails
    Delgado ruling, 144–145;
    jumps into, 146
Selena, xvii, 313
self-centered world view (HPG),
    xxv–xxvi
SER, 298
Shafer, Roy, 247–248
Shivers, Allan, 213
Shriver, Sargent, 270
Sierra, Justo, 104
Simón, Margarita, 186
Smith, George Gemmill, 232
Smith, Harold, C., 126
Smith, Preston, 283
Spanish-Speaking Congress, 167

special interest lobbying, xxxi
steadfastly loyal (HPG), xxviii
Stevenson, Adlai, 212, 214
Storm, Marion, 206
Sutherland, Tom, 124–125; 135.
    See also Good Neighbor
    Commission

teamsters, 244, 246
Tejano *patrones*, 140–141. *See
    also* political bosses
Telles, Raymond, 208, 226–227,
    229, 230
Téllez, Isabel, 186–187
Texas Rangers, 5–6, 7, 204, 245,
    286; enter García home,
    17–18
Three Rivers, Texas, xvii,
    104–105; conflicts in, 131;
    criticism of, 122; defenders
    of, 125–128; initial burial
    site, 107; investigation of,
    131–133; "whites won't like
    it," 110
Tijerina, Félix, 259
Tijerina, Reies López, 277
Tinsley, Byron, 137
Truman, Harry, 104, 171
tuberculosis: high rates, 77–78;
    Navy beds, 91; no hospital,
    81–82; rally, 95

undocumented workers, xxx–xxi.
    See also "wetbacks"
unity, 233–234, 241, 251

University of Texas, 27, 29,
    32–40
U.S. Commission on Civil
    Rights (HPG): appointed to,
    282; outburst, 281; replaced,
    287, 288; work in, 283–286

Vaughn, Harry H., 104, 120
veterans, 74, 76–77, 81–88, 90,
    86, 103, 118, 164, 173
Veterans Administration, 76, 81,
    87, 90–94, 131
Veterans of Foreign Wars, 93–94
vicarious agitation (HPG), 180
Vietnam War, xxxi, xxxiv,
    267–269, 271, 289, 301
vision of history (HPG),
    303–304
Viva Johnson clubs, 256–257
Viva Kennedy clubs, 222–224,
    234, 235, 249, 256
Viva Kennedy leaders, 224, 228,
    233

war: vicarious experience,
    xxii–xxiii; idyllic view of,
    xxv–xxvi; instilled hope, xxx
War on Poverty, 258, 259, 262,
    263, 271
Warren, Earl, 193
wetbacks, 196, 198–201
What Price Wetback?, 198–201;
    Hector uneasy with, 202
White House Conference,
    261–262, 264, 265, 266, 270

white skin advantage (HPG), 19
Williams, Roy, 179
women in Forum, 185–187;
    Hector committed to, 186
Woodman of the World,
    120–121
Woods, L.A., 170
working class, 220, 234, 279,
    281; antagonisms, xxxi; few
    opportunities, xxi–xxii; in
    college, 27
World War II, 104, 302–303,
    305; crusade for democracy,
    51; in Pacific, 105–106

Ximenes, Vicente, 183–184,
    225, 256–257, 262, 270,
    272, 273, 305

Yarborough, Don, 240–243
Yarborough, Ralph, 213–214;
    bilingual education,
    266–267; chided, 225;
    confrontation with HPG,
    233; dislikes Salinas, 228;
    PASO, 239; supportive
    constituency, 260

Zapata, Joe, 167

Additional titles in our

Hispanic Civil Rights Series

Message to Aztlán
Rodolfo "Corky" Gonzales
ISBN 1-55885-331-6

A Gringo Manual on How to Handle Mexicans
José Angel Gutiérrez
ISBN 1-55885-326-X

Eyewitness: A Filmmaker's Memoir of the Chicano Movement
Jesús Salvador Treviño
ISBN 1-55885-349-9

Pioneros puertorriqueños en Nueva York, 1917–1947
Joaquín Colón
ISBN 1-55885-335-9

The American GI Forum: In Pursuit of the Dream, 1948–1983
Henry A. J. Ramos
Clothbound, ISBN 1-55885-261-1
Trade Paperback, ISBN 1-55885-262-X

Chicano! The History of the Mexican American Civil Rights Movement
F. Arturo Rosales
ISBN 1-55885-201-8

Testimonio: A Documentary History of the Mexican-American Struggle for Civil Rights
F. Arturo Rosales
ISBN 1-55885-299-9

They Called Me "King Tiger": My Struggle for the Land and Our Rights
Reies López Tijerina
ISBN 1-55885-302-2

Julian Nava: My Mexican-American Journey
Julian Nava
Clothbound, ISBN 1-55885-364-2
Trade Paperback, ISBN 1-55885-351 0

César Chávez: A Struggle for Justice / César Chávez: La lucha por la justicia
Richard Griswold del Castillo
ISBN 1-55885-364-2

Memoir of a Visionary: Antonia Pantoja
Antonia Pantoja
2002, 384 pages, Clothbound
ISBN 1-55885-365-0, $26.95

Black Cuban, Black American
Evelio Grillo
2000, 134 pages, Trade Paperback
ISBN 1-55885-293-X, $13.95